Empires Through Time

The Rise, Reign, and Decline of Global Powers

Nino Virga

Empires Through Time
The Rise, Reign, and Decline of Global Powers

Dedicated to:

Mamma Lina

Contents

Preface

Throughout the annals of history, we find the captivating tales of super-powers that rose to unprecedented heights, only to eventually succumb to the inexorable passage of time. From the ancient dominions of China, Persia, and Greece to the modern juggernauts like the United States, these remarkable entities have left an indelible mark on the course of human civilization. Each, in its own epoch, wielded profound influence, shaping cultures, economies, and philosophical outlooks.

Painting depicting the arrival of Aeneas at Pallanteum[1]

The story of Rome, that eternal city, stands as a quintessential embodiment of this enduring legacy. It begins with the legendary flight of Aeneas, fleeing the ruins of Troy to forge a new destiny in Italy. It culminates in the awe-inspiring Roman Empire, which spanned three continents and endured for over a millennium. Rome's trajectory epitomizes the transformative power of empires, but it is but one chapter in the vast tapestry of history.

Consider the United States, a nation born of colonial origins and, in the span of just a few centuries, vaulted to global prominence, championing the ideals of democracy and individual freedom. Its influence on the world stage, reminiscent of Rome's zenith, is palpable. Across the realms of culture, economics, and military might, the United States reshaped the global order of the 20th and 21st centuries. Yet, history offers a stern reminder: even the most formidable powers, from ancient Rome to contemporary superpowers, must confront the relentless march of time and the eventual erosion of their influence.

"Empires Through Time" embarks on an immersive journey through history's corridors, traversing diverse eras and landscapes while tracing the ascendancy of these colossal entities. Beyond their territorial expanse and dominion, each empire emerges as a fusion of human aspirations, innovation, and at times, hubris. These narratives transcend mere chronicles of monarchs and battles; they encompass the realms of art, culture, commerce, diplomacy, and a myriad of forces that mold the tapestry of human societies.

This exploration is a quest for understanding. By juxtaposing the narratives of ancient and modern empires, discernible patterns emerge, revealing the universal elements that underpin the rise of great powers and their eventual decline. This knowledge equips us with a perspective to evaluate contemporary geopolitical landscapes and grasp the ever-shifting dynamics of power in the present day.

In the course of our journey, we shall unravel what set each empire apart. How did the Pharaohs of Egypt differ from the Emperors of Rome? How do the philosophical foundations of ancient Greece measure against the pragmatic strategies of modern superpowers? Amidst their undeniable grandeur, each empire harbored vulnerabilities and weaknesses that, over time, sowed the seeds of their downfall.

By grasping the driving forces behind these empires—their aspirations, challenges, groundbreaking achievements, and enduring legacies—we gain a profound appreciation for the cyclical nature of history and the determinants that govern the peaks and troughs of civilizations. Empires may rise and fall, but their impact reverberates through the corridors of time.

Embark with us on this illuminating odyssey through the annals of the world's most influential empires. "Empires Through Time" imparts not only knowledge but also wisdom, empowering readers to draw insights from the past, decipher the complexities of the present, and perhaps even glimpse into the future trajectories of nations in our ever-evolving global landscape.

Introduction: Foundations of Power

Chapter 1.
Defining Superpowers

The strong do what they can,
and the weak suffer what they must.

~ Thucydides

Spanning the vast expanse of recorded time, myriad tales of empires have emerged, captivating our collective consciousness. From the intricate lattice of socio-political dynamics in ancient realms to the complex interplay of power in modern states, these narratives have defined the ebbs and flows of human civilization. This chapter embarks on a deep exploration into these foundational stories, unearthing the nuanced elements that have shaped the ascent of empires and set the stage for their eventual decline. Dive deep into the intricacies that have sculpted our shared heritage and discover the indelible marks left by these monumental entities.

Military Dominance

Throughout history, the quest for military dominance has been a defining characteristic of superpowers. From ancient empires like the Romans and Mongols to modern nuclear-armed states, the strength and scope of armed forces have played a pivotal role in shaping global influence and achieving supremacy.

In antiquity, the power of empires was often symbolized by the size and might of their land armies. The Romans, with their gleaming armor and disciplined legions, represented not just conquerors but the vast reach of Roman civilization itself. These legions marked the boundaries of Roman influence and stood as icons of their authority. Similarly, the Mongols, renowned for their unmatched equestrian archery skills and lightning-fast campaigns, embodied the expansive spirit of the Eurasian steppe. Their swift victories underscored the potential of a finely tuned military machine.

However, the tools and methods of dominance have evolved over the centuries. Ancient fortifications and battle formations have given way to cutting-edge naval fleets, aircraft, and the ever-looming threat of nuclear conflict in the 20th and 21st centuries. While the technologies and tactics may differ, the fundamental objectives remain the same: projecting power, deterring rivals, and ensuring supremacy.

But what lies at the core of military power's enduring significance in defining superpowers? Essentially, a dominant armed force serves a dual purpose. Firstly, it acts as a deterrent, dissuading potential adversaries from challenging a clearly superior military. Secondly, in times of disputes or conflicts, a formidable military becomes a means to achieve political or economic objectives. These may include annexing territory, securing vital trade routes, or exerting influence over neighboring regions.

It's essential to recognize that military strength extends beyond sheer force. Factors such as strategic acumen, logistical capabilities, morale, adaptability, and rigorous training are often as critical as the size of an army or the sophistication of its weapons. Throughout history, we've seen examples of smaller forces employing superior tactics and psychological warfare to secure victories against numerically superior opponents. Today, the landscape of military supremacy is further reshaped by the emergence of asymmetric and cyber warfare, as well as the increasing use of drones in modern conflicts.

In summary, while the indicators of military dominance have evolved with advancements in technology, changes in societal norms, and shifts in political landscapes, its fundamental role in global power dynamics has remained constant. As we move further into the 21st century, where cyber warfare redefines the concept of combat zones and space becomes a new arena of contention, the relevance of military supremacy in determining superpower status remains as central as ever.

Economic Strength

Control over economic resources has always signified superpower status. Ancient empires held sway over vital trade routes and goods like spices and silk, whereas modern giants lead in global finance and advanced industries. The tools differ, but the essence of economic dominance persists.

Look across history's vast canvas, and economic strength emerges as a defining brushstroke. From the bustling bazaars of Samarkand, a pivotal trading hub on the ancient Silk Road, to the iconic towers of Wall Street, the message remains clear: control over economic resources is a steadfast indicator of global power.

In eras where the world was replete with enigmas, vital trade paths and goods became civilizations' pulse. The Silk Road was more than just a commercial path; it became a conduit for culture, learning, and authority, linking East and West. Empires like the Parthians, overseeing these routes, wielded colossal wealth and clout. Mastery over these paths meant more than trade; it defined the spread of ideas, innovations, and cultures.

Goods like spices from the East Indies were more than just flavor enhancers; they were status symbols, so sought after they drove exploration and ushered in the age of discovery. Likewise, Egyptian grain, feeding ancient Rome, highlighted the power of resource command. The empire's sustenance lay in who controlled this grain.

Today, the settings of economic supremacy have shifted, yet the core tenets stand firm. Modern superpowers no longer compete for spices but battle for global financial and tech industry leadership. The U.S. dollar serves as more than currency; it's a symbol of post-World War II American economic ascendancy.

Today's power centers, like Silicon Valley and Shenzhen, are battle-grounds of economic ambition. Dominance here isn't quantified by silk loads but by data volumes and market presence. The competition in areas like AI, biotech, and renewable energy reveals the modern face of economic strength. These fields, reminiscent of old trade paths, offer not just prosperity but also sway over humanity's trajectory.

Despite the shift from traditional markets to digital hubs, the heart of economic prowess remains unaltered: it's all about mastery, sway, and charting paths. This recognition isn't new; it's been the cornerstone for empires, countries, and superpowers. Economic vigor yields political clout, cultural sway

Political Influence

It has been common for superpowers to exert control in global or regional politics across history. Ancient empires controlled through vassal and tributary systems, whereas contemporary powers use international bodies and diplomatic alliances.

Political influence has always been the cornerstone in international relations. Superpowers have masterfully used this tool, dictating events, molding narratives, and showcasing their prominence on the global stage. From ancient monarchies to modern international bodies, political influence signifies superpower presence.

In ancient times, empires employed sophisticated means to exert political control. They adopted systems beyond military power, such as vassal states and tributaries.

Vassal states, semi-independent territories governed by local rulers who pledged allegiance to a dominant power, were instrumental in extending control. These states, while enjoying some autonomy, provided military aid, tribute, and loyalty. Empires like the Assyrians and Babylonians exemplify this mechanism. It wasn't just about dominance but also cultural and political propagation.

Tributary systems, notably used by Chinese dynasties like Han, revolved around acknowledging supremacy. Peripheral states or tribes gave tribute to the central empire, recognizing its dominance in return for protection or trade privileges. This system delicately balanced authority and respect, intertwining diplomacy and control.

Today, political influence is more expansive and sophisticated. Modern international organizations like the United Nations, World Trade Organization, and NATO are arenas for superpower influence.

Modern superpowers, including the USA, China, and Russia, navigate these platforms, influencing global guidelines, resolving disputes, and establishing norms. Their reach spans from economic regulations to environmental rules.

Additionally, diplomatic groups like the G7 or BRICS magnify member nations' influence, championing regional or global objectives. In these alliances, leading superpowers often dictate the agenda and discourse.

However, with great influence comes significant responsibility. Superpowers have historically been at the forefront of major events, from ancient territorial disputes to modern global humanitarian missions. Their choices impact global economies, societies, and history itself. Events like the 1962 Cuban Missile Crisis emphasize the gravity of their decisions.

In essence, political influence is a consistent indicator of superpower status. The methods have shifted, from ancient tributaries to contemporary diplomacy, but the core objective remains: to steer the global narrative. As the world evolves, political influence's role is set to become even more central.

Technological Advancement: The Catalyst of Supremacy

Spanning millennia, the ascent and dominance of global powers have been intimately tied to technological advancements. Technology, in its myriad forms, has consistently been the pivot point shifting the balance of power.

Before the digital age dawned, ancient societies grasped technology's transformational essence. Consider the Iron Age: it wasn't merely about smelting iron but reshaping warfare and agriculture's landscape. This shift allowed empires like the Romans, to craft superior tools and weapons. Their enhanced capabilities, surpassing their rivals who still relied on bronze, underpinned their ascendancy.

Likewise, the Phoenicians, with their exceptional shipbuilding skills, didn't just dominate Mediterranean trade; they ventured into uncharted waters. Their iconic triremes (ancient vessels with three rows of oars) and galleys weren't merely transport vessels; they epitomized naval supremacy. By mastering the waves, they broadened trade networks and became channels for spreading culture and influence.

Leap to the modern era, and the story echoes the same theme, albeit with today's tech marvels. The digital revolution's explosion in the 20th century's latter half redefined power dynamics. Today's superpowers brandish microchips, the internet, and AI as their scepters.

Take the United States, for instance. Silicon Valley is more than a tech hub; it's a geopolitical powerhouse. In this cradle of innovation, technological strides translate to global leadership. Dominance in data, leading AI innovations, and groundbreaking cybersecurity measures now define global supremacy.

Furthermore, space represents the ultimate arena of technological contest. The race to explore and possibly colonize celestial bodies isn't just about exploration; it's a clear assertion of superpower stature. Outer space endeavors, from planetary landings to exploiting astral resources, intertwine scientific quests with geopolitical dominance.

Analyzing superpower dynamics, one truth stands out: technological prowess isn't merely an attribute; it's a necessity. Every era has its defining innovations, and those at the vanguard of technological breakthroughs often dominate the global stage. Although the domains and instruments of innovation evolve, one principle persists: technological leaders frequently steer the course of global events.

In understanding the ebb and flow of empires and the web of power relations, technological supremacy remains a perpetual theme.

Cultural Influence: The Silent Conquest

The saga of empires and superpowers is as much about the quiet pulse of culture as it is about the loud trumpets of war and diplomacy. Often overshadowed by military might and political maneuvers, cultural influence subtly, yet indelibly, inscribes its legacy on the tapestry of time. This silent form of conquest, known as soft power, resonates deeper and often outlasts the more tangible forms of dominance, capturing not just territories but souls and sentiments.

The spread of Hellenization due to Alexander the Great's campaigns is a key example of this phenomenon. Beyond his military triumphs, Alexander seeded Greek culture throughout his conquered realms. The resulting fusion of Greek and local customs birthed cities that bore the unmistakable imprints of Hellenistic design. From art to philosophy, this melding of cultures birthed a unique identity that thrived long after political boundaries faded. Alexandria stands as a testament to this era, a confluence of knowledge, art, and diverse traditions.

In more recent times, the locus of cultural influence has notably shifted to Hollywood. The United States, leveraging its entertainment industry, broadcasted not merely films but a canvas of ideals, hopes, and a distinct lifestyle. The tales spun on Hollywood's screen, echoing themes of liberty, ambition, and allure, found eager audiences across the globe. Amplified by global media and digital networks, American popular culture sculpted global preferences, trends, and most crucially, worldviews.

The potency of cultural influence lies in its ability to foster connections. It acts as a conduit for mutual appreciation, catalyzing rapport. A song, a film, or a piece of art can transcend borders, smoothing the path for deeper diplomatic and economic ties. This soft power also crafts enduring legacies. While empires might wane and geopolitical dynamics alter, the cultural imprints remain, molding societal narratives and identities for ensuing generations.

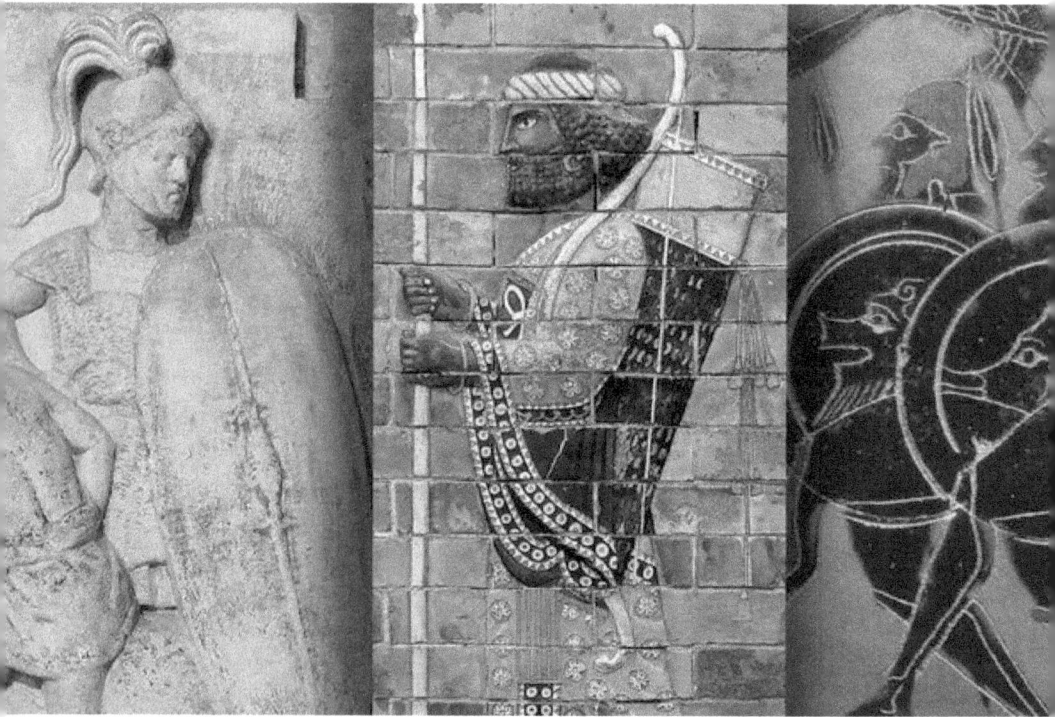

Depiction of Republican Roman Legionaries, Persian Immortals from Palace Walls at Susa and Greek Hoplite Warriors[2]

Chapter 2.
The Inevitable Decline of Superpowers

The decline of Rome was the natural and inevitable effect of immoderate greatness.

~Edward Gibbon

Introduction

History, when examined through the lens of its most powerful actors, offers a tapestry of narratives highlighting the ascent of global superpowers and, often, their eventual decline. While their rise can be attributed to a myriad of factors (as highlighted in earlier sections), their decline is also seldom a result of a singular cause. Instead, it is the culmination of interlinked vulnerabilities, internal challenges, and external threats that work synergistically, eroding the very foundations upon which their might stands.

The Snare of Success often manifests as complacency born out of long periods of unchallenged dominance. Success can breed internal discord, with factions vying for power, leading to fragmented decision-making and a loss of common purpose.

This complacency is further exacerbated by the **Fragility of Prosperity**. Economic strains often underpin the might of empires, making them vulnerable to fiscal mismanagement, unsustainable policies, and the vicissitudes of global trade dynamics.

As time progresses, the once-innovative superpowers can fall into the **Peril of Stagnation**. A technological standstill not only affects military capabilities but also impedes economic growth and adaptability to a changing world order.

The drive that propels superpowers to their peak can, ironically, become their undoing. The **Weight of Ambition** can lead to overextension, where the maintenance of vast territories and diverse populations strains resources and governance structures.

While internal vulnerabilities form one facet of decline, **Shadows on the Horizon** present external threats. Rival powers, sensing weakness, might challenge the superpower's dominance, leading to military conflicts or economic blockades.

Internally, the **Trap of Rigidity** manifests as cultural isolation. An inability or unwillingness to adapt to or absorb new cultures and ideas can stifle innovation and result in societal inflexibility.

Superpowers, despite their might, remain at the mercy of **Nature's Wrath**. Environmental calamities or health challenges, such as pandemics, can wreak havoc, challenging even the most formidable governance structures.

Central to these narratives is the role of leadership. A **Leadership Crisis** can hasten decline, where ineptitude, lack of vision, or internal conflicts prevent effective response to emerging challenges.

As we journey through this chapter, each section will delve into these intricacies, drawing from a rich tapestry of historical events, to paint a comprehensive picture of the multi-faceted dimensions of superpower declines. The ultimate aim is to understand not just the causes, but also the interplay of these factors, providing a holistic understanding of the patterns and lessons inherent in the annals of statecraft.

The Snare of Success: Internal Discord and Complacency

The journey of an empire, marked by its climb to prominence, is a spectacle that history has witnessed time and again. This progression, while admirable, comes embedded with intrinsic contradictions that, if unchecked, can precipitate its downfall.

When empires begin their ascent, they are often embodiments of enthusiasm, pioneering spirit, and camaraderie. Think of the early days of the Roman Empire, where rapid expansions and innovative governance models defined their surge to dominance. Then there's the British Empire, which, fueled by the advent of the Industrial Revolution, went on to be known as the empire where the sun never set. The dawn of the "American Empire" followed, symbolizing the epitome of new age dominance. As the United States took shape, it burst forth with dynamic fervor, casting its influential shadow from technological advancements to cultural exports. From the zeal of its Revolution to the global assertion following the World Wars, the U.S. mirrored the spirited initial stages of its European predecessors. There's a freshness, an unparalleled zeal in these initial stages, as these entities carve their niches and assert their place in the world.

However, as they continue to flourish, gaining territorial and cultural expanse, a subtle shift begins to occur. The vastness that once symbolized strength can, paradoxically, become its Achilles' heel. As territories expand, the central ethos that once bound the empire can get diluted. With increased dominance and prolonged periods of unchallenged supremacy, empires often start resting on their laurels, believing their reign to be eternal.

This is where the perils of success creep in. The institutions that once functioned seamlessly, propelled by a singular vision, now witness a slackening. Complacency replaces the hunger for innovation. The bureaucracy swells, leading to a slowdown in decision-making and execution. Corruption, once anathema, starts finding pockets of acceptance.

As empires continue on this trajectory, the political landscape undergoes a transformation. What was once a united front starts splintering.

Factions arise, each vying for power and influence. The political discourse, rather than being centered on the collective good, becomes a tussle for supremacy. This internal strife can become so pronounced that external threats are often neglected or underestimated.

Furthermore, as the elite consolidate power, they often grow distant from the very masses they govern. This disconnect manifests in socio-economic policies that favor the privileged, widening the chasm between the ruling class and the general populace. Discontent simmers, and if unchecked, can erupt into civil unrest or revolts.

The cohesive identity of the empire, carefully woven over years, starts experiencing strain. Cultural, linguistic, or regional identities, previously subsumed under the larger imperial identity, begin to reassert themselves. The once unified empire begins to feel more like a patchwork of competing interests.

In essence, the trajectory of empires, as charted by history, offers profound insights. The very factors that facilitate their rise can, in time, become the harbingers of their decline. An empire's ascent is not just a testament to its strengths but also a precursor to the challenges it will eventually face. The ebb and flow of power, thus, remain an eternal dance of rise, dominance, complacency, and decline.

The Fragility of Prosperity: Economic Strain

From the archaic realms of empires like Rome to the bustling centers of modern superpowers, the specter of economic vulnerability has perennially loomed large. Historical empires often reveled in the opulence secured from vast territories and lucrative trade routes. However, the over-reliance on singular economic channels—be it specific commodities or conquest spoils—inevitably manifested vulnerabilities. The disruption or exhaustion of these pivotal channels, whether due to external competition, overexploitation, or shifting geopolitical landscapes, often precipitated profound economic downturns.

Such vulnerabilities resonate even in the modern world, where superpowers dependent on specific economic strengths, such as oil exports or technological innovations, confront similar risks. A shift in global demand patterns, technological paradigms, or even evolving geopolitical intricacies can create economic reverberations that echo the challenges faced by their ancient counterparts.

Taxation, a crucial instrument of statecraft, has been both a bedrock and a fault line. While vital for maintaining empires and fueling growth, excessive tax burdens often precipitated widespread discontent, particularly when perceived as inequitable. Modern superpowers are no strangers to these tensions. Contemporary debates around taxation—especially those focusing on wealth distribution, corporate obligations, and economic disparities—mirror ancient challenges, revealing the timeless nature of the push and pull between state exigencies and societal expectations.

The allure and peril of borrowing present another shared narrative. Ancient empires, awash with treasures from new lands or lucrative trade, often found themselves ensnared in cycles of debt, their short-term affluence belied by underlying fiscal instability. This historical quagmire finds reflections in modern financial crises where superpowers, even those commanding vast resources, grapple with balancing fiscal discipline against growth imperatives. The recurrent specter of public debt, and the intricacies of managing it, stands testament to the universality of this challenge.

Finally, the matter of currency—its value, trustworthiness, and representation of economic health—bridges epochs. Historic actions, such as Rome's devaluation of its denarius, find resonances in the complex monetary policies of today's world. Modern superpowers, navigating the delicate waters of currency manipulation or aggressive quantitative easing, tread a path known to their ancient predecessors. Such measures, while often aimed at short-term economic relief, can entail long-term global ramifications, underscoring the intricate balance required in managing economic trust.

In this intricate tapestry of economic choices and consequences, spanning from ancient corridors to contemporary boardrooms, lies a testament to the enduring challenges of statecraft. Economic strain, whether in the heart of ancient Rome or the bustling avenues of a 21st-century superpower, remains an indomitable factor influencing the arcs of empires, emphasizing the interplay between financial prudence and the overarching stability of realms.

The Peril of Stagnation: Technological Standstill

An empire's strength is often closely tied to its capacity for innovation. However, a failure to keep pace with technological advancements can quietly erode that strength. Empires that rest on their past achievements and ignore the winds of change may find themselves overtaken by more agile and innovative rivals. Throughout history, there have been numerous examples of mighty empires left behind by technological revolutions they failed to embrace. In the grand narrative of empires, technology consistently takes center stage. From the simple tools of the Stone Age to the digital revolutions of the modern era, technological innovation has continuously shaped the fortunes of nations and empires. Yet, with innovation comes a hidden challenge: the risk of becoming too comfortable with the status quo.

For empires that have accomplished remarkable feats, there's an undeniable allure in their past successes. Architectural marvels like the Great Wall of China, the Roman aqueducts, or the majestic pyramids of Egypt, born out of the technological prowess of their times, became symbols of national pride. However, therein lies a paradox: while such achievements showcased an empire's brilliance, they also posed the risk of becoming anchors, holding them back from exploring new frontiers.

Pyramids of the Giza Necropolis[3]

The pace of technological change is not constant; there are moments in history when it accelerates exponentially. The printing press, steam engine, the internet and the recent AI revolution are just a few examples. Empires that failed to recognize these seismic shifts often found themselves grappling with obsolescence.

But why would an empire resist such change? Several reasons can be discerned. Established power structures might view innovations as threats to their dominance. Economic interests tied to older technologies might resist the new, fearing loss of revenue or relevance. Cultural or religious beliefs can also play a role, with some innovations perceived as challenging the established order or norms.

When an empire fails to adapt, the costs can be dire. Consider the fate of the Byzantine Empire in the face of gunpowder technology. Their formidable walls, which had withstood sieges for centuries, crumbled before the might of the Ottoman cannons. Similarly, the naval supremacy of the Spanish Armada, steeped in tradition and once deemed invincible, was outmaneuvered by the more agile and technologically advanced English fleet.

Every technological revolution gives rise to new power players. As some empires stagnate, others, often smaller or previously marginalized, seize the opportunity to leapfrog. They embrace and adapt to technological advancements, transforming them into strategic advantages. The rise of the Mongols can be attributed in part to their mastery of horseback warfare and advanced military strategies, enabling them to outpace larger, more established empires.

An empire's journey through time can be likened to navigating a swiftly flowing river. While past achievements provide direction and identity, it's the ability to read the currents of innovation and change that ultimately determines success. Those that halt, whether to admire the view or bask in past glories, often find themselves stranded on the banks of history as the waters of time and technology surge past.

The Weight of Ambition: Overextension

The allure of endless expansion, while tempting, comes with its own set of pitfalls. The farther an empire pushes its boundaries, the more its resources are spread thin. The task of protecting vast territories, managing distant provinces, and ensuring loyalty across diverse cultures becomes increasingly burdensome. Overextension can stretch an empire to its limits, making it vulnerable to both internal strife and external threats.

In the annals of empire-building, the thrill of conquest has proven irresistible time and again. From the shimmering deserts of Mesopotamia to the fertile plains of Eurasia, the call of uncharted territories has beckoned emperors and kings alike. However, with vast expansion comes an inherent danger, a pendulum that swings between the glory of dominion and the peril of overreaching.

Historically, the acquisition of new territories often promised untapped resources, strategic advantages, and an opportunity to spread one's culture or religion. The Roman Empire, with its ever-expanding frontiers, was fueled by the promise of wealth from new provinces and the strategic importance of securing key trade routes. Similarly, the British Empire, upon which "the sun never set," was driven by both economic motives and the ideological intent of the 'white man's burden.'

However, ruling distant lands was not merely about planting a flag and asserting dominance. The task of integrating different peoples, cultures, and economies into a single administrative framework was colossal. Roman governors faced the challenge of appeasing diverse populations, each with its distinct culture and aspirations. The British, on their part, had to grapple with myriad local customs, traditions, and resistance movements across their colonies.

Beyond governance, there was a physical challenge. The infrastructure needed to connect the heart of the empire with its farthest reaches—such as roads, naval routes, and communication systems—was a monumental endeavor. These vast networks, while facilitating control and commerce, were expensive to maintain and defend. The Great Wall of China stands as a testament to the lengths an empire would go to protect its expansive borders.

However, as empires expanded, internal fractures often began to manifest. Dissent, born out of perceived neglect or direct oppression, could simmer and eventually boil over. Regions farther from the capital often felt marginalized, leading to local uprisings or demands for autonomy. Externally, overextended borders became tempting targets for rival powers. The sheer length of the Roman frontiers made it vulnerable to Barbarian invasions, and the extensive trade routes of the Mongol Empire invited incursions.

The allure of expansion, with its promise of riches and glory, has been a siren song for empires throughout history. However, unchecked ambition, without a keen sense of its inherent challenges, often leads to an empire's downfall. As history repeatedly illustrates, the equilibrium between consolidation and expansion is delicate, and tipping the balance can set the stage for decline.

Shadows on the Horizon: External Threats

No empire exists in isolation. As one superpower rises, there are always contenders on the horizon, eager to shift the balance of power. These emerging entities, armed with ambition and often innovative strategies, can pose multifaceted threats—military confrontations, economic competitions, or ideological challenges.

The rise and dominance of an empire, while a testament to its strength, often cast shadows far and wide. In the vast theater of geopolitics, where power and influence are constantly in flux, these shadows often take the form of emerging contenders, each with its own vision for the world stage. These challengers, born from the peripheries or from the ruins of older powers, invariably shape the narrative of historical epochs.

Throughout history, power vacuums, either resulting from an empire's overextension or internal decay, have attracted new players. As the Roman Empire grappled with its internal challenges, tribes beyond its borders saw opportunities to stake their claim. The Parthians and Sassanids to the east, the Goths and Vandals from the north, each sensed the weakening giant and sought to carve their own realms from its vastness.

Yet, not all challenges are overtly militaristic. In the shadows of martial might, there are subtle wars being waged—economic rivalries, cultural confrontations, and ideological contests. The competition between the maritime republics of Venice, Genoa, and Pisa during the medieval period wasn't merely about naval dominance but also about controlling lucrative trade routes. In the modern era, the ideological divide of the Cold War saw the U.S. and the USSR engage in proxy wars, space races, and cultural exchanges, each trying to prove the superiority of its way of life.

One of the defining traits of emerging powers is their ability to innovate and adapt. Whether it's the Mongols' unparalleled mobility and communication system or the technological advancements of Germany during the late 19th and early 20th centuries, these entities often bring fresh strategies and technologies to the table. Their hunger for dominance, coupled with innovative tactics, can often catch complacent empires off guard.

Intriguingly, the relationship between an empire and its external challengers is not always antagonistic. Trade, cultural exchanges, and even alliances can be formed. The Byzantine Empire, while often at odds with its neighbors, also engaged in diplomacy and trade, weaving a complex web of interdependence. Similarly, the Ming Dynasty's tributary system in China was as much about dominance as it was about fostering diplomatic and trade relationships.

Empires, in their grandeur, can often feel invincible, viewing their dominion as the natural order of things. However, the shadows on the horizon serve as a reminder of the transient nature of power. Every towering entity must remain vigilant, for challenges do not always come as thundering armies but can manifest in the whispers of trade winds, the allure of new ideologies, or the silent march of innovation.

The Trap of Rigidity: Cultural Isolation

An empire's culture, while a source of pride, can also become its shackle. In an ever-evolving global milieu, insularity can be detrimental. Failing to appreciate, assimilate, or adapt to the cultural riches of the wider world can lead to stagnation. An empire that remains rigid, resistant to external cultural influences, can find itself isolated, both politically and ideologically.

An empire's culture is woven from threads of history, tradition, and collective experience. This becomes the emblem of identity, fostering pride and unity. Yet, as with all things, balance is key. While a culture strengthens and defines, it can also inadvertently cage, especially when it fails to evolve in a dynamically interconnected world.

The cultural identity of an empire serves as the bedrock upon which its citizens stand. This identity, forged through shared narratives, values, and experiences, can provide a sense of belonging and continuity. Think of the Renaissance in Italy or the cultural revolution of the Tang Dynasty in China. These were eras when internal culture flourished and became a beacon for surrounding regions.

However, when an empire begins to view its culture as not just unique but superior, it risks descending into hubris. This can breed an insularity, where external influences are viewed with suspicion, if not outright disdain.

The United States, a nation built on the ideals of freedom, innovation, and the 'melting pot' ethos, is no stranger to the benefits of cultural assimilation. Its music, art, literature, and even its culinary landscape have been enriched by contributions from every corner of the globe. However, in recent times, there have been undertones suggesting a retreat from this global embrace. Whether it's heightened debates around immigration, a redefining of cultural identity, or a skepticism towards international collaborations, the U.S. stands at a crucial juncture, grappling with its role in a global community.

The dangers of cultural isolation are manifold. Firstly, it narrows the intellectual horizon. When an empire shuts its doors to external cultural winds, it denies itself fresh perspectives, innovative ideas, and collaborative potential. Secondly, insularity can alienate allies and trade partners. An empire perceived as high-handed or indifferent can find itself facing diplomatic cold shoulders. Lastly, and perhaps most significantly, cultural rigidity can sow internal discord. As global exposure increases, citizens, especially the younger generation, might find themselves torn between the empire's prescribed identity and the allure of a broader global identity.

While it's natural for an empire to take pride in its cultural achievements, it must also remain open, porous, and receptive. The world, with its myriad cultures, offers a rich tapestry of ideas, art, philosophy, and innovation. An empire that chooses to isolate itself from this wealth not only impoverishes its own cultural legacy but also risks being left behind in the global narrative. In a world where borders are increasingly fluid, cultural adaptability is not just a virtue—it's a necessity.

Nature's Wrath:
Environmental and Health Challenges

The might of empires, though formidable, remains subservient to the caprices of nature. Changes in the environment, the depletion of crucial resources, or the onslaught of pandemics can play a significant role in the decline of civilizations.

In its history, humankind has continuously sought dominance over nature. From the engineering marvels of ancient aqueducts to modern dams, from herbal remedies of tribal shamans to cutting-edge medical technologies, our story is one of confrontation and adaptation to the natural world. Yet, for all our innovations and advancements, nature retains its age-old power to shape the destinies of empires.

While human empires draw borders, build cities, and weave intricate socio-political tapestries, nature operates on a grander scale. Climate shifts, whether gradual or abrupt, can transform lush landscapes into barren wastelands or inundate coastal areas. The agricultural foundations upon which many empires are built can crumble in the face of persistent drought or unpredictable flooding.

The fate of the Indus Valley Civilization serves as a poignant example. Once a flourishing society, boasting sophisticated urban centers and intricate drainage systems, it faced a dramatic downturn, with evidence suggesting a combination of climate change and river course shifts as culprits.

Similarly, the Classic Maya, with their iconic step pyramids and a deep understanding of astronomy, faced a combination of prolonged droughts and deforestation. Their reliance on rain-fed agriculture in an area with variable rainfall patterns made them particularly vulnerable.

Beyond the overt challenges of changing landscapes and depleting resources, health crises, particularly pandemics, have repeatedly shown their capacity to destabilize empires. The Plague of Justinian, the Black Death, and the more recent Spanish Flu are stark examples of nature's invisible wrath. Such health crises not only decimate populations but also strain economic structures, create political upheavals, and alter the socio-cultural fabric of societies.

In our contemporary era, these ancient tales find resonance in new challenges, such as the climate crisis and modern pandemics. Empires today, with all their technological prowess, are still racing against time to mitigate the impacts of rising sea levels, unpredictable weather patterns, and new strains of diseases. The COVID-19 pandemic, for instance, demonstrated the vulnerability of even the most advanced nations and their interconnected economies.

Nature, in its myriad forms, remains an ever-present actor on the stage of history. While human societies may rise, consolidate, and dominate, they must always reckon with the environmental and health challenges that nature presents. An empire's true strength, perhaps, lies not just in its ability to conquer other nations, but in its adaptability and resilience in the face of nature's unpredictable challenges.

Leadership Crisis: The Downfall from the Pinnacle

History has repeatedly illuminated the pivotal role that leadership plays in the trajectory of empires. Leadership is the rudder that guides a nation, for better or for worse. During the golden era of Athens, Pericles steered the city-state to unparalleled heights, epitomizing what visionary governance could achieve.

However, history also bears witness to the catastrophic outcomes stemming from inept leadership. The Roman Empire, one of history's most resplendent civilizations, didn't just decay from external pressures or internal corruption. Its series of weak and misguided emperors, especially during its waning phases, dramatically expedited its collapse. Nero's notorious reign, marked by extreme self-indulgence and negligence, and Commodus' erratic and tyrannical rule, are tales of how leadership in disarray can jeopardize the very pillars of an empire.

Shifting our gaze to contemporary times, the United States, the present-day titan, offers a lesson in the challenges of leadership in the 21st century. The presidency of Donald Trump became synonymous with discord and global uncertainty. Trump's tenure, characterized by erratic decision-making, constant staff upheavals, dismissal of traditional allies, and an often-combative approach to international diplomacy, alarmed many. While some saw him as a disruptor of a stagnant system, to many others, his leadership was a stark detour from the values that had long underpinned American global leadership. The divisiveness he sowed, both domestically and internationally, posed significant questions about the stability and direction of the 'modern empire'.

The lesson is unmistakable: while great leadership can elevate an empire, its deficiency or misdirection can be its very undoing. As empires rise and fall, the caliber of those at the helm remains an unwavering determinant of their fate.

Conclusion: Time's Teachings

In the intricate dance of history, the rise and fall of superpowers serve as timeless lessons. They underline the impermanence of power and the delicate balance on which it stands. While these empires have scripted history, their declines serve as somber reminders of the transient nature of dominance. The stories of their zeniths and eventual descents serve as both inspirations and cautions for the ages to come. Top of Form

As the pages of history turn, one prevailing truth emerges: no matter the height of their power, no empire remains immune to the sands of time. Majestic palaces crumble, illustrious cultures fade, and the corridors of power once bustling with activity, eventually succumb to silence. This impermanence isn't merely a reflection of structural weaknesses or external threats; it is an inherent quality of existence, a great equalizer that levels even the mightiest.

For the Pharaohs of Egypt, the dependence on the Nile's annual inundation was as much a vulnerability as it was a source of sustenance. Any significant deviation from its regular patterns could lead to crop failures, causing famine and socio-economic unrest. Similarly, the very architecture that testified to their greatness, like the colossal pyramids or the intricate temple complexes, necessitated vast resources and labor. Any mismanagement in this regard, be it in resource allocation or handling the workforce, could kindle discontentment and dissent.

Rome, the city that once ruled the world, had its Achilles heel too. As it stretched its limbs across continents, it grappled with the challenges of maintaining administrative coherence. The sprawling empire, with its myriad languages, cultures, and traditions, posed a colossal governance challenge. The vastness that was once a testament to its might eventually became its undoing. Decentralization, a solution to governance, led to regional powers within the empire that sometimes harbored ambitions at odds with the central authority. Additionally, economic strains, frequent leadership changes, and external pressures intensified Rome's vulnerabilities.

The Greek realm, celebrated for its philosophical profundities and democratic ideals, was also riddled with internal competitions. The rivalry between city-states, most notably Athens and Sparta, led to debilitating conflicts like the Peloponnesian War. Their regionalized structure, while allowing for diverse cultural and intellectual pursuits, made it difficult to present a unified front against external adversaries.

The modern behemoths, like the US while technologically superior and globally interconnected, are no strangers to vulnerabilities. Economic interdependencies can lead to recessions, internal political polarizations can stall governance, and the intricate web of global politics can ensnare even the mightiest. In a world more connected than ever, the ripple effects of one nation's vulnerabilities can have global repercussions.

Every superpower, in its ascendancy, writes a symphony of innovation, conquest, and cultural bloom. These melodies resonate across continents, influencing far-off lands and echoing through generations. Yet, the very notes of triumph often carry within them the seeds of their own undoing. Complacency, overextension, isolation – these are but some of the recurrent motifs that have signaled the fading crescendos of once-dominant empires.

The remnants of these great empires, from the ruins of Persepolis to the walls of the Roman Colosseum, are more than mere tourist attractions. They are silent teachers, speaking volumes to those willing to listen. Their tales caution against the trappings of unchecked ambition and the perils of insularity. Yet, they also inspire by showcasing the heights human civilization can achieve when united under a shared vision.

As the 21st century unfolds, with its unique challenges and opportunities, the stories of past superpowers hold a mirror to contemporary societies. They ask probing questions: Are we repeating the mistakes of our forebears? Are we heeding the lessons inscribed in ancient stone and parchment? They remind us that while the specific challenges might differ, the underlying themes of human ambition, adaptability, and resilience remain constant.

The cyclical rhythm of rise and decline, as observed in history's grand tapestry, offers a humbling perspective. While superpowers shape epochs and eras, they too are shaped—and ultimately reshaped—by the inexorable forces of time, nature, and human endeavor. As we look to the future, it's these lessons from the past that can guide nations and societies towards a more enduring and harmonious existence.

PART I:
Ancient Empires

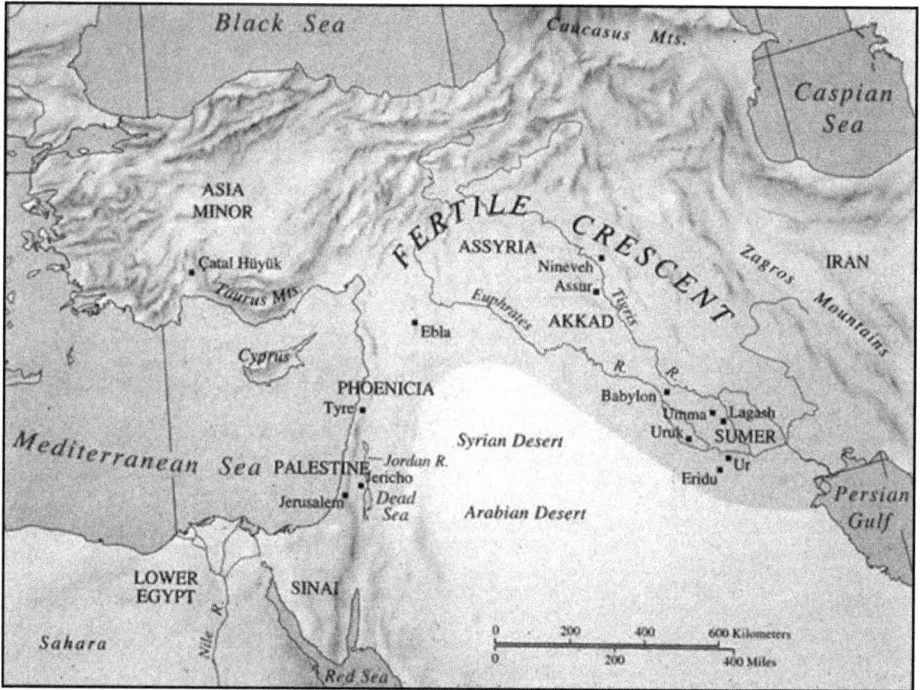

Mesopotamia

Chapter 3.
Mesopotamia: Origins, Empires and Legacy (4,500-500 BCE)

To cause justice to prevail in the land, to destroy the wicked and the evil, that the strong may not oppress the weak

~Hammurabi

Mesopotamia as the Cradle of Civilization

Mesopotamia, a Greek term translating to "land between the rivers", serves as an apt descriptor for the region nestled between the Tigris and Euphrates rivers. This area, largely corresponding to modern-day Iraq, parts of Iran, Syria, and Turkey, stands out as one of the earliest and most influential centers of human civilization.

The geographical and environmental framework of Mesopotamia was critical to its development. The Tigris and Euphrates rivers, with their annual flood cycles, transformed the region into a fertile crescent — a boon for agriculture. These fertile plains, created by silt deposits from the rivers, provided the necessary conditions for the cultivation of staple crops like barley and wheat. Over time, this consistent agricultural output fostered population growth and paved the way for sedentary societies to flourish.

However, this geographical bounty was not without its challenges. The unpredictability of floods demanded innovative solutions from the inhabitants. Through a mix of ingenuity and necessity, the early Mesopotamians devised advanced irrigation systems and flood control mechanisms, which not only tamed the rivers but also expanded cultivable land. These innovations in agriculture and infrastructure became foundational to urban development, leading to the rise of some of the world's first cities.

Beyond its agricultural innovations, Mesopotamia's location positioned it as a vital crossroads for trade and cultural exchange. It bridged the civilizations of the Indus Valley to the east and ancient Egypt to the west, facilitating the exchange of goods, ideas, and technologies. This interconnectivity, alongside its agricultural success, played an instrumental role in its ascent as a potent cultural, economic, and political hub.

As this chapter unfolds, the intricate tapestry of Mesopotamia's history will be detailed, exploring its pioneering cultures, influential empires, and the indelible marks they left on the annals of human civilization. From the innovative Sumerians and the powerful Akkadians to the resplendent Babylonians, Mesopotamia's legacy is a testament to human resilience, innovation, and the quest for knowledge.

The Sumerians and the Dawn of Civilization (circa 4500 - 1900 BCE)

In the annals of early human civilization, few societies bear as significant a mark as the Sumerians, who emerged in the fertile crescent of southern Mesopotamia. The alluvial plains between the Tigris and Euphrates rivers became a cradle for their pioneering advancements, innovations that resonate through millennia and into our contemporary world.

Mesopotamia's initial urban tapestry began with the Sumerian establishment in Eridu, which, according to various historical records, has a credible claim to be the world's inaugural city. Its existence, dating back to circa 4500 BC, was a testament to the Sumerian capacity for organized community life and governance.

By the time the calendar turned to 3200 BC, the Sumerian dominion had expanded, giving birth to a network of city-states including Uruk, Ur, and Lagash. These weren't mere settlements; they were sophisticated urban centers, each governed by a distinct ruler, encapsulated by imposing walls to ward off intruders and potential aggressors. Uruk's significance in this matrix of city-states is underscored by the eponymous Uruk period (circa 4000 - 3100 BC). This era was not merely about the physical expansion of the city but encapsulated a transformative phase in human civilization: the advent of writing.

The invention of cuneiform on clay tablets was perhaps the Sumerians' most profound legacy. As one of the earliest documented writing systems, cuneiform allowed for a broad array of administrative, literary, and educational activities, catalyzing an intellectual revolution that would shape the subsequent trajectory of other civilizations.

Architecturally, the Sumerians exhibited their aspirations towards the divine through the construction of ziggurats. These tiered temples, with their imposing stature, reached towards the heavens, epitomizing the Sumerians' religious fervor. The Ziggurat of Ur remains a testament to their architectural prowess.

An image of the Ziggurats of Mesopotamia[4]

Yet, the Sumerians weren't solely driven by the spiritual; their pragmatic innovations are evident in their mathematical systems. The implementation of the base-60 system, a precursor to our current time measurements, highlighted their sophisticated understanding of numbers.

Religion, for the Sumerians, was an intricate tapestry interwoven with their daily life. Their pantheon was expansive, comprising deities such as Anu, the sky god; Enlil, the storm god; and Inanna, the multifaceted goddess of love, war, and political power. These deities were not merely symbolic entities but played pivotal roles in the Sumerian understanding of existence and natural phenomena.

One of the crowning jewels of Sumerian literature, the "Epic of Gilgamesh", offers profound insights into their worldview. This ancient narrative, replete with themes of friendship, mortality, and the complex dynamics between gods and humans, underscores the intellectual and cultural sophistication of Sumerian society.

In this foundational stage of Mesopotamian history, the Sumerians, through their innovations and beliefs, laid the bedrock upon which subsequent empires and societies would construct their edifices.

The Akkadians: The First Mesopotamian Empire (circa 2334 - 2154 BCE)

Just as the Sumerians solidified their legacy in the annals of Mesopotamian history, a new power began to coalesce in the northern regions, spearheaded by a leader whose ambitions and capabilities were nothing short of imperial. This was the emergence of the Akkadian Empire, founded by Sargon of Akkad.

While the Sumerian city-states flourished, their independent natures and intermittent conflicts provided a strategic opportunity for consolidation. Sargon, originating from the city of Akkad, recognized this potential. Through a combination of diplomacy, military strategy, and sheer force, he embarked on a series of campaigns that would eventually subsume the Sumerian city-states and forge the Akkadian Empire. By approximately 2310 BC, cities like Uruk and Ur were under Akkadian dominion.

Yet, Sargon's ambitions transcended mere territorial gains. He envisioned an interconnected realm where trade, communication, and administration flowed seamlessly. This necessitated not only military prowess but an adept understanding of governance. To this end, he instituted systems of centralized administration, appointed loyal governors, and ensured cultural and linguistic cohesion through the propagation of the Akkadian language.

Beneath the shadow of its military conquests, the Akkadian Empire was also a hotbed of cultural and technological advancements. The use of cuneiform was refined and expanded, and Akkadian art and sculpture showcased a distinct stylistic evolution from their Sumerian predecessors, emphasizing realism and detail.

Yet, empires, no matter how vast, are not impervious to challenges. The Akkadian Empire grappled with internal rebellions, especially from the Sumerian south, highlighting the complexities of governing a heterogeneous realm. Externally, the empire's expansion brought it into contact—and occasionally conflict—with neighboring entities, most notably the Gutians, a people originating from the Zagros Mountains. The Gutians represented a formidable external challenge that eventually led to the empire's downfall around 2154 BCE.

Despite their lack of administrative sophistication and literary tradition compared to the Akkadians, the Gutians wielded sufficient military prowess to destabilize an already weakened empire beset by internal discord and environmental stressors such as drought. Their ascendancy led to a period often characterized as a 'dark age' in Mesopotamian history, marked by the decentralization of political power and a break in the tradition of centralized governance. This episode underscores the inherent vulnerabilities of imperial structures stretched thin across vast territories, unable to sufficiently manage or mitigate peripheral threats.

By around 2154 BC, the combined pressures of internal dissent, external invasions, and possibly ecological changes culminated in the decline and eventual dissolution of the Akkadian Empire. While the empire itself was transient, its impact was enduring. The very concept of a unified Mesopotamian empire served as a template for subsequent dynasties and kingdoms, notably the Third Dynasty of Ur and the Babylonian Empire.

In the grand tapestry of Mesopotamian history, the Akkadian Empire, with its audacious founder Sargon and its expansive reach, was a testament to the possibilities of human ambition and statecraft.

Babylonians: Mesopotamia's Resplendent Torchbearers (circa 1894-1595 BCE)

In the wake of the Akkadian Empire's decline, Mesopotamia bore witness to a series of shifts in power. While the Third Dynasty of Ur briefly re-established Sumerian dominance, it was the Babylonians, particularly under the leadership of Hammurabi, who would imprint an indelible mark on the historical narrative.

Babylon, situated on the banks of the Euphrates River, began its ascent as a city of significance during the early 2nd millennium BC. However, its rise to unparalleled prominence occurred under King Hammurabi, who ascended to the throne around 1792 BC. Under Hammurabi's astute leadership, Babylon extended its dominion over major parts of Mesopotamia, subsuming erstwhile powerful cities like Ur, Uruk, and Larsa.

One of Hammurabi's most enduring contributions was not born from military conquests but from legal and administrative innovation. The Codex Hammurabi, one of the earliest and most comprehensive legal codes in ancient history, was promulgated. Etched onto a stele of diorite, the code was a compilation of 282 laws covering a myriad of societal issues from trade disputes and property rights to criminal justice. Its preamble famously states its purpose as "to bring about the rule of righteousness in the land, to destroy the wicked and the evil-doers; so that the strong should not harm the weak." It underscores the intricate balance Hammurabi sought between authority, justice, and societal harmony.

While Hammurabi's Code is often at the forefront of discussions on Babylonian accomplishments, the realm also witnessed advancements in other spheres. Astronomy, mathematics, and literature flourished.

The famed Enuma Elish, the Babylonian creation myth, and the tale of the descent of the goddess Ishtar into the Underworld, offered insights into the spiritual and philosophical underpinnings of Babylonian society.

Post-Hammurabi, the Babylonian Empire faced a series of internal and external pressures, including invasions by the Hittites and the Kassites. While the city of Babylon itself would be revitalized under various dynasties, including the noted Neo-Babylonian Empire of the 1st millennium BC, Hammurabi's era stands out as a defining epoch.

The legacy of the Babylonians, encapsulated in their legal, literary, and scientific contributions, endures as a testament to the intellectual and cultural prowess of Mesopotamian civilization.

Assyrians and Neo-Babylonians: (circa 911-539 BCE)

The narrative of Mesopotamian civilization, while already rich with the accomplishments of the Sumerians, Akkadians, and Babylonians, witnessed further chapters of power and prowess with the emergence of the Assyrians and the Neo-Babylonians.

The Assyrians, originating from the northern regions of Mesopotamia, in what is now modern-day northern Iraq and parts of Syria, began their journey as a cluster of cities like Ashur and Nineveh. Around the beginning of the 1st millennium BCE, the Assyrian kingdom started to exert its dominance over Mesopotamia and beyond. By the 9th century BCE, under kings like Ashurnasirpal II and his successors, the Assyrians had created an empire that was unparalleled in its military might, administration, and territorial expanse.

Their military strategies were innovative and ruthless, employing siege engines, professional soldier classes, and an intricate network of roads to ensure rapid troop movements. The Assyrians were not mere conquerors; their administrative acumen was also evident. They established a network of vassal states, relocated potentially rebellious populations, and constructed monumental architectural projects, most notably in their capital cities of Ashur and later, Nineveh. The library of Ashurbanipal in Nineveh remains a testament to Assyrian scholarly pursuits, housing thousands of cuneiform tablets that provide a detailed window into their world.

However, the vast expanse of the Assyrian Empire became its own liability, making it increasingly susceptible to internal strife and external pressures. By the end of the 7th century BCE, the empire found itself grappling with insurrections from various subject populations. Concurrently, it faced military threats from rising entities such as the Medes and the Neo-Babylonians—the latter representing a resurgence of Babylonian power following the decline of the earlier Old Babylonian Empire around 1595 BCE. In 612 BCE, a coalition led by the Neo-Babylonians and the Medes laid siege to Nineveh, ultimately razing the city and heralding the collapse of the once formidable Assyrian Empire

In the vacuum left by the Assyrians, the Neo-Babylonians (or Chaldeans) under the leadership of Nabopolassar seized the moment to rise to prominence. His successor, Nebuchadnezzar II, is particularly noteworthy. Under his reign (604-562 BCE), Babylon flourished as never before. He undertook grand building projects, including the famous Hanging Gardens, one of the Seven Wonders of the Ancient World. The Ishtar Gate, a monumental entrance to the city, showcased the pinnacle of Neo-Babylonian art and architecture.

Furthermore, the Neo-Babylonians established themselves as formidable players in regional geopolitics. One of their most consequential actions was the capture and subsequent exile of the Judean elite, an event that profoundly impacted Jewish history and is chronicled as the Babylonian Captivity.

Nevertheless, the Neo-Babylonian Empire was relatively short-lived. In 539 BCE, the Persians under Cyrus the Great captured Babylon, integrating it into the vast Achaemenid Empire. The sun had set on the Mesopotamian dominance, but its legacy was already etched into the annals of history, influencing subsequent empires and leaving an indomitable imprint on civilization's narrative.

Trade, Cultural Exchange, and Connectivity (circa 3000-500 BCE)

Mesopotamia's geographical position rendered it not just an epicenter of civilization, but also a pivotal nexus of trade and cultural interactions. Situated between the major civilizations of the ancient world, it was a bridge connecting diverse regions, fostering an unparalleled exchange of goods, ideas, and practices.

Trade Routes and Commodities: Mesopotamia's river systems, the Tigris and Euphrates, and its overland routes facilitated trade with neighboring regions. To the east, the Indus Valley civilization was a significant trade partner, evidenced by the discovery of Mesopotamian artifacts in present-day Pakistan and northwest India. From the Indus, Mesopotamia imported luxury items like ivory, carnelian beads, and lapis lazuli. To the west, Anatolia, modern-day Turkey, provided silver, a crucial commodity for Mesopotamian economy. The south, particularly the Persian Gulf, was the route for trade with the distant Dilmun civilization (modern-day Bahrain) and the Oman peninsula, which supplied copper. Additionally, trade links with Egypt enabled the exchange of Mesopotamian grain for Egyptian gold and other luxury goods.

These trade connections were not limited to commodities. With the flow of goods came the interchange of ideas, technologies, and religious practices. Mesopotamian cylinder seals, cuneiform inscriptions, and architectural techniques have been found in sites far from its borders, indicating the profound influence of Mesopotamian culture. Simultaneously, Mesopotamia absorbed and integrated elements from other civilizations, enriching its own cultural tapestry.

Cities like Ur, Uruk, and Babylon were not only political and religious centers but also bustling hubs of commerce and trade. These cities had specialized markets or bazaars where merchants from distant lands congregated, exchanging goods and ideas. The urban populace, including the elites, depended on these markets for luxury items, metals, and rare materials not found in Mesopotamia.

The expansive trade networks and cultural interactions propelled by Mesopotamia laid the foundations for the concept of international diplomacy and treaties. Kingdoms established formal agreements to ensure the safety and fluidity of trade caravans, recognizing the mutual benefits of such arrangements. This interdependence made way for the idea of a shared humanity, connected not just by commerce but by shared aspirations, values, and challenges.

In sum, Mesopotamia, in its capacity as a trade hub, played a pivotal role in shaping the interconnectedness of ancient civilizations. The ebb and flow of goods and ideas through its cities underscore the region's significance in fostering early globalization and cultural syncretism.

Conclusion: Mesopotamia's Echoes in Time

The tapestry of Mesopotamia, intricately woven over millennia through its city-states, empires, and cultures, has created resonances that transcend its ancient boundaries. Although the political dominions of the Sumerians, Akkadians, Babylonians and Assyrians eventually ebbed, Mesopotamia's indelible imprints remain evident today.

Political entities, by their very nature, are impermanent. In the case of Mesopotamia, external invasions, internal discord, economic challenges, and environmental shifts precipitated the decline of its illustrious empires. The subsequent dominion of the Persians over this strategic region signified the end of the influential epochs of Sumer, Akkad, and Babylon.

Yet, it is the imperishable contributions of Mesopotamia that have immortalized its significance:

Cuneiform's genesis in Mesopotamia, although archaic today, epitomized humanity's profound urge to chronicle, correspond, and commemorate. It set the precedent for successive writing systems, propelling both administration and culture.

Hammurabi's Code, with its emphasis on justice, equity, and societal equilibrium, became a pioneering template in jurisprudence, influencing the foundational legal systems of future civilizations.

The legacy of **the sexagesimal system** and the meticulous observational records of celestial entities have been instrumental in shaping later advancements in these domains.

The profundity of texts such as the "Epic of Gilgamesh" and the "Enuma Elish" extend beyond **literary excellence**, offering deep insights into human existence, the divine, and the universe.

Later civilizations, from the Greeks and Romans to the luminaries of the Islamic Golden Age, while sculpting their distinctive legacies, were incontrovertibly influenced by Mesopotamian paradigms in governance, science, literature, and the arts.

Mesopotamia, often lauded as civilization's cradle, epitomizes more than a mere geographic locale. It represents an epic saga of human ambition, exploration, and creativity. While its cities may lie in ruins and its empires have merged into historical records, its ethos—a boundless quest for knowledge and an intrinsic desire to fathom the human odyssey—enduringly influences and steers the course of human advancement.

Palace of Sargon II, Khorsabad - Oriental Institute Museum, University of Chicago

Great Sphinx of Giza[5]

Chapter 4.
Ancient Egypt: The Pinnacle of Early Civilization (5000-30BCE)

All Strange and Terrible Events are Welcome,
but Comfort we Despise

~Queen Cleopatra

Egypt's Timeless Allure (from 5000 BCE)

Ancient Egypt, often encapsulated by the colossal pyramids, the Sphinx, and the intricate hieroglyphics, remains an enduring symbol of a civilization that flourished alongside the fertile banks of the Nile River. This civilization, stretching across millennia, seamlessly integrated its geographical bounty, political aspirations, and cultural innovations. Analyzing the contours of Egypt's rise and subsequent developments, it becomes apparent that the Nile was not just a river but the lifeblood that fostered the growth of one of history's most illustrious civilizations.

A confluence of factors, both natural and man-made, contributed to Egypt's prominence. The Nile's annual inundation deposited rich alluvial soil onto its banks, thereby ensuring agricultural productivity.

This consistent agricultural yield provided sustenance and, in turn, facilitated the congregation of populations, leading to the rise of complex societal structures. While the river's bounties were undeniable, it was the Egyptian populace's ability to harness these resources, coupled with their ingenuity in governance, art, and science, that positioned Egypt as a notable force in the ancient world.

Geographically insulated by vast deserts on either side, Egypt enjoyed a level of protection from foreign invasions, especially in its formative years. This natural fortification allowed for a relative continuity in its political and cultural trajectory, with only sporadic interruptions. Furthermore, the Nile served as a natural highway, fostering trade and facilitating communication between Upper and Lower Egypt, which would, in time, have profound implications for the region's political unification.

As this chapter delves into the intricate tapestry of Ancient Egypt's history, it is essential to understand that the civilization's accomplishments were not mere products of geographical determinism. They were, in large part, the result of deliberate choices, policies, and innovations by its people, who built a civilization that, even today, captures the global imagination. The forthcoming sections will navigate through Egypt's dynastic periods, its cultural zeniths, the challenges it confronted, and the indelible marks it left on the annals of human history.

Foundations: Predynastic Egypt and Early Dynastic Period (circa 5000-2686 BCE)

During the Predynastic period of Ancient Egypt, circa 5000-3100 BCE, multiple small communities settled along the Nile's fertile banks. These communities, while initially isolated, began forging links, marked by trade and occasional conflict, as they shared the river's bounties. The foundation for Egypt as a centralized state can be discerned during this period, characterized by the emergence of distinct regional cultures such as Naqada in the south and Maadi-Buto in the north.

Distinctive pottery styles, burial customs, and artifacts from this era, excavated from sites like Hierakonpolis and Abydos, offer invaluable insights into the complex socio-political structures of these early communities. Hierakonpolis, known in ancient Egyptian as Nekhen, is located on the west bank of the Nile in Upper Egypt, approximately south of modern-day Luxor. It was one of the earliest and most significant urban centers during the Predynastic period. The city held significant importance due to its strategic location at the convergence of important trade routes, further bolstered by its proximity to crucial river crossings. Abydos, on the other hand, lies some 160 kilometers to the northeast of Hierakonpolis. It was situated on the western bank of the Nile, and its significance lay primarily in its religious and ceremonial roles. Over time, it became a preferred burial place, and many pharaohs, particularly from the Early Dynastic Period, chose it as their final resting place, lending to its reputation as a sacred necropolis.

The culmination of the Predynastic period was marked by the unification of Upper and Lower Egypt around 3100 BCE, an event traditionally ascribed to the pharaoh Narmer, evidenced by the Narmer Palette, a ceremonial engraving. This unification was not merely geographical but also represented the amalgamation of the varied cultural, religious, and political entities that had evolved independently.

The concept of 'pharaoh,' an overarching ruler governing the length of the Nile Valley, originated in the wake of this unification. The term 'pharaoh' is actually a Greek adaptation of the original ancient Egyptian term 'per-aa,' meaning 'great house,' initially used to describe the royal estate but later becoming synonymous with the king himself. The pharaoh was not merely a political ruler but a divine figure, believed to be a manifestation of Horus, the falcon god, on Earth. His dual role as both a mortal king and a divine entity created a unique form of governance known as 'maat,' representing truth, balance, and cosmic order. This ideology was intrinsic to the stability and prosperity of ancient Egypt, as the pharaoh was considered the earthly guarantor of cosmic order. Thus, the formation of this unique institution of pharaohs was pivotal in the consolidation of ancient Egypt as a centralized state, infusing it with the religious, cultural, and political norms that would govern it for millennia.

The Early Dynastic Period (circa 3100-2686 BCE) witnessed the consolidation of pharaonic rule. This era saw the establishment of Memphis as a political and administrative center, situated strategically between Upper and Lower Egypt, symbolizing the unity of the two lands. First and second dynasties were established in this period with pharaohs undertaking significant construction projects, including the step pyramid of Djoser, signaling the onset of monumental architecture.

Saqqara Pyramid[6]

However, the foundations for Egypt's grandeur were laid during these initial phases, and as the Early Dynastic Period transitioned into the Old Kingdom, Egypt was poised to reach unprecedented heights in governance, culture, and infrastructure. This ascent was facilitated by the stability and administrative acumen of the early pharaohs, combined with the fertile lands of the Nile, setting the stage for the dynastic era that would etch Egypt into the annals of great empires.

The Old Kingdom: Architectural Marvels and Administrative Feats (circa 2686 - 2181 BCE)

The Old Kingdom, epitomizing the Third to the Sixth Dynasties, stands out as an era that crystallized the unique attributes of ancient Egyptian civilization. This period saw the harmonious blend of monumental architecture and a centralized bureaucracy, positioning Egypt as a dominant power in the ancient world.

The foundation of Memphis by Pharaoh Menes marked a pivotal moment in the narrative of the Old Kingdom. Its strategic location near the junction of Upper and Lower Egypt, allowed Memphis to evolve as the administrative and religious heartland. It became the focal point for trade, politics, and cultural exchange. The city's development was marked by the construction of temples, palaces, and administrative buildings, signifying its eminence in the political landscape of Egypt.

The hallmark of the Old Kingdom's legacy lies in the colossal pyramids dotting the landscape. These monumental structures served dual purposes: as eternal resting places for the pharaohs and as a demonstration of the state's unmatched power and resources.

In the early dynastic phase of Egypt, elites were typically interred in structures known as mastabas. These flat-roofed, rectangular structures, constructed from mudbricks or limestone, were characterized by a chapel for offerings and an underground burial chamber. However, as the Third Dynasty commenced, architectural ambitions evolved profoundly. The Step Pyramid of Djoser at Saqqara epitomized this transition. Instead of a traditional mastaba, Djoser's burial site was envisioned as a series of tiered mastabas stacked upon each other, culminating in a six-level step-like edifice. This innovative design, credited to the renowned vizier Imhotep, wasn't a mere architectural leap. It signified the pharaoh's ascent to divinity, forging a deeper connection between the monarch and the cosmic realm, thereby reinforcing his integral role in both the earthly and divine domains.

However, the epitome of pyramid-building manifested on the Giza Plateau. The three pyramids, dedicated to Pharaohs Khufu, Khafre, and Menkaure, dominate the skyline, with the Great Pyramid of Khufu being the most colossal. This pyramid, with its precision-aligned sides correlating with the cardinal points of the compass and originally covered in smooth, white Tura limestone, is not just an architectural masterpiece but also a testament to the Old Kingdom's advanced knowledge of geometry, astronomy, and engineering.

The Old Kingdom's administrative structure was emblematic of a tightly controlled centralized state. At its zenith, the pharaoh wielded immense power, both temporal and spiritual. Considered a divine entity, the pharaoh's rule was unchallenged, upheld by an intricate network of viziers, nomarchs, priests, and scribes. These officials played crucial roles in maintaining order, collecting taxes, overseeing agricultural production, and executing monumental construction projects.

The scribe, adept in hieroglyphic writing, was an indispensable figure in this bureaucratic machinery. They documented decrees, maintained census data, and chronicled events, ensuring that the administration's vast undertakings were methodically recorded.

Despite its monumental achievements, the Old Kingdom was not impervious to challenges. By the end of the Sixth Dynasty, the power of the pharaoh began to wane. Contributory factors included dwindling economic resources, possibly due to reduced Nile inundations, leading to decreased agricultural output. Additionally, the growing influence of nomarchs and the priesthood eroded the centralized power structure.

Environmental changes, epitomized by reduced Nile floods, strained the agrarian backbone of Egypt. The resulting famines and social unrest culminated in the fragmentation of the once-monolithic Egyptian state, leading to the onset of the First Intermediate Period.

In sum, the Old Kingdom's architectural prowess and robust administration positioned Egypt as a beacon of ancient civilization. While it had its vulnerabilities, the foundations laid during this epoch had lasting ramifications, influencing subsequent periods of Egyptian history and civilizations beyond its borders.

Interlude: First Intermediate Period – A Time of Disarray

The First Intermediate Period, spanning the Seventh to the Tenth Dynasties (circa 2181 - 2055 BCE), represents a distinct phase of disintegration in Egypt's chronological tapestry. Following the relative stability and grandeur of the Old Kingdom, this era was characterized by political fragmentation, economic upheavals, and social tumult.

The diminishing authority of the pharaohs created a vacuum that provincial rulers, or nomarchs, were keen to fill. These leaders, initially appointed by pharaohs as regional governors, began to assert their independence. This newfound autonomy was not mere opportunism but was supported by fortified provincial capitals and individual armies. The nomarchs' increased clout, coupled with their fortified strongholds, rendered Egypt a patchwork of fiefdoms, each vying for supremacy.

This socio-political fragmentation found echoes in the art and literature of the period. Tomb inscriptions and reliefs from this era divulged a departure from the formalized and idealized depictions of the Old Kingdom. Instead, they displayed a more personalized touch, emphasizing individual achievements and often reflecting a sense of pessimism. Literature, such as the "Lamentations of the Sage," echoed this sentiment, detailing the despair and chaos that had besieged Egypt.

Central to the challenges of this period were the economic difficulties exacerbated by inconsistent Nile floods. Fluctuating inundations rendered agriculture, the mainstay of Egypt's economy, increasingly unpredictable. This uncertainty led to food shortages, with the worst famine, as documented on the Famine Stele, lasting for seven years during the reign of Pharaoh Djoser. Such famines not only affected the agrarian output but also triggered societal unrest and mass migrations.

Though the First Intermediate Period was fraught with challenges, it set the stage for monumental changes. The competing factions and the overarching need for stability gradually led to the rise of two primary power centers: Heracleopolis in the north and Thebes in the south. This duality set the stage for the subsequent reunification, primarily under the Theban rulers, marking the inception of the Middle Kingdom.

In retrospection, the First Intermediate Period, despite its moniker of "disarray," was not an era of unbridled chaos. It was, instead, a transformative phase, underscoring the resilience of the Egyptian polity, its ability to introspect, adapt, and emerge renewed, laying the groundwork for the next epoch of prosperity and cultural renaissance.

The Middle Kingdom: Resurgence, Reforms, and Foreign Ventures (circa 2055 - 1650 BCE)

The Middle Kingdom, spanning the Eleventh to the Thirteenth Dynasties, epitomizes Egypt's capacity for rebirth. Following the tumultuous First Intermediate Period, the Middle Kingdom heralded an era of rejuvenation, marked by administrative reforms, architectural innovations, and strategic foreign engagements.

The advent of the Middle Kingdom is demarcated by the efforts of Theban ruler Mentuhotep II. His campaigns, culminating in the defeat of the Heracleopolitan rulers around 2055 BCE, effectively reunified Egypt. Mentuhotep II, often regarded as the second founder of Egypt, re-established the capital at Thebes, signifying both a geographical and ideological shift from the Old Kingdom's Memphis-centered governance.

With Egypt once more under centralized rule, the subsequent Twelfth Dynasty pharaohs, notably Amenemhat I and Senusret I, undertook comprehensive administrative reforms. These aimed to curtail the powers of provincial nomarchs, ensuring they couldn't amass power as during the First Intermediate Period. The country was further divided into smaller administrative units, and officials were frequently rotated, thwarting any local loyalties from becoming too entrenched.

The Middle Kingdom is recognized for its architectural and artistic endeavors. While pyramids continued to be the primary royal tombs, their design and construction materials evolved. Notably, the pyramid of Amenemhat III at Hawara, with its intricate labyrinth, stands out. Moreover, a surge in literature and art showcased more diverse themes, reflecting daily life, philosophical introspection, and even satire. The "Tale of Sinuhe," a narrative of an official's self-imposed exile and eventual return, exemplifies the literary richness of this period.

Strategically, the pharaohs of the Middle Kingdom looked beyond Egypt's borders. To the south, in Nubia, military campaigns sought control of trade routes and valuable resources, such as gold. Fortresses, like that of Buhen, were erected to solidify Egyptian dominance and protect these vital trade arteries. Diplomatic relations, exemplified by the exchange of gifts with rulers from the Levant and Crete, were also pursued, indicating Egypt's growing influence and its integration into a larger geopolitical framework.

However, by the end of the Twelfth Dynasty, signs of internal strife and external pressures began to surface. The Thirteenth Dynasty, characterized by a rapid succession of pharaohs and waning central authority, struggled to maintain the cohesion achieved earlier. The vulnerability became palpable, paving the way for foreign incursions and the subsequent Hyksos dominance.

In its entirety, the Middle Kingdom underscores Egypt's capacity for introspection and course correction. Through administrative rigor, cultural renaissance, and strategic foreign engagements, Egypt not only regained its lost grandeur but also laid the foundation for its future imperial pursuits.

Interlude: Second Intermediate Period – The Hyksos Intrigue

Spanning the end of the Middle Kingdom to the dawn of the New Kingdom, the Second Intermediate Period (circa 1650-1550 BCE) was punctuated by Egypt's fragmentation and a significant foreign presence, the Hyksos. This era, comprising the Thirteenth to Seventeenth Dynasties, is emblematic of both Egypt's vulnerabilities and its resilience.

Originating from the Levantine region, the Hyksos—often translated as "rulers of foreign lands"—began their gradual infiltration into the Nile Delta. By circa 1630 BCE, they had established a stronghold at Avaris, turning it into their capital. The Hyksos brought with them superior military technology, most notably the composite bow and the horse-drawn chariot, giving them a tactical edge over the native Egyptian forces.

With the Hyksos consolidating their power in the northern regions, Egypt experienced a bifurcation of sorts. While the Hyksos held sway in the Delta, native Egyptian rulers persisted in Thebes and other southern locales, coexisting albeit uneasily. This segmentation mirrored not only a political division but also distinct cultural and ideological realms, with the Theban rulers ardently upholding indigenous Egyptian traditions.

Contrary to earlier interpretations of the Hyksos as destructive invaders, current scholarship underscores their role in cultural fusion. While they introduced several Levantine practices and technologies, they simultaneously assimilated various facets of Egyptian culture, evident in their adoption of Egyptian titles and the worship of Egyptian deities.

The Seventeenth Dynasty Theban rulers, particularly Seqenenre Tao and Kamose, initiated campaigns against the Hyksos. However, it was Ahmose I, ascending the throne around 1539 BCE, who finally expelled the Hyksos from Avaris, reasserting Egyptian dominance and laying the foundation for the New Kingdom. This victory was not merely a military achievement but also a symbolic restoration of Ma'at, the cosmic order integral to Egyptian worldview.

The Second Intermediate Period, with its challenges and complexities, underlines the ebb and flow inherent in the annals of civilizations. The Hyksos dominion, while an interlude in pharaonic rule, fostered technological advancements and cultural exchanges, illustrating that interactions—even those rooted in conflict—can yield transformative outcomes. With the Hyksos' expulsion, Egypt was poised to embark on one of its most illustrious chapters, the New Kingdom, characterized by unprecedented territorial expansions and cultural efflorescence.

The New Kingdom: Empire's zenith and Religious Revolutions (circa 1550 - 1077 BCE)

The New Kingdom, spanning the Eighteenth to the Twentieth Dynasties, marked a zenith in Egyptian history in terms of territorial expansion, architectural accomplishments, and profound cultural shifts.

Under the Eighteenth Dynasty, two remarkable figures stood out in their leadership: Hatshepsut and Thutmose III. Hatshepsut (1478–1458 BCE), initially ascending the throne as a regent for the young Thutmose III, transitioned to a full-fledged pharaoh in her own right. Her tenure, characterized by diplomatic endeavors and ambitious building projects, culminated in the construction of the terraced mortuary temple at Deir el-Bahari. Hatshepsut's ascendancy as a female monarch in a predominantly male role underscores the occasional fluidity of gender roles within the Egyptian leadership framework.

Following Hatshepsut's death in 1458 BCE, Thutmose III (1479–1425 BCE) began to rule independently, marking a shift from peaceful diplomacy to military expansionism. He transformed Egypt into a sprawling empire, extending its territories to encompass regions like Nubia in the south, Syria-Palestine in the northeast, and parts of the Near East. The establishment of administrative hubs, notably the city of Per-Ramesses in the Delta, facilitated the efficient governance of these expansive dominions.

Arguably the most radical shift in Egyptian religious culture emerged under Amenhotep IV, who later adopted the name Akhenaten (circa 1353-1336 BCE). Transitioning from the traditional polytheistic practices, Akhenaten elevated the sun-disc god, Aten, to a supreme position, sidelining the hitherto dominant deity, Amun. This transformation was not limited to theology; it manifested in art, with more naturalistic portrayals, and politics, with the establishment of a new capital at Akhetaten (modern-day Amarna).

Post-Akhenaten's demise, there was a concerted effort to revert to the traditional religious practices. His successor and likely son, Tutankhamun (circa 1332–1323 BCE), played a pivotal role in this restoration. While his reign was short-lived, the discovery of his almost intact tomb in the Valley of the Kings in 1922 provided invaluable insights into New Kingdom art, funerary practices, and material culture.

Ramesses II (1279–1213 BCE), of the Nineteenth Dynasty, is often celebrated for his architectural endeavors, notably the construction of the Ramesseum and the rock-cut temples at Abu Simbel. Additionally, his

Photo of Abu Simbel temple[7]

reign is marked by the Battle of Kadesh against the Hittites around 1274 BCE. Although the battle's outcome was indecisive, it led to the signing of one of the earliest known peace treaties in human history.

The New Kingdom encapsulates the complexities and dynamism of Egyptian civilization. From unprecedented territorial expansions to deep introspections on religious identity, this era not only shaped the trajectory of Egyptian history but also left an indelible imprint on the broader canvas of ancient Near Eastern civilizations. As with any empire, the seeds of decline were sown within these very achievements, paving the way for external pressures and internal fissures that would manifest in the ensuing centuries.

Spiritual and Cultural Landscape: Pantheon, Afterlife, and Ceremonies

In the heart of ancient Egyptian religious life lay a diverse and intricate pantheon of gods and goddesses. Each deity was associated with specific facets of nature, society, or abstract concepts. Gods such as Ra, associated with the sun, and Amun, linked with creation, held high esteem in this divine hierarchy. Osiris, symbolic of death and resurrection, alongside his consort Isis, representing magic and motherhood, shaped Egyptian perceptions of the afterlife. Meanwhile, the deities Horus, often represented as a falcon, and Seth, the embodiment of chaos, mirrored the eternal battle between order and disorder, a theme that resonated in various cultures across time.

Integral to the worldview of the Egyptians was Ma'at, representing truth, balance, and cosmic order. Far from being a mere philosophical idea, Ma'at was the foundation upon which the rule of the pharaohs rested. It was believed that the pharaoh's duty was to ensure the continued observance of Ma'at, and any deviation from this path might lead to chaos, both in this life and in the afterlife.

The Egyptians perceived death not as a cessation but as a transformative phase in an individual's existence. Upon death, the deceased's ka, or soul, embarked on a challenging journey through the underworld. To navigate this realm and reach the Field of Reeds, an idyllic afterlife, the deceased required guidance from the "Book of the Dead," a compilation of spells and incantations. The preservation of the deceased's physical form for this spiritual journey was ensured through mummification, a meticulous process that underscored the significance Egyptians attributed to the afterlife.

In tandem with these beliefs, the construction of monumental tombs evolved. Initially, pyramids were the tombs of choice, but over time, rock-cut tombs in locations such as the Valley of the Kings gained prominence. These burial sites, inscribed with funerary texts and adorned with possessions, were meant to protect and guide the deceased in the afterlife. Adjacent to these tombs, mortuary complexes, which included temples and statues, were erected, facilitating rituals that honored the departed.

Religious ceremonies, intricately woven into the Egyptian way of life, were often tied to the agricultural calendar, emphasizing the symbiotic relationship between the land, the Nile, and the divine. Among these ceremonies, the Opet Festival in Thebes stood out, marking the rejuvenation of the king's power through his union with the god Amun. Frequent processions, where statues of deities were showcased, bridged the gap between the divine and mortal realms, offering a tangible connection to the gods.

In conclusion, the spiritual and cultural dimensions of ancient Egypt offered a rich tapestry of beliefs, practices, and rituals. This comprehensive system, evolved over millennia, not only provided a lens through which the Egyptians understood their world but also equipped them with the tools to engage deeply with existential questions and the mysteries of the cosmos.

Pillars of Legacy:
Papyrus, Hieroglyphics, Medicine, and More

Ancient Egypt's contributions to human civilization spanned a multitude of fields, many of which had enduring impacts long after the pharaohs ceased to reign. From the Old Kingdom (circa 2686 - 2181 BCE) onwards, numerous innovations emerged.

Papyrus, a material prepared from the pithy stem of the Cyperus papyrus plant, emerged around 3000 BCE and revolutionized communication. This precursor to modern paper, superseding the heavier clay tablets of contemporaneous cultures, was more versatile. Scribes across millennia, from the Old Kingdom through the New Kingdom (circa 1550 - 1077 BCE), utilized papyrus to document everything from religious decrees and administrative logs to literary works, facilitating the intergenerational transfer of knowledge.

Concurrently, by approximately 3200 BCE, hieroglyphics, ancient Egypt's formal writing system, had been established. Comprising over 700 distinct characters, hieroglyphics merged logographic and alphabetic principles. The enigma of translating these intricate scripts persisted until the 19th century when the Rosetta Stone, discovered in 1799, revealed its bilingual inscriptions in Greek and hieroglyphics. The Rosetta Stone, discovered near the town of Rashid (Rosetta) in the Nile Delta in 1799 by French soldiers during Napoleon's Egyptian campaign, stands as an exemplar of multilingualism and the interplay between ancient cultures. This granodiorite slab, dating back to 196 BCE during the Ptolemaic era, features a decree issued by King Ptolemy V Epiphanes, inscribed in three distinct scripts: hieroglyphic, demotic (a native Egyptian script), and ancient Greek. The presence of the same text in all three languages proved invaluable.

The true breakthrough in deciphering hieroglyphics came through the meticulous work of Jean-François Champollion in the early 19th century. Utilizing the ancient Greek, a language already understood by scholars, as a reference, Champollion was able to decode the hieroglyphic and demotic scripts. This decoding not only bridged a temporal chasm, granting access to the wealth of knowledge ensconced in countless hieroglyphic texts, but also emphasized the interconnectedness of ancient civilizations, where Greek rulers, adopting Egyptian customs and beliefs, facilitated a confluence of cultures.

In the realm of medicine, the Egyptians demonstrated profound insights. Ebers Papyrus, one of the most comprehensive medical documents from ancient Egypt, provides a testament to their expertise. Dating back to circa 1550 BCE, this treatise contained over 700 spells and remedies for various ailments. The surgical practices detailed in the Edwin Smith Papyrus, another crucial medical text, revealed a deep understanding of the human anatomy. Furthermore, their mummification processes, which involved the removal and preservation of internal organs, further showcased their anatomical knowledge.

Architecture in Egypt transcended mere shelter or monumentalism; it mirrored the intersection of the spiritual and the earthly. While the pyramids remain the most iconic representation of Egyptian architectural prowess, temples such as those at Karnak and Luxor epitomized the grandeur and intricacy of design. Techniques employed in erecting these colossal structures, including the use of simple tools, the establishment of precise measurements, and the organization of vast labor forces, reflected a society that valued precision, planning, and collaboration.

Art too, was an integral facet of Egyptian civilization. From the colossal statues depicting pharaohs to the intricate jewelry adorned with semi-precious stones, artistic creations were not merely aesthetic endeavors but deeply symbolic representations. They conveyed the socio-political hierarchy, religious beliefs, and cultural values.

In essence, ancient Egypt's innovations and achievements in varied domains were not isolated instances of brilliance but the outcome of a complex socio-cultural matrix that valued knowledge, creativity, and precision. Through their legacies in writing, medicine, architecture, and the arts, the ancient Egyptians paved the way for subsequent civilizations to build upon, adapt, and refine these foundations.

Conclusion: The Waning of Pharaonic Rule and Egypt's Eternal Resonance (circa 1077 - 30 BCE)

As the curtains began to descend on the illustrious age of the pharaohs, a series of external and internal factors precipitated the decline of ancient Egyptian dominance.

Post the New Kingdom, the Third Intermediate Period (circa 1077 - 664 BCE) witnessed significant political fragmentation. The centralized power that had once epitomized the Egyptian state became fractured. Tanis, in the north, emerged as a powerful center, competing with Thebes in the south. Concurrently, Libya to the west and Nubia to the south exerted influence, with Libyan chieftains gaining power in the Nile Delta and Nubian kings even ruling Egypt for a period.

By the Late Period (circa 664-332 BCE), external interventions became more frequent. The Assyrian conquest in the 7th century BCE marked a significant phase in Egypt's declining fortunes. Though the Assyrians' control was relatively short-lived, the subsequent invasion by the Persians under Cambyses II in 525 BCE signaled a deeper shift in the regional power dynamics. Despite brief resurgences of native rule, like the notable reign of Nectanebo II, Persian dominance remained a consistent challenge.

However, the landscape of power in Egypt was once again reshaped with the arrival of Alexander the Great in 332 BCE. With his conquest, he not only expelled the Persians but also endeared himself to the Egyptians by adopting traditional pharaonic titles and customs. Upon Alexander's death in 323 BCE, one of his generals, Ptolemy I Soter, became the ruler of Egypt, establishing the Ptolemaic dynasty. This Greek dynasty, while Hellenistic in nature, embraced and integrated many aspects of Egyptian culture, forging a syncretic civilization. However, the influence of the Greek rulers over time began to wane, leading to increased Roman interest and intervention.

The final blow to Egypt's autonomy was delivered not by another Eastern empire, but from the burgeoning powerhouse in the Mediterranean: Rome. Following the death of queen Cleopatra VII and her Roman ally Mark Antony in 30 BCE, Egypt was annexed as a province of the Roman Empire under Emperor Augustus. The millennia-old tradition of pharaohs, native Egyptian rulers who were deemed almost divine, was irreversibly terminated.

However, the decline of political and military dominance did not signify the erasure of Egyptian culture. In fact, its resonance was felt deeply within the Roman Empire. Temples continued to be built in the Egyptian style, Egyptian religious beliefs were integrated into Roman practices, and the city of Alexandria remained a vital hub of learning and culture.

It's critical to perceive the legacy of ancient Egypt not merely in terms of its dynastic timeline but also its profound and lasting impact on the collective consciousness of humanity. Its architectural marvels stand as testaments to human ambition; its scripts offer insights into a rich tapestry of tales, beliefs, and knowledge; its art and artifacts provide windows into a society that was complex, hierarchical, yet deeply spiritual.

It's worth pausing to consider the longevity of the Egyptian dynastic periods: the Old, Middle, and New Kingdoms spanned millennia, demonstrating remarkable resilience and adaptability. Such durations defy modern comprehension, especially when viewed through the lens of more recent geopolitically dominant entities. For instance, the United States, often perceived as a lasting world superpower, has been globally preeminent for less than two centuries. This reveals a stark contrast between the timeframes that modern audiences typically consider 'long-lasting' and the multi-millennial span of ancient civilizations. The Egyptian civilization's ability to reinvent itself, enduring periods of fragmentation and external invasions, serves as a salient reminder of the relativity of historical duration. It calls into question modern assumptions about the permanence of contemporary empires and underscores the value of adopting a longue durée perspective in the study of history.

In the annals of history, while empires may rise and wane, their legacies endure, influencing and shaping civilizations that follow. Egypt, with its grand pyramids gazing eternally towards the heavens and its intricate hieroglyphs whispering tales from epochs long past, stands as a monumental testament to this eternal truth.

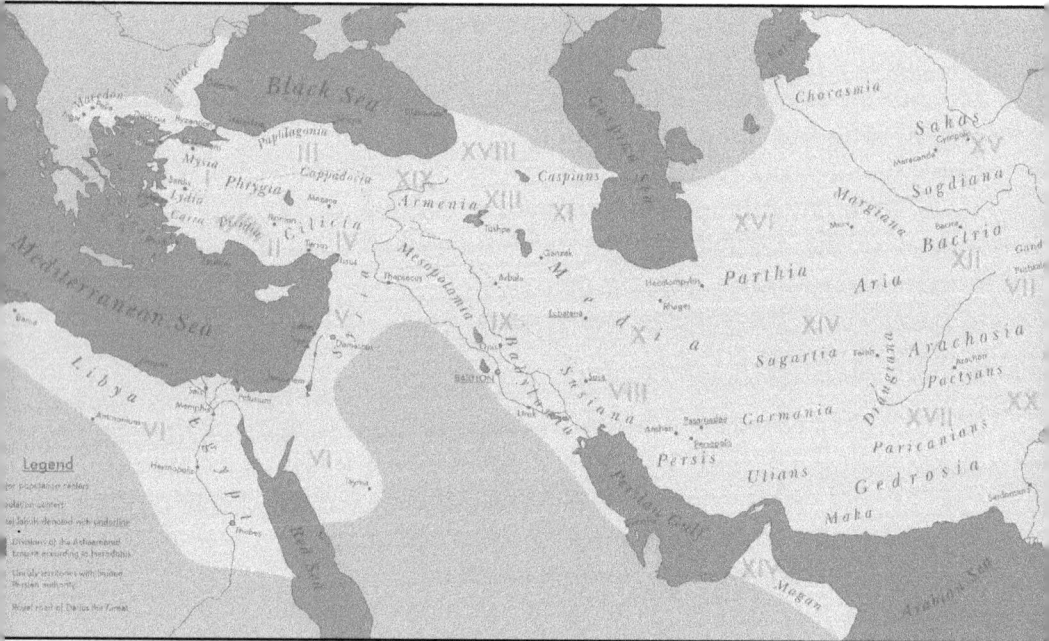

Achaemenid Empire 500 BC[8]

Chapter 5.
The Persian Empire: A Legacy of Tolerance (550-330 BCE)

Diversity in counsel, unity in command.

~*Cyrus the Great*

The Foundations of an Empire

The decline of Egyptian dominance in the ancient Near East coincided with the emergence of a potent civilization in the Iranian plateau. Geographical factors, combined with human endeavors in this region, facilitated the rise of an empire that would wield substantial influence for centuries.

Around 1500 BCE, the Aryans, an Indo-European nomadic group, migrated to the Iranian plateau, introducing their languages, traditions, and customs. These elements integrated with the indigenous cultures, thereby forming the early foundations of Persian identity, which would later be recognized for its contributions to governance, arts, and infrastructure.

By the 6th century BCE, the Medes, initially a confederation of Aryan tribes, established a dominant presence. Their ascendancy was not merely due to numerical or military superiority; their ability to unify diverse tribal factions under a single governance structure was a defining trait. Their capital, Ecbatana (present-day Hamadan), became the political and commercial hub of this growing empire. Historical records allude to the city's fortified walls constructed using gold and silver bricks. This city would remain significant for subsequent empires, including the Achaemenid, Seleucid, and Parthian.

With the Medes solidifying their control, the foundation was laid for the subsequent Achaemenid dynasty, which would further develop the empire based on principles of tolerance, extensive infrastructure, and administrative innovation.

Cyrus the Great: Conqueror and Benevolent Ruler

Cyrus II, commonly referred to as Cyrus the Great, assumed kingship in 559 BCE over Anshan, a historically relevant city in the southwest region of contemporary Iran. Originally under Elamite jurisdiction before the rise of the Persians, Anshan's prominence was underscored by Cyrus's adoption of the title "King of Anshan" prior to the inception of the Persian Empire. The strategic position of Anshan not only facilitated Cyrus's local influence but also propelled his larger vision of consolidating the Persian territories.

A depiction of Cyrus the Great [9]

By 550 BCE, Cyrus had adeptly maneuvered against the powerful Median Empire, leading to its decline and facilitating the Persian annexation of Ecbatana, the once indomitable Median capital. Cyrus's imperial objectives, however, were not confined to the Iranian plateau; his gaze turned westward to Asia Minor. In 547 BCE, utilizing effective military tactics, Cyrus managed to subjugate the Lydian kingdom, helmed by King Croesus, bringing the crucial city of Sardis under Persian hegemony.

In 539 BCE, Cyrus's diplomatic and strategic prowess culminated in the acquisition of Babylon. Instead of employing brute force, he employed a strategy that enabled him to be perceived as a liberator by the Babylonians. The Cyrus Cylinder, a cuneiform-inscribed clay artifact from the 6th century BCE, offers empirical evidence of Cyrus's administrative policies:

Policy of Tolerance. The cylinder elucidates Cyrus's endorsement of cultural and religious freedoms within his diverse empire, an early precedent for human rights declarations.

Repatriation Decree. It references Cyrus's edict allowing deported communities, notably the Jews, to repatriate and reconstruct their places of worship — an event corroborated by biblical accounts.

Historical Documentation. The cylinder provides an account of Babylon's annexation and the subsequent administrative and religious reforms under Cyrus.

Symbolic Representation. Beyond its historical relevance, the cylinder has assumed a symbolic stature in modern discourse, often invoked in discussions on human rights and diplomacy.

Cyrus's reign marked a confluence of territorial expansion, achieved not solely through warfare but also through an enlightened approach to governance that respected regional diversities. When he met his demise in 530 BCE, Cyrus left an indelible mark, having not only established an expansive empire but also bequeathed a governance model anchored in benevolence and tolerance for successive Persian rulers to emulate.

Darius I: The Architect of the Empire's Pinnacle

Upon Darius I's accession to the throne in 522 BCE, the Persian Empire's vast territories presented a tableau of both opportunity and challenges, particularly in the realm of administrative cohesion. His early reign was punctuated by the need to quell multifarious rebellions, which, by 519 BCE, culminated in a more cohesive empire. Recognizing the intricacies of governing a domain stretching from the Indus River to the Aegean Sea, Darius demonstrated a discerning approach to administrative centralization.

To institute a sustainable governance structure, Darius instigated the system of satrapies. These were essentially provincial units, helmed by satraps who, while exercising local authority, were under the overarching sovereignty of the Persian monarch. To ensure fidelity to the crown, Darius established the "Eyes of the King," a surveillance mechanism employing royal spies to oversee the satraps' activities, thus intertwining local autonomy with centralized oversight.

Darius's strategic vision was also manifested in infrastructure projects aimed at integrating the vast empire. The Royal Road exemplifies this, spanning approximately 2,500 kilometers from Sardis to Susa. This road, punctuated with strategically placed post stations, enabled efficient communication across the empire. Concurrently, Darius standardized economic transactions by introducing the daric, a gold coin, which beyond facilitating trade, symbolized the unity and economic prowess of the Persian Empire.

Among Darius's architectural endeavors, Persepolis, or "Pärsa" in Old Persian, remains preeminent. This ceremonial capital, situated in the present-day Fars region of Iran, epitomizes the architectural zenith of the Achaemenid dynasty. Its construction was not merely an exercise in grandiosity but served to enshrine the glory of the Persian Empire and Darius's expansive vision. This glory, however, encountered a temporality, with Persepolis facing devastation at the hands of Alexander the Great in 330 BCE.

Darius's infrastructural vision transcended land; he commissioned the excavation of a canal linking the Nile to the Red Sea. Although this early iteration of the Suez Canal differed markedly from its modern counterpart in scope and utility, Darius's efforts laid the groundwork for subsequent canal projects in the region, culminating in the 19th-century version known today.

By the juncture of his demise in 486 BCE, Darius had indelibly inscribed his legacy, not merely through territorial expansion but through pioneering advancements in governance, infrastructure, and cultural amalgamation.

Xerxes and the Greco-Persian Wars

In the aftermath of Darius' death in 486 BCE, the leadership mantle transitioned to his son, Xerxes. Assuming command of an empire characterized by significant territorial expanse and administrative depth, Xerxes' reign was destined to be primarily marked by a series of intricate geopolitical confrontations: the Greco-Persian Wars.

The strategic objective of annexing Greece compelled Xerxes to marshal substantial military resources, culminating in a force whose magnitude seemed to strain the very capacities of terrestrial and maritime confines. This military endeavor crystallized in 480 BCE with the Battle of Thermopylae. This particular encounter, situated within a constrained mountain pass, witnessed a strategic defensive stand by a Spartan detachment led by King Leonidas. The encounter, while highlighting Spartan martial prowess, unfortunately for them, tilted in favor of the Persian military machinery.

However, the narrative shifted in the subsequent naval engagement at Salamis. The Persian naval armada, despite its numerical advantage, encountered a resilient and strategically adept Greek naval force. The constricted straits near Athens, combined with astute Greek naval maneuvers, inflicted significant casualties on the Persian fleet. This naval setback, in conjunction with the land-based defeat at Plataea in 479 BCE, recalibrated Xerxes' ambitions, constraining further westward territorial ambitions.

These military campaigns, while not destabilizing the Persian Empire per se, illuminated certain vulnerabilities. The fiscal and logistical demands of extended military campaigns, juxtaposed against the absence of tangible territorial gains in Greece, instigated internal administrative challenges and external geopolitical recalibrations. The empire's administrative echelons, notably the satraps, started exhibiting signs of autonomy, prompting the central authority to grapple with emerging fissures in the imperial edifice.

The Greco-Persian Wars, thus, offer more than a mere military narrative. They underscore the complexities inherent in imperial expansion, highlighting the dialectic between territorial ambitions and the preservation of administrative coherence. These confrontations, while territorial in nature, also represented deeper ideological contrasts, pitting different governance paradigms against each other in a manner that would leave enduring imprints on subsequent geopolitical and philosophical discourses.

Religion: Zoroastrianism and Its Influence

The Faravahar or Frawahr - a symbol of Zoroastrianism

In the backdrop of the 6th century BCE Persia, amid the religious diversity that characterized the region, a seminal philosophical shift was underway. Central to this transformation was Zarathustra, or as the Greeks referred to him, Zoroaster. As the progenitor of Zoroastrianism, he propelled forward a monotheistic framework that would become inextricably intertwined with the identity and governance of the Persian Empire.

The theological bedrock of Zoroastrianism rested upon the supremacy of Ahura Mazda, conceptualized as an omnipotent entity embodying absolute good. However, in order to manifest the cosmological equilibrium, Angra Mainyu, a representation of chaos and malevolence, was positioned in opposition to Ahura Mazda. This intricate dualism not only demarcated the cosmic boundaries of good and evil but also postulated the role of humans as decisive actors in this cosmic narrative, with their actions possessing lasting ramifications in the metaphysical realm.

A prominent ritualistic element within Zoroastrianism was the reverence for fire. Recognized as an elemental embodiment of purity, fire became a central component of religious observances. Across the Persian Empire, fire temples, housing perpetual flames, emerged as significant religious hubs. The guardianship of these flames was entrusted to the Magi, a priestly class whose religious duties and expertise rendered them indispensable to the spiritual ecosystem of the empire.

However, Zoroastrianism's influence was not confined to the realm of spirituality alone. Its tenets and doctrines exerted profound influence on the administrative and governance paradigms of Persia. The Persian monarchs, perceiving their rule as an extension of Ahura Mazda's will, adopted a governance model rooted in divine ordainment. This Zoroastrian underpinning facilitated the maintenance of internal cohesion, offering a unified religious framework that spanned the diverse and expansive territories of the empire.

Beyond the geographical confines of Persia, the reverberations of Zoroastrianism were palpable in the subsequent evolution of the Abrahamic traditions. The foundational Zoroastrian concepts, such as the ethical dichotomy of good versus evil, the eschatological notion of a final judgment, and the anticipation of a messianic entity, found echoes and adaptions in Judaism, Christianity, and Islam.

In summation, Zoroastrianism stands as a monumental testament to Persia's rich spiritual heritage. This religious tradition, anchored in the teachings of Zarathustra and codified in scriptures like the Avesta, not only delineated the spiritual and philosophical contours of the Persian Empire but also influenced broader theological trajectories, underscoring Persia's central role in shaping the religious tapestry of the ancient world.

Tolerance and Cultural Exchange: Hallmarks of Persian Governance

The expanse of the Persian Empire, spanning from 559 BCE to 330 BCE, represented not merely territorial conquest but also a nuanced understanding of governance that defied traditional imperialistic tendencies. The fabric of the Persian realm, woven with diverse ethnic and cultural threads—such as the Medes, Babylonians, Jews, and Egyptians—attests to an administrative ethos rooted in mutual respect and inclusivity.

Through the lens of history, we find a compelling illustration of this ethos in the interactions between Cyrus the Great and the captive Jewish population in Babylon. As we've explored previously, rather than adopting the traditional role of a conqueror, Cyrus's decree revealed a disposition toward magnanimity. Cyrus act to support the freedom of the Jewish community and their rebuilding of the Temple in Jerusalem, marked his valuing benevolence over mere dominance.

The economic arteries of the empire, particularly trade routes, became conduits of cultural exchange, transcending their primary function of facilitating commerce. The Royal Road, a pivotal trade route, became emblematic of this cultural dynamism. Caravans traversing this thoroughfare transported not merely commodities, but also an eclectic blend of ideas, artistic forms, and literary traditions. This continuous interchange led to the evolution of a rich tapestry of shared knowledge and creativity.

Artistic endeavors in the empire encapsulated this ethos of cultural amalgamation. The distinctive Persian artistic lexicon, while maintaining its intrinsic identity, seamlessly incorporated elements from Egyptian, Mesopotamian, and Indus Valley traditions. Literature, another vital cultural domain, witnessed a period of vibrant diversification, imbibing myriad influences yet preserving its core essence.

However, underpinning the Persian administrative paradigm was an unwavering commitment to tolerance. By acknowledging the intrinsic value of diverse cultures, religions, and traditions, the Persian leadership established an environment conducive to internal harmony. This strategy not only buttressed the empire's internal cohesion but also became instrumental in forging external alliances, positioning Persia as a formidable entity in the ancient geopolitical matrix.

Thus, within the geographic boundaries of the Persian Empire, which extended from the Indus Valley to Thrace and from Central Asia to the Nile Delta, resonated a governance model that championed inclusion over exclusion. The Persian leadership's enduring legacy embodied a vision where their imperial mission was not merely domination but elevation, setting the stage for an enlightened era defined by tolerance and cultural exchange.

The Achaemenid Twilight and the Macedon Dawn

As the wheel of time turned towards the 4th century BCE, the illustrious Persian Empire, which had once epitomized stability, cohesion, and grandeur, began encountering formidable challenges. Economic vicissitudes and dwindling centralized authority provided fertile ground for provincial satraps to overstep their traditional bounds, leading to instances of insubordination against the imperial nucleus. The integrative fabric of the Persian realm, which had been its hallmark, appeared to be fraying.

The year 334 BCE witnessed the emergence of a potent external challenge, originating from the Hellenic West – Alexander III of Macedon. Armed with youthful zeal, unparalleled military acumen, and an insatiable drive for territorial expansion, Alexander perceived the beleaguered Persian Empire not as an impervious fortress, but as an attainable objective. His military campaigns, notably the engagements at Issus (333 BCE) and Gaugamela (331 BCE), did not merely result in Persian military reverses but symbolically marked the ebbing of an epoch.

The demise of Darius III in 330 BCE effectively terminated the Achaemenid dynastic lineage. Alexander's subsequent entrance into Persepolis, the resplendent Persian capital, and its subsequent conflagration, became emblematic of the cessation of a magnificent imperial chapter.

However, historical transitions are seldom absolute, and the eclipse of the Achaemenid realm did not signify its wholesale obliteration. Alexander's approach to governance post-conquest was marked by pragmatism and strategic assimilation. Key Persian administrative officials retained their positions, ensuring a continuity of governance. The overarching structure of local administration, a keystone of Persian governance, remained relatively inviolate.

The resulting cultural fusion between the Macedonian conquerors and Persian values ushered in the Hellenistic era, a dynamic period marked by reciprocal contributions to the domains of art, science, and philosophy.

Alexander's vast territorial expanse, while unique in its character, showcased discernible traces of Persian administrative wisdom. This was particularly evident in the concept of according localities a degree of autonomy, a principle that had been integral to the Achaemenid administrative matrix. Successor states, the Seleucids being a prominent example, exhibited pronounced Persian influences in their governance structures.

In conclusion, the fall of the Achaemenid Empire did not denote its annihilation. Instead, it transformed, influencing and merging with the cultures and empires that followed, ensuring that the legacy of Persian ingenuity, governance, and cultural contributions remained indelible in the annals of history.

Conclusion: The Persian Imprint - Enduring Influences Across Millennia

The historical tapestry of empires often reflects fluctuating trajectories marked by territorial gains, societal innovations, and eventual declines. Distinctively, the Persian Empire, even within this grand schema, carved out a niche characterized by its foresight in governance, respect for cultural multiplicity, and administrative prowess.

Central to its enduring influence was the Persian ability to assimilate and elevate rather than suppress. Their engagement with diverse cultures and traditions wasn't merely an artifact of administrative expediency; it reflected a deeper comprehension of the symbiotic nature of empire-building. This approach, as elucidated in preceding sections, transcended mere pragmatism and emerged as a paradigm, influencing subsequent epochs of governance.

The Zoroastrian philosophical undertones, which reverberated with themes of duality and morality, resonated beyond the empire's temporal boundaries, finding echoes in subsequent religious traditions. Similarly, the Persian aesthetic, an amalgam of diverse inspirations, left an indelible mark on the art and architectural lexicon of the region.

Administratively, the satrapial system, a balance of decentralization and imperial oversight, became emblematic of effective governance, serving as a template for subsequent empires. Moreover, infrastructural endeavors like the Royal Road, while instrumental during the empire's zenith, have come to symbolize the Persian commitment to cohesion and connectivity.

In encapsulating the Persian Empire's contributions, one recognizes an intricate mosaic of visionary leadership, strategic assimilation, and an unwavering commitment to societal advancement. As a conclusion to this exploration, it's evident that the empire's legacy isn't confined to the annals of history but continues to illuminate principles of statecraft and cultural engagement that remain relevant across millennia.

Sphinxes from the Palace of Darius I at Susa[10]

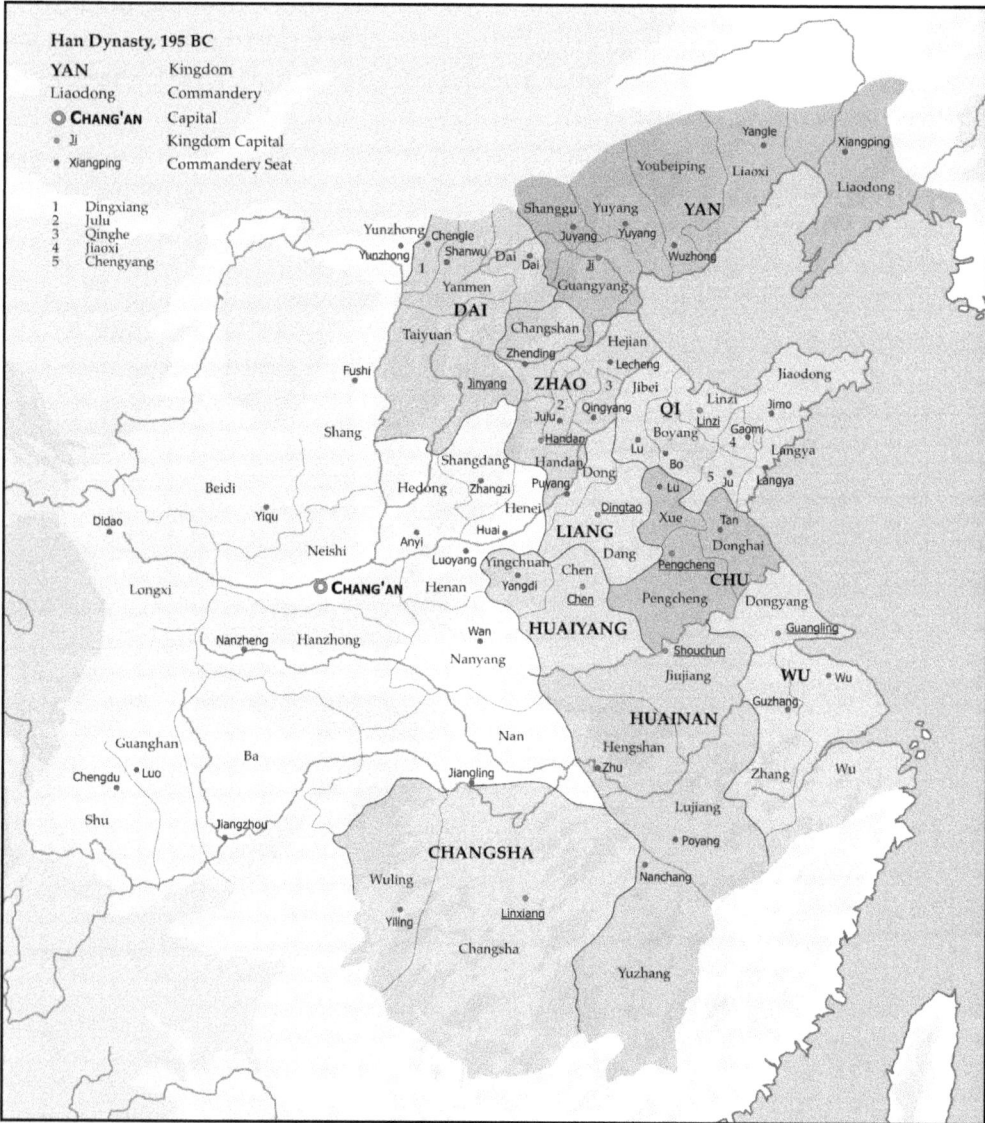

Map of Kingdoms of Han Dynasty[11]

Chapter 6.
Han Dynasty: China's Era of Enlightenment (206 BCE-220 CE)

Real knowledge is to know the extent of one's ignorance.

~Confucius

From the Ashes of the Qin Dynasty

As the historical annals of ancient civilizations unfold, one cannot help but notice the recurring patterns of power dynamics. The preceding chapter on the Persian Empire demonstrated the ebb and flow of its might, offering invaluable insights into the intricacies of empire-building and governance. In a similar vein, yet geographically distant, the rise and decline of dynasties in ancient China offer compelling parallels.

The conclusion of the Warring States period in 221 BCE marked the ascent of the Qin Dynasty, under the stewardship of Qin Shi Huang. His endeavors, from the monumental Great Wall to the awe-inspiring Terracotta Army, stand as testaments to a ruler with vast ambitions. However, for all its architectural marvels and territorial acquisitions, the Qin Dynasty was riddled with vulnerabilities. Qin Shi Huang's centralized, autocratic governance, rooted deeply in unyielding legalism, began to fracture the very foundations he sought to solidify. This societal unrest culminated in the swift decline of the Qin by 207 BCE.

Yet, as with the Persian Empire's transitions, from chaos emerges opportunity. During this period of China's uncertainty, Liu Bang, originally of modest origins, saw his opening. The Chu-Han Contention, a pivotal power struggle between Liu Bang and his rival, Xiang Yu, dominated the landscape post-Qin. This intense conflict, spread over several years, was not merely a military confrontation but also a contestation of differing visions for China's future. By its culmination in 202 BCE, Liu Bang emerged victorious, leading to the establishment of the Han Dynasty. This new era, possibly drawing lessons from the Qin's stringent policies, chose to pivot towards a governance model enriched by Confucian ideals.

Terracotta Shield Warrior,- Han Dynasty

The cyclical patterns of rise, consolidation, and decline in both the Persian and Chinese empires, albeit under different cultural and geopolitical contexts, underscore a shared human history. They echo the universality of challenges faced and the adaptability required in statecraft and governance across diverse landscapes.

Confucianism:
The Bedrock of Governance and Morality

In the labyrinth of historical trajectories that shaped ancient China, the Han Dynasty's adoption and institutionalization of Confucianism stands as a defining chapter. This philosophical system, rooted in the teachings of Confucius (Kong Fuzi), who lived during the 5th-century BCE, provided both a moral compass and an administrative guideline for the dynasty.

During the preceding Warring States Period (475-221 BCE), the myriad kingdoms grappled with socio-political instability and incessant conflict. It was a time characterized by both political fragmentation and ideological ferment. Amidst this chaos, Confucianism, with its core values of ritual, familial piety, and social harmony, emerged as a beacon of philosophical guidance. However, it was during the Qin Dynasty (221-206 BCE) that Confucianism faced stark opposition. The Qin rulers, with their unequivocal endorsement of Legalism, sought to suppress other schools of thought, even resorting to burning Confucian texts and burying scholars alive.

Yet, this suppression was transient. The Han Dynasty, particularly under Emperor Wu, who reigned from 141-87 BCE, discerned the merit in Confucianism and sought to restore its stature. Emperor Wu's reign marked a turning point, where Confucianism transitioned from being a mere philosophical school to a state doctrine. A testament to this transformative alignment was the foundation of the Imperial Academy in 124 BCE, which aimed at nurturing bureaucrats deeply entrenched in Confucian tenets. By 87 BCE, upon Emperor Wu's death, the academy had burgeoned into a preeminent institution, shaping the ethos of those who would steer the vast machinery of the Han administration.

Furthermore, the dynasty's affirmation of Confucian values was vividly evident in the civil service examination framework. The inclusion of Confucian classics in the curriculum ensured that generation after generation of bureaucrats imbibed and perpetuated its principles. This synthesis of governance and philosophy was not merely a superficial alignment but a deep-seated integration that transformed the bureaucratic structure, making it both efficient and ethically grounded.

But the realm of Confucian influence wasn't confined to the corridors of power. It permeated the very sinews of Han society. The emphasis on "ren" (benevolence), "yi" (righteousness), and "li" (ritual propriety) influenced everyday life, molding interpersonal dynamics, determining social hierarchies, and even shaping the judgments meted out in courts.

As the narrative of the Han Dynasty unfolded, with its triumphs and tribulations, the enduring legacy of Confucianism remained indisputable. Even after the fall of the Han, the seeds sown during this era ensured that Confucianism continued to be an integral component of China's cultural, ethical, and administrative landscape for millennia.

In retrospect, the Han Dynasty's alignment with Confucianism wasn't merely a strategic choice; it was a profound acknowledgment of a philosophy that encapsulated the essence of governance and morality, guiding an empire and its people toward enlightenment.

Reign of Emperor Wu: Expansion and Centralization

Traditional portrait of Emperor Wu

The annals of China's storied past are punctuated with the exploits of illustrious emperors, among whom Emperor Wu of the Han Dynasty, occupies a distinguished position. His tenure on the imperial throne, spanning over five decades, bore witness to a strategic amalgamation of territorial expansion and internal consolidation, thereby redefining the contours of the Han Empire.

Emperor Wu's reign commenced during a period when the Han Dynasty had already established a firm foundation. However, rather than resting on the laurels of his predecessors, he exhibited an insatiable desire to augment the dynasty's territorial footprint. His expansionist policies were characterized by a series of military campaigns that sought to extend Han dominion. To the north, he tackled the Xiongnu, a confederation of nomadic tribes, eventually breaking their hegemony and pushing them beyond the Ordos Desert by 119 BCE. This campaign not only ensured the security of Han's northern frontiers but also paved the way for the opening of the Silk Road, a pivotal trade route connecting China to Central Asia and beyond.

Simultaneously, his gaze turned towards the southern kingdoms, encompassing modern-day Vietnam, and the Western Regions, which is today's Xinjiang. Through a combination of military prowess and diplomacy, Emperor Wu ensured the annexation of these territories, effectively transforming the Han Dynasty into an empire with vast territorial expanse.

However, territorial expansion wasn't Emperor Wu's sole preoccupation. Parallel to these outward endeavors, he undertook significant measures to centralize administrative control. One of his most consequential reforms was the nationalization of coinage, iron, and salt industries. By wresting these vital sectors from the hands of private entrepreneurs and placing them under state control, Emperor Wu ensured a significant revenue stream for the imperial coffers, which, in turn, financed his military campaigns.

Furthermore, the establishment of commanderies and the appointment of officials directly answerable to the central authority in the newly acquired territories underscored his commitment to centralization. By doing so, he mitigated the risk of regional satraps accumulating excessive power, thereby preempting potential threats to the imperial throne. This focus on the regulation of regional power is reminiscent of the Persian system of satraps, as discussed in the previous chapter. While the term 'satrap' is rooted in Persian governance, the underlying challenge of balancing centralized control with regional autonomy is a recurrent theme in the administration of expansive empires, illustrating the universality of this governance dilemma.

Beyond administrative centralization, Emperor Wu also championed ideological consolidation. Recognizing the potential of Confucianism as a cohesive force, he endorsed it as the state ideology (as articulated in the previous section). This move, while ensuring uniformity in administrative practices, also provided a shared philosophical framework that bound the diverse regions of the empire.

However, Emperor Wu's ambitious projects were not without challenges. The incessant military campaigns and centralized initiatives strained the state's resources, leading to periods of economic challenges. Additionally, his reign, particularly in the later years, witnessed instances of dissent and criticism from scholars and officials who perceived some of his policies as overreaching.

In retrospect, Emperor Wu's reign, while marked by unparalleled territorial expansion and administrative consolidation, also serves as a testament to the complexities inherent in leading an empire. The delicate balance between ambition and sustainability, expansion, and internal cohesion continues to resonate as a lesson in the annals of statecraft. Emperor Wu, through his multifaceted reign, indelibly etched his legacy into the fabric of Chinese history, establishing benchmarks in leadership that subsequent rulers would either emulate or contend with.

The Silk Road: A Nexus of Cultural and Economic Exchange

One of the most transcendent developments of the ancient world, whose impacts reverberate even in contemporary times, is the Silk Road. The term, despite its singular appellation, refers not to a solitary thoroughfare but to a sprawling network of interconnected trade routes, extending from China in the East to the Mediterranean basin in the West. Its genesis, closely associated with the Han Dynasty, rendered it not only an artery for commerce but also a conduit for the exchange of ideas, culture, and diplomacy.

The establishment of the Silk Road can be traced back to the Han Dynasty's endeavors to secure their frontiers from the recurring threats posed by the Xiongnu to the north. By the 2nd century BCE, under the reign of Emperor Wu, the Han had managed to curtail the Xiongnu's dominance, a move that precipitated the exploration of regions beyond their immediate frontiers. Zhang Qian, a diplomat and explorer dispatched by Emperor Wu, undertook expeditions to Central Asia, forging diplomatic ties with several states. His reports upon return illuminated the opportunities that lay in establishing trade relations with these distant regions, thereby sowing the seeds for the Silk Road.

The immediate economic implications of the Silk Road for the Han Dynasty were manifold. Silk, as the name of the route suggests, was a prime commodity, coveted by the western states. In return, China imported a plethora of goods, ranging from precious stones and metals like gold and silver to exotic commodities like horses from the Fergana Valley, esteemed for their stamina and agility. However, the exchange was not limited to tangible goods alone. The route facilitated the dissemination of technological innovations, such as paper-making and printing from China, and conversely, the introduction of grape cultivation and winemaking techniques to China.

Equally consequential, if not more, was the Silk Road's role as a medium for cultural exchange. Buddhism, originating in the Indian subcontinent, found its way to China, largely via the Silk Road, thereby altering the religious and philosophical landscape of East Asia. Artistic expressions, too, were interchanged. Motifs and techniques in sculpture, painting, and architecture traversed these routes, leading to a synthesis of styles that bore testament to the confluence of diverse cultures.

Moreover, the Silk Road wasn't merely a passive conduit. The active establishments of caravanserais, inns, and trading posts along the route engendered a milieu where traders, monks, scholars, and artisans from disparate cultural backgrounds interacted, often leading to enduring relationships. These interactions, in many instances, transcended the realm of trade and culture, evolving into diplomatic ties. The Han Dynasty, through the medium of the Silk Road, established formal relations with several Central Asian states, creating a buffer against potential threats and ensuring the security of their western frontiers.

In its essence, the Silk Road, while initiated for pragmatic considerations of trade and security, metamorphosed into an entity that epitomized the interdependence of human societies. Its legacy, enshrined in the annals of history, underscores the tenet that cultures, when they interact and engage in exchanges, often lead to mutual enrichment. For the Han Dynasty, the Silk Road was not just a trade route but a symbol of its outward vision, cosmopolitanism, and the enduring impact of peaceful engagement with the world.

In a modern-day parallel, the conceptual framework behind the ancient Silk Road reverberates in China's 21st-century geopolitical strategy through the Belt and Road Initiative (BRI). Spearheaded by the Chinese government, the BRI aims to connect China to various regions across Asia, Europe, and Africa via a network of infrastructure projects. Much like the Silk Road of yesteryears, the BRI is not merely an economic venture but also a multifaceted geopolitical instrument. It serves to facilitate not only trade but also the projection of soft power, diplomatic ties, and cultural exchange. While the BRI will be discussed in greater detail in the chapter dedicated to modern China, its evocation here serves to underline the historical continuity in China's approach to external engagement, commerce, and diplomacy.

Technological and Scientific Milestones of the Han Era

The Han Dynasty firmly established itself as a nexus of scientific and technological evolution, underscoring China's status as a pioneering center of innovation in the ancient world. The confluence of state patronage, a quest for administrative efficiency, and an intrinsic cultural emphasis on knowledge acquisition spurred a cascade of inventions and insights that resonated through subsequent Chinese epochs and the broader world.

Arguably, one of the most transformative innovations of this period was the refinement of paper-making techniques. Prior to this, inscriptions were predominantly made on bone, bamboo slips, or silk, which, while effective, were either labor-intensive or prohibitively costly. Circa 105 CE, Cai Lun, an official in Emperor He's court, heralded a paradigm shift by introducing a paper-making process using mulberry bark, old rags, hemp, and fishnets. This innovation not only democratized knowledge dissemination but also galvanized literary and scholarly pursuits, shaping the contours of Chinese intellectualism for centuries to come.

Parallel to this, the realm of metallurgy witnessed pivotal advancements. The Han era was characterized by the more prevalent use of iron, a departure from the earlier Shang and Zhou periods which leaned heavily towards bronze. Innovations such as the double-acting piston bellows enabled higher temperatures in blast furnaces, facilitating the conversion of cast iron to wrought iron and subsequently to steel. Such metallurgical progress yielded sharper agricultural implements, sturdier construction materials, and more formidable weaponry, profoundly impacting various facets of Han society.

Agriculturally, the Han dynasty's technological ingenuity manifested in the development of the iron moldboard plow. This device, designed with a central ridge to channel soil to the sides, optimized tilling, enhancing agricultural yield. Coupled with the introduction of crop rotation systems and state-mandated granaries, these innovations underpinned the dynasty's food security framework, supporting its growing populace.

The scientific pursuits of the Han era, though intrinsically tied to practical applications, also exhibited a deep reverence for empirical observation and methodological documentation. Notably, Zhang Heng, a polymath of the Eastern Han period, circa 132 CE, engineered the world's first seismoscope—a sophisticated apparatus capable of detecting distant earthquakes. This invention, emblematic of the Han's scientific temperament, seamlessly melded intricate craftsmanship with keen observational acumen.

Furthermore, the period ushered in significant advancements in the domain of medicine. The Han era bore witness to the collation and systematization of medical knowledge, encapsulated in foundational texts like the "Huangdi Neijing" (The Yellow Emperor's Inner Canon). These works not only codified diagnostic techniques, therapeutic methodologies, and surgical procedures but also emphasized the philosophical underpinnings of health, echoing the Confucian harmony ethos.

In essence, the Han Dynasty, with its rich tapestry of technological and scientific milestones, fortified its position as an epoch of enlightenment, setting benchmarks that would influence both native and foreign civilizations in manifold ways. The innovations of this era, both tangible and conceptual, serve as enduring testaments to a society's relentless quest for progress and understanding.

Legalism and Confucianism: Equilibrium in Governance:

During the Han Dynasty, governance was not defined by a singular philosophical current but by an intricate equilibrium forged between two seemingly disparate ideologies: Legalism and Confucianism. While these doctrines were rooted in different foundational principles, the Han rulers skillfully amalgamated them to forge a cohesive administrative apparatus that leveraged the strengths of both.

Legalism, which initially gained prominence during the Qin Dynasty under the stewardship of statesmen like Li Si and Lord Shang Yang, was characterized by its strict codification of laws and its unwavering focus on state control. This philosophy propounded the necessity of robust laws and centralized autocratic rule, emphasizing punishment over reward. It argued that human nature was inherently selfish, and thus, rigorous laws were imperative to maintain order and discipline. The short-lived Qin Dynasty, albeit marked by its brutal enforcement of Legalist doctrines, laid down a centralized bureaucratic structure, which the subsequent Han Dynasty found expedient to retain, albeit with modifications.

Contrastingly, Confucianism, a doctrine stemming from the teachings of Confucius in the 5th century BCE, emphasized moral rectitude, familial piety, and societal harmony. In the Confucian paradigm, rulers were to lead by example, fostering benevolence, righteousness, and wisdom. The ruler-subject relationship was analogous to the father-son relationship, emphasizing mutual respect and obligations.

During the Han Dynasty, particularly under the reign of Emperor Wu (circa 141-87 BCE), there was a significant paradigm shift. Wu recognized the utility of Confucianism in legitimizing his rule, reinforcing societal values, and facilitating efficient governance. The doctrine's emphasis on education, meritocracy, and bureaucratic aptitude resonated with the administrative challenges of the expansive Han territory. Consequently, Confucianism was institutionally integrated into the state apparatus, especially with the establishment of the Imperial Academy in 124 BCE, focusing on Confucian classics.

Yet, the Han Dynasty did not completely eschew Legalism. Instead, it ingeniously combined Legalist principles, particularly its structured administrative techniques and rigorous legal frameworks, with the moral compass and ethical grounding of Confucianism. This fusion manifested in various domains: rigorous yet just legal codes, a centralized yet morally guided bureaucracy, and an emperor who was both an autocratic figure and a paragon of Confucian virtues.

This confluence of ideologies provided the Han Dynasty with a multi-faceted governance model. Legalism's structured mechanisms ensured state stability and efficient rule, while Confucianism's moral underpinnings fostered societal harmony and legitimized the ruler's mandate.

In the annals of Chinese history, the Han Dynasty's governance equilibrium, delicately balancing Legalist pragmatism with Confucian morality, stands as a testament to the nuanced understanding of statecraft. This equilibrium not only facilitated the dynasty's longevity but also established a governance model that future Chinese dynasties would draw upon, underscoring its enduring relevance.

Han Economic Systems and Trade

The Han Dynasty presided over one of China's most economically vibrant epochs, characterized by profound innovations in monetary systems, tax structures, trade dynamics, and infrastructural developments. This period not only witnessed the consolidation and expansion of the Chinese economy but also its integration into a broader intercontinental commercial network.

Central to the Han economy was the institution of a standardized monetary system. The "Wu Zhu" coin, introduced during the reign of Emperor Wu, became the predominant currency. Its standardized weight and inscription enhanced its credibility and facilitated its widespread use. This currency standardization played a pivotal role in stimulating trade and ensuring fiscal uniformity across the expansive Han territories.

On the taxation front, the Han administration adopted a multifaceted approach. Land taxes, assessed based on the amount and quality of land held, formed a significant chunk of the state's revenue. Additionally, a poll tax was levied on adult males, and produce taxes on harvests, notably grains, were collected. The state also profited from monopolies, particularly on salt and iron. By 117 BCE, Emperor Wu had nationalized both these essential industries, thereby ensuring the state's direct control over production and distribution, which simultaneously bolstered the imperial treasury and diminished the economic power of certain elites.

Trade, both internal and external, was a linchpin of the Han economic matrix. Domestically, the construction of a vast network of roads and canals, including parts of the imperial highway known as the Gaoji Causeway, fostered connectivity between different regions of the empire. This infrastructural backbone enabled the efficient movement of goods, people, and information, synchronizing the diverse economic pulses of the Han dominion.

Externally, the Han Dynasty is inextricably linked with the genesis and proliferation of the Silk Road, the transcontinental trade network connecting China with Central Asia, the Indian subcontinent, Persia, and eventually the Mediterranean world.

Furthermore, Han China was not isolated to overland trade; maritime routes, particularly those navigating through the South China Sea, opened avenues to Southeast Asia and the Indian Ocean, further expanding the Han's commercial outreach.

In summation, the Han Dynasty's economic framework was an intricate amalgamation of centralized state control, innovative monetary and tax systems, and dynamic trade networks. The blend of internal economic consolidation with external commercial outreach ensured the Han Dynasty's economic prosperity and its indelible mark on the global economic tapestry. Through its sophisticated economic strategies and expansive trade routes, the Han Dynasty not only fortified its own imperial coffers but also sowed the seeds for China's enduring legacy as a central node in global commerce.

Han Social Dynamics: An Exploration Beyond Imperial Walls

The Han Dynasty ushered in a society that was complex, diverse, and culturally rich. While numerous historical accounts have centered on the imperial court and its corridors of power, the essence of the Han Dynasty resonated in the daily lives of its people, the structures of their society, their cultural manifestations, and the philosophical dialogues that molded their perspective on the world.

Societal structures during the Han era were largely hierarchical, rooted in Confucian principles that emphasized filial piety, moral integrity, and respect for authority. The society was predominantly agrarian, with the majority of the populace engaged in farming. Agriculturists, by virtue of producing the essential sustenance for the empire, were held in high regard, second only to scholars in the Confucian societal hierarchy. Merchants, despite their increasing wealth and influence, especially with the burgeoning trade routes, were positioned lower in this hierarchy due to Confucian reservations about profit-seeking ventures.

At the foundation of Han society was the family unit, which was patriarchal in nature. Ancestor veneration remained central to familial rituals, reflecting the deep-rooted belief in the continuity between the living and the ancestral worlds. Marriage was an integral societal institution, often arranged, serving not just as a union between individuals but as an alliance between families.

In the domain of literature, the Han era was particularly transformative. This period saw the compilation of historical records, such as Sima Qian's 'Records of the Grand Historian' (Shiji), which remains a seminal text providing insights into Chinese history up to the Han period. Poetry, especially the fu style that combined prose and verse, became a notable literary form. Literature wasn't merely an elite pursuit; it permeated various strata of society, facilitated by the increasing accessibility to texts with the advent of paper, an innovation of the Han Dynasty.

Artistically, the Han period was characterized by intricate bronzework, jade carvings, and pottery, most notably the painted ceramics from the Han tombs. Murals adorned tomb walls, illustrating daily life, mythology, and cosmology, serving as windows into the Han psyche. Architecturally, while wood remained the predominant building material, there was a growing prevalence of stone and brick, especially in constructing city walls and fortifications.

Religiously and philosophically, the Han era was a melting pot. While Confucianism became the state ideology, Taoism, with its emphasis on living in harmony with the Tao or the natural way of things, garnered substantial followers. Furthermore, Buddhism began making inroads into China during the later Han years, carried by missionaries and traders along the Silk Road.

Cultural festivals and communal gatherings were integral to Han society, often centered around agricultural cycles, celebrating harvests, and appeasing deities for bountiful yields. Music and dance were vital components of these celebrations, and a myriad of musical instruments from zithers to flutes embellished Han orchestras.

In encapsulation, the Han era's social fabric was a vibrant tapestry, woven from threads of tradition, innovation, and cultural synthesis. The societal structures, artistic expressions, and intellectual discourses from this epoch collectively contribute to a nuanced understanding of Han China, offering a holistic perspective that transcends mere political or military narratives. Through its societal intricacies and cultural nuances, the Han Dynasty carved out a distinct identity, with reverberations felt deeply in the successive epochs of Chinese history.

Downfall:
Interplay of Domestic Turmoil and External Pressures

The Han Dynasty's decline, like many great empires, was not precipitated by a single event but rather by a complex interplay of internal and external factors that unfolded over time.

Domestically, the later years of the Han Dynasty were marked by increasing instability and turbulence. Factional struggles within the imperial court became a recurring issue, often pitting the eunuch factions against other court officials, thereby undermining the efficacy and integrity of governance. This political infighting and corruption not only weakened central authority but also disrupted the smooth administration of the vast empire.

The central authority's waning control made way for the rise of regional warlords, each commanding their own territories and armies. Their growing influence further fragmented the empire, and as their power grew, loyalty to the central Han rulers dwindled. This decentralization of power made cohesive governance and unified responses to external threats increasingly challenging.

Economically, the empire grappled with issues of land ownership. Large tracts of land became concentrated in the hands of a few wealthy families, leading to widespread landlessness among the peasants. The consequent socio-economic disparity resulted in numerous uprisings, with the Yellow Turban Rebellion of 184 CE being particularly significant. Such widespread rebellions not only drained the empire's resources but also highlighted the pervasive discontent with the Han rule.

Externally, the Han Dynasty faced escalating threats from nomadic groups along its borders. The Xiongnu, a confederation of nomadic tribes, posed a perennial challenge. While the Han Dynasty had, at times, managed to subdue or placate them through military campaigns or diplomatic means like the "heqin" (marriage alliances) policy, by the dynasty's later stages, these external groups grew bolder, sensing the weakening internal structure of the Han.

Additionally, the Han's extensive trade routes, especially the Silk Road, while economically beneficial, also exposed the empire to external influences and potential vulnerabilities. The extensive network, which facilitated cultural and commercial exchanges, at times, also became conduits for external threats.

As these domestic and external pressures compounded, the resilience of the Han Dynasty was tested to its limits. The efforts of some late Han emperors to reform and restore the dynasty's former glory proved insufficient against the tide of challenges. In the year 220 CE, the final Han emperor was deposed, ushering in the era of the Three Kingdoms and signifying the conclusion of one of China's most remarkable dynastic eras. The combination of internal strife and external pressures proved insurmountable, signaling the close of a chapter in China's expansive history.

Conclusion:
Enduring Influence on Chinese Civilization:

The Han Dynasty, with its profound legacy spanning over four centuries, indelibly shaped the trajectory of Chinese civilization and left an indelible mark on the annals of global history. Despite its eventual decline, the dynasty's influence persisted, deeply embedding itself into the cultural, political, and societal realms of subsequent Chinese eras.

In terms of governance, the Han Dynasty institutionalized the bureaucracy, relying on merit-based examinations rooted in Confucian thought. This tradition, originating from the establishment of the Imperial Academy, became a cornerstone of Chinese governance, extending into the late Qing Dynasty and influencing other East Asian states. The integration of Confucianism with statecraft, where ethical considerations and governance converged, set a philosophical precedent that later dynasties emulated, albeit with variations.

Scientifically, the Han era was a cradle of innovation. From papermaking to seismographs, its technological advancements not only enhanced domestic productivity and administration but also enriched the wider world. The spread of these innovations, notably paper, along trade routes such as the Silk Road, played a pivotal role in stimulating intellectual progress in distant lands.

Economically, the establishment of the Silk Road under the Han Dynasty was momentous. This vast network of trade routes fostered economic, cultural, and diplomatic exchanges that transcended the confines of empires. Goods, ideas, and religious beliefs traversed these routes, linking the Han with the Roman Empire in the West and influencing regions as diverse as Central Asia and the Indian subcontinent.

Culturally, the Han Dynasty witnessed the flourishing of arts, literature, and historiography. The historical records penned by Sima Qian, a foundational figure in Chinese historiography, provided a comprehensive chronicle that future historians revered and emulated. Additionally, the artistry of the period, from intricate pottery to sophisticated jade carvings, set aesthetic standards that later epochs would strive to match or reinterpret.

Societally, the interplay of Legalist and Confucian philosophies during the Han era molded societal structures and norms. The emphasis on filial piety, reverence for ancestors, and the ethical responsibilities of rulers and subjects became ingrained in Chinese society. These tenets, over time, evolved but retained their foundational importance, underscoring the societal equilibrium that the Han Dynasty championed.

In the broader canvas of world history, the Han Dynasty's synchronicity with the Roman Empire provides a captivating comparative study. Both empires, in their respective realms, established enduring administrative, cultural, and economic systems that exerted influence far beyond their immediate territories and epochs.

In conclusion, the Han Dynasty's legacy is multifaceted and enduring. It crystallized principles of governance, pioneered scientific advancements, laid economic foundations, and enriched cultural tapestries that subsequent Chinese dynasties would inherit, adapt, and refine. Its influence, extending beyond China's borders, underscores the dynasty's pivotal role in shaping not only Chinese civilization but also broader global historical narratives.

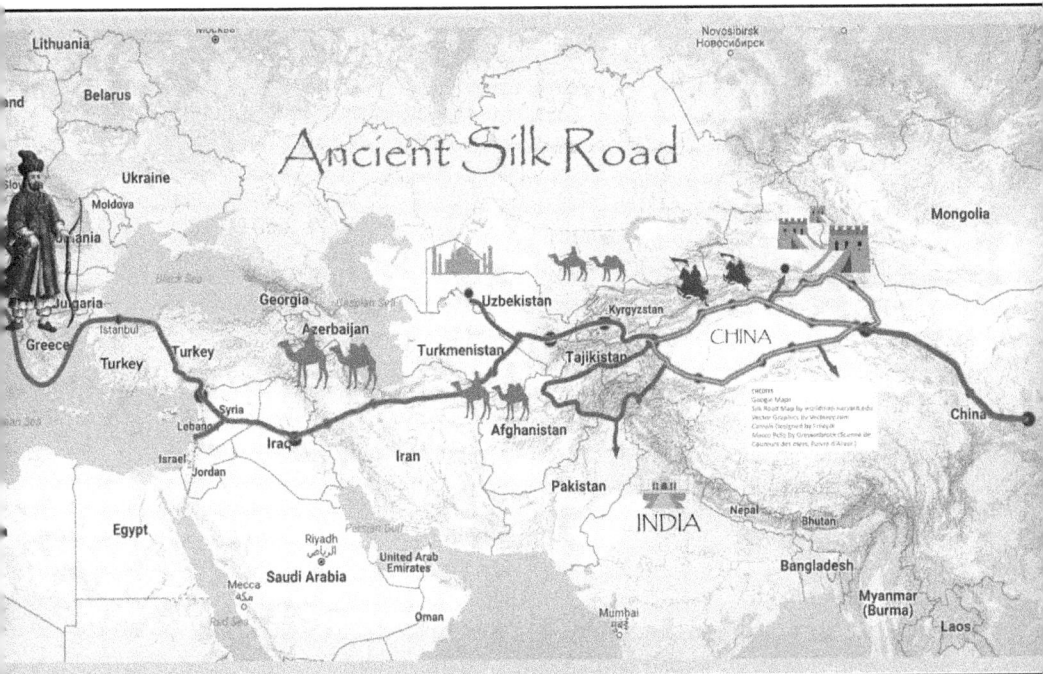

Map of the Silk Road[12]

Greek-City-States[13]-

Chapter 7.
Ancient Greece: the Cradle of Western Democracy (800-146BCE)

Just because you do not take an interest in politics doesn't mean politics won't take an interest in you.

~Pericles

The Genesis of Western Thought

As the expansive Han Dynasty thrived in the vast landscapes of the East, a contrasting narrative was unfolding in the West. Nestled on a rugged peninsula extending into the azure waters of the Mediterranean was Ancient Greece. Its geophysical intricacies—ranging from towering mountains to idyllic islands—catalyzed the emergence of numerous independent city-states, each nurturing its distinct ethos amidst the challenges and opportunities posed by the land.

Unlike the vast monolithic entity of the Han Dynasty, Greece's character was inherently fragmented. The geographical divisions fostered autonomous polities, which, despite being part of the overarching Hellenic identity, retained their unique socio-political and cultural fabric. This was not a singular, unified empire, but rather a constellation of city-states, contributing diverse chapters to the annals of Greek civilization.

In this intricate landscape, tales of heroism epitomized by figures like Achilles and Odysseus took shape, immortalized in epics that have endured the test of time. Concurrently, intellectual hubs birthed thinkers of unparalleled profundity, such as Socrates and Plato, who would lay the cornerstone of Western philosophical discourse. The Greek ethos was not merely content with storytelling; it fostered a climate of rigorous inquiry, debate, and introspection, seeking profound understanding of existence, morality, and the fabric of society.

In analyzing Ancient Greece, it becomes evident that its fragmented geographical configuration, combined with a relentless pursuit of knowledge and understanding, rendered it the birthplace of seminal Western concepts, notably democracy, philosophy, and the arts. As we navigate through the chronicles of Greece, we find ourselves traversing a realm where the boundaries of human curiosity, intellect, and ambition were ceaselessly expanded, leaving an indelible imprint on the trajectory of Western civilization.

Early Aegean Civilizations and Transition

Prior to the classical age's radiance, the Aegean basin witnessed the evolution of two distinctive civilizations: the Minoans, concentrated on Crete, and the mainland Mycenaeans. Although individualistic, both civilizations became precursors to the broader Hellenic sphere.

From approximately 2000 BCE to 1450 BCE, the Minoans' presence was evident through their intricate palatial structures, notably in Knossos, and vivid frescoes detailing their religious and everyday life. As proficient mariners, their influence stretched across the Mediterranean. The undeciphered Linear A script attests to their sophisticated administrative systems.

By 1450 BCE, Minoan influence receded, ushering in the Mycenaean era. Originating from the Peloponnese, they assimilated aspects of Minoan culture, yet maintained a distinct identity showcased by formidable fortresses like Mycenae and Tiryns with their notable "Cyclopean" walls. The deciphered Linear B script revealed its linguistic affinity to early Greek.

However, circa 1100 BCE, Mycenaean civilization experienced a downturn, instigating the Greek Dark Ages. Monumental structures that once epitomized Mycenaean might were forsaken or devastated. Previously flourishing trade routes crumbled, inducing economic regression and population decline.

Despite the apparent descent, this era was a crucible of transformation, spawning the foundational concept of the polis or city-state. This age saw Greek migrations to Asia Minor's Aegean coast and the gradual emergence of novel artistic expressions, heralding an impending cultural revival.

A quintessential legacy from this transitory phase was the perpetuation of heroic myths and deities through spoken word. Later, luminaries like Homer would enshrine these narratives in classics like the "Iliad" and "Odyssey." Such epics bridged the divide between the bygone Mycenaean epoch and the burgeoning Archaic city-states, offering the Greeks a unified cultural anchor and a beacon illuminating their path to resurgence.

Polis Emergence: Athens, Sparta, and Inter-Polis Dynamics

By the 8th century BCE, post the Greek Dark Ages, the distinctive construct of the polis, or city-state, commenced its ascendancy. Each polis, marked by its fervent autonomy, was a Hellenic microcosm, replete with distinct governance, defense mechanisms, and societal norms.

Athens, ensconced in Attica, became the vanguard of democratic governance. By the 5th century BCE, under luminary leadership like that of Pericles, it metamorphosed into a bastion of direct democracy. Herein, citizenry actively steered policy decisions. The Athenian Agora, teeming with civic activity, epitomized the city's unwavering commitment to discourse and collective involvement.

In stark contrast, Sparta, anchored in the austere terrains of Laconia, etched its identity as a martial juggernaut. Spartan societal edifices rested on stringent discipline and martial excellence. From their infancy, Spartan males were inducted into an exacting military regimen, chiseling them into adept combatants. Their governance, a synthesis of monarchical and oligarchic elements, accentuated communal welfare over individualism, solidifying Sparta's military pre-eminence in the Peloponnese.

These very attributes of staunch independence and unyielding identity occasionally engendered discord amongst the city-states. The Peloponnesian War, epitomizing the deep-seated animosity and distrust between Athens and Sparta, is a salient reflection of the intricate dynamics within the Hellenic polis framework.

Within this historical context, Greece manifested not merely as a territorial expanse, but as a kaleidoscope of contrasting ideologies, administrative architectures, and societal conventions. These city-states, despite their divergent trajectories, collectively forged the multifaceted narrative of Ancient Greece.

Persian Conflicts and the Advent of the Delian League

Amidst their intellectual and cultural zenith, the Greek city-states also emerged as martial adversaries of note. This prowess was soon to be examined against a formidable behemoth of the era: the Persian Empire.

Intent on European territorial augmentation, the Persian sovereign, King Darius I, viewed the Ionian Revolt — an insurrection by the Greek polities in Asia Minor against Persian dominion — as the precursor to a wider altercation. Athens' alliance with the Ionians invoked Darius' ire, prompting a military sortie against it in 490 BCE, culminating at Marathon. Here, despite being outnumbered, Athenian strategists Miltiades and Callimachus orchestrated a decisive Athenian triumph. This confrontation, beyond its immediate military implications, became a symbolic representation of a free citizenry's defiance against imperial expansionism. Additionally, Pheidippides' reputed marathon run from Marathon to Athens, proclaiming victory, has bequeathed a legacy of resilience and fortitude embodied in the contemporary marathon race.

Yet, Persian imperial aspirations persisted. Under Darius' successor, Xerxes I, as previously covered, a formidable invasion was mobilized, instigating the subsequent Persian Wars. The Thermopylae pass bore witness to Spartan King Leonidas I and his hoplites' exemplary tactical acumen, momentarily stalling the Persian juggernaut. Concurrently, at the naval theater in Salamis in 480 BCE, Themistocles of Athens employed Greek trireme dexterity, subverting the vast Persian armada. This series of confrontations culminated at Plataea in 479 BCE, where a unified Hellenic force cemented Persian retreat from the Greek mainland. These encounters not merely epitomized martial engagements but also underscored a collision of cultural, administrative, and ideological paradigms, with Greek victories symbolizing the preservation of Hellenic autonomy and ethos.

The 5th century BCE heralded the inception of the Delian League, a coalition of city-states with Athens at its helm. Envisioned as a bulwark against Persian resurgence, members were obligated to replenish a central coffer, initially domiciled in the impartial sanctuary of Delos. However, Athens' escalating ascendancy culminated in the treasury's translocation to Athens in 454 BCE. Though positioned as a precautionary measure, this relocation amplified Athenian fiscal dominion. Consequently, resources, once earmarked for collective defense, were increasingly diverted to Athenian architectural endeavors, exemplified by the Parthenon's edification. This fiscal redirection, from collaborative security to Athenian aggrandizement, instigated intra-league disaffection, gradually eroding its foundational principle.

Athens' Pinnacle: The Advent of Democracy and Cultural Flourishing

Following the cessation of Persian hostilities, Athens, bolstered by its successes, ascended to a position of prominence in the Aegean. The tenure of Pericles, spanning 461 BCE to 429 BCE, heralded Athens' illustrious "Golden Age," demarcated by an efflorescence in governance, artistic endeavors, philosophical discourse, and architectural innovation.

Arguably, the epoch's most transformative legacy was the institutionalization of democracy. While antecedent Athenian reforms had sown the seeds of democratic governance, it was under Pericles that these tenets were robustly actualized. The Pnyx, an Athenian hill, became the congregation point for citizens deliberating on civic affairs within the "Ekklesia" assembly. This direct democratic apparatus was complemented by the "Boule," a council of 500, selected by sortition, entrusted with streamlining the Ekklesia's deliberative agenda.

Simultaneously, the arts witnessed a renaissance. Playwrights like Sophocles, Euripides, and Aeschylus crafted theatrical masterpieces, delving into the intricate tapestry of human existence, fate, and ethical conundrums. Contrasting these profound narratives were satirists like Aristophanes, whose comedic oeuvre critiqued and caricatured the socio-political zeitgeist. The annual Dionysia festival became the nexus of these theatrical performances, celebrating the deity Dionysus.

Philosophical discourse burgeoned, with luminaries like Socrates, Plato, and Aristotle sculpting the foundational edifice of Western philosophical inquiry.

Architecturally, Athens underwent metamorphosis. The city's Acropolis became the locus of monumental edifices, with the Parthenon, consecrated to Athena, epitomizing Athenian architectural acumen and religious piety.

Yet, the very magnitude of Athenian ascendancy nurtured rivalries, especially with the militaristic Sparta. This burgeoning antagonism foreshadowed a confrontation, threatening to eclipse the luminosity of Athens' Golden Age.

The Peloponnesian War: Dynamics of Ideological and Military Confrontation

The intricate tapestry of Greek politics and society in the 5th century BCE bore witness to the Peloponnesian War, a comprehensive conflict from 431 BCE to 404 BCE, pitting the Delian League, under Athenian hegemony, against the Peloponnesian League, steered by Sparta. More than territorial dominion, this war symbolized an ideological schism: Athens, a beacon of democracy, naval prowess, and cultural dynamism, was juxtaposed against Sparta's austere militarism and oligarchic governance.

Analytically, the war's trajectory can be segmented into three salient phases:

The Archidamian War (431-421 BCE). Named in recognition of Archidamus II, the Spartan monarch, this phase was marked by recurrent Spartan incursions into Attica and reciprocal Athenian naval sorties targeting the Peloponnesian coastline. The Athenian strategy, devised by Pericles, revolved around evading terrestrial engagements with Sparta's formidable infantry, instead capitalizing on the fortified Athenian walls and maritime supremacy. This modus operandi, though pragmatic, bore consequences. The concentration of the populace within Athens' walls exacerbated the impact of a virulent plague between 430-426 BCE, severely depleting Athenian demographics and leading to the demise of Pericles.

Sicilian Expedition (415-413 BCE). Emboldened by ambition, Athens endeavored to annex Sicily. This expedition, however, culminated in a grievous Athenian debacle, culminating in extensive naval and infantry losses.

Decelean War (413-404 BCE). The latter phase of the war witnessed augmented Persian patronage for Sparta. This external support facilitated the Spartans in fortifying Decelea, proximate to Athens, and orchestrating a naval force to challenge Athenian maritime ascendancy. This culminated in the naval confrontation at Aegospotami in 405 BCE, where Athens faced a crushing naval defeat.

By 404 BCE, the cumulative strains of protracted warfare led to Athens' capitulation, relegating it to the exigencies of Spartan terms.

The repercussions of the Peloponnesian War reverberated through-out the Greek landscape. The once-vibrant city-states grappled with economic and military enervation. Democratic tenets, once Athens' hallmark, receded, supplanted by oligarchic establishments, often under Spartan auspices. This tumultuous period underscored the inherent fragilities of the polis framework and foreshadowed the ascent of Macedon, under the aegis of Philip II and subsequently, his progeny, Alexander the Great.

Conclusion:
Greece's Intellectual and Cultural Imprint

The trajectory of Ancient Greece, spanning its variegated polities and temporal epochs, left an indelible imprint on the annals of human civilization. Nestled within the complex geographical contours of islands and peninsulas, the Greeks cultivated an intellectual and cultural milieu that would resonate through millennia.

At the helm of the intellectual revolution were luminaries like Socrates, Plato, and Aristotle. Their seminal inquiries into existence, ethics, and political structures provided foundational pillars for Western philosophical thought. Their rigorous method of dialectics and questioning spurred intellectual traditions that endure in contemporary academia.

Athens stands as a testament to the nascent endeavors of establishing a polity driven by its citizens. The democratic institutions and ideals birthed in this city-state not only steered its own political course but became a reference point for subsequent democratic movements and statecraft.

The Greek landscape pulsated with artistic and scientific fervor. Playwrights like Sophocles delved into intricate explorations of human emotions and conflicts, while architectural feats, epitomized by structures like the Parthenon, mirrored their penchant for geometric precision and aesthetic equilibrium.

While the Greek civilization shimmered with achievements, it was not devoid of internecine conflicts. The Peloponnesian War stands as a poignant reminder of the potential descent into chaos, precipitated by overreach and political miscalculations.

Beyond tangible achievements, the Greek spirit catalyzed monumental intellectual epochs. Their unyielding faith in human reason and inquiry germinated seeds for the European Renaissance, the Enlightenment, and the scientific surges that followed. These movements, while geographically and temporally distanced from Ancient Greece, bore the unmistakable echoes of its ethos.

In sum, a contemplative dive into Ancient Greece is not merely an academic exploration of a bygone era. It's an engagement with an intellectual and cultural dynamism, a spirit that, despite the vicissitudes of time, continues to permeate, guide, and inspire the contours of contemporary thought and society.

The Parthenon in Athens[14]

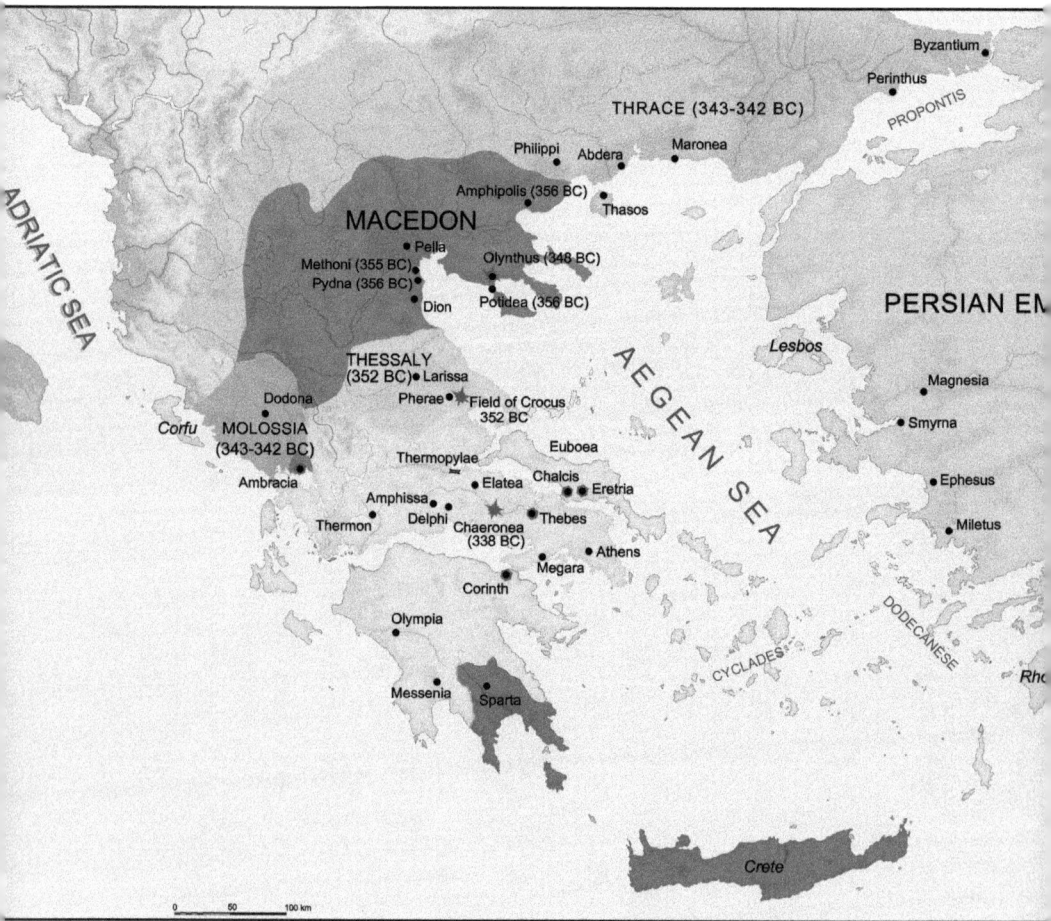

The Kingdom of Macedonia[15]

Chapter 8.
Macedon: from Kingdom to Colossus (359-320BCE)

There is nothing impossible to him who will try.

~Alexander the Great

A Kingdom on the Fringe of Greatness

Ancient Greece's pantheon of influential city-states, from the philosophical brilliance of Athens to the military prowess of Sparta, was counterbalanced by the steady rise of Macedon to the north. This region, marked by its diverse terrains ranging from Pindus Mountains to expansive plains, nurtured a distinct populace known for their horsemanship and warrior ethos. These geographical factors played a crucial role in shaping their military and strategic orientations.

By the 4th century BCE, a confluence of internal and external factors positioned Macedon for a significant ascent in the regional hierarchy. The aftermath of the Peloponnesian War left many Greek city-states in a weakened state, creating a power vacuum and presenting Macedon with both challenges and opportunities. King Amyntas III, during his reign, made preliminary efforts to unite the fragmented tribes within Macedon, achieving a semblance of cohesion that had been elusive for the region. His strategies involved not only military campaigns but also diplomatic endeavors to strengthen Macedon's regional position.

However, it was under Philip II, Amyntas III's successor, that Macedon truly began its transformative journey. Philip II's comprehensive reforms in the military sector, especially the introduction of the phalanx formation, combined with his diplomatic acumen, allowed Macedon to start exerting influence over the fractured Greek city-states. His reign witnessed significant territorial expansions and strategic alliances, setting the stage for Macedon to transition from a peripheral state to a dominant power.

In sum, the 4th century BCE marked a pivotal era for Macedon. Amidst the backdrop of a recovering Greek world, Macedon, through a combination of leadership foresight, strategic reforms, and geopolitical circumstances, positioned itself to play a central role in the evolving dynamics of the region. The kingdom was no longer just an entity in the shadow of greater powers; it was charting its path to preeminence.

The Ascendancy of Philip II: Rise of a Powerhouse

Macedon's trajectory towards becoming a formidable power in the ancient world is intrinsically linked to the leadership and policies of Philip II. When he assumed the throne in 359 BCE, Macedon was in a precarious position, beset by external threats from neighboring tribes like the Illyrians, Paeonians, and Thracians. Concurrently, the fractured nature of Greek city-states and their inter-state competitions presented potential avenues for strategic advantage.

One of Philip's initial undertakings was a comprehensive overhaul of the Macedon military apparatus. He instituted the Macedon Phalanx, a tactical formation distinguished by the use of the Sarissa, a lengthy spear extending beyond 6 meters. This formation enhanced the army's cohesion and offensive capabilities. Beyond the infantry, Philip emphasized the role of cavalry and introduced advanced siege techniques, elevating the Macedon military from a regional force to one capable of challenging the established powers of the time.

Parallel to his military reforms, Philip exhibited astuteness in diplomacy. His marriage to Olympias, a princess from the Molossian dynasty, was not merely a personal union but a strategic alliance, emblematic of his broader approach to foreign relations. Furthermore, leveraging the wealth accrued from gold mines in Pella, Philip embarked on a dual strategy of military expansion and diplomatic inducements. He utilized these resources to secure the allegiance of influential figures within the Greek political landscape and to fund mercenaries, thereby amplifying Macedon's influence.

This combination of military innovation and diplomatic strategy culminated in the Battle of Chaeronea in 338 BCE. Here, Philip's Macedon forces confronted an alliance of Athenian and Theban troops. Despite the valor and historical military competence of the Greek city-states, they were unprepared for the disciplined might of the Macedon Phalanx. Philip's victory was not just a military conquest; it was a symbolic assertion of Macedon's newfound preeminence. The subsequent establishment of the League of Corinth under Macedon oversight was a testament to Philip's vision: to dominate the Greek world without resorting to direct annexation.

In essence, during Philip II's reign from 359 BCE to 338 BCE, Macedon underwent a transformative evolution. Through a blend of strategic military reforms, shrewd diplomacy, and economic investment, Philip II not only stabilized his kingdom but also positioned it as the leading power in the region. His leadership encapsulates the emergence of Macedon from a peripheral state to a central player in the geopolitical dynamics of the ancient world.

Alexander the Great: Mastery in Strategy and Statecraft

Emerging from the foundational stability established by Philip II, Alexander III, commonly known as Alexander the Great, took the reigns of Macedon and furthered its territorial and cultural influence. Born in 356 BCE in the Macedon capital of Pella, Alexander was inculcated not only with military training but also with intellectual enrichment, having been mentored by the renowned philosopher, Aristotle.

Mosaic of Alexander the Great with Horse Bucephalus

This combination of martial and intellectual guidance prepared him for an era of conquests and cultural assimilations.

Upon his father's assassination in 336 BCE, Alexander's initial challenges stemmed from consolidating his rule, given the subsequent revolts within Greece. Demonstrating both military adeptness and a grasp of governance, he swiftly pacified these insurrections. Once consolidated, Alexander embarked on a mission of expansion that marked a new chapter in the annals of empire-building.

By 334 BCE, Alexander's campaign outside the Greek realm commenced with his strategic move across the Hellespont into Asia Minor. One of the defining battles during this phase was the confrontation at Issus in 333 BCE, where Alexander's tactical brilliance resulted in the defeat of the Persian Emperor, Darius III. His subsequent campaigns saw the incorporation of key geopolitical territories like Tyre, Gaza, and Egypt into the Macedon domain. The conquest of Babylon in 331 BCE epitomized the rapidity and efficiency of his expansionist strategy.

Yet, Alexander's ambitions were not constrained by the known boundaries of the time. His forays into Central Asia encountered formidable adversaries, but through a combination of military strategy and diplomacy, regions like the Sogdian Rock and territories of the Scythians were annexed. By 326 BCE, his expedition reached the Beas River, marking his easternmost penetration into the Indian subcontinent.

Beyond mere territorial conquests, Alexander's reign was characterized by cultural and administrative amalgamations. The establishment of Alexandria in Egypt was emblematic of his vision—a city that would amalgamate Greek and Eastern knowledge, serving as a nexus of intellectual and cultural exchange for centuries. The era that followed his conquests, known as the Hellenistic Age, marked a synthesis of Greek and Eastern cultural norms, architectures, and ideologies.

In 323 BCE, at the age of 32, Alexander's sudden demise in the palace of Nebuchadnezzar II in Babylon marked the end of a transformative reign. Despite the brevity of his life, his expansive empire—from Greece to the fringes of India—stood as a testament to an astute amalgamation of military strategy, cultural assimilation, and visionary statecraft. Alexander's legacy wasn't merely in the territories he conquered, but in the profound impact of the Hellenistic culture that persisted long after his passing.

The Hellenistic Era:
Confluence of Greek and Eastern Traditions

The expansive territories acquired during Alexander's campaigns set the stage for an unprecedented period of cultural and intellectual amalgamation, with the Macedon court, especially under leaders like Philip II and Alexander, serving as a nexus for this synthesis. This era, now referred to as the Hellenistic Period, bore witness to the fusion of Greek paradigms with the rich tapestries of Eastern cultural norms, all under the aegis of Macedonian leadership.

Urban centers like Alexandria, founded in 331 BCE, and Pella, the designated capital of Macedon, encapsulated this evolution. Alexandria rapidly burgeoned into a hub of Hellenistic intellectualism, as evidenced by its library—arguably the most comprehensive repository of its time—and architectural marvels such as the Pharos lighthouse. Meanwhile, Pella mirrored the aristocratic affluence through its architectural marvels and intricate artistic creations, serving as the core from which the Macedonian rulers projected their power and cultural stewardship.

The artistic sphere experienced an apotheosis, with state patronage enabling artists to venture beyond the classical paradigms of Greek artistry towards nuanced realism emblematic of the Hellenistic era. In both Pella and far-reaching regions encompassing Bactria and extending to contemporary Afghanistan, the artistry showcased discernible Hellenistic influences, manifesting in both architectural edifices and sculptural forms.

However, the integration was not limited to artistic pursuits alone. The intellectual landscape thrived, exemplified by the education Alexander received from the eminent philosopher Aristotle. With the empire's territorial expansion, urban centers like Alexandria became crucibles for academic exploration. Emergent philosophies like Epicureanism and Stoicism not only enriched Hellenistic introspection but also made lasting impacts on subsequent Roman intellectual traditions.

In regions stretching from Anatolia to the Indus Valley under the Seleucid Empire, and concurrently in the Indian subcontinent under the Mauryan dynasty, discernible Hellenistic influences were manifested in various spheres of life. Strategic positioning and diplomatic engagements enabled the promulgation of Greek traditions within the intricate fabric of Asian cultural milieu. This was further facilitated by formal relations established through the medium of trade routes, reminiscent of Alexander's eastern campaigns.

Anchoring this Hellenistic fusion was the foundational ethos of the Macedon court, which envisaged a symbiotic relationship between political ascendancy and cultural stewardship. It underscored the realization that an empire's true grandeur lay not just in its territorial dominions, but in its capacity to be a custodian of knowledge, foster artistic ingenuity, and nurture ideas for posterity.

Thus, the Hellenistic Period transcended mere coexistence or assimilation of diverse elements. It represented an epoch wherein political power and cultural dynamism converged, mutually enriched, and collaboratively scaled unprecedented zeniths of human evolution.

The Military Foundations of Macedon Supremacy: The Phalanx and Comprehensive Warfare

The trajectory of Macedon's ascendancy in the geopolitical landscape of antiquity was underscored by its revolutionary military innovations. Central to this was the Macedon phalanx, a strategic formation that fundamentally altered the mechanics of warfare. Comprising tightly packed infantry ranks wielding the sarissa, a spear of formidable length, the phalanx became emblematic of an overwhelming force that adversaries found daunting to penetrate. Incepted during Philip II's reign in the latter segment of the 4th century BCE, this formation fortified the Macedon army's strategic advantage, rendering it the predominant force on numerous battlegrounds.

However, the comprehensive scope of Macedon military capabilities extended well beyond the confines of infantry tactics. Under the aegis of Alexander's leadership, the Macedon military apparatus demonstrated a remarkable adaptability, deploying an amalgamated approach that integrated cavalry, archery, and advanced siege methodologies. This was evident in confrontations with resilient adversaries, exemplified by the Siege of Tyre in 332 BCE, where the Macedon military utilized an array of innovative siege instruments including mobile towers and battering mechanisms, while simultaneously imposing maritime blockades, thereby neutralizing even the most fortified of defensive structures.

Additionally, in the domain of naval warfare, Macedon strategies evidenced a marked evolution. Although Macedon's historical foundation was not steeped in naval traditions, the confluence of Hellenistic maritime expertise with resources garnered from subjugated territories facilitated the development of a potent naval fleet. This naval reinforcement proved instrumental during campaigns in regions such as Egypt.

The underlying catalyst for these military transformations, however, was the strategic acumen inherent in Macedon leadership. This encompassed Philip II's adept unification strategies as well as Alexander's visionary and adaptive battle tactics. Confrontations with diverse adversaries, be it the mounted archers of the Scythian steppes or the imposing war elephants encountered in the Indian subcontinent, saw Macedon strategies demonstrating resilience, adaptability, and ingenuity.

In summation, the Macedon military ethos was not confined to sheer conquest. It was characterized by a propensity to assimilate, adapt, and innovate. This holistic military paradigm transitioned Macedon from its historical position as a marginal entity to an empire of unparalleled might, with its tactical legacy influencing subsequent generations of military thinkers and strategists.

Wealth and Strategy: Macedon's Economic Expansion

The economic prowess of ancient Macedon was inextricably linked with its strategic territorial acquisitions and foresighted governance. The region was endowed with natural resources, most notably the gold deposits in the Pangaion Hills and the silver-rich environs of Amphipolis. However, it was the astute management and expansionist policies of leaders like Philip II and Alexander that transformed this inherent wealth into a sophisticated, interconnected economic framework.

By 336 BCE, Philip II's strategic conquests in Thrace not only expanded Macedon's territorial boundaries but also granted them direct access to crucial mineral resources. This influx of precious metals financed multifaceted endeavors, from military expeditions to infrastructural projects, consequently amplifying the state's financial reserves. Yet, the economic canvas of Macedon was poised for even broader strokes under Alexander's reign. The subjugation of the Achaemenid Persian Empire, an economic titan in its own right, led to a monumental transfer of wealth. The treasuries of prominent Persian cities like Susa, Persepolis, and Ecbatana were integrated into the Macedon fiscal system, marking a scale of economic amalgamation rarely witnessed in ancient times.

Beyond mere acquisition, the Macedon leadership displayed remarkable acumen in systematizing its economic infrastructure. The advent of a uniform coinage, exemplified by the gold stater adorned with depictions of Athena and Nike, not only standardized monetary transactions but also facilitated commerce across the empire's vast territories, stretching from the European heartlands to the Asian peripheries.

The strategic dominance over crucial trade conduits, especially those bridging the Mediterranean and the Orient, further entrenched Macedon's economic hegemony. Consequently, trading hubs experienced an upsurge in activity, catalyzing the movement of commodities, intellectual paradigms, and diverse populations.

However, the true hallmark of Macedon economic strategy lay in its governance. The establishment of judicious economic policies, with a pan-Macedon purview, stimulated commerce and prosperity. Urban centers, both historical and newly founded, thrived under this regime. Alexandria, for instance, emerged as a quintessential embodiment of this economic and cultural synthesis, bridging trade and Hellenistic enlightenment.

In synthesizing this economic narrative, it becomes evident that Macedon's financial vitality was not solely a byproduct of its conquests but also a testament to its integrative and strategic governance. The empire's legacy underscores the confluence of wealth, strategy, and administrative vision, reaffirming that an empire's resilience is anchored as much in its economic robustness as in its military might.

Dissolution and Resurgence: The Aftermath of Alexander's Demise and the Rise of the Diadochi

The sudden demise of Alexander in 323 BCE precipitated an existential crisis for the vast Macedon Empire. Bereft of a universally acknowledged heir and centralized authority, the empire's integrity dangled precariously. The ensuing power vacuum catalyzed the ambitions of the Diadochi, Alexander's seasoned generals, who were now grappling not just for territorial control but for the stewardship of the Alexandrian legacy.

From 323 BCE to the dawn of the 3rd century BCE, the geopolitical landscape was in constant flux, punctuated by the so-called Successor Wars. These conflicts were not merely territorial skirmishes; they were high-stake endeavors underpinned by the aspirations of generals-turned-monarchs. Key figures such as Antigonus Monophthalmus, Seleucus I Nicator, Ptolemy I Soter, and Cassander emerged not as transient warlords but as potential founders of lasting dynasties.

The contours of the erstwhile unified empire were redefined:

> **The Antigonid Dynasty** took control over Macedon and substantial territories in Greece. Their reign symbolized a return of Macedon hegemony, albeit confined primarily to the European continent.

> **The Ptolemaic Dynasty** found its epicenter in Egypt. Ptolemy's establishment of Alexandria as the capital ensured that the city's luminescence in culture and knowledge persisted under the aegis of a new ruling class.

> **The Seleucid Empire**, under Seleucus, exhibited expansive territorial ambitions. From Anatolia in the west to the eastern thresholds of the Indus Valley, the empire presented a mosaic of cultures, all unified under the overarching Hellenistic umbrella.

These transformations, while carving up the monolithic Macedon Empire, paradoxically ensured the endurance of Hellenistic civilization. Each of these emergent polities, despite their distinct political identities and trajectories, championed Hellenistic traditions. The Greek language, artistic conventions, architectural styles, and philosophical discourses found new audiences and patrons. Thus, while the political unity Alexander had achieved may have disintegrated, the cultural and intellectual synthesis he fostered not only endured but also proliferated across these successor states.

Conclusion: Reflections on Macedon Magnificence - The Precursor to a New Dawn

In the vast continuum of history, the journey of empires presents a captivating tapestry of ascent, zenith, decline, and legacy. The Macedon Empire, with its meteoric rise and unparalleled conquests, offers a rich case study for those eager to understand the interplay of power, culture, and ambition.

Several analytical observations arise from this momentous chapter of antiquity

The Power of Military Innovations: Beyond just their prowess in battle, Macedon military strategies encapsulated the brilliance of strategic adaptation, ensuring their dominance across varied terrains and against diverse adversaries.

The Synthesis of Cultures: The Macedon epoch wasn't merely about assimilation. It was a symphony of cultures, where Hellenistic traditions harmoniously intertwined with local customs, birthing an era of unmatched artistic and intellectual renaissance.

A Legacy of Economic and Administrative Mastery: The Macedon's economic achievements were not solely hinged on territorial acquisition. They laid the groundwork for a system that interlinked vast stretches of land, promoting trade and mutual prosperity.

Centers of Knowledge and Enlightenment: The safeguarding and propagation of knowledge, most notably through institutions like the Library of Alexandria, ensured that the echoes of this era would reverberate through successive ages.

As the vast empire, rich with diverse cultures and landscapes, started to unravel without a unifying successor, the Diadochi emerged, carving out their realms from this once-colossal edifice. Despite the fragmentation, they continued to embody the spirit of the Hellenistic ethos within their respective domains.

The complex dynamics of the Macedonian era, characterized by moments of cultural fusion and periods of political division, established the groundwork for the following phase in history. As the shadows grew longer on the Macedon landscape, and its luminosity waned, the stage was set. A hushed anticipation gripped the Mediterranean. Out of these very shadows, awaiting its moment in the annals of time, arose an entity destined to leave one of the greatest impacts in world history. This emerging force, observing, learning, and biding its time, was none other than... Rome.

Mosaic of Romulus and Remus Suckling A Wolf[16]

Chapter 9.
Rome: From City-State to World Power (753-27 BCE)

Alea Jacta Est (The die is cast)

~Julius Caesar

Rome Unfolded

Rome: a name synonymous with grandeur, representing a civilization that once spanned continents, and an empire that indelibly marked history's pages. Originating from myths surrounding the hero Aeneas, who evaded Troy's fall and sought refuge in Italy, to its notable decline, Rome's narrative has captivated and enlightened many. Beyond tales of conquests and battles, it encompasses narratives of governance, culture, and the very essence of humanity. This narrative underscores human resilience, an insatiable quest for power, and the recurring patterns of ascendancy and decline.

Located among the Seven Hills by the Tiber River, Rome emerged as a modest settlement. Aeneas's odyssey, as detailed in Virgil's Aeneid, positions him as a precursor to Romulus and Remus, and a pivotal entity in Rome's foundational myths. Tracing its trajectory, one witnesses Rome's burgeoning influence, spanning from North Africa's sunlit terrains to Britain's rain-swept landscapes, and from the Iberian Peninsula to the expansive Middle East. Our chronicle starts with these ancient legends and Rome's establishment in 753 BCE, progressing to the Western Roman Empire's decline in 476 CE. A nod is also given to the Eastern Roman Empire or Byzantium's lasting legacy, which persisted for an additional millennium.

The Roman tale is intricate, interweaving destiny and human aspiration. Delving into its annals, one grasps why Rome, even after numerous centuries, stands as an exemplar of civilization and a beacon of profound historical import.

Founding Myths and Early History

In ancient Italy, narratives and traditions converged, resulting in the foundation of what would become a pivotal global empire: Rome. Rome's origin tales serve as an interface between myth and reality, merging human endeavors with divine interventions. This confluence shapes Rome's political and cultural foundations through tales transmitted across generations.

Central to Rome's beginnings is the legend of Romulus and Remus. Born to Rhea Silvia, a Vestal Virgin, and the deity Mars, they faced potential execution by King Amulius of Alba Longa due to an ominous prophecy. Despite being abandoned in the Tiber River, the brothers survived, with a she-wolf providing sustenance until a shepherd, Faustulus, and his spouse, Acca Larentia, adopted them. Their heritage manifested in leadership abilities. After overthrowing King Amulius and restoring their grandfather Numitor, they aimed to establish their city around 753 BCE. A location dispute resulted in Romulus fatally wounding Remus, leading to the naming of the city as Rome.

Subsequent to this legendary establishment, Rome underwent governance by seven consecutive kings from 753 to 509 BCE. These rulers, despite wielding absolute power, set the groundwork for the forthcoming republic. Post founding Rome, Romulus incepted pivotal societal structures and segmented the populace. His successor, Numa Pompilius (c. 717-674 BCE), was pivotal in institutionalizing Rome's religious customs. The subsequent rulers, ranging from Tullus Hostilius to Lucius Tarquinius Superbus, were instrumental in Rome's early developmental phase, forging infrastructures and widening territorial boundaries. Lucius Tarquinius Superbus's autocratic reign resulted in his expulsion and initiated the Roman Republic era in **509 BCE**.

This phase, rich in myths and early historical occurrences, was foundational for Rome's subsequent political evolutions. It instilled principles of governance, sacrifice, and preordained roles. References to these initial tales of divine interplay, leadership vision, and societal structuring were recurrently cited in ensuing eras, underpinning the Roman sociopolitical fabric.

The Roman Republic: Rise of a Democratic Power

Emerging in response to the monarchic excesses and cognizant of an increasing societal demand for equitable governance, the Roman Republic was conceptualized as a groundbreaking democratic model. Spanning approximately five centuries (509 BCE - 27 BCE), this structure oversaw Rome's ascendancy from local dominance to Mediterranean supremacy.

The reign of Lucius Tarquinius Superbus culminated in widespread disapproval due to his blatant disdain for established Roman conventions and the Senate's autonomy. The rape of Lucretia, a noblewoman, by Sextus Tarquinius, the king's son, was a pivotal event that incited widespread anger and led to a revolt against the monarchy. This uprising was led by Lucius Junius Brutus and Lucius Tarquinius Collatinus, both of whom were related to the royal family. Their actions eventually resulted in the overthrow of Tarquinius Superbus and the establishment of the Roman Republic.

In the Republic's infancy, a stark demarcation existed between the Patricians — aristocratic lineage holders — and the Plebeians, encompassing the majority including artisans, merchants, and agriculturalists. The Patricians held exclusive rights over religious and administrative positions, sidelining the Plebeians from significant state affairs. This disparity triggered the "Conflict of the Orders" (5th - 3rd century BCE), during which the Plebeians, in their quest for enhanced political clout and economic protections, periodically demonstrated, causing sizable disruptions. Their tenacity culminated in pivotal reforms, epitomized by the inauguration of the 'Twelve Tables' — Rome's seminal codified laws — and the eventual elevation of Plebeians to prestigious roles, inclusive of the Consulship.

Externally, the Republic, bolstered by an augmented military acumen, transitioned from a defensive stance against immediate neighbors to aggressive territorial ambitions. Following the Samnite Wars (343-290 BCE), Rome solidified its control over central Italy. Subsequently, its confrontations with the southern Greek colonies culminated in the Pyrrhic War (280-275 BCE). Despite the derivation of the term "Pyrrhic victory" from this conflict, Rome emerged triumphant, ensuring its dominion over the Italian Peninsula by the 3rd century BCE's culmination.

This Republic era meticulously instilled an ethos within Rome, which valorized its democratic structures, championed adaptability, and encouraged territorial aspirations. These foundational tenets would subsequently steer the Republic during engagements with prominent Mediterranean adversaries and its eventual imperial evolution.

Military Innovations and Expansion

Rome's ascension to its esteemed position in the annals of antiquity was intricately tethered to its formidable military framework, not merely its political sagacity or cultural magnetism. The Republic phase was instrumental in the recalibration of Rome's military doctrines, thus fortifying its dominion over the Italian Peninsula and subsequently facilitating its sprawling Mediterranean expanse.

At the heart of Rome's military triumphs lay the Roman Legion, an embodiment of versatility and discipline. Initially, Rome's military alignment was with the phalanx formation, a paradigm borrowed predominantly from the Greeks and Alexander the Great. Yet, as the Republic matured, a shift to the manipular formation transpired. A standard legion, usually encompassing approximately 4,800 troops, was segregated into 'maniples', delineated further into the hastati, principes, and triarii. This hierarchical structuring, fortified by steadfast discipline and an ingrained camaraderie, permitted seamless adaptability across diverse terrains, enhancing infantry efficacy.

The tapestry of Rome's military strategy was underscored by its engagements with Carthage in the Punic Wars. These prolonged confrontations (264-146 BCE) were determinative of western Mediterranean supremacy. Rome's ability to rapidly construct a navy, despite Carthage's maritime dominance during the First Punic War (264-241 BCE), underscored its adaptable military ethos. The Second Punic War (218-201 BCE) spotlighted Rome's resourcefulness and strategic tenacity, culminating in its victory despite Hannibal's audacious campaigns. By the Third Punic War's cessation (149-146 BCE), Rome had effectively annexed vital regions like Sicily, Sardinia, Corsica, and parts of North Africa.

Having secured the western Mediterranean, Rome's gaze shifted eastward, culminating in the Macedon Wars (214-148 BCE) and the eventual subjugation of Greece by 146 BCE. Greece's incorporation brought with it cultural treasures, inducing a pronounced Hellenization of Roman society.

Rome's insatiable territorial appetite further propelled it into Asia Minor and against the Seleucid Empire. Consequently, by the Republic's twilight, Roman territories had expanded to encompass regions synonymous with contemporary Turkey, Syria, and parts of Mesopotamia.

Cumulatively, Rome's meticulous military reforms, astute strategic deployments, and undeterred ambitions transmuted it from a nascent power within the Italian Peninsula to an uncontested Mediterranean behemoth.

Late Roman Republic's Socio-Political Landscape

During the 2nd century BCE, Rome's external might was juxtaposed with its internal tumult. Tiberius and Gaius Gracchus, progeny of a venerable Roman family, were emblematic of this societal discord. In 133 BC, driven by glaring economic disparities, Tiberius Gracchus inaugurated a comprehensive land redistribution initiative, targeting the vast estates of Rome's elite. Predictably, the Senate, predominantly an aristocratic entity, perceived this as a direct encroachment upon their interests.

Exerting his influence through the Public Assembly, Tiberius galvanized significant popular backing, thereby exacerbating the pre-existing political rifts. Gaius Gracchus, his sibling, subsequently sought to build on this momentum, introducing reforms in 123 BC that spanned agricultural distribution, grain prices, and military induction parameters. Although these endeavors held promise for the Roman plebeians, they simultaneously unsettled the prevailing societal order, culminating in the assassinations of both brothers – Tiberius in 133 BCE, followed by Gaius in 121 BCE.

The ramifications of the Gracchi's ventures were multifaceted. The chasm between Rome's affluent upper echelons and its economically marginalized populace widened, casting a shadow over the Republic's foundational democratic ideals. Public assemblies, historically revered as democratic bastions, morphed into theaters of acute confrontation, with both populistic factions and the steadfast Senate grappling for political dominance.

Transitioning to the modern era, particularly 21st-century America, one can discern parallels with the Gracchian epoch. The emergence of figures like Donald Trump catalyzed societal divisions, echoing the schisms that plagued the late Roman Republic. While populism often promises societal enhancement, beneath such assertions lurks the potential for exacerbating existing inequalities, deepening societal divides, and stoking volatility.

Amid the tumultuous socio-political landscape of Rome in the late 1st century BCE, the stage was set for the rise of an individual of extraordinary strategic brilliance. In this tempestuous epoch, where ambition met opportunity, one figure's actions would not merely redefine the contours of Rome but would cast a long shadow over subsequent chapters of global history. That man was none other than Julius Caesar.

The emergence of Julius Caesar and the Gallic Wars

Julius Caesar, an iconic figure in Roman history, commenced his ascent within the political spheres of Rome much before his military expeditions. Born into the Julian gens, Caesar's early life was punctuated by challenges, including a period of hiding post Sulla's proscriptions.

Emerging from these adversities, he quickly showcased an astute understanding of Rome's political matrix, often leveraging alliances to propel his ambitions.

One of Caesar's most seminal alliances was the formation of the First Triumvirate in 60 BCE. This was an unofficial coalition with Gnaeus Pompeius Magnus (Pompey) and Marcus Licinius Crassus. This union was not born out of mutual respect but rather out of mutual necessity. Caesar needed financial and military backing for his proconsular command in Gaul, Crassus sought military command in the East, and Pompey wanted ratification of his eastern settlements. It's pivotal to understand that this was a marriage of convenience, each member recognizing the potential advantages it offered in the short term.

The territories of Gaul, lying beyond Rome's established frontiers, presented both a challenge and an opportunity. Comprising a mosaic of distinct tribes, Gaul was a region marked by its rich resources and strategic importance. The military campaigns initiated by Caesar against the Gauls weren't merely territorial expansions; they were strategic endeavors to solidify his position back in Rome. Each victory in Gaul augmented Caesar's coffers, supplemented his legions, and enhanced his reputation.

The tribes of Gaul, such as the Helvetii, the Aedui, and the Arverni, under leaders like Vercingetorix, exhibited formidable resistance. However, the Roman legions, supported by a highly sophisticated logistical network and an unparalleled command structure, consistently outmaneuvered and subdued the tribal confederations. The Siege of Alesia in 52 BCE, wherein Caesar's forces besieged and defeated Vercingetorix, epitomized Roman military prowess and marked the culmination of the Gallic Wars.

Parallel to his military campaigns, Caesar undertook an extensive documentation effort in his "Commentarii de Bello Gallico." This text, while providing a detailed account of the campaigns, also functioned as a political instrument. By portraying the Gauls as barbaric and emphasizing Roman civility, Caesar projected himself as Rome's protector, paving his way into the heart of Roman politics.

Post the Gallic Wars, Caesar's amassed wealth and strengthened legions amplified his political weight. The fragile equilibrium of the First Triumvirate disintegrated with Crassus's death in 53 BCE at Parthia. This, combined with Caesar's increasing clout, exacerbated tensions with Pompey. The proverbial point of no return was Caesar's decision to cross the Rubicon River in 49 BCE, in direct violation of the Senate's edict. This act catalyzed a civil war, with Caesar eventually emerging victorious.

However, this victory did not signify a stable reign. Caesar's rapid reforms and power consolidation fomented concerns among the Senate's traditionalist faction. In 44 BCE, this latent tension culminated in Caesar's assassination, a watershed moment signifying the decline of the Roman Republic and the inception of the Roman Empire.

In analyzing Caesar's trajectory, it becomes evident that his career was not just a product of personal ambition but was intricately intertwined with the socio-political dynamics of Rome during his era. The Gallic Wars, hence, weren't mere military conquests but were instrumental in reshaping Roman history.

Conclusion: From Republic to Empire - Political Transformations

The late Roman Republic was marked by intense social, political, and economic upheavals. A multitude of factors, ranging from widening class divides, administrative inefficiencies, to the rise of influential generals with personal armies, undermined the Republican framework. The assassination of Julius Caesar, while being a culmination of this tumult, ironically propelled Rome further into instability.

The power vacuum post Caesar's death introduced the Roman polity to the Second Triumvirate in 43 BCE. Composed of Gaius Octavius Thurinus (later Augustus), Mark Antony, and Lepidus, this alliance was distinctly different from its predecessor. Endowed with constitutional legitimacy for a tenure of five years, it wielded proscription as a tool, targeting not just political rivals but also accumulating wealth from confiscated properties.

A pivotal element in this era's political matrix was the evolving relationship between Mark Antony and Cleopatra. Beyond their personal bonds, this alliance had deeper ramifications. Egypt, with its immense grain supplies, was critical to Rome's sustenance. Antony's alignment with Cleopatra posed not just as a political challenge but as a potential threat to Rome's food security. Additionally, Antony's donations of Roman territories to Cleopatra's children exacerbated tensions with Octavian, who capitalized on this to fuel anti-Antony sentiments in Rome.

The ensuing conflict culminated in the Battle of Actium in 31 BCE. Antony and Cleopatra's defeat wasn't merely a military setback; it symbolized the end of one of the last vestiges of the Republican era. Octavian's ascendancy post Actium was methodical. Instead of asserting overt dominance, he embarked on a calculated strategy. In 27 BCE, his apparent gesture of ceding powers back to the Senate was a masterstroke, as it portrayed him as the Republic's preserver. The Senate's reciprocation, bestowing upon him the title 'Augustus,' signaled a nuanced transition. While the title meant 'the revered one,' it was devoid of overt monarchical connotations, aligning with Octavian's narrative of being the Republic's guardian.

However, beneath this veneer of republicanism, Augustus systematically centralized authority. Positions like the 'tribunicia potestas' and 'imperator' were crucial in this design. While outwardly, these positions were in line with the Republican framework, in essence, they concentrated legislative, military, and religious authority in Augustus.

Simultaneously, Augustus initiated comprehensive reforms, understanding that an empire's stability necessitated robust administrative structures. The creation of a standing army, the 'Praetorian Guard,' establishment of the 'cursus honorum' to streamline administrative careers, and the delineation of senatorial and imperial provinces ensured better governance. He also fostered a cultural renaissance, patronizing luminaries like Virgil and Horace, thereby intertwining the empire's political identity with its cultural ethos.

This transition from Republic to Empire was indeed more than a mere shift in titles or individuals in power. It was a structural evolution, driven by socio-political necessities and shaped by individuals' astuteness. The Republican ideal, premised on collective governance, morphed into a more centralized, autocratic system under the Empire. The subsequent Pax Romana, spanning approximately two centuries, stands testament to the effectiveness, albeit not without challenges, of this transformation. This period not only defined the Roman identity but also influenced the conceptualization of governance, culture, and administration in the Western world's subsequent epochs.

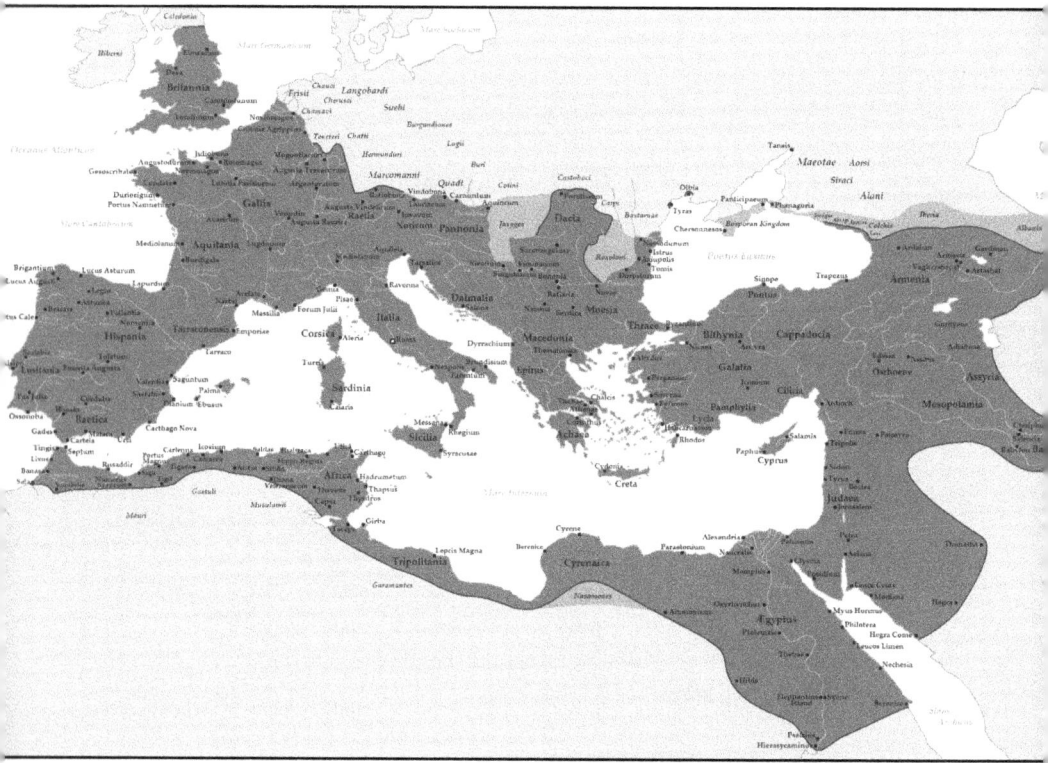

The Roman Empire · 117 CE[17]

Chapter 10.
The Roman Empire
(27 BCE-476 CE)

The object of life is not to be on the side of the majority, but to escape finding oneself in the ranks of the insane.

~ Marcus Aurelius

Foundational Transition: From Republic to Empire

The rise of the Roman Empire from the ruins of the Republic outlined the transformative nature of Roman politics and leadership. The assassination of Julius Caesar, a pivotal juncture, initially threatened to mire Rome in unremitting instability. Contrarily, this upheaval catalyzed the emergence of an empire, vast in its territorial magnitude and superior in influence compared to its Republican antecedent.

It was Octavian, subsequently adopting the title Augustus, who adeptly steered Rome through this political quagmire. His initiatives segued Rome from its republican governance—where authority was, at least notionally, dispersed—to an imperial structure characterized by centralized dominion. This paradigmatic shift indelibly reconfigured the Roman sociopolitical fabric.

The empire's vast territorial mosaic, stretching from Germania's temperate forests to Egypt's arid expanses, manifested an impressive cohesion. This unity was in part due to the Pax Romana, an Augustan policy that fostered a shared Roman identity across diverse cultures and topographies. The intricate network of Roman roads served dual purposes: they were conduits for commerce and communication and vectors for transmitting Roman cultural and societal norms.

Rome, as the empire's epicenter, underwent significant infrastructural evolution during Augustus's tenure. Architectural marvels like the Pantheon and the Forum of Augustus emerged as physical testaments to Rome's pinnacle of cultural and aesthetic achievements. Concurrently, the proliferation of Latin, initially restricted to the Italian precincts, began resonating from Carthage's vibrant markets to the intellectual environs of Athens.

Though the empire's inception heralded transformative policies, it did not lead to a wholesale abandonment of Republican legacies. Institutions like the Senate retained significance, albeit with attenuated powers. Similarly, the Roman legions, emblematically bearing their eagle standards, persisted as territorial custodians.

While the empire's territorial expansion facilitated the assimilation of myriad cultures, it concurrently presented unprecedented challenges. Nonetheless, the foundational strategies and structures, instituted by Augustus and predicated upon the Republic's terminal lessons, affirmed Rome's position not merely as a geopolitical entity but as a luminous paradigm of civilization and the immutable potency of Roman principles.

The Pax Romana Epoch: Constructing Unity and Prosperity

Spanning from 27 BCE to 180 CE, the Pax Romana—literally translating to "Roman Peace"—was not merely an interlude of tranquility but a strategic initiative established by Augustus that aimed to instill cohesion, stability, and advancement throughout the expansive Roman dominions.

Emerging from the tumultuous backdrop of political disarray and confrontations characterizing the Republic's denouement, Augustus's empire endeavored to mend its internal schisms while projecting an aura of both strength and benevolence. The nomenclature "Pax Romana" itself distilled this aspiration, positioning Rome as a unifying force, amalgamating diverse territories under its equanimous governance.

A salient feature of this epoch was its infrastructure-centric development. Arterial roads such as the Via Augusta and Via Domitia bisected the empire, catalyzing trade, expediting communication, and enabling swift military deployments. These infrastructural veins ensured that the quintessence of Roman cultural, economic, and administrative practices permeated from Rome's nucleus to its peripheral territories.

Urbanization witnessed an uptick during the Pax Romana. Metropolises like Ephesus, Tarraco, and Lugdunum evolved into epitomes of Roman architectural innovation, punctuated with infrastructural marvels like amphitheaters, aqueducts, and sanctuaries. While these cities imbibed and reflected indigenous customs, they simultaneously showcased Roman urbanistic features—from structured street layouts to Latin-laden inscriptions.

Commercial activities thrived in this era. The Mediterranean, colloquially dubbed 'Mare Nostrum' by the Romans, teemed with trading vessels ferrying a panoply of commodities—from Gaul's renowned wines to the orient's aromatic spices. The empire's sheer territorial magnitude facilitated a confluence of commodities, philosophies, and cultures, engendering a dynamic milieu of intercultural dialogues and trade.

Outside the domains of trade and infrastructure, the Pax Romana emphasized the paramount importance of legal principles. Laws and legal tenets, many formulated during this epoch, were pivotal in ensuring judicious governance. The principle of "civis romanus sum" conferred certain rights and privileges, fostering a cohesive Roman identity amongst a demographically diverse populace.

Moreover, this period's relative tranquility became conducive to cultural and scholarly endeavors. Literary luminaries such as Virgil, Ovid, and

Seneca crafted timeless masterpieces, encapsulating the zeitgeist of a flourishing empire.

However, the Pax Romana's luminosity was occasionally overshadowed by adversities, including external aggressions, frontier altercations, and internal factionalism. However, the strategic foundations established by Augustus, reinforced by the administrative skills of subsequent leaders, solidified the Roman Empire's role as a stronghold of stability in the unpredictable ancient world.

Sociocultural Evolution in the Roman Landscape

Under the aegis of the Pax Romana—characterized by stability and cohesion—the sociocultural canvas of the Roman Empire witnessed a metamorphosis. With burgeoning trade conduits and urban centers, the societal composition of the empire transitioned, assimilating diverse elements from its extensive territories, thus evolving the core Roman identity.

Central to the societal matrix of Rome was the 'familia' construct. Anchored by the 'paterfamilias', typically the eldest male member, these family units mirrored the empire's hierarchical design. However, the integration of multifarious cultures into the Roman fold gradually nuanced traditional family tenets, heralding a more globalized perspective.

Roman society's stratification was multifaceted. The Senatorial and Equestrian echelons epitomized the elite, while the 'plebeian' segment constituted a significant majority. Nevertheless, the Pax Romana's economic vigor facilitated the ascendancy of affluent plebeians, subtly eroding the demarcations of entrenched class systems. Concurrently, the institution of slavery—regrettably integral to Roman society—underwent a transformation. An amalgamation of slaves, hailing from various geographies and imbibing distinct cultural nuances, indelibly influenced facets of Roman existence, spanning culinary preferences to artistic endeavors.

In the realm of education, the Roman elite exhibited proficiency in both Greek and Latin literary, philosophical, and historical paradigms.

Educational establishments, diverse in their formalities, mushroomed throughout the empire. This educational sprawl ensured that Roman progeny, predominantly from the wealthier strata, were beneficiaries of a comprehensive pedagogical experience.

Recreational activities occupied a central position in Roman cultural life. Rome's Colosseum, a structural exemplar, frequently resonated with the spectacles of gladiatorial confrontations and chariot expeditions. Theatrical venues, platforms for works by luminaries such as Plautus and Terence, metamorphosed into cultural epicenters in Roman urban locales. Furthermore, an array of festivals, spanning religious observances to secular celebrations, punctuated the Roman temporal cycle, offering both diversions and avenues for community cohesion.

Religious practices remained pivotal. While the conventional Roman deities—encompassing Jupiter, Mars, and Venus—retained their reverence, the empire's geographical expanse ushered in diverse religious tenets. The incorporation of the Egyptian Cult of Isis, Persian Mithraism, and emerging Christian doctrines highlighted the religious diversity and integration that thrived within Roman territories.

The empire's sartorial, artistic, and culinary domains mirrored its global outreach. Romans, often draped in togas, developed culinary palettes incorporating eastern spices, resided in abodes graced with Hellenistic artistry, and imbibed musical rhythms influenced by remote geographies.

In summation, during the Pax Romana, the Roman sociocultural fabric emerged as an intricate amalgam, a nexus where time-honored traditions interfaced with novel influences. The stability and affluence of this period, instantiated by Augustus and perpetuated by subsequent rulers, catalyzed a cultural flourishing, perpetually refining and extolling the Roman identity.

The Roman Empire in Transition: From Unity to Dichotomy

As the Pax Romana's luminosity dimmed, the structural and cultural edifice of the Roman Empire, painstakingly built over centuries, began confronting multifarious stresses. Factors which had erstwhile cemented the empire's cohesion and magnificence subsequently engendered fissures and bifurcations.

The empire's vast territorial sprawl, once a crucible of diverse cultures and intellectualism, emerged as an administrative conundrum. The logistics of governing territories as geographically and culturally disparate as the fog-shrouded realms of Britannia and the arid landscapes of Egypt from a singular nucleus like Rome grew increasingly labyrinthine. The latency in communication, burgeoning regional asymmetries, and insurrectionary tendencies started undermining the monolithic authority Rome once wielded.

Economic frameworks, previously robust and dynamic, displayed signs of fraying. The complex trade matrices—once the arteries of Roman affluence—were compromised by maritime piracy in the Mediterranean and transgressions by frontier tribes. Urban loci, key cities and towns once emblematic of Roman ascendancy, witnessed regression. The economic vibrancy characteristic of the Pax Romana era metamorphosed into periods of stagnation in these formerly bustling hubs, precipitating demographic shifts from urban to agrarian settings and attenuating the quintessential Roman urban ethos.

On the religious front, the heterogeneity that once defined the empire's spiritual landscape became a crucible for discord. Christianity's ascendancy, premised on monotheistic doctrines, was frequently at odds with Rome's entrenched polytheism. As the Christian fold expanded, it sporadically invoked the empire's ire, primarily because it was perceived as an affront to both the customary Roman religiosity and the emperor's divinity.

From a militaristic standpoint, the once indomitable Roman legions grappled with exogenous and endogenous challenges. Transgressions by external entities, notably the Germanic tribes, intensified. Concurrently, the internal fabric of the legions, increasingly reliant on non-Roman conscripts owing to recruitment impediments, witnessed dwindling loyalties. This engendered sporadic mutinies and sporadic elevations of 'Barracks Emperors', indicative of the military's diminishing cohesiveness.

In an attempt to arrest this multifactorial decline, Emperor Diocletian, in 285 CE, instigated a profound reconfiguration by bifurcating the empire into the Eastern and Western Roman entities. This division, predicated on creating a streamlined administrative apparatus, signalled a paradigmatic shift. The monolithic Roman Empire, previously emblematic of unity and expansiveness, commenced its evolution into two distinct entities, each navigating its trajectory in an increasingly tumultuous global milieu.

The Roman Empire: From Pinnacle to Precipice

The bifurcation of the Roman Empire, segregating it into Eastern and Western dominions, signified not merely a geopolitical realignment but underscored the looming tribulations that would hasten the latter's eclipse. The Western Roman Empire, with the illustrious city of Rome as its nucleus, confronted these adversities head-on, with consequences that would reshape the historical trajectory.

Economically, the opulence synonymous with the Pax Romana era had receded into historical annals. The intricate trade arteries, which had once pulsated with vibrant commerce, now encountered perturbations stemming from both internal flux and external menaces. The majestic urban epicenters, erstwhile bastions of Roman societal and cultural zenith, manifested signs of desolation, with many metamorphosing back into pastoral terrains.

Externally, barbarian onslaughts became a chronic concern. Ethnic groups such as the Visigoths, Vandals, and Huns, impelled by both migratory exigencies and the allure of Roman affluence, persistently penetrated Roman defenses. The audacious desecration of Rome by the Visigoths in 410 CE epitomized the waning Roman impregnability. This was accentuated by the Vandalic appropriation and devastation of Carthage in 439 CE, eroding the Western Empire's territorial dominion.

The internal political tableau was riddled with volatility. Imperial ascensions were frequently orchestrated through military subterfuge, eschewing traditional avenues of hereditary succession or senatorial ratification. Such incessant political oscillations eroded centralized potency, rendering holistic governance an elusive ideal.

In the realm of spirituality, the ascendant trajectory of Christianity persisted. The promulgation of the Edict of Milan in 313 CE by Constantine the Great enshrined Christian religious freedoms, pivoting away from erstwhile periods of antagonism. As the 4th century culminated, Christianity's enshrinement as the state religion heralded a discernible rift from Rome's ancestral polytheistic tenets.

Contrastingly, the Eastern Roman dominion, termed Byzantium, with the strategically poised Constantinople as its capital, navigated these tribulations with relative resilience. Byzantium's geographically advantageous position, fortified bulwarks, and robust economic infrastructure endowed it with a longevity that would witness the Western Empire's decline, ensuring its continuity for a subsequent millennium.

The Western Roman Empire's denouement materialized in 476 CE, orchestrated by Odoacer, a Germanic potentate, culminating in the dethronement of the terminal Roman sovereign, Romulus Augustulus. This watershed moment, emblematic of the Western Roman Empire's 'fall,' delineated the cessation of Rome's political dominion in the Western hemisphere. Nevertheless, Rome's indelible legacy, spanning jurisprudence to cultural paradigms, would indomitably influence Europe's subsequent historical arc.

Byzantium:
An Evolutionary Continuation of Roman Legacy

As the Western Roman Empire grappled with an intricate web of predicaments culminating in its dissolution, its Eastern counterpart, colloquially termed Byzantium, epitomized adaptability and endurance. This division of the ancient Roman world not only navigated the vicissitudes that precipitated the West's decline but also flourished, serving as an anchor of civilization, commerce, and geopolitical influence in the medieval epoch.

Central to Byzantium's tenacity was its capital, Constantinople. Its geographically strategic nexus, bridging Europe and Asia and straddling the pivotal junction between the Black Sea and the Mediterranean, rendered it an epicenter of trade. The city's monumental fortifications, a legacy of Emperor Theodosius II's foresight in the 5th century, bolstered its defensive capabilities, repelling a myriad of siege attempts across the ages.

From an economic vantage, Byzantium's ascendancy was facilitated by its dominion over profitable trade conduits and its fertile agricultural expanses. The gold solidus, the emblematic Byzantine monetary unit, emerged as a touchstone in global commerce, underscoring the empire's fiscal influence. Furthermore, Byzantium's intermediary position fostered its role as a conduit facilitating the interplay of commodities, intellectual thought, and technological advancements between the East and West.

On the cultural frontier, Byzantium was an amalgamation. Retaining the structural vestiges of Roman governance and jurisprudence, it concurrently imbibed Hellenistic influences, Christian ideologies, and subsequently, diverse Asiatic cultural elements. This syncretic tapestry birthed distinctive artistic, architectural, and scholarly expressions. The Hagia Sophia, commissioned by Emperor Justinian I in the 6th century, encapsulated Byzantine architectural magnificence and ingenuity.

In the religious sphere, Byzantium was a crucible of Christian orthodoxy. The theological maelstroms that resonated within its precincts, exemplified by debates like the Iconoclast Controversy, were instrumental in sculpting Christian tenets. The empire's hosting of the Ecumenical Councils was pivotal in delineating and cementing Christian dogmas.

Byzantium's interactions with burgeoning powers in its vicinity were multifaceted. Encounters with entities like the Sassanian Empire and subsequent Islamic Caliphates oscillated between adversarial confrontations and constructive engagements in diplomacy, commerce, and cultural reciprocity. Byzantium's acumen in adaptation, diplomatic overtures, and its propensity to integrate extraneous cultural facets bolstered its sustained relevance.

The specter of the Western Roman Empire's downfall perennially loomed in Byzantine consciousness. This historical precedent served as an instructive lodestar, accentuating the imperatives of adaptability, robust centralized stewardship, and the cultivation of socio-economic and cultural symbioses both internally and with exogenous powers.

To encapsulate, as the luminescence of the Western Roman Empire dimmed, Byzantium emerged as its torchbearer. This beacon, albeit refracted through a distinct lens, perpetuated the brilliance of Rome, illuminating the medieval epoch and forging a bridge between antiquity and posterity.

Rome in Context:
Comparing With Other Ancient Superpowers

The evaluation of Rome's expansive legacy is augmented when positioned alongside other formidable ancient empires. Through comparative analysis, not only does Rome's distinctive trajectory emerge, but the recurrent dynamics shaping numerous empires across diverse geographies and timelines become discernible. The synthesis of these shared experiences and distinct identities provides an intricate understanding of Rome's enduring influence and offers a vantage point into the cyclical patterns of empire development.

Rome and Mesopotamia. Mesopotamia, often characterized as the genesis of civilization, heralded urban governance through its early city-states, including Uruk, Akkad, and Babylon. Both the Roman and Mesopotamian empires perceived the pivotal role of codified laws. The Code of Hammurabi and Rome's Twelve Tables respectively, underscored justice and societal harmony. Notably, the architectural prowess of both civilizations was evident in their development of complex aqueducts and canal systems, exemplifying the importance attached to water resource management.

Rome and Egypt. The Nile-centric Egyptian civilization, recognized for its uninterrupted dynastic rule, shares intriguing parallels with Rome. Both the Roman Emperors and Egyptian Pharaohs were venerated as semi-divine entities, bridging the terrestrial and the divine realms. Architectural preferences also drew parallels; while Egyptian pyramids and temples reflected a religious zeal and beliefs about the afterlife, Roman amphitheaters and forums were manifestations of societal ethos and vibrant public engagement. Furthermore, meticulous record-keeping was a hallmark of both empires, with Egypt employing hieroglyphics and Rome using Latin inscriptions.

Rome and Persia. The expansive Achaemenid Persian Empire offers an illuminating comparison with its intricate administrative apparatus. Both empires, despite their vastness, favored a degree of decentralization; the Persian Empire had its satrapies, and Rome appointed provincial governors. Communication and trade arteries, like Persia's Royal Road and Rome's Via Romana, bound their territories together. Noteworthy is the religious tolerance practiced in both empires, with Persia recognizing various regional deities and Rome eventually endorsing Christianity.

Rome and the Han Dynasty. The Han Dynasty of China, roughly contemporaneous with the Roman Empire, introduces an eastern perspective. Both empires, despite geographical separation, recognized the mutual benefits of trade, facilitated by the iconic Silk Road. Furthermore, the security challenges posed by vast territorial expanse resonated in both contexts, with Rome confronting Germanic tribes and the Han addressing the Xiongnu threat. The emphasis on knowledge preservation was mutual, exemplified in Roman libraries and the Han academies.

Rome and Macedon. Alexander the Great's rapid expansion and the subsequent proliferation of Hellenistic culture elucidate the dynamics of swift territorial acquisition and cultural assimilation. Unlike Rome's gradual territorial incorporation, Alexander's conquests were meteoric. Yet, both faced the intricate challenge of cultural amalgamation. Notably, the Hellenistic influence on Roman domains in various spheres, from art to philosophy, underscored Macedon's residual influence post its disintegration.

Conclusion: Echoes of Rome in Today's World

The trajectory of Rome, from its legendary origins to its emergence as a formidable power, has been seminal in the annals of human history. Its evolution from a nascent city-state on the Tiber banks to an expansive empire straddling three continents offers insightful parallels to the dynamics of ascendancy, zenith, and decline characteristic of prominent civilizations. Rome's narrative underscores the foundational pillars that buttressed the edifice of much of Western civilization.

Contemporary societies exhibit an enduring Roman imprint in manifold aspects. Architectural marvels like the Colosseum and the Pantheon find their modern counterparts, and legal doctrines pioneered during the Roman era inform the judicial frameworks of several present-day nations. Roman deliberative practices have bequeathed philosophical tenets that continue to influence the contours of modern governance and diplomacy.

Roman architectural motifs, such as arches, columns, and domes, continue to inspire contemporary designs. The democratic ethos rooted in the Roman republic—though it has undergone myriad transformations—resonates in modern democratic setups. Legislative entities across nations have borrowed both nomenclature and structural attributes from the Roman Senate.

The Roman legal framework, with its emphasis on justice, equity, and individual rights, has bequeathed enduring principles. Modern legal paradigms, spanning from the presumption of innocence to contract law's foundational principles, owe their genesis to Roman legal traditions.

Tangible remnants of Roman genius, in the form of roads, aqueducts, and amphitheaters, punctuate landscapes across Europe and North Africa. Contemporary infrastructural undertakings frequently derive inspiration from Roman engineering marvels. Modern urban planning methodologies, characterized by grid layouts and zoning considerations, mirror Roman city planning insights.

The cultural sphere is replete with Roman influences. Latin, Rome's linguistic legacy, though ostensibly dormant, permeates scientific nomenclature, legal aphorisms, and the lexicons of Romance languages. Roman literary contributions, spanning the gamut from Seneca's philosophical deliberations to Virgil's monumental epics, have indelibly influenced Western literary canon and thought processes.

Narratives centered on Roman myths, deities, and historic figures have undergone reinterpretation and adaptation across diverse media, fostering a vibrant tapestry of art, literature, and drama.

A consequential aspect of Rome's legacy is its indelible religious influence. Emperor Constantine's endorsement of Christianity in the 4th century CE was pivotal in sculpting the religious milieu of the Western domain. The ascendancy of the Papacy in Rome, coupled with the propagation of Christianity, set the stage for the religion's expansive outreach.

In summation, Rome transcends its historical confines, resonating vibrantly in the contemporary epoch. Its multifaceted influence underscores the monumental scope of human endeavors, the perennial nature of human pursuits, and the transcendent essence of human accomplishments. As the tapestry of history unfurls, with empires oscillating through cycles of rise and decline, Rome's indelible imprints serve as an enduring testament to the inexorable spirit of civilization—a spirit that birthed an illustrious empire from a fledgling city-state and continues to shape our collective odyssey.

The Pantheon in Rome[18]

The Colosseum,in Rome[19]

PART II:
From Rome's Ashes: Empires that Shaped a Millennium

Introduction

Subsequent to the waning influence of Rome, the global tableau did not descend into inertia. The vast vacuum resulting from Rome's receding dominion swiftly witnessed the ascendancy of potent entities, each inscribing its indelible mark on the historical tapestry. These new empires, spanning geographies from the arid expanses of Arabia to the icy stretches of Mongolia, often evoked Rome's monumental grandiosity, but also incorporated their unique principles, technological advancements, and civilizational blueprints.

Rome's decline did not connote a termination; rather, it heralded a period of flux, marking the transmutation of ancient legacies into novel epochs of human ingenuity and imperial enterprise. The fervent religious milieu of the Arabian Peninsula gave birth to a formidable caliphate, weaving together an intricate mosaic of cultures, scholarly pursuits, and pioneering innovations, stretching its influence from the Iberian Peninsula to the Indian subcontinent. Concurrently, Europe, once the epicenter of Roman magnificence, underwent a transformative phase with its disparate regions consolidating under the aegis of Charlemagne, thus signaling the advent of a distinct renaissance. In parallel, the expansive, rugged terrains of Mongolia became the crucible for a nomadic wave led by Genghis Khan, eventually coalescing into an unprecedentedly vast empire that recalibrated norms of commerce, diplomatic engagements, and militaristic strategies. Additionally, when contrasted with the context of the Byzantine territory, Anatolia's landscape served as the crucible for the emergence of an empire destined to bridge the East and West—the formidable Ottomans.

While Rome's influence was undeniable and its legacy profound, it did not possess a monopoly on global shaping forces. The ensuing millennium, post-Rome, was a vibrant arena where empires oscillated through cycles of emergence and dissolution. This period was emblematic of a renewed thirst for knowledge, a fervor for safeguarding and disseminating wisdom, and a reinvigorated engagement in the multifaceted ballet of diplomacy, commerce, and territorial expansions. Our ensuing exploration of this era will escort us across diverse landscapes—from majestic imperial residences to animated commercial hubs—narrating the chronicles of those formidable entities that arose from Rome's remnants to sculpt a millennium's narrative.

Chapter 11.
The Islamic Caliphates (632-1258 CE)

The best richness is the richness of the soul.

~Caliph Umar

Setting the Stage for Islamic Expansion

In the vast deserts of the Arabian Peninsula, historically characterized by nomadic lifestyles and active trade routes, the 7th century CE bore witness to a transformation of profound consequence. Specifically, in the city of Mecca, the emergence of Islam, founded by Muhammad—a former merchant-turned-prophet—was poised to significantly alter the geopolitical and religious terrains.

Muhammad's prophetic journey commenced in 610 CE with a series of revelations. These divinely inspired messages, which would later be meticulously compiled into the Quran, laid the foundational doctrine for a burgeoning faith whose influence would soon eclipse the borders of the Arabian sands. Notably, within a relatively short span, Muhammad's monotheistic teachings garnered a substantial following, thereby positioning them in direct opposition to Mecca's entrenched polytheistic practices.

Historical records suggest that prior to the ascendancy of Islam, Mecca already held a prominent position within the Arabian Peninsula as both a commercial and religious nexus. Central to Mecca's religious landscape was the Kaaba—a cuboidal edifice believed to have been constructed by the Prophets Abraham and Ishmael. While intrinsically linked to the Abrahamic tradition, over the centuries, the Kaaba became increasingly associated with the various deities worshiped by different Arabian tribes. Consequently, by Muhammad's era, it was a repository of a diverse array of idols, symbolic of the myriad deities revered by these tribes. This intricate web of religious beliefs, combined with Mecca's role as a pilgrimage center, meant that the city witnessed a confluence of tribes, each bringing its unique religious practices, trade commodities, and cultural expressions. This intricate blend of polytheistic practices was not merely a religious phenomenon; it was deeply interwoven with the socio-economic dynamics of Meccan society.

Given this backdrop, Muhammad's proclamation of a strict monotheism posed more than a theological challenge. It represented a significant disruption to the established socio-economic balance of Mecca, as the emerging faith, with its unwavering focus on a singular deity— Allah—stood in direct counterpoint to the city's established polytheistic tenets and the associated power hierarchies.

A pivotal juncture in this transformative journey was reached by 630 CE, when Mecca, recognizing the irrevocable momentum behind Muhammad and his teachings, acceded to his influence. This was symbolized most poignantly by the rededication of the Kaaba exclusively to Allah. This seminal event was not merely of religious significance; it heralded the onset of a distinct socio-political paradigm.

The ensuing years post Muhammad's demise in 632 CE showcased the breathtaking pace at which Islam proliferated. The consolidation of the historically divided tribes of the Arabian Peninsula under the banner of Islam established a robust base.

This consolidation was instrumental in facilitating the meteoric rise of the Islamic caliphates, entities that would etch an indomitable legacy in the annals of global history.

The Rightly Guided Caliphs:
Foundations of an Empire

The void left by Prophet Muhammad's passing in 632 CE precipitated a pivotal juncture in the nascent stages of Islamic history: the question of leadership succession for the rapidly expanding Muslim community. The ensuing period ushered in the Rashidun era, signifying the "Rightly Guided" Caliphs—a sequence of four eminent leaders who meticulously crafted the foundational strategies and principles of the burgeoning Islamic Empire.

First in this lineage was Abu Bakr, an intimate companion of Muhammad. Upon taking on the role of the Caliphate in 632 CE, he skillfully addressed and maneuvered through the intricate challenges of the Ridda Wars. These military engagements, though intense, served to consolidate the fragmented Muslim territories by suppressing insurrections, thereby ensuring the Arabian Peninsula's continued allegiance to Islamic governance.

The baton of leadership subsequently transitioned to Umar ibn al-Khattab in 634 CE. His tenure was marked by a methodical and audacious expansionist strategy. As a testament to his military acumen and diplomatic prowess, vast swathes of the Byzantine and Sassanian Empires capitulated to the advancing Muslim armies. It is worth noting that the Sassanian Empire, which had been a dominant regional power ruling from 224 CE until its collapse in 651 CE, was a highly organized state with advanced administrative, military, and cultural systems. It was the last pre-Islamic Persian Empire and a formidable rival to the Byzantine Empire, engaging in prolonged conflicts that left both empires weakened. This phase of relentless expansion culminated in the symbolic and strategic acquisition of Jerusalem in 637 CE. Merely a few years later, by 651 CE, the vestiges of the formidable Sassanian Empire were seamlessly assimilated into the Islamic dominion, with many of its administrative and cultural practices subsequently integrated into the Islamic Caliphate.

Uthman ibn Affan, ascending to the exalted position of Caliph in 644 CE, encountered a tapestry of internal challenges and dissent. However, his reign is predominantly remembered for an unparalleled scholarly endeavor: the unification and standardization of the Quranic verses into a singular canonical text. This scholarly exercise provided a bedrock for the consistent transmission and preservation of Islamic tenets for subsequent generations.

Lastly, Ali ibn Abi Talib commenced his leadership in 656 CE, a period marred by intricate political convolutions. While his tenure as Caliph was punctuated by civil strife and ultimately culminated in his tragic assassination in 661 CE, his enduring legacy lies in his profound theological and intellectual contributions to Islam. Notably, his unwavering emphasis on principles of justice and equity remains an intrinsic part of Islamic jurisprudence and ethos.

In retrospection, the Rashidun epoch, encapsulating a timeframe of approximately 30 years, was transformative. It facilitated the ascendancy of an empire whose territorial boundaries extended from the arid Arabian deserts, traversed the fertile crescent, and eventually encompassed regions as distant as Spain and the frontiers of India.

The Umayyad Dynasty: Expansion and Consolidation

At the end of the Rashidun era, after Ali's assassination in 661 CE, the political leadership shifted to the Umayyad Dynasty, which was deeply rooted in the bustling urban environment of Damascus. The Umayyad regime charted a distinctive trajectory characterized by ambitious territorial annexations juxtaposed with intricate administrative fine-tuning.

Muawiya I, inaugurating the Umayyad reign as its foremost Caliph, instigated pivotal reforms in governance. Eschewing the erstwhile tribal configurations, he instituted a centralized bureaucratic architecture, meticulously calibrated to oversee the empire's sprawling territories that now bridged three distinct continents. This marked a significant paradigm shift from ad-hoc tribal governance to a more structured, efficient administrative paradigm.

The Umayyad expansionist vision was relentless. To the west, the formidable Muslim legions, bearing the Umayyad insignia, ventured deep into North Africa, eventually reaching the Atlantic shoreline by 711 CE. Concurrently, in an audacious maritime endeavor, Tariq ibn Ziyad, a Berber general of considerable repute, navigated across the Strait of

Gibraltar, precipitating the swift Islamic subjugation of the Iberian Peninsula.

Simultaneously, the eastern frontiers of the empire were incrementally pushed into the Indian subcontinent, effectively integrating regions corresponding to contemporary Pakistan. Notably, these territorial inclusions were not mere military dominations. They engendered vibrant urban centers like Cordoba and Kairouan, where a confluence of Islamic, Christian, and Jewish intellectual traditions coalesced, fostering an era of unparalleled scholarly effervescence.

Yet, the Umayyad aspirations were not merely hemmed in by geographical boundaries. Their territorial voracity propelled them deep into the European heartland. By 732 CE, having firmly entrenched themselves in Spain, Umayyad battalions ventured further, clashing with Charles Martel's Frankish phalanxes at the Battle of Tours. This monumental engagement, often delineated as a fulcrum in the annals of European historiography, delineated the zenith of Umayyad incursions into Europe. Furthermore, the battle's aftermath provided the impetus for the ascendance of the Carolingian lineage within the Frankish territories as we will cover in a later chapter.

Nevertheless, the sheer expanse of the Umayyad dominion inevitably incubated fissures. Despite their remarkable external conquests, the Umayyad leadership contended with a cauldron of internal strife. Latent tensions, particularly between indigenous Arab Muslims and the Mawali – the non-Arab Muslim converts – threatened the empire's cohesion. The latter, despite their newfound religious affiliation, grappled with systemic marginalization, which sowed seeds of discontent.

The crescendo of these multifaceted tensions manifested in the Abbasid Revolution of 750 CE, culminating in the Umayyad Dynasty's unceremonious ouster. In this tumultuous transition, a solitary Umayyad scion, Abd al-Rahman I, evaded the pervasive bloodshed, seeking refuge in Al-Andalus. There, he laid the foundations for what would evolve into the illustrious Caliphate of Cordoba.

In summation, the Umayyad era, with its amalgamation of military dexterity, administrative ingenuity, and cultural stewardship, reinforced the Islamic Empire's stature in the medieval global tapestry. Their indelible imprints, discernible both in oriental and occidental realms, epitomize a period rife with territorial augmentations and nuanced cultural amalgamations.

The Abbasid Era:
An Epitome of Enlightenment and Evolution

The tumultuous denouement of the Umayyad dynasty in 750 CE heralded the ascent of the Abbasids, a lineage that would indelibly shape the Islamic realm's intellectual and cultural contours. Transferring the imperial seat from Damascus to the meticulously crafted urbanity of Baghdad, the Abbasid reign infused this nascent city with an aura of scholarly luminance, technological advancement, and artistic exuberance.

Caliph Al-Mansur, ascending as the dynasty's second sovereign, spearheaded the architectural genesis of Baghdad in 762 CE. With a strategic vantage point proximate to historically significant trade corridors, Baghdad rapidly metamorphosed into a magnet for intellectual and commercial pursuits. Scholars, traders, and skilled craftsmen, drawn from diverse geographical quarters, converged upon the city. Esteemed institutions, epitomized by the illustrious House of Wisdom, meticulously curated an array of ancient manuscripts, facilitating the translation and dissemination of Greek, Persian, and Indian treatises within the Islamic milieu.

Under the aegis of visionary caliphs like Harun al-Rashid and Al-Ma'mun, the Abbasid epoch bore witness to an intellectual efflorescence. Luminary figures emerged, with the likes of Al-Khwarizmi pioneering algebraic methodologies and algorithmic constructs. Concurrently, polymaths such as Ibn Sina, colloquially known as Avicenna, crafted seminal works, notably the 'Canon of Medicine,' which remained a touchstone in medical discourse across both oriental and occidental realms for ensuing centuries. Literary avenues thrived, buoyed by poetic virtuosos like Al-Mutanabbi and erudite scholars including Al-Jahiz, whose treatises spanned an eclectic range from linguistic mastery to the intricacies of natural selection.

The geographical expanse of the Abbasid domain rendered it a crucible for multifaceted cultural interchanges. The fabled Silk Road, safeguarded under Abbasid stewardship, morphed into an arterial network for the transference of commodities, ideologies, and innovations. Techniques of paper fabrication, originating from Chinese realms, revolutionized the domain of Islamic manuscript production. Concurrently, Persian bureaucratic intricacies were seamlessly assimilated, enhancing the administrative framework of the Abbasid hegemony.

However, such luminance was interspersed with periods of profound challenges. The empire's territorial aggrandizement engendered complex governance dilemmas. Powerful provincial governors, equipped with considerable autonomy, occasionally manifested defiance towards the centralized Abbasid authority. Furthermore, the geopolitical landscape bristled with external adversarial entities, ranging from a resurgent Byzantine Empire to the ascendant Seljuk Turks, perpetually testing the Abbasid martial resilience.

By the advent of the 10th century, fissures in the empire's political edifice became increasingly conspicuous. Although the caliphal institution retained its spiritual sanctity, tangible political influence frequently resided with military potentates or emergent regional lineages. The monumental invasion by the Mongols in 1258 CE, which resulted in the fall of Baghdad, marked the waning phase of the eastern Abbasid domain. Nevertheless, a vestige of the dynasty lingered in Egypt under Mamluk suzerainty until its subjugation by the Ottomans in 1517.

In retrospection, the Abbasid chronicle, punctuated by its monumental strides in scientific exploration, philosophical discourse, and artistic endeavors, stands as an emblematic testament within historical annals. This epoch encapsulates a juncture when the Islamic world, radiating scholarly brilliance, epitomized enlightenment, proffering a legacy that continues to illuminate subsequent eras.

Evolution from Centralized Caliphate to Mosaic of Regional Powers

As the annals of history chronologically unfurled, the grandeur epitomized by the Islamic Caliphates, hallmarked by territorial aggrandizement and a fervent era of cultural rejuvenation, inevitably encountered an evolutionary trajectory characterized by decentralization and fragmentation. Commencing in the waning years of the 9th century, the Abbasid Caliphate's vast territorial dominions and its inherently heterogeneous demographic composition instigated pronounced administrative complexities.

The geographic vastness of the Abbasid realm inherently rendered a centralized governance model progressively impracticable. Emirs, or regional potentates, started to manifest an increasingly pronounced proclivity for autonomy, often circumventing or even defying the central edicts of the caliphal establishment. For instance, in the Iberian Peninsula, the Umayyad remnants, diverging from the Abbasid sphere, instituted an independent caliphate in Córdoba. Simultaneously, North Africa witnessed the ascendancy of the Fatimid dynasty, a Shi'a entity, which audaciously juxtaposed itself against the predominant Sunni orthodoxy championed by the Abbasids.

The economic substratum of the empire also underwent profound perturbations. Historically, the Silk Road had functioned as the principal arterial conduit facilitating transcontinental commerce. However, with the advent of enhanced maritime navigational capabilities, sea-borne trade routes emerged as formidable competitors. Consequently, erstwhile pivotal commercial nexuses, such as Baghdad and Samarkand, grappled with relative economic diminution.

Externally, the Abbasid domain was assailed by multifarious adversarial forces. The Crusades, initiated in the 11th century from the European heartland, were underpinned by the ambition of recapturing the Holy Land from Muslim suzerainty. While the initial Crusader offensives registered successes, the Islamic territories eventually coalesced under astute military tacticians, notably Salah ad-Din, commonly known as Saladin. Despite the eventual Muslim resurgence against the Crusader enclaves, these military engagements exacted a heavy toll, both in terms of resources and the exposed vulnerabilities of the Islamic realm.

However, the most cataclysmic external challenge emanated from the expansive steppes of Central Asia. The 13th-century Mongol onslaughts, spearheaded by formidable commanders including Genghis Khan and his progeny, wrought devastation upon vast regions of the Islamic domain. The sacking of Baghdad in 1258 CE by Hulagu Khan not only symbolized a grievous military capitulation but also signified the obliteration of a revered cultural and scholarly haven.

Yet, in the face of these myriad challenges, the intrinsic resilience of the Islamic ethos remained undiminished. Successive power centers materialized, with entities like the Mamluks in Egypt, the Safavids in Persia, and the Ottomans in Anatolia each assimilating and augmenting the caliphal legacy. This ensured that the luminescence of Islamic civilization persisted, undeterred by external vicissitudes.

In summation, the transformation from a monolithic caliphal construct to a kaleidoscope of regional dynastic entities, while symbolizing the culmination of one historical epoch, simultaneously augured the genesis of subsequent eras, each embroidering intricate patterns onto the expansive fabric of Islamic historiography. The dynamism, tenacity, and adaptative capacities of these multifarious Islamic societies reinforce their quintessential relevance within the overarching global historical discourse.

Conclusion:
Broader Implications of the Caliphate Epoch

The narrative of the Islamic Caliphates is not confined merely to territorial dominions or political triumphs; it spans a multifaceted spectrum, encompassing intellectual revolutions, intricate cultural syntheses, and far-reaching economic ramifications. These entities, from their nascent inception in the Arabian Peninsula to the zenith of their influence in regions such as Al-Andalus and the fertile crescent, delineated a trajectory that intricately wove together strands of culture, innovation, and knowledge.

In the domain of intellectual pursuits, the caliphates emerged as formidable patrons. The intricate tapestry of scientific exploration and philosophical inquiry was enriched by luminaries such as Al-Khwarizmi, whose elucidations in algebra paved the foundational pathways for subsequent mathematical discourses. Similarly, figures like Ibn Sina and Al-Razi extrapolated and expanded upon the Hellenistic compendium of medical knowledge, effectively transmitting this enhanced understanding to European intellectual bastions during the Renaissance era. This intellectual transference was facilitated by institutions like the House of Wisdom in Baghdad, which served as crucibles for translation, debate, and innovation.

From a cultural standpoint, the Islamic Caliphates epitomized a melting pot of diverse traditions. The confluence of Persian poetic nuances, Indian mathematical rigor, and Greek philosophical paradigms with indigenous Arab intellectual traditions engendered a distinctive civilization. Architectural marvels, such as the Alhambra in Andalusia (Southern Spain) with its intricate geometric patterns and the spiraling minaret of the Great Mosque of Samarra (in central Iraq), remain testament to this unparalleled synthesis.

On the economic front, the Caliphates were instrumental in nurturing and safeguarding expansive trade networks. Notably, the Silk Road, which historically functioned as the lifeline of transcontinental commerce, experienced a renaissance under the aegis of the Caliphates. This not only facilitated the exchange of tangible commodities but also engendered the dissemination of ideas, technological innovations, and intellectual paradigms.

Perhaps one of the most profound legacies of the Caliphates resides in their instrumental role in promulgating the tenets of Islam. Through a combination of strategic conquests, deft diplomacy, and commerce, Islam permeated diverse territories, ranging from the African hinterlands to the steppes of Central Asia. Today, the core principles delineated during the epoch of the Caliphates, encompassing justice, piety, and scholarship, resonate with a significant proportion of the global populace.

In summation, the overarching narrative of the Islamic Caliphates transcends mere political or military delineations. They symbolize an era where multifarious domains, from science to architecture, experienced profound advancements. This epoch, with its myriad contributions to global civilization, underscores the profound relevance and enduring impact of the Caliphate epoch on contemporary societal constructs.

Chapter 12.
The Carolingian Empire and Feudal Europe (768-843 CE)

To have another language is to possess a second soul.

~Charlemagne

The Merovingian Prelude:
Foundations of the Frankish Realm

As the Islamic Caliphates thrived in the East, forging pathways for intellectual, cultural, and economic synthesis, Western Europe was undergoing its own transformative epoch. The decline of the Western Roman Empire had left a power vacuum, much like the Arabian Peninsula before the rise of Islam, inviting an array of tribal entities to assert their dominance. The legacy of the Caliphates, marked by the transference of ancient knowledge and the flourishing of scientific and philosophical inquiry, presents a compelling juxtaposition to Western Europe's state of fragmented governance and socio-political unrest. This chaotic European landscape, marked by divergent ambitions and shifting allegiances, bore witness to rising powers that sought to reconstitute the mantle of civilization, albeit through a different cultural and religious prism.

Among those seeking to fill the post-Roman void, the Franks, a Germanic tribe with a history intertwined with the Romans, began to assert their dominance. Originating from the Lower and Middle Rhine regions, they had served as Roman foederati, blending Germanic traditions with Roman administrative practices.

The Merovingian dynasty, with roots tracing back to the chieftain Merovech, emerged as a stabilizing force in this chaotic landscape. By the 6th century CE, they had carved out an expansive realm, its borders stretching across what is now France, Germany, and beyond.

Clovis I, crowned in 481 CE, stands as a pivotal figure in this dynasty. His conversion to Christianity in 496 CE, following a victorious battle, was more than a personal epiphany. It symbolized the Frankish realm's alignment with the Roman Catholic Church, forging a bond that would deeply influence European politics and religion for centuries.

However, the Merovingian reign was not without its challenges. The tradition of dividing territories among heirs led to fragmentation and infighting. By the 7th century, the 'do-nothing kings' of the Merovingian line were mere figureheads, with the real power vested in palace officials known as the 'mayors of the palace.'

Amidst this backdrop of political maneuvering and shifting allegiances, the stage was set for the ascent of the Carolingians, a dynasty poised to reshape the European landscape.

Charles Martel and the Battle of Tours

In European history, few figures loom as large as Charles Martel, the Frankish statesman and military leader. Born in 688 CE, Charles, whose surname 'Martel' means "the Hammer," would come to forge a legacy that would shape the trajectory of the European continent. He rose to power as the Mayor of the Palace, a position that, over time, overshadowed the Merovingian kings in actual authority.

Charles' defining moment came in 732 CE, near the city of Tours as briefly outlined in the previous narrative about the Islamic Caliphates. The Umayyad Caliphate, having expanded rapidly across North Africa and into Spain, posed a significant threat to the Christian heartland of Europe. Their forces, led by the governor of Al-Andalus, advanced deep into Frankish territory. The stage was set for a confrontation that would echo through the annals of history.

The Battle of Tours, sometimes referred to as the Battle of Poitiers, was not just a military engagement; it was a clash of civilizations. On one side stood the seasoned Umayyad forces, their banners bearing witness to their conquests from the Middle East to Spain. On the other, the Frankish army, determined to halt the Muslim advance into Europe.

The battle raged, and when the dust settled, Charles Martel emerged victorious. This triumph didn't just secure the Frankish realm; it halted the northward expansion of the Umayyad Caliphate, ensuring that Christianity remained the dominant faith in Western Europe.

Charles Martel's leadership laid the foundation for the Carolingian dynasty. His grandson, Charlemagne, would further expand the empire, but it was Charles, with his hammer, who struck the first blow, shaping the destiny of a continent.

The Ascendancy of Charlemagne: Europe's First Emperor since Rome

Charlemagne, or Charles the Great, stands in European history as a colossus, bridging the chasm between ancient empires and the medieval world. Born in 742 CE, Charlemagne was the grandson of Charles Martel and inherited a realm already on the ascent.

From the outset, Charlemagne's reign was marked by relentless expansion. He waged campaigns against the Saxons in the north, integrating their territories into his empire after decades of conflict. To the south, the Lombards in Italy felt the weight of his military might, and by 774 CE, Charlemagne was crowned King of the Lombards, asserting control over the Italian Peninsula.

Yet, his ambitions were not solely territorial. Charlemagne envisioned a Christian empire that echoed the grandeur of Rome. He fostered learning and culture, initiating what historians term the 'Carolingian Renaissance'.

Charlemagne

Monastic schools flourished, classical texts were preserved, and scholars like Alcuin of York thrived at his court, laying the intellectual foundations for Europe's later medieval renaissance.

However, it was on Christmas Day in the year 800 CE that Charlemagne's legacy was truly cemented. In St. Peter's Basilica in Rome, Pope Leo III crowned him "Emperor of the Romans," a title that had lain dormant in the West since the fall of the Western Roman Empire. In that moment, Charlemagne resurrected the concept of a unified Christian empire in the West, drawing a direct lineage from the Caesars of old.

His reign, which lasted until 814 CE, saw the establishment of administrative reforms and legal codes, like the Capitulare de Villis, which standardized regulations across his vast territories. These decrees, while administrative in nature, were instrumental in consolidating the diverse regions of his empire, from the Iberian Peninsula to Central Europe.

Upon his death, Charlemagne left behind an empire that spanned modern-day France, Germany, the Low Countries, Switzerland, Austria, and parts of Spain and Italy. While the empire would face divisions and challenges in the subsequent years, Charlemagne's vision of a united Christian Europe laid the groundwork for the Holy Roman Empire and the idea of a European Christendom.

In Charlemagne, Europe found its first great unifier since the days of the Roman Caesars, a beacon that illuminated the path from the fragmented realms of the Dark Ages to the dawn of a new European epoch.

The Carolingian Renaissance: An Intersection of Cultural Continuity and Innovation

Amidst the geopolitical machinations and territorial augmentations of the Carolingian Empire, an intellectual and cultural ferment, designated by historians as the "Carolingian Renaissance," marked a distinctive phase. This epoch, predominantly under Charlemagne's aegis, bore witness to a rejuvenation of literary, artistic, and scholastic endeavors, echoing the intellectual rigor of ancient Rome and Greece.

Charlemagne's patronage of learning was not a mere whimsical pursuit but a strategic endeavor. His sponsorship led to the foundation of both monastic and palace schools, with the Palace School of Aachen emerging as a focal point, drawing scholars from diverse European locales. These educational establishments, especially monasteries, evolved into hubs of erudition. The scriptoria became vital in the transcription of ancient manuscripts, ensuring that invaluable classical treatises—works of stalwarts like Virgil, Cicero, and Ovid—were not relegated to obscurity.

A salient figure of this renaissance was Alcuin of York. Originating from Northumbria (medieval kingdom in Northern England) and armed with profound scholastic credentials, Alcuin was entrusted by Charlemagne to helm educational and ecclesiastical reforms. Among Alcuin's most consequential undertakings was the standardization of Latin script, culminating in the evolution of the "Carolingian minuscule." This script was characterized by clear, legible characters with consistent spacing, eschewing the complexities and ambiguities inherent in earlier scripts. It thereby eliminated many ligatures and allowed for easier identification of individual letters and words. This reform had not merely aesthetic but pragmatic implications. By fostering uniformity in transcriptions, Carolingian minuscule facilitated the more accurate copying of texts, thereby minimizing transcription errors. This was a critical development for the propagation of canonical and theological works, given that scribes often worked on texts of great import, where even minor errors could produce substantive doctrinal discrepancies. Beyond immediate considerations, the script's influence persisted into the Renaissance and beyond, serving as a basis for the development of humanist minuscule and, eventually, the typefaces that dominate Western print culture today.

Artistically, this period marked a convergence of classical inspirations with emerging Carolingian aesthetics. This synthesis was manifest in various mediums, from illuminated manuscripts to intricate metalwork. Architecturally, structures like the Palatine Chapel in Aachen epitomized this blend, integrating classical design principles with Carolingian innovations.

Beyond the arts and humanities, the Carolingian Renaissance also invigorated theological discourse. There was a renewed engagement with biblical texts and the writings of the Church Fathers, engendering a more cohesive Christian theological framework across Charlemagne's territories.

In summation, the Carolingian Renaissance, while temporally circumscribed, etched an indelible mark on the annals of European cultural history. It functioned as a conduit, transmitting the intellectual legacy of the classical era to nascent medieval Europe. Nevertheless, the era's intellectual and cultural stability was an ephemeral phenomenon, ultimately incapable of staving off the political fragmentation that was to come. Despite its remarkable accomplishments in art, learning, and theology, the Carolingian Empire was on a trajectory toward disintegration, a process formalized by the Treaty of Verdun in 843 CE. This decline in centralized authority and territorial cohesion would sow the seeds for the socio-political transformations that dominated the ensuing medieval period, which will be the subject of our subsequent discussion.

The Dissolution of the Carolingians and the Emergence of Regional Dominance

The Treaty of Verdun, intended as a diplomatic resolution among Charlemagne's grandsons, inadvertently precipitated the empire's fragmentation into West Francia, East Francia, and Middle Francia, with each segment charting its distinct historical path.

West Francia witnessed the ascendancy of the Capetian dynasty, initiated by Hugh Capet's reign in 987 CE. This dynasty, beyond its territorial ambitions, embarked on a concerted effort to centralize monarchic power. This centralizing aspiration inevitably engendered conflicts with entrenched regional lords and, notably, with the English crown, prefiguring the geo-political animosities of subsequent centuries.

Conversely, East Francia would evolve into the Holy Roman Empire, a complex political entity aiming to resurrect the Christian Roman Empire ideal within predominantly Germanic territories. Under the Ottonian dynasty, and notably Otto I, a nuanced strategy emerged to reconcile the ecclesiastical authority of the Pope with the secular ambitions of the Empire. The Holy Roman Empire eventually coalesced into a labyrinthine web of semi-autonomous entities, theoretically unified under an elected emperor. Its existence, spanning several centuries, was fraught with both internal contradictions and external pressures, particularly from the Papacy and Italian city-states.

Middle Francia, bereft of the political stability its counterparts enjoyed, witnessed a dilution of its territories, which were annexed by its neighbors. Notably, Lotharingia emerged as a strategic fulcrum, eliciting territorial interests from both the emergent French and German polities.

Parallel to these continental shifts, the peripheries of the erstwhile Carolingian domain saw regional assertiveness. In the British Isles, the reign of Alfred the Great (871–899 CE) marked a critical juncture in the creation of a unified English polity. Prior to Alfred's rule, the land that would become England was fragmented into several kingdoms, often at odds with one another, and frequently under attack from Viking raiders. Alfred's military reforms, including the development of a standing army and fortified burhs (fortified settlements), were pivotal in staving off Viking invasions, particularly at the Battle of Edington in 878 CE. More than a military leader, Alfred also sought to cultivate the intellectual and cultural dimensions of his kingdom, promoting literacy and education in line with the Carolingian Renaissance occurring on the continent. Thus, Alfred's reign did not merely militate against external aggressors but also laid the intellectual and administrative foundation upon which the Kingdom of England would subsequently build.

On the Iberian Peninsula, the period saw an intensification of the Reconquista, a series of campaigns that aimed to retake territories held by Muslim powers. While the Reconquista had been a long-term process that stretched across several centuries, this era was particularly significant due to the emergence of unified Christian kingdoms like Castile, Aragon, and León. These kingdoms, bolstered by a combination of religious zeal and political ambition, began launching more coordinated military campaigns against Muslim dominions such as the Emirate of Granada. The Reconquista also benefited from the military orders, such as the Order of Santiago and the Knights Templar, who were ideologically motivated to reclaim Christian lands. The Treaty of Alcaçovas in 1479 effectively marked the completion of the Reconquista with the integration of the Kingdom of Granada into Castile in 1492, thereby consolidating Christian dominance in the Iberian Peninsula.

Therefore, while the Carolingian Empire's fragmentation facilitated the emergence of disparate, regionalized political systems within its former territory, it concurrently set the stage for ascendant, unifying trends in other geographical areas. This complex patchwork of dissolution and unification highlighted a broader European milieu, one characterized by a dynamic interplay of centrifugal and centripetal forces. These developments collectively served as a prologue to a medieval epoch shaped by intricate diplomatic negotiations, martial ambitions, and reciprocal cultural exchanges, thus setting the stage for the next chapter in European history: the institutionalization of feudalism as the backbone of medieval society.

Feudalism: The Backbone of Medieval Europe

The unraveling of the Carolingian Empire, a sequence of events detailed in the preceding section, led to a multilayered socio-political vacuum across Europe. This vacuum was partly filled by the emergence of feudalism, an intricate system of mutual obligations, land tenures, and hierarchical relationships that became the structural foundation of medieval European society.

The concept of "fief" functioned as the central pillar of feudalism, transcending mere geographical territory to become a nexus of authority, economic viability, and societal standing. Within the ambit of this hierarchical construct, monarchs and high-ranking nobles allocated fiefs to vassals. The allocation was contingent upon the vassals' commitment to provide military service and other forms of support, echoing the fractal division of Carolingian territories and their respective rulers' needs for localized military strength. This process of fief allocation was further complicated by an iterative layering of power, whereby primary vassals sub-divided and allocated portions of their fiefs to sub-vassals.

The manorial estate stood as another cornerstone of the feudal architecture. Its economic role was not isolated from its social implications; the estate served as a microcosm of the feudal hierarchy. Serfs and peasants, tethered to the lands they cultivated, contributed to the agricultural output essential for sustaining both the estate's population and the lord's military commitments. In this way, the estate system represented an evolved form of localized governance and economic self-sufficiency, filling the governance void left by the Carolingian disintegration.

But feudalism was more than a mere transactional arrangement. The system was fortified by oaths of fealty, solemn pledges that defined the relationship between lords and vassals. These oaths were ceremonies fraught with symbolic gravitas, encapsulating the mutual obligations and manifold responsibilities inherent in the feudal system. These rituals can be viewed as formalized expressions of the same allegiance dynamics that once held the Carolingian Empire together, albeit in a significantly more localized context.

A thorough analysis of feudalism unveils its inherent structural complexities. The decentralization that allowed regional lords significant autonomy often led to power dynamics wherein these lords could rival even monarchs, paralleling the regional assertiveness that arose following the Carolingian split. This decentralization, though stabilizing at a local level, also fostered inter-noble conflicts and presented significant challenges to the concept of a unified, centralized authority.

Moreover, feudalism perpetuated a systemic imbalance. While it offered a degree of stability and security, it imposed severe restrictions on the serfs and peasants who made up the majority of the population. Their limited rights, economic constraints, and social immobility reflect a darker aspect of the system, highlighting the asymmetric distribution of privileges and obligations.

In hindsight, feudalism was both a byproduct of the Carolingian fragmentation and a precursor to the regional entities that would later dominate European history. Through its labyrinthine structure of obligations and privileges, feudalism contributed to the emergence of socio-political identities that were both localized and part of a broader European tapestry. These nascent entities, enriched by unique combinations of cultural, economic, and political factors, were instrumental in shaping the contours of European history, marking the transition from a Carolingian epoch to a new, complex era characterized by regional powers with distinct identities.

Conclusion: Legacy of the Carolingian Empire

The Carolingian Empire, despite the ephemerality of its political zenith, engendered enduring ramifications on the European historical continuum. By meticulously analyzing these legacies, one discerns that its influence permeated diverse domains such as governance, culture, and ecclesiastical affairs, molding Europe's trajectory in intricate ways.

In terms of governance, Charlemagne's architectural approach synthesized Roman administrative paradigms with Germanic tribal conventions. This amalgamation fostered a governance model characterized by centralized authority underpinned by decentralized administrative units, a prototype that subsequent European monarchies would adapt and refine.

During a period frequently characterized as the "Dark Ages," the Carolingian Renaissance stands in stark contrast. The emphasis on erudition, the conscientious preservation of classical literature, and the assiduous patronage of the arts constituted a deliberate endeavor to maintain Europe's tether to its classical lineage. Analytically, this intellectual and artistic renaissance can be viewed as a precursor, setting the stage for subsequent epochs of cultural resurgence.

From an ecclesiastical perspective, the Carolingian Empire's maneuvers significantly sculpted Europe's Christian tapestry. Aligning strategically with the Papacy, spreading the Benedictine monastic customs, and standardizing Christian ceremonies enhanced Christianity's prominence as a unified religious institution across the continent.

Societally, the Carolingian paradigm facilitated the crystallization of the feudal system, a framework that would profoundly define medieval Europe's socio-political landscape. The entrenchment of concepts such as vassalage and the reciprocal nature of land tenures for military allegiance showcased the empire's profound influence on social contracts.

On the geopolitical front, the Treaty of Verdun in 843 CE, while primarily an instrument for the Carolingian partition, inadvertently charted the embryonic contours of emergent European polities. Analyzing these delineations, one observes precursors to contemporary territories such as France, Germany, and the Low Countries.

The emblematic title of the "Holy Roman Emperor," conferred upon Charlemagne by Pope Leo III, transcended its immediate political milieu to persist as a symbol evoking both authority and ecclesiastical unity. The Holy Roman Empire, embodied by this title, encapsulated the aspirational vision of a unified Christian Europe under cohesive secular stewardship.

The disintegration of the Carolingian Empire, culminating in the Treaty of Verdun in 843 CE, not only mapped out the initial borders of rising European nations but also planted the roots for territorial disputes and division. The sprawling Carolingian lands, in their post-Verdun configuration, began to grapple with the complexities of defining sovereignty, territorial integrity, and the relationship between church and state.

As territories continued to evolve, the splintered Carolingian regions faced ongoing tensions. The vestiges of centralized Carolingian rule were juxtaposed against the aspirations of burgeoning regional powers. These entities, while recognizing their Carolingian legacy, also sought to assert their autonomy and distinctive identities. The quest for territorial consolidation and regional dominance inevitably laid the groundwork for protracted struggles and confrontations.

Religious discord, too, finds its antecedents in the post-Carolingian landscape. The Empire's alignment with the Papacy, while consolidating Christianity's influence, also fostered a dual challenge of temporal versus spiritual authority. As the Church sought to assert its influence, individual monarchies and regions navigated their relationship with Rome, leading to both alliances and confrontations. The religious fissures that would prominently erupt during the Reformation and the Thirty Years' War (1618-1648) can trace their origins, in part, to these early power dynamics.

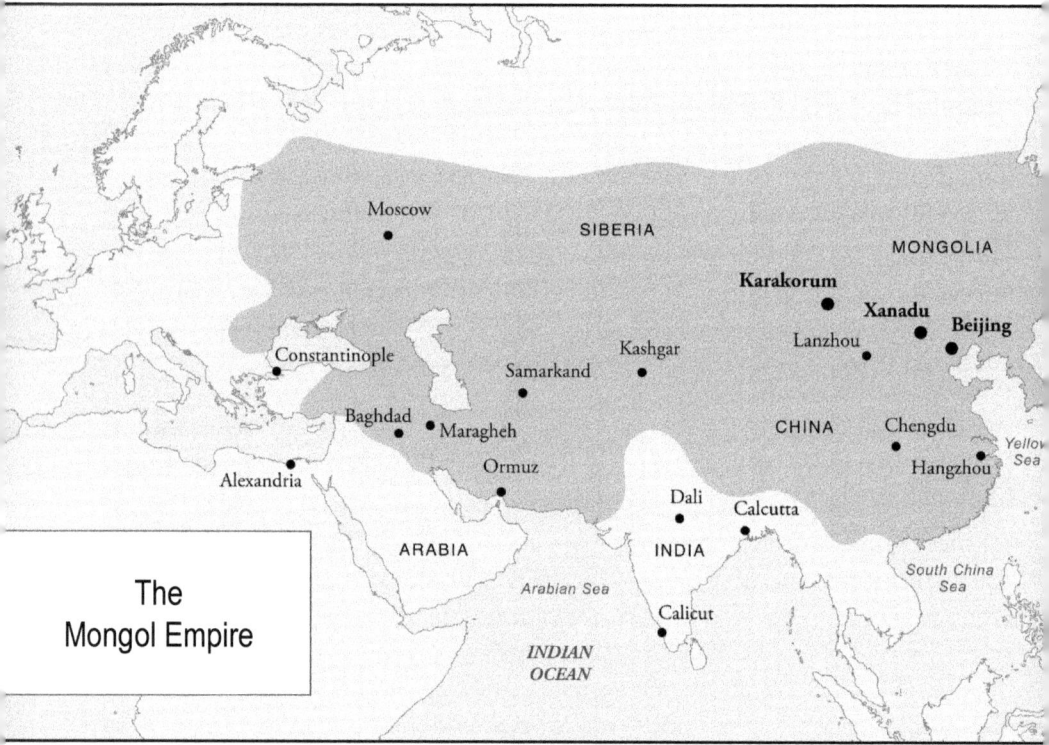

The
Mongol Empire

Moscow

SIBERIA

MONGOLIA

Karakorum

Xanadu

Beijing

Lanzhou

Constantinople

Samarkand

Kashgar

Baghdad

Maragheh

CHINA

Chengdu

Ormuz

Hangzhou

Yellow
Sea

Alexandria

Dali

Calcutta

ARABIA

INDIA

Arabian Sea

South China
Sea

Calicut

INDIAN
OCEAN

Mongol Empire 1260 CE[20]

Chapter 13.
The Mongol Empire
(1206-1368 CE)

A leader can never be happy until his people are happy.

~Genghis Khan

The Steppes of Central Asia:
Birthplace of the Mongol Horde

While the Carolingian Empire's decline in the late 9th century marked the dissolution of one of Western Europe's most formidable power structures, the early 13th century bore witness to the emergence of another dominant force in the Eurasian landscape: the Mongol Empire. In contrast to the disintegration of the Carolingian realm, where internal fragmentation and external pressures led to a weakening of centralized power, the Mongol Empire represented a surge in imperial consolidation, spearheaded by Genghis Khan in 1206.

The end of the Carolingian dynasty, which had been marked by decentralization and the relegation of the Carolingian monarchs to ceremonial roles, contrasted sharply with the Mongolian emphasis on a centralized, militaristic power structure. Whereas the Carolingians had been ensnared by feudal complexities and increasingly fragmented polities, the Mongols operated with a focus on rapid territorial expansion, enabled by their highly mobile, disciplined cavalry and a unique form of governance that deferred much to tribal loyalties but was nonetheless autocratic in nature.

The Central Asian steppes, spanning from modern-day Mongolia to Kazakhstan, presented a challenging yet liberating environment. The expansive open lands, characterized by biting cold winters and fleeting summers, molded the Mongols into a hardy and versatile people.

This itinerant lifestyle cultivated a profound sense of community and mutual reliance. Tribes were united by blood ties and shared traditions, with family being the societal bedrock. The Mongols' very existence hinged on their collective efforts, be it in erecting their yurts (tents) or in the realms of hunting and combat.

Mongol warfare mirrored their daily existence. The composite bow, an ingenious piece of weaponry, enabled them to strike with precision while mounted. Their strategies underscored swiftness, adaptability, and the element of surprise, often employing deceptive retreats to lure adversaries into traps.

Yet, the steppes were not just lands of pastoral serenity; they were arenas of ceaseless conflict. Clashes over territories and resources among tribes were frequent. Amidst this volatile backdrop, a young Temujin would emerge, confronting insurmountable odds, only to unify these combative tribes and carve out one of history's most dominant empires.

Temujin: From Outcast to Genghis Khan

The story of Temujin, who would later be known as Genghis Khan, began in the year 1162. His life, from its very outset, was marked by profound hardship and adversity. At the tender age of nine, tragedy struck when a rival tribe poisoned his father, Yesugei. This act of treachery thrust young Temujin into a world of power struggles and betrayal, setting the stage for a life of extraordinary challenges.

The death of his clan leader, Yesugei, led to a devastating betrayal by his own tribe, who believed the family was too weak to lead. This abandonment forced Temujin, his mother, Hoelun, and his siblings into the unforgiving wilderness. In this harsh and desolate environment, they were left to fend for themselves, facing the constant threat of starvation, exposure to the elements, and attacks from other nomadic tribes.

These early years of adversity were the crucible in which Temujin's character was forged. He learned invaluable lessons about the importance of loyalty and the dangers of betrayal, lessons that would shape his leadership style in the years to come. From a young age, he exhibited qualities of resilience, cunning, and determination that would later define his rule as Genghis Khan.

As Temujin grew into a young man, he began to display exceptional prowess as both a warrior and a leader. Through a combination of strategic alliances, often sealed through marriage, and audacious military campaigns against rival tribes, Temujin steadily began to consolidate power among the disparate Mongol clans. His leadership style was innovative and distinctive, setting him apart from other tribal leaders of his time.

One of the most remarkable aspects of Temujin's leadership was his commitment to meritocracy. Unlike many leaders who relied on lineage and familial ties to reward followers, Temujin promoted individuals based on their abilities and contributions. This meritocratic approach not only ensured the unwavering loyalty of his followers but also attracted warriors from other tribes who were impressed by this progressive system.

In addition to his approach to leadership, Temujin introduced groundbreaking military strategies that were far ahead of his time. His campaigns incorporated elements of espionage, psychological warfare, and disciplined troop movements. These innovations gave him a significant advantage on the battlefield and contributed to his string of victories.

By the year 1206, after a series of triumphant campaigns and diplomatic maneuvers, Temujin had achieved the seemingly impossible: the unification of the fiercely independent and often warring Mongol tribes. In a grand kurultai, a traditional assembly of Mongol chieftains, he was acclaimed as "Genghis Khan," a title that would translate to

Ghengis Khan[21]

"universal ruler" and become synonymous with his legendary achievements.

Genghis Khan's rise heralded the close of the Mongols' disjointed tribal phase and inaugurated an age of relentless territorial expansion, forming an empire that would eventually span from the Pacific shores to Europe's core. His remarkable journey, from the harshest of beginnings to becoming one of history's most formidable leaders, serves as a testament to the indomitable spirit of a man who would leave an indelible mark on the world.

Blitzkrieg Across Continents: Mongol Military Tactics and Conquests

The astonishing rise of the Mongol Empire was not solely the result of sheer numbers or brute force; it was a demonstration of military innovation and strategic brilliance. At its core was the formidable Mongol military machine, a force that seamlessly blended unparalleled mobility, precision archery, and a profound understanding of psychological warfare.

The Mongol warrior was a product of the unforgiving steppes, where they honed their skills from a young age. Proficiency in horse riding and archery was not just encouraged but ingrained in their very existence. Central to their military success was the composite bow—a compact yet potent weapon that allowed them to shoot with remarkable accuracy while mounted on horseback. This unique capability made them exceptionally lethal adversaries in open combat. However, it was not merely their weaponry that set them apart but also their extraordinary mobility.

Mongol warriors traveled light and fast, often covering vast distances that left their enemies bewildered and unprepared. Each warrior maintained multiple mounts, ensuring that fresh horses were readily available. This practice gave them the ability to outpace and outmaneuver their adversaries with astonishing speed, confounding those who sought to engage them.

Yet, the Mongol strategy was far more nuanced than raw combat prowess alone. Genghis Khan and his accomplished generals were masters of psychological warfare. They artfully employed tactics such as the feigned retreat, luring unsuspecting enemies into carefully laid ambushes. They were adept at spreading rumors and misinformation, sowing discord and fear among their opponents long before the battlefield was even reached. Prior to engaging in actual combat, the Mongols ensured that their adversaries were mentally defeated, with chilling tales of Mongol ferocity circulating far and wide.

The efficacy of these tactics was vividly demonstrated in their conquests. The invasion and subjugation of the Khwarezm Empire serve as a remarkable testament to Mongol military genius. In response to the murder of his trade envoy, Genghis Khan launched a relentless campaign against the vast Khwarezmian territories. Through a meticulously executed series of sieges, battles, and strategic maneuvers, the Mongols systematically dismantled the Khwarezmian forces, capturing their cities, and effectively erasing the empire from the annals of history in just a few short years.

China, a formidable adversary with its fortified cities and immense armies, presented a distinct challenge. Employing a blend of adept siege tactics, strategic partnerships, and resolute tenacity, the Mongols achieved dominance over the Jin Dynasty to the north, and subsequently, the Song Dynasty in the south, consolidating China under Mongol governance.

The tremors of the Mongol onslaught were felt as far as Europe. The Mongol incursions into Eastern Europe, particularly their decisive victories at the Battle of the Kalka River and their invasion of Hungary, sent shockwaves throughout the continent. The Mongols, with their seemingly supernatural speed and efficiency, appeared to be an invincible force, sweeping through territories and leaving a trail of awe and fear in their wake.

In essence, the Mongol military campaigns were not merely about conquest; they were a symphony of strategy, psychology, and raw combat skill. Through the mastery of these elements, a nomadic tribe from the vast steppes of Mongolia managed to carve out the world's largest contiguous land empire, forever etching their name in the annals of history.

Pax Mongolica: The Mongol Peace and its Implications

Amidst the settling dust of conquests, as the Mongol Empire extended its dominion from the vast steppes of Central Asia to the very gates of Europe, a unique era emerged—a period often referred to as the "Pax Mongolica" or "Mongol Peace." This epoch, spanning much of the 13th and early 14th centuries, bore witness not to the thunderous gallop of hooves or the clashing of swords but to an unprecedented surge in trade, cultural exchange, and relative stability.

The Mongol Empire, in its sheer magnitude, encompassed a kaleido-scope of diverse cultures, civilizations, and intricate trade routes. Among these, the Silk Road, the ancient network of trade pathways connecting the East to the West, gained particular significance. Under the protective canopy of the Mongol Empire, this ancient route experienced a renaissance. Merchants, traders, and travelers could now traverse these paths with a degree of safety and assurance that had been hitherto unheard of. The Mongol administration established an elaborate system of relay posts and waystations across the empire, facilitating swift communication and the unhindered movement of goods.

Yet, the revitalized Silk Road served as more than a conduit for commodities; it became a thoroughfare for the exchange of ideas, technologies, and knowledge. Revolutionary developments such as papermaking techniques, printing technology, and even gunpowder found their way from China to the distant corners of the West. Simultaneously, the flow of European knowledge and innovations ventured eastward, enriching societies along the way.

Cultural exchange flourished, driven in part by the pragmatic approach to governance undertaken by the Mongols. Acknowledging the diversity of their subjects, the Mongols embraced a policy of relative religious tolerance. While they maintained their traditional beliefs, they refrained from imposing them on their subjects. Instead, they generously supported various religious institutions, be it Christian churches, Muslim mosques, Buddhist monasteries, or Daoist temples. This policy not only ensured smoother administration but also fostered an environment where scholars, artists, and religious figures from diverse backgrounds could interact, collaborate, and flourish.

However, the Pax Mongolica was not merely a consequence of Mongol benevolence; it was a deliberate and calculated strategy. By facilitating and promoting trade, they enriched their own coffers and expanded their influence across vast territories. By allowing religious and cultural freedom, they minimized resistance and rebellion. The Mongols, with a sagacity that transcended mere military might, recognized that the true strength of an empire lay not solely in its dominion over land but also in its capacity to harmoniously integrate and unite diverse peoples.

In retrospect, the Pax Mongolica stands as a remarkable testament to the multifaceted nature of the Mongol Empire. Beyond their formidable reputation as conquerors, they exhibited astute administrative prowess and a deep appreciation for the arts and culture. While their initial reign resonated with the clamor of conquest, it eventually paved the way for an epoch where the East and West interacted more intimately, laying the groundwork for a world increasingly intertwined, with the flux of thoughts and trade continuing to influence historical trajectories.

The Fragmentation of an Empire: The Khanates

The sprawling expanse of the Mongol Empire, stretching from the vast Pacific Ocean to the heart of Europe, was both its strength and its Achilles' heel. As the 13th century gave way to the 14th, the once-unified empire began to splinter, birthing distinct political entities known as Khanates. Each Khanate, rooted in the legacy of the Mongols, embarked on a unique evolutionary path, deeply influenced by the cultures, traditions, and challenges of their respective regions.

Founded by Kublai Khan, the grandson of Genghis Khan, **the Yuan Dynasty** marked the Mongols' intriguing entry into the complex realm of Chinese governance. Kublai Khan, with a decisive move of the capital to present-day Beijing, sought to meld Mongol martial prowess with the administrative expertise of China. While this era saw remarkable advancements in the arts and the unification of China under a single rule after years of fragmentation, it also encountered significant resistance from the Han Chinese populace, who viewed the Mongols as foreign occupiers. Over time, internal strife, economic difficulties, and natural disasters contributed to the Yuan Dynasty's decline, ultimately culminating in their overthrow by the Ming Dynasty in 1368.

Established by Hulagu Khan, another of Genghis Khan's grandsons, **the Ilkhanate** encompassed territories in modern-day Iran and parts of Iraq. In its early stages, the Mongols were ruthlessly efficient in their conquest, most notably with the brutal sack of Baghdad in 1258. However, as time passed, they began adopting Persian customs, administrative practices, and even the Islamic faith. This cultural amalgamation transformed the Ilkhanate into a rich tapestry of Mongol, Turkic, and Persian influences. Nevertheless, the Ilkhanate faced economic challenges and internal disputes that led to its gradual decline by the mid-14th century.

Named after Genghis Khan's second son, Chagatai, this Khanate extended across the vast Central Asian steppes and encompassed sections of the Silk Road. Serving as a crucial bridge between the East and the West, **the Chagatai Khanate** played a pivotal role in facilitating trade. However, it also became a region rife with constant power struggles, both internally and against neighboring entities, eventually leading to its fragmentation and dissolution.

Under the leadership of Batu Khan, the Mongols surged into the Russian steppes, giving rise to **the Golden Horde**. This Khanate, with its capital at Sarai, exerted a profound influence, extracting tribute from Russian principalities for centuries. While the Mongols did not directly administer these territories, their presence left an indelible mark on Russian political dynamics, military strategies, and trade. The Golden Horde's dominance gradually waned during the 15th century, especially after the ascent of the Muscovite principality.

In essence, the division of the Mongol Empire into these distinct Khanates represented not just a political fragmentation but also a cultural evolution. Each Khanate, while bearing the unmistakable imprint of its Mongol origins, transformed into a unique entity, profoundly shaped by its interactions with indigenous cultures, religions, and the myriad challenges it confronted. The legacy of the Mongol Empire, therefore, transcends mere conquests; it resides in the intricate tapestry of states it nurtured, each contributing to the rich mosaic of human history.

The Decline and Legacy of the Mongol Empire

The Mongol Empire, at its zenith, was an unparalleled force, its shadow stretching across continents. Yet, like many empires before it, it was not immune to decline. The vastness that once was its strength became a challenge, as distances strained governance and communication.

The vast territories of the Mongol Empire, each with its unique challenges and cultures, demanded decentralized governance. This decentralization, over time, led to power struggles among various Mongol leaders. Succession crises were frequent, with various claimants vying for the title of the Great Khan. These internal conflicts sapped the strength of the empire, making it vulnerable to external threats.

The Mongol Empire thrived on conquest, with war spoils often bolstering its economy. However, as the pace of conquest slowed, the empire faced economic challenges. Overextension of military campaigns drained the coffers, and the vast territories made trade regulation challenging. Additionally, the empire's sheer size made it difficult to maintain the infrastructure, like the famed Silk Road, which once facilitated trade and communication.

As the Mongol Empire's internal cohesion weakened, external entities sensed opportunities. From the Mamluks in Egypt to the growing power of the Muscovite principality in Russia, regional powers began to resist and push back against Mongol dominance. These external pressures, combined with internal strife, created a perfect storm, leading to the gradual disintegration of the empire.

Despite its decline, the Mongol Empire's impact on the world is undeniable and multifaceted. The Pax Mongolica, or Mongol Peace, facilitated trade across Asia, making the Silk Road a conduit for not just goods but ideas, technologies, and cultures. This exchange enriched regions from China to the Middle East, leading to a renaissance of sorts in arts, sciences, and literature.

In terms of governance, the Mongols introduced a degree of meritocracy, often employing administrators based on capability rather than lineage. Their relative religious tolerance allowed for the flourishing of multiple faiths within their territories.

Linguistically, the Mongol influence can still be seen in the Turkic languages of Central Asia. Architecturally, from the grandeur of the Ilkhanate structures in Persia to the Yuan Dynasty's constructions in China, the Mongol legacy stands tall.

In summation, while the Mongol Empire, like all empires, faced its sunset, its legacy endures. It serves as a testament to the indomitable spirit of the nomadic warriors from the steppes of Central Asia who carved an empire that changed the course of history.

Conclusion: The Mongols in World History - A Re-evaluation

The Mongol Empire, with its vast expanse and indomitable spirit, has often been a subject of both admiration and vilification in historical narratives. As with many empires of such magnitude, myths and misconceptions have clouded our understanding of the Mongols and their place in world history.

One of the most pervasive myths about the Mongols is their portrayal as mere barbaric conquerors, leaving destruction in their wake. While they were undoubtedly fierce warriors, this narrow view overlooks their administrative acumen, their promotion of trade, and their patronage of arts and sciences. The Mongols were not just destroyers; they were also builders and integrators of the vast territories they conquered.

Another misconception is the portrayal of the Mongols as an ethnically homogenous group. In reality, the Mongol Empire was a melting pot of various ethnicities, cultures, and religions, all coexisting and interacting under the Mongol aegis.

The Mongol Empire's significance transcends its military conquests. Their rule facilitated one of the most extensive cultural and economic exchanges in history. The Silk Road, under Mongol protection, became a conduit for the flow of goods, ideas, and technologies between the East and West.

Furthermore, the Mongols' religious tolerance, especially during the reign of Kublai Khan, allowed for the flourishing of various religious practices, from Christianity and Islam to Buddhism and indigenous shamanistic traditions. This religious pluralism became a hallmark of their rule and set a precedent for subsequent empires.

The Mongol administrative system, which prioritized merit over lineage, was revolutionary for its time. It laid the groundwork for more structured and efficient governance in the territories they ruled, influencing subsequent empires and states.

Finally, in re-evaluating the multifaceted legacy of the Mongols in world history, it is crucial to explore their progressive stance on gender relations, which set them apart from many of their contemporaries. Within the vast expanse of the Mongol Empire, women enjoyed a degree of freedom and participation in society that was notably advanced for their era. Mongol women were active participants in economic activities such as herding, trade, and agriculture, contributing significantly to the empire's prosperity. Moreover, some women held influential positions in politics, serving as advisors and wielding considerable authority. The Mongols' practice of religious tolerance extended to women's religious freedoms, allowing them to freely practice their faiths. This unique approach to gender equality, marked by economic autonomy, political agency, and religious freedom, underscores the Mongols' complex and lasting impact on world history.

In conclusion, the Mongols, often relegated to the role of mere conquerors in popular narratives, were pivotal players in shaping the course of world history. Their empire, though transient, left an indelible mark, fostering connections and integrations that would shape the trajectory of Eurasia for centuries to come. The Mongol Empire stands not just as a testament to the prowess of a nomadic tribe but as a beacon of the interconnectedness and shared heritage of human civilizations.

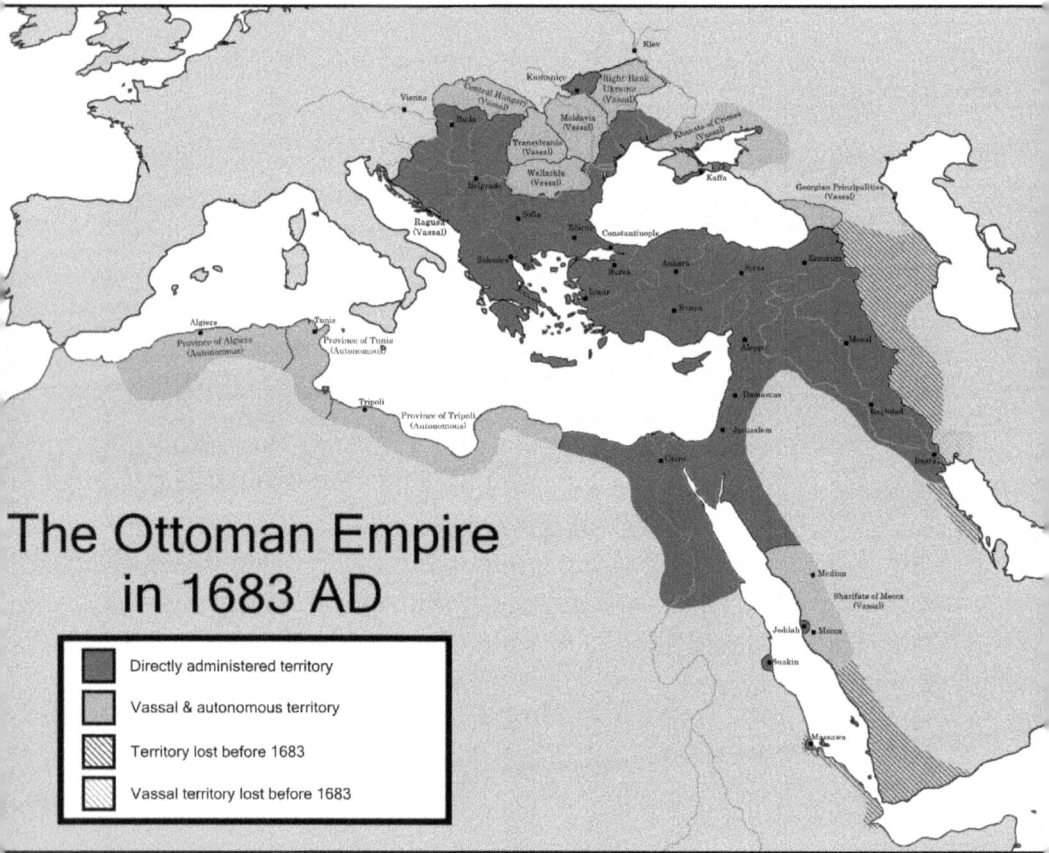

The Ottoman Empire
in 1683 AD

■	Directly administered territory
▨	Vassal & autonomous territory
▨	Territory lost before 1683
▨	Vassal territory lost before 1683

Ottoman Empire[22]

Chapter 14.
The Rise of the Ottoman Empire (1299-1922)

*I, the Sultan of Sultans, and the strongest ruler, the loftiest
king who defeats the kingdoms around the world.*

~ Suleiman the Magnificent

Origins: From Nomadic Tribes to Empire Builders

In the wake of the Mongol Empire's epochal influence on Eurasia—a
reign that was far more nuanced than mere conquest, characterized
by its innovative administrative structures, promotion of cultural
exchange, and fostering of religious pluralism—the stage was rife for
the rise of other formidable powers that would extend and adapt these
legacies. Among these were the Oghuz Turks, propelled westward from
their Central Asian homelands by the Mongol invasions. Their arrival
in Anatolia, a historically significant region that had been the theater
for the rise and fall of multiple empires, coincided with the decline of
the Byzantine Empire.

Much like the Mongols, who were mistakenly portrayed as solely
destructive when their rule in fact presented a multi-dimensional
amalgam of administration, cultural amalgamation, and religious

tolerance, the Oghuz Turks under Osman were not mere conquerors. They were empire builders, synthesizing governance strategies in ways that echoed the Mongol priority on meritocratic administrative systems. The early Ottomans embraced Islam as a unifying ideological framework, a feature that parallels the Mongols' inclusive approach to religious practice during periods of their rule.

Furthermore, the Oghuz Turks emerged at a time when the Mongols had significantly disrupted existing power structures, creating vacuums and opportunities that were ripe for exploitation. As such, the early Ottomans were agile actors, capitalizing on the resultant political instability to initiate their military campaigns, which went beyond territorial acquisition to focus on the establishment of governance structures. The early Ottoman state thus mirrored the Mongol Empire in integrating a variety of ethnic and religious groups into their administrative ambit, although under the banner of Islamic unity.

By the time of Osman's death in 1324, the foundations of an empire had been laid—an empire that would inherit, adapt, and extend the complexities and innovations introduced to Eurasia by the Mongols. The emergence of the Ottoman Empire, therefore, was not an isolated event but a sequel in the extended narrative of political and cultural transformations set in motion by the Mongols.

The Conquest of Constantinople: A New Era Dawns

Constantinople, perched strategically between Europe and Asia, was more than just a city; it was a beacon of medieval civilization. For over a millennium, it stood as the proud capital of the Byzantine Empire, a successor to ancient Rome's grandeur. Its formidable walls, intricate palaces, and majestic Hagia Sophia spoke of a city that had witnessed empires rise and fall.

Enter Mehmed II, a young and ambitious sultan, often referred to as Mehmed the Conqueror. By the time he ascended the Ottoman throne in 1444, he harbored a dream that many before him had: to capture Constantinople. The city, with its double walls and strategic position, had repelled numerous sieges in the past. But Mehmed was determined to make history.

Mehmed's preparations for the siege were meticulous. He spent years amassing resources and assembling a vast army, which included soldiers from various backgrounds and regions of the Ottoman Empire. His forces were well-equipped with an array of innovative siege equipment, including the formidable Great Bombard, a massive cannon capable of breaching Constantinople's famed walls. This siege cannon was an engineering marvel of its time, demonstrating the Ottomans' commitment to taking the city.

In 1453, Mehmed marshaled his army and began a relentless assault on Constantinople. For 53 days, the city endured a continuous and devastating barrage. The defenders, led by the Byzantine Emperor Constantine XI, displayed remarkable resilience, but the odds were stacked against them. The Great Bombard, which had been positioned on a massive wooden platform to facilitate its movement, played a crucial role in pounding the city's defenses.

On May 29, 1453, the unthinkable happened: Constantinople fell to the Ottomans. The city's legendary walls were breached, marking the end of the Byzantine Empire. The Ottoman victory was a testament to both the determination of Mehmed and the effectiveness of his siege tactics.

But for the Ottomans, this was not just a military victory; it was a symbolic one. Mehmed, understanding the city's historical and cultural significance, aimed not to destroy but to transform. He declared Constantinople, now renamed Istanbul, the new capital of the Ottoman Empire. Churches were converted into mosques, with the Hagia Sophia being the most notable transformation. Yet, in a testament to his vision, Mehmed ensured that the city remained a hub of cultural and religious diversity.

The conquest of Constantinople was a watershed moment. It not only solidified the Ottomans' dominance in the region but also shifted the balance of power in the medieval world. The city, once the heart of the Byzantine realm, now pulsed with Ottoman vigor, serving as a bridge between the East and West and heralding a new era in the annals of empire-building.

The Ottomans as Caliphs: Bridging Historical Legacies

The ascension of the Ottoman Empire cannot be fully understood without addressing its claim to the esteemed title of Caliph, symbolizing both spiritual and political authority within the Muslim world. This assertion allowed the Ottomans to seamlessly weave their narrative into the broader continuum of Islamic governance, positioning themselves as the legitimate inheritors of a grand Islamic tradition.

As detailed in Chapter 11, the Caliphate held significant religious and political importance within the Muslim world. By the time the Ottomans came to power, the once-mighty Abbasid Caliphate had experienced a decline, with the Abbasid line holding symbolic authority in Cairo under the protection of the Mamluks.

The pivotal moment for the Ottomans occurred in 1517, when Sultan Selim I's conquest of Egypt led to the transfer of the caliphal title from the last Abbasid representative in Cairo to the Ottoman Sultan. This was not merely a ceremonial acquisition; it cemented the Ottomans' position as the preeminent leaders of the Sunni Islamic world.

Endowed with the dual mantle of Sultan and Caliph, the Ottoman ruler stood as both a temporal monarch and a spiritual leader. This duality informed the empire's governance structure, blending traditional Islamic jurisprudence with Ottoman administrative innovations. Consequently, the empire was perceived as a bastion of Sunni Islam, its laws and edicts echoing the combined authority of both sultanate and caliphate.

The claim to the caliphal title also had pronounced implications for Ottoman diplomacy. Within the Islamic realm, the Ottomans, referencing their caliphal status, could assert moral and religious superiority, influencing smaller Muslim states and regions either directly or indirectly. This caliphal mantle also played a role in their interactions with non-Muslim powers, presenting the empire as the singular representative of the Muslim world.

In anchoring themselves to the legacy of past caliphates, as elaborated in Chapter 11, the Ottomans skillfully employed history to buttress their rule, intertwining religious authority with political prowess. This synthesis of sultanate and caliphate would have lasting ramifications, shaping the empire's administrative ethos, its diplomatic ventures, and its self-perception as the vanguard of the Islamic world.

Sultan Suleiman and the Ottoman Empire at Its Zenith

Sultan Suleiman, crowned in 1520, bore the immense responsibility of an empire's legacy. Under his leadership, the Ottoman Empire achieved unparalleled grandeur, earning him the title "The Magnificent."

Suleiman's reign was a testament to the zenith of Ottoman power. Europe quaked at his military ambition as he embarked on a series of conquests that expanded the empire's borders and influence. Territories like Hungary, Rhodes, and significant parts of the Balkans fell under Ottoman dominion, reshaping the map of southeastern Europe. The Mediterranean, a vital trade route, saw the Ottomans challenge formidable powers like Venice and Spain. The siege of Vienna in 1529, though not successful, marked the empire's audacious reach and the palpable threat it posed to Christian Europe.

But Suleiman was not just a warrior; he was a visionary reformer. Recognizing the need for efficient governance, he introduced robust administrative measures that streamlined the empire's vast bureaucracy. The legal system underwent significant enhancements during his reign. Suleiman personally oversaw the codification of laws, ensuring a just and orderly society within his territories.

However, the empire's brilliance extended beyond its military conquests and administrative reforms. This period witnessed a flourishing of culture and the arts. Istanbul, the empire's capital, was transformed into a hub of architectural marvels, with the majestic Suleymaniye Mosque standing as a testament to this era's brilliance. Arts found a nurturing environment within the empire; poetry, literature, and painting flourished, with the sultan himself contributing as an accomplished poet.

Spanning 46 years, Suleiman's reign represented not just the pinnacle of the Ottoman Empire but a golden era of culture, administration, and military prowess. The empire's boundaries stretched from Vienna's gates to Mesopotamia's ancient lands, from Russia's steppes to North Africa's shores. Suleiman was more than a conqueror; he was an emperor who recognized the intricate balance between might and enlightenment.

The Ottoman Administrative and Military System

The Ottoman Empire's vast expanse, spanning diverse cultures and territories, necessitated a unique administrative and military structure. This system, deeply rooted in Islamic traditions while remarkably adaptive, played a pivotal role in maintaining control and ensuring stability across the empire.

Central to the empire's military prowess was the Devşirme system. Instituted in the 14th century, this practice involved the periodic collection of Christian boys from their families, primarily from the Balkans. These young recruits underwent rigorous training in the imperial capital, where they received education in Islam, statecraft, and martial arts. This transformative process produced the empire's administrative and military elite.

From this pool of young recruits emerged the Janissaries, the empire's elite infantry units. Distinguished by their unique hats and known for their disciplined formations, the Janissaries became the backbone of the Ottoman military. Their extensive training, unwavering loyalty to the sultan, and access to advanced weaponry made them a formidable and highly effective fighting force. They played pivotal roles in major campaigns and sieges throughout the empire's history.

On the administrative front, the Ottoman Empire was divided into provinces, each overseen by a Pasha or a Bey. These high-ranking officials were appointed directly by the sultan and were entrusted with the responsibility of maintaining order, collecting taxes, and ensuring the overall well-being of their respective regions. However, their authority was deliberately counterbalanced by the influence of local leaders and institutions, ensuring a degree of regional autonomy while still upholding central control.

One of the most enlightened policies of the Ottoman Empire was the Millet system. Recognizing the empire's rich tapestry of religious diversity, this system allowed various religious communities, including Christians, Jews, and others, to govern themselves according to their own religious laws and under the leadership of their respective religious authorities. While these communities were subject to Ottoman imperial authority and contributed through taxes, they enjoyed a significant degree of autonomy in their internal affairs.

This delicate blend of centralized authority and localized autonomy, coupled with a formidable military apparatus like the Janissaries, allowed the Ottoman Empire to maintain its dominance and ensure stability across its vast and diverse territories. The Ottoman administrative and military systems serve as a testament to the empire's remarkable ability to balance the intricacies of power, pragmatism, and pluralism.

Challenges, Stagnation, and Reforms

The Ottoman Empire, once an unrivaled power at its zenith, encountered a series of mounting challenges by the 17th century. These challenges, both internal and external, would shape the empire's trajectory and ultimately contribute to its transformation.

Externally, the emergence of European powers began to pose a significant threat to Ottoman dominance. Advancements in naval technology and the Age of Exploration enabled European nations to establish new trade routes, effectively bypassing Ottoman-controlled territories. This shift in trade dynamics diminished the empire's economic influence and disrupted its longstanding trade networks. On the battlefield, the Ottomans faced substantial territorial losses, particularly in Europe, as resurgent powers like Russia, Austria, and Poland contested Ottoman rule and expanded their own territories at the empire's expense.

Internally, the empire grappled with economic difficulties. The once-thriving trade routes that had been a cornerstone of Ottoman prosperity were now overshadowed by European maritime routes. This shift in global trade dynamics led to inflation within the empire, placing significant strain on its economy. Moreover, the Ottoman administrative machinery, which had been renowned for its efficiency, began to show signs of corruption and inefficiency, further exacerbating internal challenges.

Recognizing the pressing need for change, the Ottoman Empire embarked on a series of modernization efforts, most notably the Tanzimat reforms of the 19th century. These reforms were aimed at restructuring the empire's legal, administrative, and military systems, drawing inspiration from European models. One of the most significant aspects of these reforms was the proclamation of equal rights for all citizens, regardless of their religious affiliation. Infrastructure projects, educational reforms, and a revamped legal system were all part of a comprehensive effort to rejuvenate the ailing empire.

Parallel to these administrative changes, the empire experienced a cultural and intellectual renaissance. European ideas on nationalism, governance, and science found eager proponents within Ottoman intellectual circles. This influx of new ideas sparked lively debates about the empire's identity and future direction. Some advocated for a return to Islamic traditions, emphasizing the empire's heritage, while others championed a more secular, European-inspired path toward modernization.

In essence, the Ottoman Empire, particularly in its later years, stood at a crossroads. As it sought to adapt and evolve in response to mounting challenges, the very fabric of the empire—its identity, its governance, and its place in the world—underwent profound transformations. This period of challenge, stagnation, and reform set the stage for the empire's final chapters in the tumultuous 20th century.

The Decline of the Empire and the Road to World War I

The 19th century marked a period of gradual erosion for the Ottoman Empire, particularly in its European territories. As nationalist movements gained momentum across the empire, regions that had been under Ottoman control for centuries began to assert their desire for independence. Nowhere was this nationalist fervor more pronounced than in the Balkans, a region of immense strategic and cultural significance to the Ottoman Empire.

The Balkan Wars of 1912 and 1913 were pivotal moments in this process of territorial loss. A coalition of Balkan states, united by their nationalist aspirations, squared off against the Ottoman Empire. These wars resulted in significant territorial losses for the Ottomans, further weakening their grip on Europe.

The decline of the Ottoman Empire did not go unnoticed by the major European powers, each of which had its own strategic interests in the region. The so-called "Eastern Question" emerged as a central issue in European diplomacy: What would become of the Ottoman territories as the empire continued to crumble? Britain, France, Russia, and Austria-Hungary all sought to influence the empire's disintegration to their advantage. Key prizes included control of the Straits, which connected the Black Sea to the Mediterranean, and access to the rich oil fields of the Middle East.

Amidst this complex web of external pressures and internal decay, the Ottoman Empire sought allies to bolster its position on the international stage. Germany, itself a rising power in Europe, saw an opportunity in forming an alliance with the Ottomans. Such an alliance could provide a counterbalance to the other European powers, especially Russia. This alliance, formalized in 1914, would have profound implications for the empire's future.

The outbreak of World War I marked a pivotal moment in the history of the Ottoman Empire. While the empire had faced challenges and territorial losses in the past, the scale and intensity of World War I were unparalleled. The decisions made during this period would not only determine the empire's fate but also shape the geopolitical landscape of the Middle East for the century to come. The Ottomans, allied with Germany, found themselves pitted against a coalition of powers that included Britain, France, and Russia. This conflict would prove to be the final chapter in the story of the once-mighty Ottoman Empire, setting the stage for the empire's dissolution and the redrawing of borders in the Middle East.

Conclusion: Legacy of the Ottoman Empire

The dissolution of the Ottoman Empire marked the beginning of a new era, as the modern Republic of Turkey emerged from its ashes. At the helm of this transformation was Mustafa Kemal Atatürk, a visionary leader who sought to steer Turkey towards modernity and progress. Atatürk championed secularism, introduced a new legal system, and promoted education. His vision was to create a modern and progressive state founded on principles of democracy and nationalism, while still preserving and respecting Turkey's Ottoman heritage.

The legacy of the Ottoman Empire extends far beyond the realm of politics. It has left an indelible mark on art, architecture, and culture. Iconic landmarks like the Hagia Sophia in Istanbul, with its stunning blend of Persian and Byzantine influences, continue to resonate with visitors today. The intricate designs of Iznik tiles serve as a testament to the Ottoman aesthetic, which has influenced artistic traditions across regions.

Ottoman culinary traditions have also made a lasting impact, enriching kitchens from the Balkans to the Middle East. Dishes like kebabs, baklava, and Turkish delight have become beloved staples in international cuisine.

But the Ottoman Empire's legacy extends even further. It served as a vital bridge between the East and West, facilitating trade, diplomacy, and cultural exchange. The millet system, which granted religious communities a degree of autonomy, offers valuable insights into early forms of pluralistic governance. The empire's administrative and legal frameworks provided blueprints for many modern states in the Middle East and the Balkans.

In the vast narrative of world history, the Ottoman Empire stands out as a dynamic and influential civilization. It exemplifies the capacity of civilizations to shape the trajectory of history. While the empire itself has receded into the annals of history, its legacy continues to influence our contemporary world, serving as a reminder of the enduring impact of past civilizations on the present.

Chapter 15.
Italian City-States: The Rise of Commerce and Culture (14th-17th Centuries)

The ends justify the means

~Nicolo' Macchiavelli

The Geopolitical Context

As the Carolingian Empire witnessed its gradual decline throughout the 9th century, a seismic shift in the distribution of power was set in motion across the European continent. The empire's disintegration into regional territories, epitomized by the Treaty of Verdun in 843 CE, catalyzed a weakening of centralized authority. This geopolitical fragmentation was an enabling context for various local power structures to assert their autonomy. The Italian Peninsula was no exception to this continental transformation. Its assortment of city-states—Venice, Florence, Milan, and Genoa, among others—emerged not as empires in the conventional sense, but as potent polities whose influence stretched across economic, cultural, and, to a lesser extent, military realms.

Within the broader context of global powers, the city-states defy facile categorization. Although they never coalesced into an empire, their outsized impact echoed some imperial paradigms. Where empires wield their force through territorial expansion and subjugation, the Italian City-States leveraged their power through mercantile networks, pioneering financial instruments, and cultural patronage. Their emergence was not an isolated phenomenon; rather, it was intricately entangled with global forces such as the Crusades in the 11th to 13th centuries, the Reconquista in Spain culminating in 1492, and the rise of the Ottoman Empire, particularly post-1453 with the capture of Constantinople.

The aforementioned events were not mere backdrops but interactive agents that shaped the destiny of the Italian City-States. The Crusades opened up trade routes to the East, in which Italian merchants played a pivotal role, thereby contributing to a redistribution of wealth and knowledge. The Reconquista, by expelling the Moors and Jews who had played a significant role in the Iberian economy, further paved the way for Italian mercantile hegemony. Lastly, the rise of the Ottoman Empire, while initially seen as a threat, became an economic opportunity as Italian City-States, particularly Venice, engaged in commercial agreements with the Ottomans, thereby acting as intermediaries between the East and West.

In essence, the Italian City-States emerged as pivotal actors on the European stage, not through the conventional methods of empire building, but through mercantile and financial prowess, intellectual ferment, and diplomatic acumen. Their rise can be seen as a reflection of the fragmentation of power in post-Carolingian Europe, even as they themselves took part in reshaping the continental and, indeed, global balance of power. As we delve into this complex milieu, it becomes evident that while they were not empires, the Italian City-States nonetheless offer essential insights into the dynamics of power that shaped empires and influenced the course of global history.

It was within this context that the city-states of Venice, Genoa, Florence, and Milan asserted their ascendancy, albeit through divergent means.

Venice carved out its unique identity as a maritime republic. Its strategic position at the crossroads of the Adriatic and Mediterranean Seas provided unparalleled advantages in trade. By the late 13th century,

Venice had established a complex network of overseas territories, known as the "Stato da Màr," which included key ports like Dubrovnik and parts of the Dalmatian coast. These territories not only amplified Venice's naval capabilities but also buttressed its mercantile endeavors, allowing for an effective control of trade routes to Asia Minor and the Levant.

Genoa, Venice's maritime rival, followed a somewhat parallel trajectory but was more heavily oriented toward the western Mediterranean. Established trade connections with North Africa and the control of Corsica and Sardinia were crucial elements of Genoese geopolitical strategy. In competition with Venice, Genoa also participated in the Crusades, which further provided it with an extended network of trading posts and colonies, notably in the Black Sea region.

Florence, unlike its maritime counterparts, emerged as the epicenter of banking and commerce on the Italian Peninsula. Largely landlocked, Florence deployed its resources toward the development of textile industries, particularly wool and silk. Florentine banks became pivotal in European commerce, devising financial instruments like the bill of exchange and facilitating commerce across the continent. Families like the Medici were emblematic of the convergence of commerce, politics, and cultural patronage that distinguished Florence.

Milan, strategically situated at the crossroads of trade routes between the Italian Peninsula and Northern Europe, was a hub for land-based commerce and manufacturing, particularly in arms and armor. Governed primarily by a series of oligarchic and later monarchical authorities, including the Visconti and Sforza families, Milan played a central role in the often-fractious regional politics of Northern Italy.

The internal dynamics of these city-states were not insulated phenomena but were deeply integrated into broader geopolitical frameworks. Venice's mercantile networks, Genoa's naval colonies, Florence's financial systems, and Milan's manufacturing capabilities did not merely serve local or even national interests but were instrumental in shaping international trade routes, technological advancements, and even political alliances across Europe.

While none of these city-states ascended to the status of an empire, their collective and individual contributions to geopolitics were out of proportion to their geographical expanse. They each epitomized a fragment of power that, when considered within the context of declining Carolingian influence and the ascendant Ottoman Empire, shaped the European terrain in ways both subtle and profound. Their influence echoed beyond mere commerce, extending into the intellectual and cultural currents of the time, thus setting the stage for the period's defining conflicts and transformations.

The Economic Revolution: Merchants and Moneylenders

Building on the complex geopolitical framework elucidated in the prior section, the economic revolution incited by the Italian City-States warrants particular attention. It is essential to contextualize their emergent banking systems and mercantile networks as transformative forces that transcended mere economic implications, evolving to shape political and even cultural paradigms across Europe.

One of the pivotal economic innovations was the systematization of banking by Italian institutions, primarily Florence. Florentine banks developed groundbreaking financial mechanisms that are foundational to contemporary banking, including double-entry bookkeeping, the establishment of holding companies, and the promulgation of financial instruments like the bill of exchange and promissory notes. The Medicis, for instance, expanded their banking operations beyond Florence, establishing branches in key European cities, thereby facilitating seamless transcontinental trade. This was an economic coup of unprecedented scale, essentially laying the groundwork for a rudimentary form of globalized finance.

Concurrent to these financial developments were the mercantile endeavors by Venice and Genoa. As maritime powers, these city-states were pivotal in the establishment of intricate trade networks that spanned the Mediterranean and beyond. Venice, in particular, was instrumental in developing trade links to the East, contributing to a thriving trade in spices, silks, and precious stones. Genoa, in contrast, focused on the western Mediterranean but was equally instrumental in its mercantile influence, particularly in trading goods like wool, grain, and salt.

These mercantile networks did not evolve in isolation; they had substantive interactions with the Ottoman Empire, which by the late 15th century had become a preeminent power in the Mediterranean. Trade treaties, such as the Capitulations granted by the Ottomans, allowed for reciprocal trade arrangements that extended mutual benefits. Venice, especially, enjoyed a complex relationship with the Ottomans, characterized by periods of both collaboration and conflict. While geopolitical tensions occasionally flared up—such as during the Venetian-Ottoman Wars of the 16th and 17th centuries—the broader economic symbiosis was mutually advantageous. The exchange of goods like Venetian glass for Ottoman spices and textiles highlighted the intricate interplay between these political entities.

Overall, the banking and mercantile systems pioneered by the Italian City-States revolutionized European economies and solidified their transcontinental linkages. These systems were not mere vehicles of economic growth but acted as arbiters in the redistribution of power, thereby aligning with the book's central theme regarding the rise, reign, and decline of global powers. They shaped European trade routes and even dictated the contours of European interactions with rising powers like the Ottoman Empire, thereby entrenching themselves as vital elements in the dynamic tapestry of late medieval and early modern geopolitics.

The Renaissance: Intellectual and Cultural Contributions

The intellectual and cultural dimensions of the Italian City-States offer another layer of complexity to their already multifaceted impact on European civilization. In line with the preceding discussion on economic transformation, it is imperative to address how these city-states served as crucibles for intellectual developments that eventually transcended their local confines and disseminated throughout the European continent. This intellectual migration was emblematic of the overarching theme of this book—namely, how power manifests, waxes, and wanes across disparate realms of human endeavor.

Renaissance humanism, which placed humans and human intellect at the center of the world, took root primarily in these Italian cities. Grounded in the study of classical antiquity, humanism represented an intellectual shift that celebrated the individual, thereby challenging long-standing medieval collectivist ideals upheld by both feudal and religious authorities. Florence was the fertile ground where this intellectual metamorphosis germinated, with thinkers like Petrarch and Boccaccio laying the cornerstone for this paradigmatic shift. Their work elevated vernacular literature and prompted a re-evaluation of classical texts, casting a profound influence not only on literature but also on philosophy and educational theory.

The School of Athens. Woodcut engraving by Raffaello Sanzio

The City-States' patronage of the arts resulted in an artistic explosion, aptly encapsulated by the careers of Leonardo da Vinci, Michelangelo, and Raffaello. These artists' masterpieces were not solely aesthetic triumphs but were imbued with scientific curiosity and methodological rigor, reflecting the confluence of art and science characteristic of the period. Their work in anatomy, perspective, and natural sciences rendered them not merely artists but polymaths whose contributions spanned multiple disciplines.

In the realm of science, the Italian City-States, particularly Venice, contributed to advances in cartography and navigational technology, critically aiding maritime trade and exploration. The invention of the printing press in the mid-15th century, although not an Italian innovation per se, found rapid and transformative adoption in Italy. Johannes Gutenberg's technology was quickly assimilated into the Venetian economy, making Venice a hub for the dissemination of both classical and contemporary knowledge. The widespread printing of books like Dante's "Divine Comedy" and Machiavelli's "The Prince" empowered these texts to catalyze intellectual developments well beyond Italy's borders.

Collectively, these intellectual and cultural contributions emanating from the Italian City-States did more than enrich the world of ideas; they redefined how society interacted with these ideas, creating avenues for critical thought, artistic expression, and scientific inquiry. These developments, in synergy with economic and geopolitical shifts previously discussed, cement the City-States' role as integral players in the matrix of power dynamics that have shaped the course of human history.

Governance and Political Structures

The governance and political structures of the Italian City-States offer compelling insights into the divergent paths that political systems can take within the European context, especially when examined against the backdrop of prevalent feudal structures that dominated much of the continent during the same period. These disparate systems serve as a testament to the fluidity and adaptability of governance models, a topic that aligns with the broader focus of this book on the ebb and flow of power structures.

Certainly, the governance systems of the Italian City-States—ranging from Republics to Duchies to Oligarchies—reveal unique modes of rule that were shaped by distinct historical, economic, and social factors. In Florence, governance was structured around the Signoria, an executive council composed of nine men. However, the selection of these council members was far from a democratic process; it was instead heavily influenced by the ruling guilds, exclusive organizations of the economic and social elite. Furthermore, influential families like the Medicis had significant sway over these guilds, thereby indirectly steering governance. Thus, while appearing to foster civic participation, Florence maintained a rigidly structured hierarchy that concentrated power among the elite.

In Venice, governance was even more complex, with a hierarchical system of councils presided over by a Doge, whose powers were rigorously confined to ceremonial roles. The real authority lay with the Council of Ten, a powerful oligarchic body designed to avert the risk of monarchical rule. Through this meticulously structured governance system, Venice was able to achieve stability and adaptability in its rule, even if the power remained with a privileged minority.

Turning to Milan, which was governed as a Duchy primarily under the Sforza family, the system sharply contrasted with the Republics. Rather than a participatory or oligarchic rule, Milan exhibited traits akin to a military dictatorship. The Sforzas entered into strategic alliances, often secured by marital unions, to consolidate their centralized authority. While commercial and guild interests existed, they were subordinate to this autocratic governance structure.

Each of these models of governance was not an isolated phenomenon but was deeply responsive to both internal dynamics and the external geopolitical context. These structures played a fundamental role in how each city-state interacted with the broader European landscape, showcasing the diverse ways in which similar geographies and cultural milieus could spawn divergent governance systems.

Oligarchic systems, often found in maritime powers like Genoa, consisted of powerful families or guilds exerting collective control. These systems occasionally gave way to temporary autocratic rulers during periods of crisis, as evidenced by the rise of Andrea Doria, who restored Genoan independence and instituted an oligarchic constitution, thereby enhancing the city-state's mercantile and naval strength.

The coexistence of these varied forms of governance within a relatively confined geographical space underlines the City-States' role as laboratories for political experimentation. This heterogeneity in governance models offers crucial insights into how different systems adapted to both internal challenges and external pressures, be they economic, social, or geopolitical.

In summary, the Italian City-States serve as fascinating case studies in the diversity of governance structures that can arise even within closely interconnected communities. Their political innovations, combined with their contributions to economics,

Influence on Modern Capitalism

The ascent of the Italian City-States in the late Medieval and early Renaissance periods provides an indispensable backdrop for understanding the emergence of modern capitalism. This intersection of economic theory and historical occurrence dovetails with the overarching theme of the rise, reign, and decline of global powers. By unraveling the economic practices within these City-States, we gain insight into the nascent forms of capitalism that would later become instrumental in shaping global economic frameworks.

Significantly, these City-States were the nurseries for financial innovations that have contemporary echoes. Among the remarkable advancements were the establishment of early capital markets, maritime insurance, and groundbreaking banking systems. Families such as the Medicis in Florence and the Sforzas in Milan were not merely political powerhouses but also early capitalists who contributed to the development of these financial mechanisms.

The Medici family, with its banking empire, serves as a quintessential example. The Medici Bank, founded in 1397 by Giovanni di Bicci de' Medici, was not the first banking institution but stands as a paragon of early modern banking innovation. The Medici Bank distinguished itself through its extensive branch network across vital European trading cities from London to Constantinople. Utilizing financial instruments like bills of exchange, the bank facilitated international trade without the logistical risks and inefficiencies tied to the transportation of physical currencies like gold and silver. These bills served as written orders, obligating one party to pay another a set sum at a predetermined future date, often involving transactions in multiple currencies.

Additionally, the Medici Bank was instrumental in the widespread adoption of double-entry bookkeeping, enhancing transparency and accounting accuracy. This accounting innovation has enduring relevance and serves as the bedrock of modern financial systems.

In relation to the cultural milieu of the period, it's worth noting the etymology of the term "bankruptcy," which derives from the Italian "bancarotta." This term originated from the practice of breaking a moneylender's bench to signify insolvency. The act was not merely symbolic but served a practical purpose: it constituted a public declaration of financial failure and thereby barred the individual from future business dealings. This historical idiom attests to the pivotal role that financial practices played in the socio-cultural landscape of the time. Collectively, these advancements contributed to the fluidity and globalization of capital, thereby laying the groundwork for contemporary banking systems.

The Sforza family, who governed Milan, also invested heavily in economic enterprises but were more focused on land-based assets and military endeavors. Nonetheless, their financial practices, such as the levying of taxes and the use of paid mercenaries, displayed an early form of state capitalism that involved close cooperation between merchants and rulers to achieve mutual economic objectives.

Venice and Genoa, both maritime republics, made invaluable contributions to maritime insurance. Recognizing the immense risks involved in seafaring trade, these city-states developed early forms of insurance contracts that would indemnify the loss or capture of merchant ships. The Venetian "Colleganza" and the Genoese "Commenda" were contractual agreements that enabled investment in maritime trade voyages, offering a model for risk-sharing and investment that laid the groundwork for future joint-stock companies.

These City-States were not isolated economic entities but were intricately connected to broader European and Mediterranean trade networks. This includes interactions with the Ottoman Empire, as previously examined in a previous section. The rise of the Ottoman Empire had dual effects: it created challenges due to the disruption of overland trade routes, yet also provided new trading opportunities, particularly in spices and luxury goods, that the Italian City-States skillfully exploited.

In summary, the economic systems that emerged from the crucible of the Italian City-States serve as a prologue to modern capitalist structures. By institutionalizing early forms of banking, investment, and insurance, these City-States crafted financial models that would be refined and expanded upon in later centuries, shaping the economic landscape of the modern world. Their role in this evolution affirms their lasting influence and contributes to our broader understanding of how economic systems rise, evolve, and, at times, precipitate the decline of empires.

Conclusion: Geopolitical Shifts and Decline

As history has amply demonstrated in the cases of various empires and powers, the zenith of influence is seldom perpetual. The Italian City-States, despite their numerous contributions to economics, art, and culture, were not insulated from this inescapable cycle of rise, reign, and decline. This decline was due to a confluence of internal and external factors, each intricating with the other in complex ways that underscore the City-States' vulnerability to broader geopolitical shifts.

Externally, the rise of trans-Atlantic trade following Columbus's voyages in 1492 significantly diverted economic focus away from Mediterranean trade routes, which had been the lifeblood of these City-States. This shift was further exacerbated by the circumnavigation of Africa by Portuguese navigators, offering a sea route to India and the East, thereby bypassing the Mediterranean middlemen. The ascendancy of powerful nation-states, particularly France and Spain, posed another grave challenge. These nations had larger territories, greater resources, and more cohesive military structures. The Italian Wars, which occurred between 1494 and 1559, saw the French and Spanish monarchies vie for control over parts of Italy, drastically altering the balance of power and diminishing the independence and influence of individual City-States.

Internally, the City-States were victims of their own fragmented political structures. The lack of centralized authority made them vulnerable to internal strife, often stoked by rival families vying for control. For example, the Medici family returned to power in Florence in 1530 after years of exile, but this was only possible due to the city's weakened state and internal divisions. Such rivalries depleted resources and diverted focus from larger existential threats. Governance mechanisms, ranging from republics to oligarchies, struggled to evolve in ways that could mitigate these burgeoning challenges, thereby stifling any concerted response to the tidal shifts in geopolitics and economics.

Furthermore, the decline was not simply a matter of military and economic setbacks but was also intellectual and cultural in nature. The humanist vigor of the Renaissance began to wane by the late 16th century, succeeded by the Baroque era, which, while artistically significant, did not offer the same transformative socio-political energy. Consequently, the City-States lost their role as the epicenters of European intellectual life.

In this respect, the decline of the Italian City-States can be seen as an outcome predetermined by their own structural limitations and the inexorable shifts in the geopolitical landscape. These shifts are instructive in a broader analysis of how regions rise to prominence based on certain advantageous conditions but later recede when those conditions are altered by internal decay or external competition. This analytical lens reaffirms the City-States' inclusion in a study focused on the rise, reign, and decline of global powers, for their decline illustrates the intricate dance between internal governance, economic innovation, and external forces that shapes the trajectory of influential entities throughout history.

Chapter 16.
Thirty Years' War: Bridging Ancient to Modern Empires (1618-1648)

War is one of the scourges with which it has pleased God to afflict men

~Cardinal Richelieu

Europe's Religious Cauldron

As dawn broke over Europe in the 17th century, storm clouds had been gathering, heralding one of the most transformative and devastating conflicts in its history: The Thirty Years' War (1618-1648). This prolonged strife, which ravaged the heart of the continent, was not merely a clash of arms but also a crucible in which the world's geopolitical landscape was forever changed.

This tumultuous era became a profound transformational epoch, a hinge upon which the world pivoted from the grandeur of ancient empires to the dawn of modern nation-states.

The millennia before had seen the majestic rise and fall of empires—mighty pharaohs had built timeless pyramids across the Nile, Roman legions had marched across continents, and the Persian realm had connected the East and West through its sprawling territories. These empires commanded allegiance, through military might and also through the shared cultural and administrative ethos that stitched vast lands together. They were the stalwarts of the old world order, where the fates of many were determined by the ambitions of a few.

By the time of the Thirty Years' War, Europe was divided along religious lines. The north and west, including regions like Scandinavia, England, had largely embraced Protestantism. Meanwhile, the south, including Spain, Italy, and the Papal States, remained staunchly Catholic. Central Europe was a mosaic of religious affiliations, with pockets of Calvinism, Lutheranism, and Catholicism often existing side by side.

Engraving depicting the Siege of Magdeburg

Religious tensions were further exacerbated by the Catholic Counter-Reformation, an aggressive campaign by the Catholic Church to reclaim lost territories and souls. The inception of the Jesuit order, coupled with the determinations of the Council of Trent, strengthened Catholic principles and rituals, laying the foundation for a reinvigorated affirmation of the faith.

Thus, as the 17th century dawned, Europe was a tinderbox of religious rivalry, political ambition, and territorial disputes. The spark of the Thirty Years' War, while rooted in specific events in Bohemia, was, in reality, the culmination of decades of religious tension and political maneuvering.

As the first salvos of the Thirty Years' War were fired, the tectonic plates of global power began to shift. Sovereignty, a concept once reserved for emperors and kings, was being redefined, inching closer to the idea of nationhood that we recognize today.

Emerging from this crucible of war were the nascent structures of modern diplomacy and statecraft. The Peace of Westphalia in 1648, which concluded the war, signaled the beginning of a new world order. Sovereign states with recognized borders began to take precedence over sprawling, multi-ethnic empires.

Thus, as we delve deeper into this chapter, we journey through a transformative period that bridged two epochs. From the remnants of the illustrious ancient empires, the foundation stones of today's world were laid, shaping the geopolitical dynamics of the ensuing centuries. The Thirty Years' War, with its intricate web of alliances, betrayals, and aspirations, stands as a testament to humanity's enduring quest for evolution and identity.

The Holy Roman Empire and the Prelude to War

As we covered in a previous chapter, from the remnants of the Carolingian Dynasty's dissolution emerged the Holy Roman Empire, an intricate multi-ethnic confederation that epitomized the evolving fabric of European geopolitics. This vast agglomeration, encompassing a diverse mosaic of duchies, principalities, kingdoms, and free cities, was emblematic of a Europe undergoing profound transformations.

The intricate bond between the Holy Roman Emperors and the Papacy, though symbolically significant, was fraught with tensions creating frequent conflicts in the delicate balance of religious and secular power.

By the dawn of the 16th century, the Holy Roman Empire stood at a crossroads. The Protestant Reformation, catalyzed by Martin Luther's Ninety-Five Theses in 1517, wasn't just a theological upheaval. It signaled a tectonic shift in the European socio-political landscape. As Protestant doctrines gained adherents, particularly in the Empire's northern territories, they inevitably came into conflict with the prevailing Catholic orthodoxy. Yet, these theological disputes mirrored deeper geopolitical fissures, as regions sought greater autonomy and influence within the Empire's vast expanse.

Such divisions manifested dramatically in events like the Defenestration of Prague in 1618, an act where religious dissent reached a violent climax. During this pivotal event, Protestant nobles threw two Catholic regents and their secretary out of a window of Prague Castle, symbolizing a stark rejection of Habsburg Catholic hegemony. Though they survived the fall, the incident inflamed tensions to such an extent that it served as the immediate catalyst for the Thirty Years' War. This war, which embroiled numerous European powers, led to catastrophic loss of life and upheaval, altering the continent's political and religious landscape indelibly. Thus, the Defenestration was not merely an act of localized insurrection but a touchstone in a larger European crisis—a quest for autonomy, the recalibration of power, and the redefinition of territorial and religious boundaries.

In essence, the Holy Roman Empire, despite its moniker evoking a sense of grandeur and uniformity, was more aptly described by Voltaire's famous quip that it was "neither holy, nor Roman, nor an empire." This realm was a cauldron of diverse interests and allegiances, and its internal complexities, intricately interwoven with the broader religious ferment of Europe, positioned it at the epicenter of an impending storm: the Thirty Years' War that would engulf the continent.

The Shift From Empire to Nation-State

It's overly simplistic to view the Thirty Years' War solely as a religious confrontation. While its genesis can be traced back to religious frictions between the Catholic and Protestant states of the Holy Roman Empire, the war, over its course, morphed into a broader contest of power among Europe's leading dynasties and states.

Central to understanding the war's trajectory is the unique construct of the Holy Roman Empire. As articulated in the previous section this naturally engendered power vacuums and intricate political maneuvering due to its lose definition and significant decentralized structure.

Cardinal Richelieu of France, a devout Catholic, was a masterful strategist who introduced the doctrine of 'raison d'état'. This principle placed the welfare and supremacy of the state above religious or moral obligations. In line with this, Richelieu, despite France's Catholic allegiance, supported Protestant forces against the Catholic Habsburgs of the Holy Roman Empire. This was a strategic move, stemming from his recognition of the overarching threat the Habsburgs, with their expansive territories, posed to France.

However, France wasn't the only country driven by geopolitical ambitions. Spain, for instance, although led by the Habsburg dynasty, was primarily motivated by its rivalry with France and its desire to consolidate territories in the Low Countries. Meanwhile, Denmark entered the war to expand its influence in Northern Germany and to counter the rising Catholic forces. Sweden, under Gustavus Adolphus, saw an opportunity to assert dominance in the Baltic region and to protect Protestant interests.

As the war's canvas broadened, Europe's landscape turned into a chessboard of geopolitics, where religious motivations often became subordinate to territorial and dynastic aspirations. The Peace of Westphalia in 1648 epitomized this transition. Beyond recognizing the religious rights of individual states within the Holy Roman Empire, it signified the rise of the nation-state—emphasizing well-defined territorial borders and national identities.

But why did the concept of the nation-state gain prominence? One of the primary inefficiencies of sprawling empires was their heterogeneous nature, which often led to internal divisions. The vast territories, each with its own customs and laws, posed administrative challenges. Coupled with religious and cultural differences, this often led to internal conflicts and hampered cohesive policymaking. The Holy Roman Empire, for instance, constantly grappled with disputes among its member territories. The nation-state, offering unity and a more centralized structure, emerged as a compelling alternative in this backdrop.

Furthermore, as mercantilism gained ground, the need for stable trade routes and economic policies accentuated the appeal of centralized power and well-defined territorial boundaries. This shift signaled the decline of vast, sprawling empires and heralded the rise of nation-states.

By the time the curtains fell on the Thirty Years' War, the political contours of Europe were being redrawn. The tapestry of empires was unraveling, making way for nation-states that would shape the geopolitical landscape in the ensuing centuries.

Balance of Power:
The New European Political Doctrine

In the aftermath of the Thirty Years' War, with its extensive devastation and the immense disarray it brought to Europe's political landscape, the continent's monarchs and decision-makers confronted a critical juncture. They recognized the inherent perils of allowing unchecked dominance by any single entity. This revelation underscored the need for a new geopolitical doctrine to prevent future upheavals: the principle of the "Balance of Power."

Fundamentally, the Balance of Power posited that no nation should amass enough strength to imperil others. Should such a hegemonic rise be observed, it became an implicit obligation for other states to counteract, either through forming alliances or direct intervention. While antecedents of this principle can be traced back to earlier epochs, its salience and formalization emerged in the European geopolitical milieu post the Thirty Years' War.

The Peace of Westphalia can be interpreted as a nascent manifestation of this doctrine. While its explicit objectives revolved around arbitrating religious discord, its broader implications underscored the sovereignty of states and the mutual respect of their territorial and political integrities.

This principle of balance found expression in a plethora of subsequent European events. Consider the War of the Spanish Succession (1701-1714). Here, the looming specter of a single Bourbon dynasty potentially controlling both Spain and France led to the formation of a coalition—comprising powers like England, the Dutch Republic, and Austria—to curtail such an ascendancy. The Napoleonic Wars offer another exemplar. A series of coalitions arose in response to France's expansionist aims under Napoleon, striving to rein in the Napoleonic juggernaut.

The Congress of Vienna (1815) stands as another significant milestone. In the post-Napoleonic era, it convened representatives from major European powers to reconfigure the continent's political delineations. The overarching objective? Ensuring that no single power could unilaterally disrupt the continental equilibrium. This gave birth to the "Concert of Europe" – a tacit consensus among these nations to maintain balance, favoring diplomatic engagements over armed confrontations as the primary mode of conflict resolution.

However, one must not romanticize the Balance of Power as an infallible panacea. There were instances where the very coalitions and alliances designed under its aegis inadvertently precipitated conflicts, as evident in the intricate web of alliances that set the stage for World War I.

Seen against the backdrop of the historical transition from vast empires to the rise of nation-states and eventually to the emergence of global superpowers, the Balance of Power serves as Europe's adaptive mechanism. It was an effort to establish a self-correcting system to counter hegemony and prioritize stability, profoundly influencing European geopolitics and establishing precedents that continue to inform contemporary international diplomacy.

Economic Repercussions and the Rise of Capitalism

The Thirty Years' War, although primarily framed within religious and political contexts, had profound economic implications, laying the groundwork for the incipient stages of capitalism and sounding the death knell for the waning feudal system.

One of the most pressing concerns in the wake of the war was its staggering financial toll. The costs associated with mobilizing, equipping, and maintaining large-scale armies strained the coffers of many states.

Especially for smaller states, this expenditure spiraled into crippling debts. In this fiscal maelstrom, the emergent European merchant and banking class assumed a pivotal role. By bankrolling states, these early capitalists gained substantial leverage, which began to erode the once unassailable dominion of the traditional nobility.

The war's concomitant effect on agrarian dynamics was another facet of this economic transformation. With vast territories of agricultural land decimated by warfare, land valuations in numerous regions experienced precipitous declines. This devaluation often forced minor landowners, burdened by debt, to divest their holdings. Consequently, lands were amalgamated into larger estates. Furthermore, there was a palpable shift in agricultural strategies – transitioning from predominantly subsistence-based farming to a market-centric model, wherein produce was cultivated with broader markets in mind, rather than local sustenance.

In terms of trade, the war's disruptions had lasting ramifications. Traditional trade hubs and routes were beleaguered, necessitating the exploration of alternative avenues. This quest synergized with the broader Age of Exploration, where European states were already extending their territorial ambit, establishing colonies that would serve dual purposes: sources of raw materials and novel markets for European commodities.

Urban landscapes too bore the economic imprints of the war. Cities like Amsterdam, either unscathed or strategically neutral during the hostilities, emerged as nexuses of commerce, finance, and innovation. The Amsterdam stock exchange, inaugurated in 1602, accentuated its global significance in the war's aftermath, becoming a linchpin in international financial transactions.

The epoch also witnessed the ascent of joint-stock companies, epitomized by entities like the Dutch East India Company and the British East India Company. Operating at the intersection of state sanction and private entrepreneurship, these corporations became instrumental in the propagation of early capitalism. Their influence transcended mere commerce, impacting politics and territorial control.

Surveying the broader historical continuum from vast empires to the dawn of modern superpowers, it is evident that the economic metamorphosis catalyzed by the Thirty Years' War occupies a pivotal position. While not its explicit objective, the war inadvertently cultivated a milieu conducive to the growth of capitalism. This emergent economic doctrine, predicated on private enterprise and expansive trade, not only bolstered European states but also laid the foundational blueprint for today's global economic architecture.

Cultural and Social Shifts: From Divine Right to National Identity

The transformative aftershocks of the Thirty Years' War extended far beyond the circumscribed spheres of politics and economy. They permeated the cultural and social edifice of Europe, instigating a recalibration of deeply entrenched beliefs and heralding an era that prioritized national consciousness over divine providence.

Historically, European monarchs were proponents of the 'Divine Right of Kings,' an axiom asserting that their reign was sanctioned by divine decree, thus positioning them at an elevated pedestal where their rule was beyond temporal reproach. This doctrine was emblematic of the era's confluence of religion and statecraft, where spiritual doctrine often underpinned political legitimacy.

Yet, the magnitude and duration of the war, fraught with its shifting allegiances and religious nuances, precipitated a gradual disillusionment with this divinely ordained monarchic model. The relentless conflict and accompanying human toll engendered skepticism towards the notion that monarchs, ordained by God, were championing righteous causes for their subjects.

This burgeoning skepticism catalyzed a pivot towards a nascent form of nationalism. In the wake of the war, there was a discernible inclination towards identifying with shared cultural, linguistic, and historical markers, as opposed to mere religious tenets. The salience of a shared national identity began to overshadow purely religious affiliations.

The burgeoning print culture, leveraging the capabilities of the printing press, was instrumental in this cultural metamorphosis. By facilitating the dissemination of literature, national epics, and nascent forms of journalism, it sculpted a collective cultural consciousness, increasingly divorced from religious paradigms.

Moreover, the Peace of Westphalia's stipulation of cuius regio, eius religio, while ostensibly reiterating the monarch's prerogative to delineate the state's religious fabric, simultaneously emphasized the primacy of territorial sovereignty, subtly diminishing the universality of religious mandates.

Post-war Europe also bore witness to an evolution in the perception of the individual within society. Transitioning from passive subjects beholden to divinely anointed monarchs, individuals began to be perceived as active citizens, possessing distinct rights and duties vis-à-vis their evolving nation-states.

Synthesizing this period of transition, it becomes evident that the Thirty Years' War was instrumental in reshaping European identities. It engendered a departure from divine-centric ideologies and fostered the ascendancy of nationalistic sentiments. This tectonic shift laid the groundwork for the modern nation-state paradigm, which would subsequently steer the course of global geopolitics, fundamentally molding the contours of the contemporary world order.

Conclusion:
The Thirty Years' War - a Nexus between Eras

Historically, wars, with their profound upheavals, have acted as inflection points, redrawing not only territorial boundaries but also the contours of societal thought. The Thirty Years' War, however, stands distinguished in this pantheon, serving as a confluence of myriad currents that shaped the course of global history.

Initiated as a religious dispute within the confines of the Holy Roman Empire, the war illuminated the intricate interplay of power, diplomacy, and strategy, where religion became one of many variables in a complex equation of statecraft.

The Peace of Westphalia, a seminal diplomatic conclave, emerged as the harbinger of modern international discourse. This accord not only terminated the immediate conflict but also crystallized principles that would undergird global diplomacy for centuries: sovereign integrity, diplomatic dialogue, and mutual non-interference.

Drawing lessons from the war's devastation, European powers gravitated towards the Balance of Power as their new geopolitical doctrine. This doctrine, prioritizing equilibrium over hegemony, marked a discernible departure from erstwhile paradigms centered on divine mandates and imperial universality. Implicitly, European powers acknowledged that their aspirations for ascendancy were better served through collaborative equilibrium, underpinned by commerce, diplomacy, and extraterritorial expansions. Interestingly four centuries later, in the early 20th century, when the United States emerged as a global power, it reintroduced elements of the universalist approach to international relations. The United States believed that its mission was to improve humanity, partly rejecting the longstanding "rough" European practice of the Balance of Power concept, which had been in use for centuries.

The economic reverberations of the war also catalyzed a paradigm shift, moving away from feudal remnants and ushering in nascent capitalist principles. This economic transformation, intertwined with profound cultural and societal evolutions, set the stage for seismic changes. Nationalistic fervor, individual liberties, and a redefined relationship between the state and its citizenry became the new norms, gradually displacing earlier, divinely ordained societal constructs.

Viewed in the continuum of history, the Thirty Years' War occupies a unique locus, acting as the fulcrum between antiquated empires and modern state entities. This conflict dissolved long-held doctrines and paradigms, replacing them with the nascent principles that would come to define modern statecraft and global dynamics.

In synthesizing our understanding of contemporary geopolitics and the ascent of present-day superpowers, the echoes of the Thirty Years' War remain palpable. This conflict, with its profound ramifications, undeniably stands as the crucible that shaped the trajectory of the modern world.

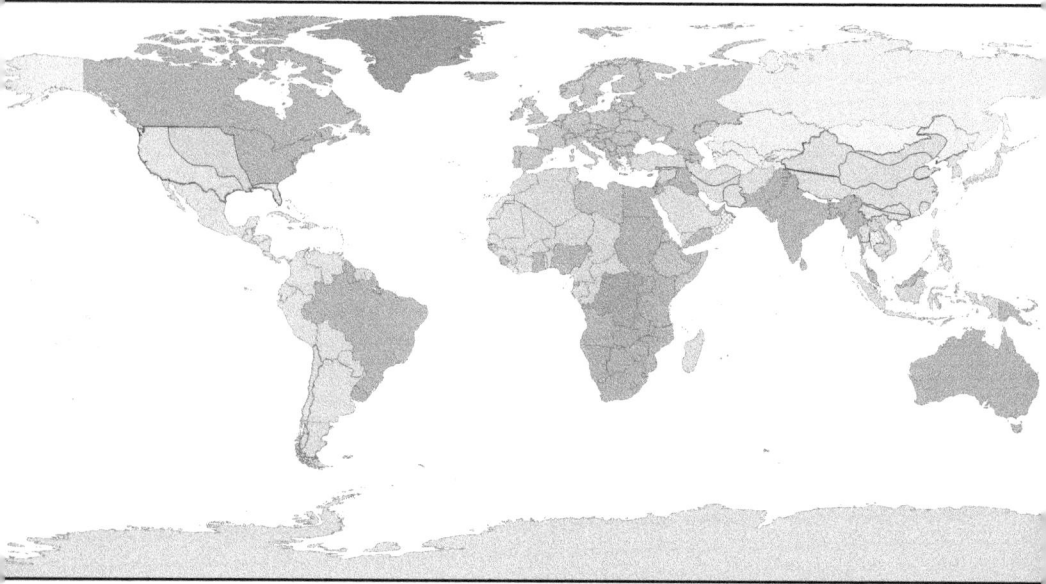

European Empires[23]

PART III:
The Age of
Empires

Depiction of Columbus landing on Hispaniola[24]

Chapter 17.
Exploration, Colonization and the Industrial Revolution (15th-19th Centuries)

*You can never cross the ocean unless you have the courage to
lose sight of the shore.*

~Christopher Columbus

Introduction

Emerging from the aftermath of the Thirty Years' War, European
nation-states encountered a set of circumstances that propelled them
onto the global stage. Driven by technological advancements, burgeoning mercantile ambitions, and an intensified quest for knowledge,
these nations embarked on ventures beyond their traditional boundaries. Distinctly differing from prior empires that expanded by annexing
proximate territories, this era witnessed European powers navigating
across vast oceans to establish dominions on previously unknown lands.
Such expansion had multifaceted implications, reshaping the global
milieu in domains spanning society, culture, economics, and politics.

Concurrent to the colonial epoch, the waning years of the 18ᵗʰ century marked another pivotal transition: the onset of industrialization. Initially germinating in Britain, this transformation rapidly extended its influence globally. This was not a mere change in the source of power, with steam supplanting muscle, or a simple transformation of landscapes with the advent of factories. Instead, it signified a paradigm shift in the nexus of power. The mastery of the Industrial Revolution emerged as a defining criterion for nations aspiring for global pre-eminence. This chapter aims to elucidate the intricate interplay between the age of colonial exploration and the ascendancy of industry, both of which collectively paved the way for the emergence of the subsequent superpowers.

The Dynamics of European Colonization

In the 15ᵗʰ century, Europe, emerging from internal disruptions, found itself grappling with an imperative: the need to forge direct trade connections with Asia. This compulsion, accentuated by the cutting-edge technological innovations of the era, inaugurated what historians recognize as the Age of Exploration.

The early 15ᵗʰ century saw the Iberian Peninsula emerging from the shadows of the Christian Reconquista, an arduous mission to reclaim territories from the Moors—an extension of the Islamic caliphates, as delineated in prior chapters. Portugal, having this recent accomplishment under its belt and boasting a formidable maritime lineage, became a pioneer in the maritime exploration landscape. Prince Henry the Navigator, cognizant of the potential of maritime dominion, established a navigational center in Sagres, congregating eminent minds in seafaring. This concentrated endeavor culminated in 1498 when Vasco da Gama pioneered a maritime passage to India, substantially altering the mechanics of global trade.

Simultaneously, Spain, casting its gaze westward, commissioned Christopher Columbus in 1492 to discover a westward conduit to Asia. His landing in the Caribbean, while unintended, precipitated a cascade of Spanish territorial endeavors. The consequent Spanish expeditions, helmed by figures like Cortés and Pizarro, subdued mighty civilizations, including the Aztecs and Incas, fortifying Spain's geopolitical standing.

Concurrently, Africa began to factor prominently in European designs. The Portuguese, having initiated coastal explorations, established thriving trade stations along the African seaboard. Besides the flourishing commerce in commodities such as gold and ivory, the transatlantic slave trade began its dark trajectory, resulting in the forced migration of a significant number of Africans to the Americas.

The era represented more than mere geographical explorations; it manifested the unyielding determination of European powers to leave indelible marks on history. These colonial endeavors, animated by the twin desires for affluence and supremacy, realigned global geopolitics, setting the stage for modern-day diplomatic interactions.

Britain, recognizing the strategic value of colonies, broadened its horizons to the New World in the latter part of the 16th century. With colonies stretching from North America to the Indian subcontinent, by the 19th century, Britain's colonial matrix had become unrivaled.

France, in its quest for colonial preeminence, carved out territories ranging from Canada to specific sectors of India and extended its influence into the African hinterlands. The French colonial legacy, marked by sophisticated governance structures and cultural amalgamation, still resonates, particularly in African nations.

The Dutch, capitalizing on their maritime prowess, oriented their aspirations towards the East. The Dutch East India Company commanded a significant presence along pivotal trade channels, with territories like Indonesia falling under its ambit. In the Western hemisphere, Dutch aspirations manifested in regions spanning Brazil to New Amsterdam, now recognized as New York City.

In their pursuits, these European powers didn't merely expand territories; they facilitated the amalgamation of diverse cultures, providing the underpinnings for the present-day globalized paradigm.

Industrial Britain: Genesis and Ramifications

As Britain transitioned into the latter half of the 18th century, it found itself on the precipice of an unparalleled transformation. This industrial metamorphosis, germinating in Britain, would not just recalibrate its domestic socio-economic terrain but would also modulate international geopolitics for the ensuing centuries.

The initiation of this groundbreaking revolution traces back to the textile sector. Circa 1764, the textile industry witnessed James Hargreaves' introduction of the spinning jenny—a machinery that brought about an unparalleled surge in production efficiency. Contrasted against the previous manual labor-intensive spinning process, the spinning jenny, equipped with multiple spindles, enabled a worker to concurrently produce multiple threads. This technical advancement was pivotal in catalyzing the textile industry's mechanization during the Industrial Revolution.

In tandem with this development, Richard Arkwright's water frame emerged. This machinery, by leveraging natural water currents to activate wheels and subsequently power looms, epitomized the progression from cottage industries reliant on manual labor to mechanized factory setups.

The innovations did not plateau here. In 1781, James Watt unveiled a revamped steam engine, distinguished by its superior efficiency. Initially designed to expel water from mines, the utility of this steam engine soon permeated myriad sectors, from industrial to transportation realms. Concurrently, the demand for coal, integral to these steam-propelled industries, escalated. Mining operations delved deeper into the earth's strata, excavating the vital coal reserves integral to Britain's burgeoning industrial prowess.

Parallel to these advancements, the British iron industry experienced a spike in production. This abundant iron availability became the cornerstone for expansive infrastructural projects. Among the most consequential was the railway network, a brainchild of George Stephenson. This network, by facilitating rapid goods transportation and integrating previously isolated regions with urban epicenters, reshaped Britain's internal dynamics.

Two urban centers emerged as the epitome of this industrial age. Manchester, with its ceaseless factory operations and distinctive industrial ambiance, became emblematic of textile manufacturing. Conversely, Birmingham, christened the 'Workshop of the World', diversified its production spectrum, crafting everything from rudimentary buttons to intricate steam engines, catering to both local and global markets.

However, this industrial surge was not constrained to technological and economic dimensions. It had profound societal repercussions. An observable population drift from rural to urban regions transpired, as individuals sought enhanced employment opportunities within urban factories. This demographic shift precipitated the ascendance of the urban proletariat, resulting in significant socio-cultural modifications in British societal constructs.

On the economic front, the implications were multifaceted. As production costs diminished and output escalated, Britain's economic orientation pivoted from being a predominant importer to an export juggernaut. Consequently, British global trade infrastructures expanded exponentially, with the steam and iron-powered British merchant fleet asserting its dominance on maritime routes.

This industrial acumen and economic ascendancy were instrumental in the ensuing expansion and fortification of the British Empire. The industrial innovations endowed Britain with a pronounced advantage in exploration, annexation, and colonization. The domestic factories, in their quest for raw materials, looked towards the colonies. These colonies, in turn, served dual purposes: they supplied the required raw materials and simultaneously acted as guaranteed markets for finished commodities. This symbiotic relationship foreshadowed the dawn of an empire renowned for its vastness—an empire where the sun perpetually shone.

Industrialization's Global Ripples

Emerging from the precincts of Britain, the industrial phenomenon soon echoed across international terrains, redefining both economic structures and socio-cultural dynamics. As Britain burgeoned as the vanguard of industrialization, it inadvertently cast a mold, which many nations, particularly in Europe, deemed imperative to emulate or even supersede.

France, sensing the reverberations of Britain's industrial crescendo, was quick to respond. The earliest transformations were discernible within the textile sector, as it integrated mechanized methodologies. French urban landscapes metamorphosed, marked by proliferating factory complexes. Indispensably, the Napoleonic era ushered in reforms which recalibrated transportation and communicative frameworks, effectively accelerating France's industrial ascendance. By the midst of the 19th century, these strategic shifts had propelled France to the forefront of industrial powers.

Germany, during its pre-unification phase, although a mosaic of individual states, was not devoid of its intrinsic industrial propensity. With the coal-abundant Ruhr Valley as its nucleus, Germany initiated its industrial trajectory. Post the seminal unification of 1871, the consolidated German Empire amplified its industrial pursuits, in certain realms even posing stiff competition to its British and French counterparts.

Across the Atlantic, the expansive United States discerned the virtues of industrial integration. Harnessing knowledge from European forerunners, and buoyed by local innovators like Samuel Slater and Eli Whitney, the U.S. underwent a transformative industrial metamorphosis. Noteworthy urban hubs, such as Pittsburgh and Detroit, surfaced as stalwarts in steel and automobile sectors, respectively. The sprawling railroad infrastructures, beyond just aiding transportation, effectively consolidated the vast nation, both economically and socio-culturally.

Japan's industrial narrative underscores its resilience and foresight. Extricating itself from its erstwhile isolationist posture, the Meiji Restoration era delineated Japan's resolve to modernize. By meticulously amalgamating European technological prowess with inherent Japanese disciplines, Japan orchestrated an unparalleled industrial resurgence. Metropolises like Osaka and Tokyo, within a relatively compressed temporal frame, emerged as fulcrums of global industrial activities.

However, the repercussions of this industrial epoch transcended mere technological advancements and altered deeper societal constructs. Traditional artisanal communities, once pivotal to economic matrices, grappled with the overwhelming magnitude and efficiency ushered in by mechanized production. Economic paradigms, historically anchored to agrarian cycles, now resonated with the cadence of steam engines and the industrial milieu.

Additionally, the global politico-strategic arena was recalibrated by these industrial undertones. Nations, buoyed by their industrial prowess, envisioned amplified political aspirations. Enhanced industrial capacities often translated into fortified military competencies, thus reshaping geopolitical equations. Diplomatic affiliations evolved, age-old hostilities magnified, and global politico-strategic dynamics were redefined, with industrial undertones as the underlying motif.

Britain, as the progenitor of this sweeping revolution, adroitly utilized its industrial advantage to fortify its global ascendancy. The innovations emanating from its industrial bastions not only galvanized domestic advancements but also strategically augmented its colonial pursuits. Endowed with state-of-the-art machinery, augmented transportation networks, and burgeoning production capacities, Britain envisaged an expansionist blueprint for its empire—a discourse to be elaborated upon in the ensuing chapter.

Industrialization's Role in Reshaping Global Hegemony

The 19th-century industrial metamorphosis that permeated Europe had repercussions that transcended its continental confines, and its tendrils intertwined with the intricate designs of global imperialism. European powers, chiefly Britain and France, equipped with newfound industrial capacities, found themselves poised to augment their colonial pursuits, backed by mechanized naval fleets and technologically advanced armaments.

This epoch witnessed a departure from conventional colonial objectives. Instead of merely territorial annexations, it was an evolution in the paradigm of colonial governance. As Europe surged with a plethora of industrial commodities, ranging from textiles to advanced machinery and firearms, these products found eager markets in their colonies. The colonies, in turn, were restructured to serve as resource repositories, ensuring a constant supply to fuel Europe's burgeoning industrial apparatus. A salient example of this can be discerned in the British colonial relationship with India. The subcontinent, abundant in cotton, was methodically transformed into a significant supplier for British mills. Paradoxically, this raw material's final product, finished textiles, found their way back to India, effectively saturating local markets.

Africa's abundant natural wealth similarly succumbed to Europe's imperialistic endeavors. Resources, ranging from the mineral-rich southern regions to rubber from the Congolese heartland, became integral cogs in the European industrial machine.

The arteries of global trade, concomitantly, experienced a paradigmatic shift. Historical trade thoroughfares, renowned for the exchange of spices and ornate fabrics, were now inundated with commodities reflective of the industrial age—coal, steel, and mechanized goods. The inauguration of the Suez Canal in 1869 stands as a testament to Europe's intent to streamline its industrial and imperial endeavors. This objective was further epitomized with the Panama Canal's operationalization in 1914, signaling a transformative phase in global trade mechanisms.

However, this industrial-imperial symbiosis was not without its ramifications. Colonies, traditionally celebrated for their indigenous industries and artisanal expertise, found themselves dwarfed by the colossal shadow of European mechanization. Local craftsmen, erstwhile revered for their skill, now confronted the inexorable onslaught of mass-produced goods. This economic marginalization, as history would attest, sowed seeds of disillusionment, gradually nurturing sentiments of nationalism and self-assertion. Despite their economic subjugation to European metropoles, aspirations for political autonomy, self-governance, and sovereignty germinated within these colonies. This juxtaposition—European imperial ascendancy juxtaposed against a subterranean undercurrent of colonial resistance—precipitated the socio-political landscape of the 20th century, where empires would grapple with the very nationalist movements they inadvertently engendered.

Societal Evolution in the Shadow of Industrialization

With the 19th century's onset, societies within nations at the fore-front of industrialization experienced a profound recalibration of their structural dynamics. Predominantly agrarian communities, historically synchronized with the ebb and flow of agricultural cycles, now found their rhythms disrupted by the relentless drone of industrial machinery. Emblematic of this shift were cities such as Manchester and London in Britain, which not only burgeoned demographically but also signi-fied a significant societal migration from pastoral settings to industrial heartlands.

This transition wasn't merely geographical; it signified an alteration in the quotidian existence of these migrants. The agricultural calendar, which had erstwhile provided temporal structure to their lives, was supplanted by the regimented schedules dictated by factories. Yet, such precipitated urbanization came accompanied by its suite of complica-tions. Densely populated urban quarters, often bereft of adequate san-itation and infrastructure, emerged as crucibles for health crises and societal disquiet.

Against this backdrop, the stratifications of society also underwent redefinition. At one end of this spectrum stood the industrial bour-geoisie—newly minted magnates endowed with immense economic leverage, which invariably translated to political clout. Conversely, the proletariat, essential for the smooth functioning of the industrial machinery, found themselves ensnared in often debilitating working environments. This socio-economic chasm catalyzed the genesis of movements seeking to champion the cause of these workers, leading to the institutionalization of labor unions.

The cultural domain was not insulated from this era's pulsations. Artistic and literary endeavors began mirroring the complexities and contradictions intrinsic to this period. Whether through the literary tapestries woven by Dickens or the poignant brushstrokes of Realist painters, the spectrum of industrial-era experiences—from the deso-lation of factory life to the opulence of the emergent affluent class—found representation.

A consequential offshoot of this epoch was the transformation of educational paradigms. The burgeoning industrial establishments necessitated skilled manpower, which, in turn, led to the inception of mass education systems. These foundational educational reforms would serve as precursors to the intellectual and cultural oscillations that would characterize the subsequent century.

Nevertheless, the implications of these societal shifts weren't confined to the geographical boundaries of industrial pioneers. Emboldened by their industrial and, consequently, imperial ascendency, these nations' societal structures and ideologies permeated their colonial territories. Thus, the sociological metamorphoses of the 19th century didn't merely sculpt the contours of the societies nested within the epicenter of the Industrial Revolution but also cast shadows upon the global fabric of empires.

Conclusion: Legacy of Colonialism and Industrialization in the Modern World

Colonial legacies indelibly etch the tapestries of contemporary global landscapes. The dominance of languages—like English, French, Spanish, and Portuguese—in vast geographical terrains stands testament to the pervasiveness of bygone colonial hegemonies.

In the realm of literature, the colonial shadows are intricately interwoven into narratives. Luminaries such as Chinua Achebe, Salman Rushdie, and Derek Walcott not only interrogate and challenge the embedded colonial Weltanschauung but also deftly explore the nuanced terrains of post-colonial identities.

Economic vestiges of the colonial epoch persist in erstwhile colonies. Predominantly extractive infrastructures, instituted by colonial overseers, continue to influence these nations' economic blueprints. For instance, India's endeavor to metamorphose into a service-centric economy coexists with sectors that hark back to its colonial past. Malaysia, capitalizing on its geographically strategic locus, emerges as a nexus in global commerce. Meanwhile, Nigeria wrestles with the intricate dynamics of steering a resource-abundant nation within the post-colonial milieu.

On the political front, the repercussions of colonial governance models are palpable. While certain nations gravitate towards democratic paradigms, others manifest tendencies towards more autocratic governance architectures. The remnants of arbitrarily delineated colonial borders continue to ignite regional tensions, exemplified by the unrest witnessed in regions like Sudan and the Congo.

The ramifications of industrialization, akin to colonialism, are inextricably embedded in modern socio-economic fabrics. Numerous contemporary urban conglomerations owe their origins to the industrial impetus of yesteryears. Trade conduits, initially conceptualized to bolster industrial expansion, now form the arterial networks of global economic systems. Additionally, technological strides of the present, while advanced, often trace their foundational ideologies to innovations birthed during the industrial epoch.

The realm of modern geopolitics is invariably colored by the hues of its colonial antecedents. Contentious issues ranging from calls for reparations, nuanced trade dynamics, to territorial conflicts can be traced back to the colonial matrix.

In summation, the legacies of colonialism and industrialization, far from being confined to history, persistently influence and shape the contours of present-day nation-states, reminding us of the intricate webs of history and their lasting impact on the evolving global narrative.

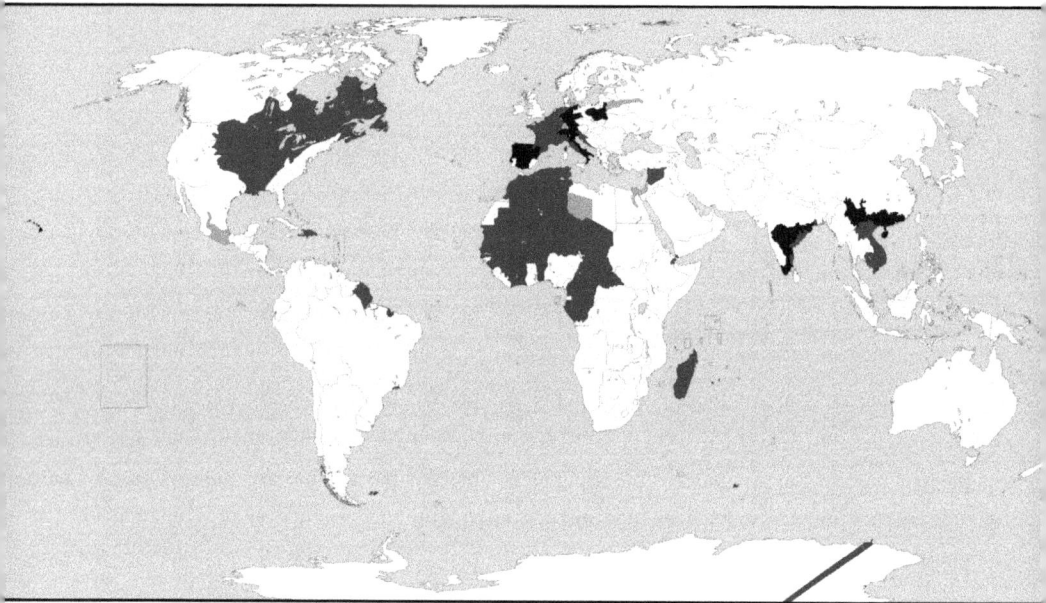

The French Colonial Empire

Chapter 18.
The French Empire: Richelieu to Napoleon (17th-19th Centuries)

History is the version of past events that people have decided to agree upon

~Napoleon Bonaparte

France's ascent

In the early 17th century, as previously seen, Europe was a patchwork of monarchies, principalities, and city-states. It was an age of political fragmentation, where the concept of the modern nation-state was still in its infancy. Amidst this backdrop, Cardinal Richelieu emerged as the mastermind of a transformational vision. A man of cunning diplomacy and unwavering ambition, he understood that to become a global power, France had to consolidate its authority and emerge as a formidable nation-state.

Centralizing authority and weakening the influence of rival nobility was imperative for Richelieu. One of his key accomplishments was the establishment of a network of spies and informants, enabling the crown to monitor and suppress dissent among the nobles, thereby solidifying the monarchy's control.

Financial reform was another cornerstone of Richelieu's agenda. He restructured the tax system, imposing levies on the nobility and clergy, who had long enjoyed tax exemptions. These reforms not only bolstered the royal coffers but also asserted the supremacy of the crown over the privileged classes.

Simultaneously, Richelieu pursued an assertive foreign policy. He involved France in the Thirty Years' War as detailed previously, not out of religious conviction, but as a calculated move to limit the power of the Habsburg dynasty, whose extensive holdings encircled France. This involvement marked a strategic shift, as France transitioned from being a spectator to a participant in the continent's conflicts.

France's ascent during Richelieu's tenure is not solely attributed to its political might but also its cultural and linguistic consolidation. Richelieu established the Académie Française in 1635, an institution that remains pivotal nearly four centuries later. Designed to centralize and standardize the French language, the Académie has been instrumental in fostering cultural unity and national identity. Comprising esteemed members known as "les Immortels", it not only crafts the definitive dictionary of the French language but also ensures the language's evolution, reflecting societal shifts and technological progress. While Richelieu's support for luminaries like René Descartes added intellectual gravitas, the enduring influence of the Académie has cemented France's reputation as a beacon of global culture and linguistic heritage.

By the time of his death in 1642, Richelieu had laid the foundations for a more centralized, powerful, and assertive French state. His policies and reforms would serve as a blueprint for future French leaders, setting the stage for France's rise as a dominant European and global power in the centuries to come.

But the story of France's ascendancy doesn't stop with Richelieu's nation-building. The Enlightenment, a period of intellectual ferment, swept across Europe like wildfire, and France was its epicenter. Visionaries like Voltaire, Rousseau, and Montesquieu championed reason, liberty, and the pursuit of knowledge. Their ideas seeped into the collective consciousness of the French people and beyond, igniting a fervor for change.

As the pages turn, you'll witness the eruption of one of the most seismic events in human history: the French Revolution. Born out of social inequality, economic strife, and a thirst for political representation, the Revolution stormed the Bastille and ignited the flame of liberty, equality, and fraternity. It was a cataclysmic upheaval that would resonate far beyond the cobbled streets of Paris.

France's revolutionary fervor soon transcended its borders. The ideals that had driven the Revolution, framed within the Declaration of the Rights of Man and of the Citizen, became a beacon for oppressed peoples worldwide. From the American colonies to the far reaches of Europe, the French Revolution served as both an inspiration and a warning—a call to arms for those who sought to challenge the shackles of monarchy and aristocracy.

And then, amidst the tumultuous aftermath of the Revolution, emerged a military genius—Napoleon Bonaparte. His meteoric rise from a Corsican artillery officer to the ruler of France was as audacious as the era itself. Napoleon's conquests knew no bounds. His armies swept through Europe, redrawing maps and challenging the old order. The Napoleonic Code, a testament to his visionary legal reforms, would serve as a blueprint for justice and equality in many parts of the world.

But as with many empires, the zenith is often followed by a precipitous fall. In the midst of his imperial ambitions, Napoleon's forays into Russia, his defeats at Leipzig, and ultimately, his exile to Elba would mark the beginning of the end.

This chapter is a chronicle of a nation's journey from a fractured state to a global power, from the drawing rooms of Versailles to the blood-soaked streets of the Revolution. It is a tale of innovation, enlightenment, and upheaval, one that would echo through centuries of political thought and inspire countless revolutions. The rise of France from Richelieu to Napoleon is a testament to the enduring power of visionaries, revolutionaries, and the relentless pursuit of a place on the world stage. As we traverse this transformative period, the French Empire's influence on the world will become apparent, for it was an empire that, in its rise and fall, shaped the course of history.

Louis XIV and the Age of Absolutism

Louis XIV, recognized as the Sun King, took the French throne in 1643 at the age of four, initiating a reign spanning over seven decades. This period was marked by Louis's persistent drive for absolutism, aiming to centralize authority and assert the dominance of the French monarchy.

Central to this endeavor was the architectural marvel, the Palace of Versailles. Located a short distance from Paris, this expansive palace not only served as the seat of royal power but also became a symbol of the monarch's absolute authority. Elements such as the Hall of Mirrors highlighted the stature of the French monarchy on a global stage. This projection of power was not merely for domestic consumption; European monarchs, observing the consolidation of power at Versailles, sought to emulate Louis XIV's blend of political control and regal display.

Louis XIV's vision extended beyond France's borders, leading to colonial endeavors in regions including North America and the Caribbean. This push for overseas territories and the establishment of trade networks signaled France's ambitions on a global scale, influencing the trajectory of global geopolitics.

The age of Louis XIV, marked by a commitment to absolutism, extravagance, and territorial expansion, provided profound lessons for subsequent rulers. It showcased the potentials and pitfalls of centralized authority, redefined European political structures, and emphasized France's ambitions in global colonial dynamics. Through these actions, the Sun King's reign underscored the multifaceted repercussions of autocratic governance.

The Enlightenment and France

As Louis XIV's reign concluded, France transitioned into a period often designated as the Enlightenment. This era, also known as the "Age of Reason," signified a notable shift in human thought. Stemming from the Scientific Revolution's challenges to traditional paradigms—particularly as Europe grappled with empirical contributions from figures like Galileo and Newton—a renewed zeal for knowledge and skepticism towards established order took root.

France became a central nexus for this burgeoning intellectual movement. Within Paris's salons, a confluence of philosophers, writers, and scholars—among them Voltaire, known for his critiques of religious orthodoxy; Rousseau, the proponent of social contract theory; Diderot, orchestrating comprehensive knowledge dissemination; and Montesquieu, delineating the separation of powers—converged to critically examine societal and governmental structures. Their deliberations and writings not only altered the intellectual discourse but also catalyzed widespread societal introspection, especially among France's literate classes.

As the 18th century approached its conclusion, the Enlightenment's ideals, now deeply embedded in French societal consciousness, culminated in the transformative French Revolution. The Revolution's motto, "Liberté, égalité, fraternité," resonated beyond France, becoming emblematic of democratic aspirations globally.

In analyzing France's engagement with the Enlightenment and its revolutionary aftermath, it becomes evident that this period was pivotal in reframing societal norms, challenging conventional authority, and recalibrating the state-individual dynamic. The confluence of Enlightenment ideals and revolutionary impulses forged a path for the ascendency of reason, liberty, and equality, serving as influential touchstones for subsequent eras.

The French Revolution

In the 18th century, France's socio-economic fabric was marred by stark disparities. Louis XVI's monarchy, ensnared in years of fiscal imprudence marked by lavish expenditures and costly military endeavors, teetered on the edge of financial ruin. This economic burden was disproportionately shouldered by the Third Estate, which encompassed the vast majority of the French populace, from the bourgeoisie and urban laborers to the peasantry. Despite representing about 98% of the population, their political influence was dwarfed by the privileged First and Second Estates, who enjoyed many tax exemptions. To address the fiscal crisis of 1789, Louis XVI convened the Estates-General, drawing representatives from all three estates. However, facing underrepresentation and inequitable voting practices, the Third Estate took a decisive step: they broke away and proclaimed themselves the 'National Assembly,' asserting that they were the true representatives of the French people. This pivotal move, coupled with rising tensions, led to the iconic storming of the Bastille, heralding the onset of the revolution,

Post this pivotal event, France's political landscape underwent significant metamorphosis. The emergent National Assembly, predominantly representing the bourgeoisie, took radical steps: they nullified feudal entitlements, promulgated the Declaration of the Rights of Man and of the Citizen, and embarked on land redistributions. Drawing inspiration from Enlightenment tenets, these revolutionaries endeavored to dismantle the entrenched ancien régime, fostering a society based on justice and egalitarianism.

In the evolutionary trajectory of the French Revolution, the period between 1793 and 1794, known as the Reign of Terror, stands out prominently. Led by the Jacobins, particularly figures like Maximilien Robespierre and Louis Antoine de Saint-Just, this phase was marked by stringent measures to eliminate perceived threats to the revolutionary cause. The Committee of Public Safety, under Robespierre's guidance, became the de facto ruling body of France. Its period of dominance was fraught with internal strife, as the ideals of the revolution often found themselves in conflict with the realities of governance. The Reign of Terror, while seeking to solidify the gains of the revolution, also became infamous for its extensive use of the guillotine. Notable figures, including King Louis XVI and Queen Marie Antoinette, were executed alongside many others—both aristocrats and revolutionaries who were perceived as either threats or insufficiently radical.

As the Terror waned, post-Robespierre, France's governance experienced multiple shifts. The radical fervor of the Jacobins, who had been instrumental in key revolutionary acts such as the abolition of the monarchy and the establishment of the First French Republic, began to decline.

After Robespierre's execution in 1794 and emerging from the Jacobins' decline, the Directory was established in 1795. It was a body designed to represent a more moderate phase of the revolution. This new form of republican government, characterized by a bicameral legislature and an executive of five directors, sought to stabilize the revolutionary gains while guarding against both individual autocracy and a potential return to monarchic rule. Yet, the Directory's era was fraught with difficulties. From 1795 to 1799, economic challenges, often rooted in warfare and disruptions in agriculture, plagued France.

The Directory, marked by internal corruption and an evident lack of popular legitimacy, struggled to find solutions. Moreover, political purges aimed at both royalist sympathizers and lingering Jacobin sentiments showcased its tenuous grip on power. Such challenges rendered the Directory increasingly unpopular and paved the way for its eventual downfall.

Externally, France found itself besieged. The revolutionary and anti-monarchial fervor alarmed other European monarchies, leading to the formation of coalitions. Countries like Britain, Prussia, and Austria sought to contain and, if possible, reverse the revolutionary tide, fearing its spread might destabilize their own territories. This resulted in the Revolutionary Wars, where France, despite its internal chaos, managed to not only defend its revolutionary principles but also lay the groundwork for Napoleonic ambitions.

Thus, while the French Revolution aimed to establish liberty, equality, and fraternity, its path was marred by extremes, from the internal purges during the Reign of Terror to external confrontations with European coalitions.

In summary the tumultuous aftermath of the French Revolution in the late 18th century, marked a combination of socio-political disarray and external threats, provided a fertile ground for the ascent of an adept military tactician: Napoleon Bonaparte.

Napoleon Bonaparte: Rise and Rule

Napoleon's Corsican birth in 1769 heralded a life that would pivotally reshape both French trajectories and broader European geopolitics. The early stages of his military career were marked by his astute grasp of artillery tactics and a notable ability to inspire and lead troops. Even in the nascent years of his service, during the Revolutionary Wars, Napoleon displayed an innate talent for strategy and organization. The Siege of Toulon in 1793, where he ousted British forces and was subsequently promoted to brigadier general at the age of 24, showcased his rising prominence.

During the transformative period of France's revolutionary face-offs against European monarchies, Napoleon Bonaparte emerged as a pivotal figure, particularly underscored by his military campaigns.

In the Italian Campaigns of 1796-1797, Napoleon confronted the Habsburg-led coalition, which prominently included Austria. It's worth noting that during this period, various regions of Italy were under Habsburg Austrian control, making the Italian Campaigns integral to France's broader strategic objectives against the Austrian Empire. Utilizing innovative tactics, his forces achieved crucial victories at Montenotte, Rivoli, and Arcole. These successes led to the Treaty of Campo Formio in 1797, which not only resulted in territorial acquisitions such as Lombardy for France but also disrupted the established balance of power in the region, significantly diminishing Habsburg dominance in Italy.

The Egyptian Expedition of 1798-1799, while driven by a strategic objective to undermine British influence in the Indian trade route via Egypt, was multi-faceted. Following a conclusive victory at the Battle of the Pyramids, the French faced a setback at the naval Battle of the Nile against Admiral Horatio Nelson's British fleet. However, beyond its military endeavors, the campaign had a profound cultural impact. Napoleon's inclusion of scholars in the expedition led to monumental discoveries like the Rosetta Stone, propelling advancements in the field of Egyptology and reinforcing France's stature in scientific and cultural domains.

However, it wasn't just Napoleon's military successes that propelled him forward. His keen understanding of propaganda meant that even setbacks were presented in a favorable light, bolstering his reputation. By 1799, with France's revolutionary governance mired in the inefficacies of the Directory and riddled with dissatisfaction, the stage was set for change. Napoleon, recognizing the moment, collaborated in the coup of 18 Brumaire, leading to the Directory's overthrow and the establishment of the Consulate. As First Consul, his ascendancy from the Corsican aisles to the zenith of French governance was complete.

Under Napoleon's stewardship, France underwent sweeping reforms. The Napoleonic Code, promulgated in 1804, stands as a testament to his transformative governance. This legal framework, prioritizing equality and individual rights, subsequently informed legal structures globally. However, Napoleon's ambitions transcended domestic governance. As he marshaled forces across Europe, territories from the Iberian Peninsula to the Russian steppes witnessed the might of the French Empire. Establishing client regimes and designating loyal confidants as monarchs, Napoleon sought a cohesive European order under French aegis. By 1804, consolidating his power, he proclaimed himself Emperor of the French.

The protracted Napoleonic Wars, which saw France clash with shifting European coalitions, indelibly shaped the continent. Key battles such as Austerlitz and Borodino underscored Napoleon's military ingenuity, while the wars also engendered significant civilian distress. Napoleon's attempt at economically isolating Britain through the "Continental System" had substantial repercussions, leading to economic strains and geopolitical tensions. Moreover, Napoleon's dominion inadvertently sowed the seeds of nationalism, as subjugated regions aspired for autonomy.

Interpreting Napoleon Bonaparte's legacy necessitates a balanced approach. His contributions, from military strategies to legal reforms, undoubtedly molded European dynamics. Simultaneously, the human costs of his ambitions and the European resistance to

Napoleonic hegemony merit critical scrutiny. In essence, Napoleon's epoch functioned as a bridge: transitioning from the revolutionary ideologies of the 18th century to the intricate power interplays of the 19th century, and thereby laying foundational stones for modern Europe's political architecture.

The Fall of Napoleon

As the 19th century dawned, Napoleon Bonaparte's influence on European geopolitics was unparalleled. In a matter of only few years his European campaigns had significantly reconfigured European political and territorial landscapes.

The crux of Napoleon's rule hinged on his unyielding ambition, a trait that was abundantly evident between 1803 and 1815, a period dominated by the Napoleonic Wars. These conflicts weren't sporadic battles but a systematic series of confrontations wherein France, under Napoleon's leadership, faced various shifting European alliances.

The War of the Third Coalition in 1805, primarily formed by Britain, Austria, and Russia against France, saw significant confrontations both at sea and on land. While the Battle of Trafalgar posed challenges in naval terms, the Battle of Austerlitz — the "Battle of the Three Emperors" — displayed Napoleon's land strategy, as he defeated the Austro-Russian forces.

The subsequent Peninsular War from 1808 to 1814 featured Spain, Portugal, and Britain rallying against Napoleon's attempts to control the Iberian Peninsula. The terrain and the adept use of guerrilla warfare by the Spanish, amplified by British military support, consistently tested the mettle of the French forces.

The War of the Fifth Coalition in 1809 saw a resurgence of Austria, backed by Britain, attempting to curb the expanding French influence. Yet, despite their concerted efforts, the Battle of Wagram solidified Napoleon's dominance, leading to the Treaty of Schönbrunn, which imposed territorial concessions upon Austria.

Guided by the formidable Grande Armée, Napoleon's campaigns significantly expanded his empire's territories in Europe. However, the relentless pace of these conquests, compounded by the inherent economic and logistical challenges, also intensified the undercurrents of resistance against French supremacy, foreboding later trials in his reign.

In 1812, Napoleon, at the peak of his power, took a step that would drastically alter the course of his empire's fate. Embarking on a bold campaign, he sought to expand his dominion by invading Russia. Advancing deep into Russian territory, the Grande Armée found themselves ensnared in an unanticipated quagmire. Confronted by a tactical scorched-earth strategy employed by the Russians and subsequently decimated by the unforgiving winter, their ambition turned to despair. This monumental miscalculation, echoing through the annals of history, would eerily resurface about a century later. The 20th century would bear witness to another formidable force repeating a similar grave error in its invasion of Russia—underscoring the cyclical nature of strategic blunders and the haunting specter of history's repetition. This formidable force repeating Napoleon strategic miscalculation would be none other than Adolf Hitler's Nazi Germany.

Napoleon's misadventures in Russia emboldened various European nations, culminating in a formidable coalition against him. One of the coalition's significant confrontations against Napoleon transpired during the Battle of Leipzig in 1813, often termed the "Battle of the Nations." This united European front not only arrested the French advance but also initiated the decline of the Napoleonic empire. By 1814, the geopolitical landscape shifted, relegating Napoleon to exile on Elba.

Yet, the year 1815 observed a temporary reversal of fortunes. Napoleon's audacious escape from Elba and his subsequent re-entry into France led to a period termed the Hundred Days. This interlude concluded with the pivotal Battle of Waterloo in June 1815, where a coalition, including the forces under the Duke of Wellington and Prussian Field Marshal Blücher, defeated Napoleon. Subsequently, Napoleon was exiled to Saint Helena, where he met his demise on May 5, 1821.

Napoleon's passing symbolized the end of an epoch defined by revolutionary fervor and the emergence of powerful military leaders. The post-Napoleonic era saw European leaders convene at the Congress of Vienna in 1815, striving to reinstitute equilibrium in a continent scarred by upheavals. Notwithstanding his fall, the indelible marks of Napoleon's reign, encapsulated in legal reforms and military doctrines, persisted, underscoring his enduring impact on European systems and societies.

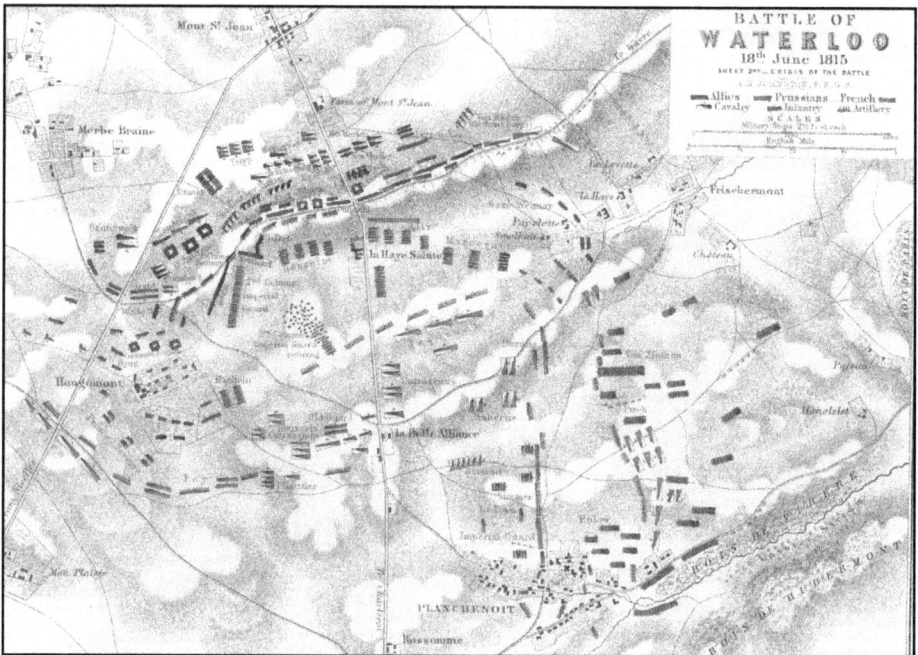

Battle of Waterloo, 18 June 1815[25]

Conclusion: Legacy of the French Empire

The ripple effects of the French Empire, under the stewardship of Napoleon Bonaparte, spanned continents and eras, dramatically reshaping the historical trajectory. This monumental legacy was not merely an artifact of the Napoleonic era; it infiltrated military doctrines, judicial structures, and foundational political thoughts.

The French Empire, birthed from the tumultuous currents of the French Revolution, played a pivotal role in molding foundational political philosophies. The revolutionary ideals of liberty, equality, and fraternity became the bedrock of democratic notions that prioritized governance rooted in the people's will. Throughout subsequent centuries, these ideals ignited a plethora of global revolutions and independence movements.

On the military front, Napoleon's indelible mark remains unsurpassed. He introduced warfare strategies that merged artillery, swift mobilization, and infantry assaults. The "Corps system" decentralized armies into agile units, influencing future military structures. His campaigns, however driven by territorial ambition, became archetypes for logistical brilliance and strategic deployment.

However, the brilliance of Napoleon's strategic insights had its shadows. His relentless military campaigns and territorial ambitions resulted in immense human tolls. The expansiveness of his wars led to significant societal disruptions, economic hardships, and immense suffering for the common populace.

In the realm of jurisprudence, the Napoleonic Code emerged as a defining contribution. Replacing France's complex laws, this code emphasized legal equality, property rights, and evidence-based trials. But it wasn't devoid of criticisms. While it streamlined legal systems, the Code also regressed on some societal advancements, notably curtailing certain rights previously extended to women during the early days of the Revolution.

Post Napoleon, the Congress of Vienna sought to stabilize a tumultuous Europe. This gathering represented more than territorial realignments; it epitomized Europe's shared aspirations for peace, paving the way for subsequent diplomatic overtures.

In summation, Napoleon Bonaparte's French Empire carved influential pillars that touch diverse aspects of modern existence. From disseminating revolutionary ideals, reshaping military tactics, framing global legal structures, to underlining Europe's intertwined fate, Napoleon's legacy is robust. Yet, as with any historical titan, his reign was not devoid of complexities and critiques, and it remains imperative to perceive his contributions within this multifaceted prism.

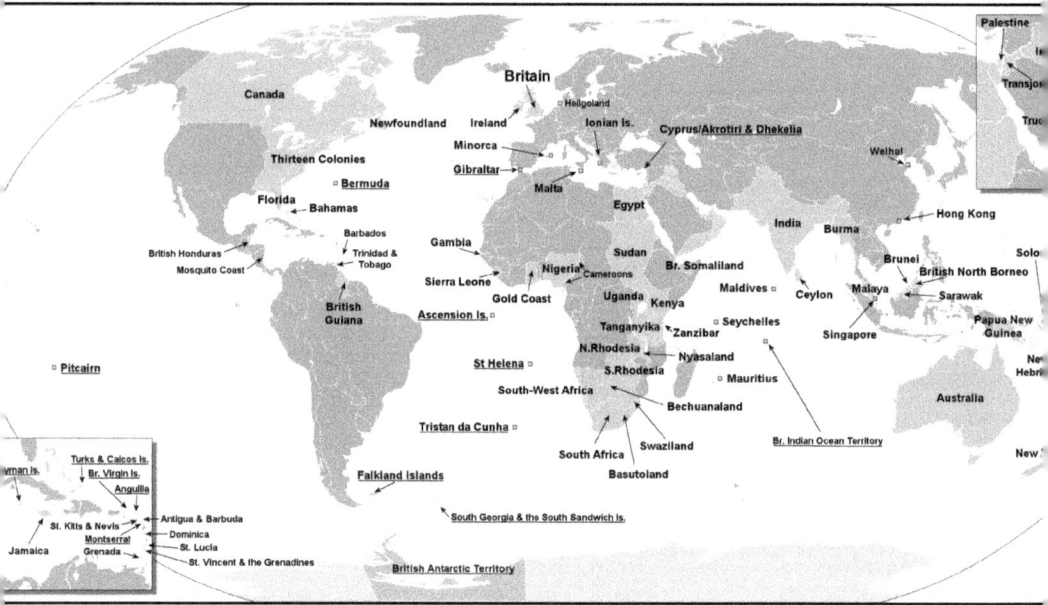

The British Empire[26]

Chapter 19.
The British Empire: The Sun Never Sets (16ᵗʰ-20ᵗʰ Centuries)

We are not interested in the possibilities of defeat;
they do not exist.

~Queen Victoria

The Rise of a Global Hegemon

As previously indicated from the late 15ᵗʰ century onwards, geopolitical shifts, technological advancements, and mercantile ambitions sowed the seeds for the growth of global empires. It is within this context that Britain began its ascent as an empire, its trajectory influenced by the confluence of exploration, colonization, and the Industrial Revolution, previously discussed in Chapter 17.

Initiating its colonial endeavors in the 16ᵗʰ century, the British Empire's territories burgeoned by the 19ᵗʰ and 20ᵗʰ centuries, eventually encompassing an unprecedented expanse. By the zenith of its power in the mid-19ᵗʰ century, Britain presided over an intricate web of territories spanning multiple continents. Methodical strategies — encompassing diplomacy, strategic alliances, and military conquests — were employed to secure these vast expanses. Notably, Africa, with its abundant resources, vast tracts in Asia, with India being paramount, and territories across Oceania came under British dominion. In terms of sheer territorial volume and population, the British Empire was unparalleled, controlling approximately a quarter of the world's land and populace.

The Treaty of Tordesillas in 1494, orchestrated by Pope Alexander VI, delineated the spheres of influence in newly discovered lands between Spain and Portugal. This treaty played an instrumental role in shaping England's colonial endeavors. Initial attempts, such as Sir Walter Raleigh's expedition to Roanoke in the 1580s, were marred by setbacks. However, these were precursors to more concerted and successful efforts in subsequent centuries.

Beyond territorial acquisitions, the British Empire became a crucible for cultural, linguistic, and economic exchanges. It wielded significant influence in determining global trade paradigms, facilitated the proliferation of the English language, instituted legal structures, and even played a role in popularizing sports like cricket and rugby. Britain's maritime prowess, further fortified after the pivotal 1588 defeat of the Spanish Armada, was pivotal in cementing its global standing.

Yet, the trajectory of the British Empire was not an uninterrupted tapestry of successes. It was punctuated with instances of indigenous resistance, episodes of exploitation, and complex socio-cultural interactions. Consequently, while the empire's influence was vast, it was also variegated, and this chapter seeks to unravel the multi-dimensional facets of an empire on which the sun proverbially never set.

The Genesis of British Imperialism

Between the late 15th and the entirety of the 16th centuries, an intricate tapestry of socio-political, economic, and religious factors provided the impetus for the embryonic stages of the British Empire. The matrix of European exploration and colonization was but one aspect; embedded within were profound economic motivations, escalating European rivalries (that would eventually culminate in the thirty-years was), nascent religious fissures, and advancements in maritime capabilities.

In the timeline stretching from 1485 to 1603, termed the Tudor Epoch, England underwent transformative phases. An epochal event, the Battle of Bosworth Field in 1485, saw Henry VII's ascendance, marking the cessation of the Wars of the Roses—fraught conflicts over the English throne's legitimacy. The sequential reigns of the Tudor monarchs—Henry VII, followed by Henry VIII, Edward VI, Mary I, and concluding with Elizabeth I—imparted definitive directions to England's trajectory. Noteworthy was Henry VIII's tenure, which precipitated the English Reformation and subsequently birthed the Church of England. Elizabeth I's reign, often encapsulated as the "Elizabethan Era," stood out for its confluence of cultural efflorescence and maritime advancements. It's salient to note that, despite confronting larger and resource-laden adversaries like Spain and France, England's ambitions transcended its boundaries. The quest for establishing alternative trade conduits, circumventing the control exerted by the Ottoman Empire and dominant Italian city-states, underscored this aspiration. This intent manifested tangibly in John Cabot's 1497 voyage, culminating in his arrival in present-day Canada.

The subsequent century marked England's incursions into Asia, emblematic of which was the inception of the East India Company in 1600. Anointed with a royal charter by Elizabeth I, this entity secured exclusive trading privileges in the waters of the Indian Ocean. Evolving over decades, its role morphed from pure mercantile endeavors to wielding political clout, culminating in its militaristic and administrative dominion over substantial sections of India.

Parallelly, the 17th century witnessed England's forays into the New World of North America. This was a terrain where imperial powers, chiefly Spain and Portugal, had already staked claims. Colonization efforts materialized with the foundation of Jamestown in 1607 and Plymouth in 1620. The economic calculus, while paramount, was complemented by a quest for religious autonomy. This is exemplified by the voyage of the Mayflower in 1620, which ferried the Pilgrims— primarily English Separatists—to the New World. Their objective was dual: to extricate themselves from religious straitjackets and to institute novel governance models, evident in the Mayflower Compact. Their interactions with indigenous communities added another layer to this colonial narrative.

Europe in the 17th century was a crucible of competitive dynamics. England's engagements with contemporaneous powers, notably the Dutch and the French, accentuated these rivalries. A series of naval confrontations, known as the Anglo-Dutch Wars spanning 1652-1674, were seminal in asserting England's maritime preeminence. Culminating these confrontations was the Treaty of Utrecht in 1713, which marked the cessation of the War of Spanish Succession. This treaty facilitated England's ascendancy as a paramount naval entity, bequeathing it territories like Newfoundland and Gibraltar.

In summation, the foundational phase of the British Empire was a complex interplay of global occurrences and localized European dynamics. As the empire's territorial ambit expanded, it simultaneously grappled with multifaceted challenges, laying the groundwork for its unparalleled imperial dominance in subsequent centuries.

Ascendancy in Asia: Britain's Pinnacle Possession

Asia, an expanse characterized by its vast territorial spread, abundant natural resources, and intricate cultural mosaics, emerged as a magnet for European imperialist aspirations. Within this extensive continent, Britain's gaze fixated primarily on India, subsequently anointing it as "The Jewel in the Crown" of their imperial portfolio.

Transitioning to the mid-18th century, historical dynamics within the Indian subcontinent witnessed the gradual ebbing of the Mughal Empire—a colossal entity that had previously sprawled across significant swathes of the region. Within this flux, the East India Company, discerned the potential to embed itself deeper within the Indian fabric. Simultaneously, the Company navigated the competitive landscape, especially countering French encroachments. A watershed moment in this tussle for dominance manifested in the Battle of Plassey in 1757. Under the leadership of Robert Clive, Company forces clinched a decisive victory against the Nawab of Bengal. The ramifications of this military triumph crystallized in the Treaty of Allahabad, enacted in 1765. This accord endowed the East India Company with revenue collection rights spanning the agriculturally opulent provinces of Bengal, Bihar, and Orissa.

The dawn of the 19th century witnessed an exponential consolidation of the Company's territorial footprint in India. This dominion was sustained and augmented through a multifaceted approach encompassing military expeditions, strategic treaties, and fostering alliances with indigenous chieftains and monarchs.

In tandem with their Indian endeavors, Britain cast its eyes towards China, a nation steeped in millennia of history and economic potential. However, initial interactions were marked by hesitancy from the Qing dynasty, which exhibited circumspection regarding expansive trade engagements with Western entities. Confronted with a trade disequilibrium stemming from Britain's surging demand for Chinese tea, a recourse was sought in the form of opium exports from India to China. This trade strategy, while momentarily addressing the fiscal imbalance, inadvertently unleashed a pervasive addiction crisis within China, culminating in multifarious socio-economic upheavals. The Qing dynasty's stringent measures to curb the opium influx instigated a series of confrontations known as the Opium Wars, spanning 1839-1842 and 1856-1860.

The cessation of these confrontations witnessed the formulation of treaties skewed heavily in Britain's favor. The Treaty of Nanking, ratified in 1842, is particularly noteworthy. Its provisions facilitated British acquisition of several port cities, with Hong Kong's annexation being the most significant. Labelled as "Unequal Treaties," these accords epitomized the broader paradigm of Western subjugation of China during the 19th century.

Conclusively, by the mid-19th century, Britain's imprint on Asia was unmistakable, characterized by a potent blend of strategic acumen and martial supremacy. While India emerged as the linchpin, ensuring unparalleled fiscal inflows, it concurrently became the epicenter of burgeoning resistance narratives, foreshadowing future nationalist insurgencies and Britain's eventual retreat from the Asian theater.

Africa: The Contest and Britain's Endeavor

The African continent, characterized by its vast geographies, pivotal geostrategic significance, and abundant resource wealth, evolved into a crucible for European imperial aspirations during the late 19th century. This intense and multifaceted European incursion is aptly delineated as "The Scramble for Africa." Central to this endeavor was Britain, whose aspirations and maneuvers underscored its imperialist appetite.

By the latter segment of the 19th century, a confluence of technological breakthroughs, epitomized by innovations such as the Maxim gun and advancements in tropical disease mitigation, capacitated European entities to penetrate previously inaccessible African hinterlands. This deeper incursion was further facilitated by pressing economic imperatives underscored by the quest for untapped raw material reserves and emergent market opportunities. Further galvanizing these colonial undertakings was an undercurrent of burgeoning nationalism, propelling European polities to assert and expand their territorial footprints.

Britain, leveraging its expansive global territorial portfolio, approached Africa with a multifaceted rationale. Strategic imperatives converged with economic considerations, further amplified by the overarching objective of forestalling and counteracting the territorial ambitions of competing European powers, principally the French and the Germans.

Given the frenetic pace of territorial annexations and the attendant risk of inter-European conflicts, a regulatory mechanism was deemed essential. This precipitated the Berlin Conference spanning 1884-1885, a diplomatic conclave aimed at streamlining the African colonization process. Notably absent from this gathering were African stakeholders. Post-conference stipulations endowed Britain with significant territories, reinforcing its control over pivotal African regions.

A salient feature underscoring Britain's African pursuits was its focus on the Suez Canal, operationalized in 1869. This engineering marvel dramatically truncated maritime transit times between Britain and India. Grasping its strategic indispensability, Britain endeavored to assert control over Egypt. Initially, this was a collaborative venture with France, but subsequent geopolitical dynamics led to Britain's singular dominance. The Nile, integral to Egypt's agrarian and economic vitality, beckoned British ambitions, culminating in expeditions into Sudan and sporadic confrontations with competing colonial forces, notably the French.

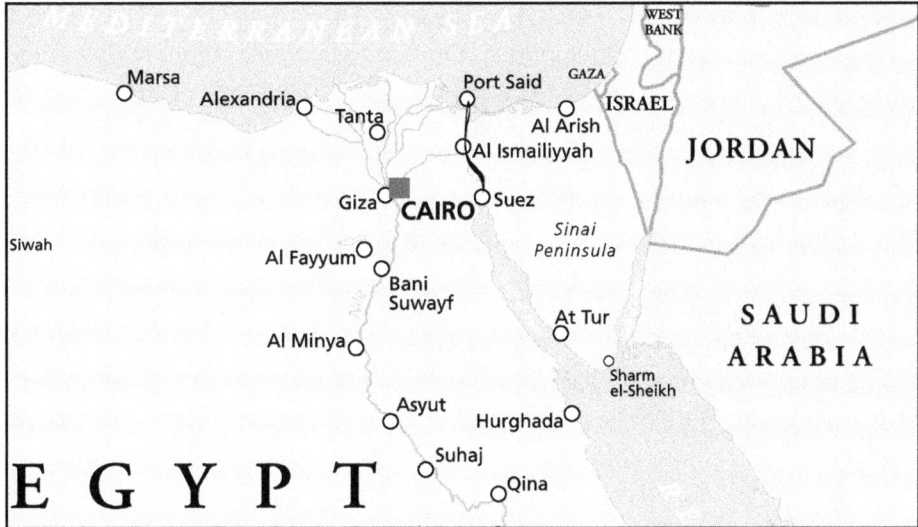

The Suez Canal[27]

The southern extremity of the continent, South Africa, attracted British attention with the 1814 annexation of the Cape Colony. The subsequent decades amplified British interests, particularly post the discovery of diamonds and gold in the latter half of the 19th century. This resource bonanza engendered economic buoyancy but also ignited tensions with the Boers, descendants of early Dutch colonial settlers. The resulting friction culminated in the Anglo-Boer Wars. The conflict's cessation witnessed British triumph and the 1910 establishment of the Union of South Africa, a dominion within the British imperial framework. During this epoch, a young British officer, manifested his tenacity and ingenuity with a daring escape after being taken prisoner. His traits, displayed in his South African adventure, would later underscore his transformative global contributions. His name that would later become legendary, was Winston Churchill.

As the 20th century dawned, Britain's African dominion spanned from the northern confines of Egypt to the southern reaches of South Africa. While these territorial gains fortified Britain's global stature, they concurrently incubated nationalist sentiments among indigenous African populations, heralding future decolonization movements.

Oceania: Britain's Pacific Endeavors

Oceania, with its extensive archipelagos and dispersed island entities in the Pacific, held both allure and intricacy for the British imperial agenda. While the Pacific expanse did not encounter the fervent colonization race observed in Africa and Asia, its strategic geography and economic potential did not escape the British Empire's gaze.

The British foray into Australia commenced in 1788, marked by the inauguration of a penal colony in New South Wales. This establishment emanated from Britain's imperative to address its prison population surplus. While its penal origins are undisputed, the subsequent trajectory of British presence in Australia evolved rapidly. Pioneers and surveyors undertook extensive explorations across the expansive Australian landmass. The mid-19th century witnessed a transformative phase with the Gold Rush and agrarian prospects magnetizing an influx of settlers, leading to the rapid metamorphosis of the Australian colonial landscape.

However, British colonization in Australia significantly impacted the indigenous inhabitants, the Aboriginal communities. These populations grappled with multifaceted challenges, encompassing dislocation, the introduction of alien diseases, and direct confrontations with the colonizers. These adversities precipitated substantial demographic declines and disrupted long-standing Aboriginal societal structures.

Adjacent to Australia, in New Zealand, the British navigated their relationship with the Maori, the indigenous Polynesian communities. By 1840, in a bid to systematize British colonization and concurrently recognize Maori entitlements, the Treaty of Waitangi was formalized. Nonetheless, the ensuing period witnessed discrepancies in the treaty's interpretation between British and Maori stakeholders. This incongruence catalyzed the New Zealand Wars spanning 1845 to 1872. The conflict's cessation left the Maori populace with considerable territorial losses. Subsequent years have witnessed endeavors to address and reconcile the historical breaches of the Treaty's stipulations.

Beyond the confines of Australia and New Zealand, the British expanded their Pacific footprint. Establishing colonial dominions and protectorates in diverse locales like Fiji, Papua New Guinea, and the

Solomon Islands, the British pursued varied objectives. These ranged from establishing coaling depots facilitating naval operations to tapping into regional commodities, including copra and sandalwood.

In summation, the British colonial chapter in Oceania underscores its relentless quest for global ubiquity. Albeit geographically remote from the empire's nucleus, these Pacific territories were instrumental in bolstering trade, military strategization, and amplifying British geopolitical influence in the Pacific corridor. The vestiges of this epoch persist as contemporary nations navigate their post-colonial identities, juxtaposing historical legacies with contemporary global challenges and prospects.

The Caribbean: An Intersection of Commerce, Culture, and Exploitation

The Caribbean archipelago, strategically positioned in the midst of the Americas, crystallized into an indispensable asset for the British Empire. These isles became arenas of profound economic enterprise, intricate cultural amalgamations, and, regrettably, instances of severe human exploitation.

Central to Britain's engagement in the Caribbean was the burgeoning demand for sugar. By the 17th century, British colonial endeavors were manifest in Barbados, which subsequently proliferated to incorporate territories such as Jamaica, the Bahamas, and a host of additional islands. While sugar plantations burgeoned, the substantial economic gains accrued were predicated upon the labor of enslaved Africans, catapulting the transatlantic slave trade into an instrumental, albeit morally reprehensible, component of the Caribbean's economic architecture.

The British Caribbean colonies evolved into formidable economic entities. Commodities encompassing sugar, rum, and molasses not only catered to British consumption but also permeated markets across Europe and the broader Americas. This intricate commercial web concurrently precipitated profound cultural interchanges. The convergence of African heritages with European conventions birthed distinct Creole cultures, manifestations of which—spanning music, dance, and folklore—continue to reverberate across the Caribbean milieu.

Transitioning into the late 18th and early 19th centuries, a discernible shift in British sentiment began crystallizing against the transatlantic slave trade. Pioneered by figures like William Wilberforce, this movement culminated in the 1807 Slave Trade Act, prohibiting the transportation of slaves. This legislative trajectory continued with the 1833 Slavery Abolition Act, which pronounced the cessation of slavery across the majority of the British Empire. The aftermath of these acts instigated a significant recalibration of the Caribbean's economic modus operandi. The emancipated populace transitioned into wage-earning roles or small landholding positions, and to bridge labor shortfalls, indentured laborers, predominantly from India, were integrated into the Caribbean labor landscape.

From a strategic vantage point, the Caribbean's significance extended beyond economic contours. Isles such as Bermuda and the Bahamas crystallized into pivotal naval and mercantile hubs, fortifying Britain's Atlantic preeminence. As global geopolitical tensions escalated, particularly as the 20th century dawned, the British Caribbean's role in sustaining naval supremacy and ensuring unimpeded trade corridors became paramount.

In synthesizing the Caribbean's trajectory within the ambit of British imperial history, it emerges as a region of profound economic vitality, juxtaposed against the moral quandaries emblematic of the Empire's operational ethos. While the vestiges of colonial exploitation linger, the Caribbean's indomitable spirit, enriched cultural tapestry, and resilience underscore its integral placement within global historical narratives.

Global Geopolitical Dynamics: the British Empire Amidst Rivalries and Alliances

In the intricate matrix of global geopolitics, Britain's journey in buttressing and amplifying its empire necessitated adept maneuvering amidst the crosscurrents of international rivalries and relations. This era witnessed the Empire not as an insular entity but as an integral component within a vast and interconnected geopolitical architecture, often bringing it into friction with analogous imperial endeavors.

Foremost among Britain's imperial adversaries was France. Historical antecedents trace their confrontations back to North America, evidenced in the Seven Years' War (1756-1763), which later rippled into African territories, exemplified by the Fashoda Incident in 1898. Additionally, Britain's imperial pursuits frequently intersected with the Dutch ambitions in Southeast Asia, a testament to which are the Anglo-Dutch Wars in the 17th century.

One of the more nuanced and prolonged confrontations, 'The Great Game' in the 19th century, saw Britain and Russia jostling for dominance in Central Asia. At its core, it was a quest for geopolitical ascendancy, but a parallel objective was safeguarding the corridors to India, Britain's invaluable colony. Instead of overt warfare, this engagement was predominantly characterized by intelligence operations, adept political tactics, and the establishment of strategic alliances.

The European diplomatic milieu of the 19th century was primarily underpinned by the Balance of Power principle, striving to forestall the overwhelming dominance of any singular entity. The Congress of Vienna in 1815 was emblematic of this ethos, envisaging a continental stability post the tumult of the Napoleonic Wars, with Britain invariably aligning its diplomatic stances to bolster its imperial interests.

However, the interlude between 1815 and the onset of World War I in 1914, characterized as 'Pax Britannica', marked an era of relative tranquility. This period spotlighted Britain's unparalleled naval and industrial preeminence, with the Empire orchestrating the enforcement of international accords and standards.

Transitioning into the 20th century, the emergence of assertive powers, most notably Germany under Kaiser Wilhelm II, began to impinge upon Britain's hitherto unchallenged supremacy. The burgeoning German naval fleet and its colonial pursuits, coupled with events such as the 1911 Agadir Crisis, encapsulated the mounting geopolitical frictions.

To distill the British Empire's trajectory within this age of heightened imperial dynamics, it emerges that its path was indelibly influenced by global politics. The oscillation between alliances and rivalries during this epoch not only dictated the Empire's strategies but also prefaced the monumental global confrontations that would ensue in the 20th century.

Imperial Governance: Structures, Strategies, and Underlying Ideologies

The British Empire's governance was undergirded by intricate systems that straddled diverse terrains and socio-political landscapes. The enormity of its territorial reach compelled adaptability in its administrative methodologies. Yet, foundational to these strategies was an entrenched ideological stance premised on the notion of a 'civilizing mission'.

Central to this mission was an unwavering conviction in European ascendancy and an ensuing imperative to bring enlightenment to societies perceived as less advanced. This was eloquently, albeit controversially, epitomized by Rudyard Kipling's "The White Man's Burden" in 1899, a poetic articulation endorsing the civilizational onus borne by Western powers, irrespective of resistance from the colonized.

The Empire's governance strategies oscillated between two primary modes:

Direct Rule. This was invoked predominantly in regions devoid of robust governance structures or in scenarios demanding meticulous British oversight. Post the Sepoy Mutiny of 1857, India exemplified this approach, with the British administrative machinery exerting comprehensive control over resources and overarching policies.

Indirect Rule Envisioned for territories with pre-existing leadership hierarchies, such as certain African regions. This allowed traditional leaders to retain their status, albeit under the aegis of British supervision. Leveraging the inherent societal reverence for these leaders often translated into a more seamless administrative process and economized on resources.

The Empire's administrative acumen was further fortified by infrastructural advancements. The inception of railways, telegraphic networks, and ports augmented not merely the extraction of resources but also consolidated administrative coherence. The Indian Railways epitomized this dual objective, emblematic of both British engineering proficiency and the ambition to integrate vast geographic swathes.

Legal reforms were integral to the Empire's governance. The promulgation of English common law tenets and the establishment of judiciary and policing mechanisms modeled after British paradigms often supplanted indigenous legal frameworks. Concurrently, the initiation of English-centric educational infrastructures aimed to engender a loyalist administrative cadre. Paradoxically, these very institutions occasionally became crucibles for nationalist fervor.

While the Empire's governance often encountered acquiescence, it was not devoid of contestations. Sporadic insurrections and organized resistance underscored colonial discontent. The British countermeasures oscillated between tactical reforms and stringent suppressions, often deploying strategies to fracture collective opposition.

To encapsulate, the administrative edifice of the British Empire was an intricate confluence of practical exigencies and deep-seated ideologies. The tangible legacies in infrastructure and legal frameworks endure in many erstwhile colonies. However, the pervasive threads of racial hierarchies and imperial presumptions not only steered colonial engagements but continue to reverberate in contemporary post-colonial discourses.

Nationalism Emerges: Transformation of Colonial Landscapes

Against the vast territorial canvas of the British Empire, the dawn of the 20th century saw the rise of a powerful opposing force: nationalism. Characterized by a fervent aspiration for autonomy and a rejuvenated reverence for indigenous histories and cultures, nationalism poised a substantive challenge to the bedrock of imperial governance.

The advent of modern education, often a byproduct of British colonial initiatives, precipitated an intellectual resurgence in numerous colonies. A new echelon of leaders and thinkers crystallized, adept in Western intellectual traditions, yet profoundly anchored in their native cultural matrices. This cadre critically scrutinized the merits and moral authority of external domination.

India, by virtue of its demographic magnitude and geopolitical import, emerged as the crucible of anti-colonial dissent. Intellectuals like Dadabhai Naoroji delineated the fiscal hemorrhaging from India to the British coffers. Advocates like Bal Gangadhar Tilak championed the ethos of 'Swaraj' or self-governance. The subsequent decades, particularly the 1920s and 1930s, witnessed the ascendancy of figures like Mahatma Gandhi, whose advocacy for 'Satyagraha' – a commitment to non-violent resistance – became emblematic of India's quest for emancipation.

In the African context, the articulations of nationalism manifested slightly later but with commensurate intensity. Visionaries like Jomo Kenyatta and Kwame Nkrumah emerged as the standard-bearers of African autonomy. Concurrently, the Pan-African ethos envisaged a unified African resistance against the shackles of colonialism.

The Caribbean witnessed an amalgamation of labor-centric movements coalescing with demands for political self-determination. Icons like Marcus Garvey, through the Universal Negro Improvement Association, propagated a narrative of Black empowerment and self-sufficiency, leaving indelible imprints beyond just the Caribbean.

The global conflagrations of the two World Wars inadvertently catalyzed nationalist sentiments. Colonial subjects, having contributed to the wartime efforts with expectations of subsequent political liberalization, discerned the dissonance between wartime rhetorics of liberty and the realities of their subjugation. Such incongruities amplified calls for decolonization.

Following the cessation of the Second World War, Britain confronted escalating fiscal and diplomatic exigencies in retaining its colonies. Coupled with mounting nationalist pressures and evolving international paradigms, the pendulum inexorably swung towards decolonization.

Conclusively, as the luminescence of the British Empire began its inexorable dimming, the luminance of nationalism amplified, signaling the impending culmination of an imperial epoch that spanned continents and centuries.

Complexities of the British Empire's Economic Legacy

Spanning diverse geographies and encompassing a plethora of cultures, the British Empire's economic footprint was both vast and profound. Its overarching dominance in global commerce and finance reshaped the economic contours of regions, seeding the antecedents of the contemporary global economic structure.

The British Empire engineered an extensive framework for global commerce. Many colonies were earmarked for specialized economic functions, delineated by the raw materials they furnished or the markets they provided for British industrial products. This schematic allocation, in many ways, set the preliminary blueprint for the modern-day global trading ecosystem.

Concomitant with the British Industrial Revolution, the appetite for raw materials surged, reinforcing the economic salience of the colonies. These regions became pivotal conduits supplying resources to satiate the industrial machinery of Britain. Illustratively, cotton procured from Indian or Egyptian hinterlands was channeled to the looms of Manchester, metamorphosing into textiles that subsequently permeated global markets.

The diffusion of British economic paradigms and infrastructures was evident across the Empire's expanse. Financial systems, commercial legislative frameworks, and capital market institutions in the colonies mirrored British archetypes. Entities like the East India Company, while instrumental in the imperial enterprise, simultaneously conceptualized the template for the present-day multinational corporate entities.

In juxtaposition to infrastructural advancements such as rail networks, there was undeniable economic depletion experienced by several colonies. A significant tranche of wealth was siphoned off to Britain, engendering capital attrition in numerous colonized territories.

The global conflagrations of the two World Wars imposed formidable economic exigencies on Britain. The aftermath of the First World War witnessed a relative erosion of Britain's economic hegemony, juxtaposed against the ascendant economic trajectory of the United States. To finance these military endeavors, colonies were subjected to onerous fiscal impositions, exacerbating existing economic imbalances.

By the mid-20th century, an amalgam of economic pressures and burgeoning nationalist articulations rendered the colonial territories less as assets and more as encumbrances. The financial burden of sustaining expansive overseas territories, juxtaposed with the emergence of alternate global economic hubs, factored into the calculus leading to the Empire's fragmentation.

In aggregate, the British Empire, while acting as a catalyst for global economic integration and engendering certain infrastructural legacies, concurrently instantiated economic asymmetries. The nexus between imperial economic dividends and colonial exploitation remains a nuanced and contentious facet of the Empire's legacy, subject to intricate academic and political dissections.

Conclusion:
Commonwealth and Cultural Influence

The eclipse of the British Empire's political dominion did not denote the culmination of its influence. Rather, the empire's dissolution engendered a complex tapestry of cultural and institutional legacies, rendering the empire's reach not just territorial but also ideational.

Emerging from the shadows of decolonization was the Commonwealth of Nations. Incepted in 1949, this congregation of erstwhile British territories epitomizes the voluntary allegiance to shared ethos encompassing democracy, human rights, and economic evolution. While devoid of political tethering, the Commonwealth, with the British monarch at its helm, underscores the persisting affiliations forged during the imperial epoch.

An indelible mark of the British Empire is the ascendancy of the English language, evolving into a predominant medium of global communication. This linguistic bequest extends to the literary realm, with authors hailing from former British territories, such as Nigeria's Chinua Achebe or India's Salman Rushdie, augmenting the breadth and depth of English literature with their multifaceted narratives.

Legal architectures in numerous former colonies, spanning India to Canada, carry the hallmarks of British jurisprudence, mirroring the tenets of British common law. Parallelly, the administrative scaffolding in these nations often echoes British bureaucratic paradigms, engendering a modicum of governance congruence across these diverse territories.

The empire's pedagogical initiatives have metamorphosed into premier educational edifices in the post-colonial world. Institutions, whether it be the University of Delhi, the University of the Witwatersrand, or the University of Malaya, trace their genesis to British academic templates and have burgeoned into eminent centers of scholastic pursuit.

Sporting affinities, be it cricket, football, or rugby, disseminated by the British, have entrenched themselves in the cultural psyche of many ex-colonies. Cricket, in nations such as India or the West Indies, has transcended its recreational dimension, morphing into a cultural institution, with matches often evoking historical reminiscences from the imperial era.

The cultural osmosis was bidirectional. As much as the colonies assimilated facets of British culture, the British socio-cultural milieu was permeated by its colonies' artistic, culinary, and musical influences, resulting in a richly interwoven tapestry of shared cultural heritage.

In essence, the British Empire's dissolution did not culminate in its evanescence. Through constructs like the Commonwealth and through profound cultural and institutional legacies, the empire's resonance lingers, shaping, and often complicating, the intricate dynamics between former colonies and Britain.

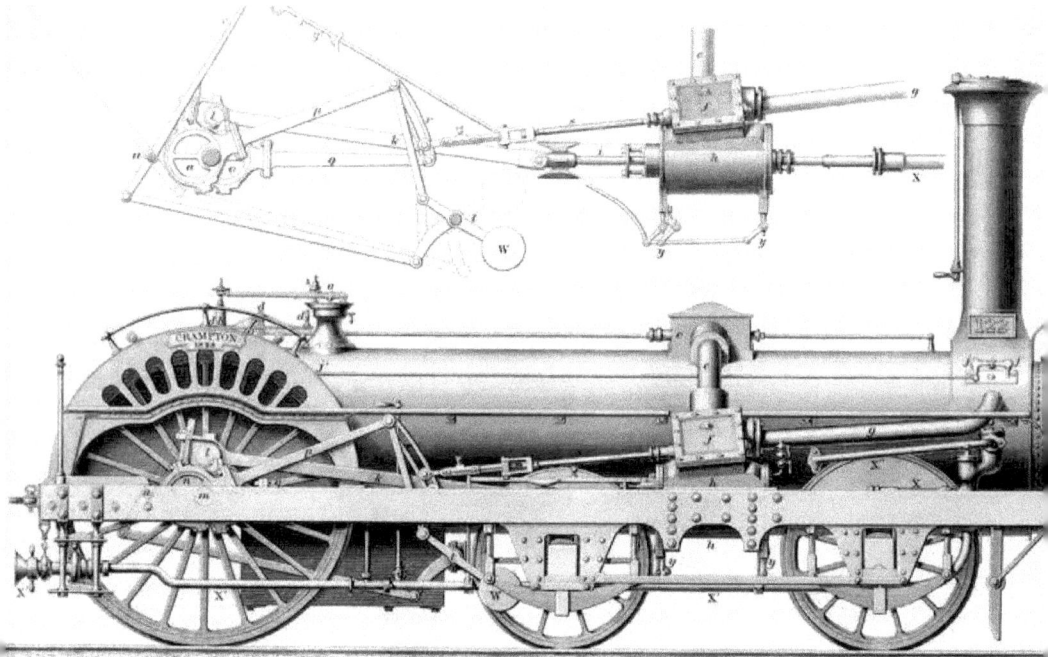

Cramptons Railway Locomotive Engine[28]

Chapter 20.
The 19ᵗʰ Century: Rising Powers and Global Tensions

Politics is the art of the possible

~Otto von Bismarck

The "Long Century": Dynamics and Transformations

The 19ᵗʰ century, frequently characterized as the "long century," encapsulated pivotal transitions on a global scale. As the 1800s unfurled, the British Empire, buoyed by its maritime prowess, sophisticated infrastructural capabilities, and a robust economy underscored by its colonies, augmented its territorial grasp as covered in the previous chapter. By mid-century, its jurisdiction spanned across diverse topographies, from India's pulsating harbors to Africa's expansive landscapes and the frigid stretches of Canada. Markets became repositories of global commodities, English emerged as the prevalent lingua franca in numerous regions, and London crystallized its position as the globe's financial nucleus.

Meanwhile, the United States confronted its internal convulsions. The Civil War, spanning from 1861 to 1865, posed existential challenges to the nation's foundational tenets. The subsequent phase, illuminated by the doctrine of 'Manifest Destiny', witnessed the U.S. extending its reach westwards. By the close of the century, the country had solidified its stature as an industrial behemoth and economic juggernaut.

In Europe, tectonic shifts were palpable. The Germanic territories, traditionally fragmented by linguistic and cultural distinctions, coalesced into the German Empire in 1871. This newly industrialized conglomerate, steered by Otto von Bismarck, exerted a transformative impact on Europe's geopolitical contours. Similarly, the Italian states, united by shared aspirations, cohered into a singular nation, shedding historical parochialism.

Concurrently, the Ottoman Empire, erstwhile a colossus, grappled with diminishing influence. Termed the "sick man of Europe", it was beleaguered by internal discord and external exigencies. The complexities surrounding its territories morphed into the "Eastern Question", interrogating the ramifications of its potential dissolution.

The Industrial Revolution, having germinated in Britain in the late 18th century, permeated globally. Innovations like steamships, railways, and telegraphy metamorphosed trade and communication frameworks. Traditional agrarian orientations gave way to burgeoning urban ecosystems, signaling the advent of a novel, interconnected era.

Post the Napoleonic Wars and subsequent to the Congress of Vienna in 1815, the European continent gravitated towards stability, aided in part by the Concert of Europe. This consortium of diplomatic dialogues, encompassing major European stalwarts, emerged as an arbiter of continental tranquility. Their intent was dual: to arbitrate conflicts and to deter hegemonic ascendancy by any single European power. One of this period's salient legacies was its ability to circumscribe large-scale European confrontations, bolstering the century's image as a phase of comparative pacifism. Nonetheless, beneath this veneer of calm, the intricate lattice of alliances and obligations was surreptitiously laying the groundwork for the profound upheavals of the 20th century, testing long-held assumptions of 19th-century stability.

The Epoch of Technological Transition and Global Power Realignment

As the 19th century evolved, marked by territorial expansions of empires, intricate political maneuverings, and internal societal realignments, it concurrently bore witness to an era of unprecedented technological innovation. The shifts, as elucidated in the preceding section, from the sprawling British Empire's dominance to the consolidation of fragmented European territories, all converged on a strategic landscape transformed by technology. While the geopolitical contours were redrawn through diplomacy and warfare, the very mechanics of these undertakings were being redefined by the epoch of technological transition.

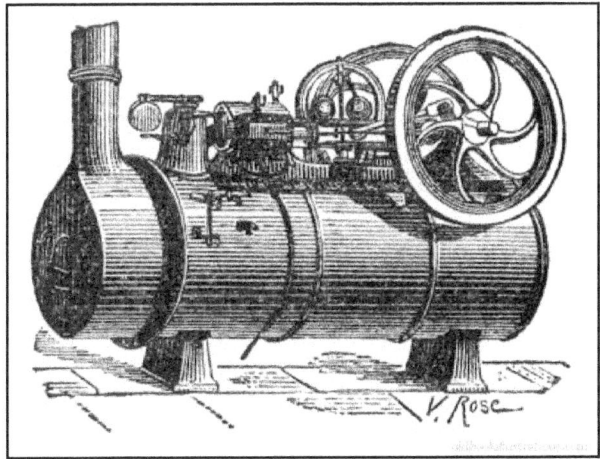

The steam engine, initially fueled by coal and subsequently by oil, epitomized this metamorphosis. This mechanized marvel precipitated a transportation paradigm shift, expediting the translocation of commodities, individuals, and intellectual constructs. Consequently, railways emerged as arterial networks, melding disparate urban centers and engendering a cohesive national fabric.

This railway infrastructure, however, bore ramifications transcending domestic confines. It enhanced not only the rapid deployment capabilities of military contingents but also streamlined resource procurement and dissemination across expansive colonial territories. This logistical prowess fortified imperialistic assertions and control.

Parallel to this, the telegraph materialized as an innovation par excellence in the realm of communication. It dismantled geographical and temporal barriers, enabling instantaneous intercontinental exchanges.

This nascent era heralded an unmatched global integration, rendering the world increasingly interwoven.

Industrialization manifested prominently through the proliferation of factories in urban nuclei, eliciting a significant demographic migration. An exodus from agrarian milieus to industrial epicenters became evident as individuals pursued occupational avenues in manufacturing sectors. This urban influx underscored industrialization's overarching societal reconfiguration.

The concomitant economic ramifications were palpable. Industrialized states enjoyed discernible economic ascendancies. Revenue streams emanating from industrial sectors fortified imperial expansions and augmented military competencies. Consequently, the Industrial Revolution emerged as an impetus for the emergence and consolidation of certain global actors. Their economic vitality invariably segued into military supremacy and territorial annexations.

Furthermore, the era was characterized by a technological contestation among imperial entities. Each vied for supremacy by appropriating avant-garde innovations across diverse domains, including armament, transit, and communication. Technological advancements were inextricably linked with hegemony, and entities averse to adaptation risked obsolescence.

Beyond the archetypal steam engines and telegraphs, the 19th century witnessed a plethora of scientific revelations and engineering accomplishments. Projects such as the Suez Canal's excavation underscored this innovative zeitgeist, amplifying global interconnectivity and reinforcing imperial influence.

In summation, the 19th century was distinguished by its technological strides that bore profound implications on global hegemonic architectures. Industrial dynamism, transportation novelties, and communication breakthroughs collectively redefined the geopolitical terrain. These innovations underpinned the ascendency of specific empires, their territorial consolidations, and prefigured the 20th century's intricate challenges and confrontations. The historical trajectory of empires was intertwined with their adeptness at assimilating these technological shifts to fortify their global prominence.

German Unification and Its Geopolitical Implications

The late 19th-century unification of Germany fundamentally altered the geopolitical landscape of Europe and presaged the seismic shifts that would engulf the world in the 20th century. At the helm of this transformative episode was Otto von Bismarck, Chancellor of Prussia, who navigated through intricate political terrains by employing the principles of Realpolitik. The term, often attributed to Ludwig von Rochau, emphasizes the primacy of power and practical considerations over ideological or ethical constraints. Bismarck's adroit application of these principles enabled him to maneuver within a multipolar European environment to create a unified German nation-state under Prussian leadership.

Otto von Bismarck

Otto von Bismarck's meticulous engineering of geopolitical scenarios was nowhere more evident than in his handling of the Austro-Prussian War of 1866. Recognizing the Austrian Empire as the primary obstacle to Prussian supremacy within the German Confederation, Bismarck skillfully navigated diplomatic channels to isolate Austria. He concluded secret treaties with Italy and exploited tensions over the administration of Schleswig-Holstein, a region both Austria and Prussia had jointly administered since defeating Denmark in 1864. The treaties were tactically designed to disallow the possibility of Austria receiving any significant external support. When war broke out, the Prussian military, empowered by its superior Krupp artillery and efficient railway mobilization, swiftly defeated Austria within seven weeks. The Treaty of Prague formalized Austria's exclusion from German affairs and allowed Prussia to dissolve the old German Confederation, replacing it with the North German Confederation led by Prussia itself. The Austro-Prussian War thus eliminated Austria as a contender for leadership in German-speaking Europe, allowing

Bismarck to orchestrate a federation that excluded Austrian influence but increased Prussian hegemony.

Following the isolation of Austria, Bismarck then focused on consolidating Prussian dominance through a calculated engagement with France, an endeavor epitomized by the Franco-Prussian War of 1870-1871. Bismarck understood that a conflict with France could solidify the union of the southern German states with the North German Confederation, thereby achieving his objective of unification under Prussian aegis. The diplomatic stratagem to achieve this was the Ems Dispatch, a manipulated account of a meeting between King Wilhelm I of Prussia and the French ambassador. Bismarck altered the wording of the original dispatch to make it appear as if both sides had insulted the other, thereby infuriating public sentiments in both France and Prussia. As expected, France declared war, appearing as the aggressor, and thus triggering the defensive alliances between Prussia and the southern German states. Following the eventual capture of Emperor Napoleon III at the Battle of Sedan and the Siege of Paris, the war culminated in the German Empire's proclamation in the Hall of Mirrors at Versailles on January 18, 1871. Through astute maneuvering, particularly his masterful use of the Ems Dispatch as a diplomatic catalyst, Bismarck achieved German unification and significantly altered the European balance of power.

This empire did not merely reflect military triumphs; it also encapsulated Bismarck's nuanced understanding of diplomatic equilibrium. His meticulous crafting of treaties and alliances, such as the Dual Alliance with Austria-Hungary in 1879, the Triple Alliance incorporating Italy in 1882, and the Reinsurance Treaty with Russia in 1887, revealed his capacity to deftly balance power dynamics and protect Germany from the risk of a two-front war. His system functioned as a bulwark against the upheavals that would later unravel the European order.

However, the subsequent misuse of this power serves as a cautionary tale. Following Bismarck's dismissal in 1890, the subsequent stewards of German policy lacked his sagacity and finesse. Notably, they failed to renew the Reinsurance Treaty with Russia, facilitating an environment that led to the diplomatic encirclement Bismarck had diligently sought to prevent.

The shrewdness and subtlety with which Bismarck executed his foreign policy stood in stark contrast to the lack of nuance exhibited by his successors, who proved unable to manage the empire's complex network of alliances and interests, contributing to the catastrophic conflicts of the 20th century.

In summary, the narrative of Germany's rise under Bismarck showcases the dual edge of empire-building. While the Chancellor's Realpolitik forged an entity of unparalleled might, the inability of his successors to responsibly manage this power constituted a critical failing, triggering far-reaching geopolitical disasters. The German example, thus, stands as a complex testament to the ascendancy and vulnerabilities inherent in the lifecycle of global empires, offering a multifaceted perspective on the dynamics of power, statecraft, and historical contingency.

Austro-Hungarian Imperial Endeavors and Regional Confrontations

As Otto von Bismarck masterminded the ascendance of a unified German state through Realpolitik, another European powerhouse, the Austro-Hungarian Empire, navigated its own set of complex challenges.

Over several centuries, the Habsburg dynasty astutely employed matrimonial ties, political schemes, and territorial conquests to establish a diverse empire. By the 1800s, this empire, known as the Austro-Hungarian Monarchy, epitomized a potent political entity. Emperor Franz Joseph I's reign saw the empire's aspirations entwined with burgeoning nationalism and intricate geopolitical dynamics, particularly pronounced in the Balkans.

As previously outlined, Austria's defeat to Prussia in the Austro-Prussian War of 1866 marginalized it in German politics and necessitated a reevaluation of its strategic priorities. The Treaty of Prague, which concluded this conflict, explicitly removed Austria from German affairs and dismantled the German Confederation in favor of the North German Confederation under Prussian hegemony. This strategic setback led the Austro-Hungarian leadership to shift its geopolitical focus, increasingly setting its sights on south-eastern Europe, primarily the ethnically complex and politically fragmented Balkans.

The Balkan Peninsula, rich with a mix of ethnicities and national fervors, became a focal point for the empire's ambitions. Intent on augmenting its territorial hold and reinforcing its dominion, the Austro-Hungarian Empire often found itself in contention with other regional powers. These confrontations ranged from contestations with the declining Ottoman Empire to engagements with a resurgent Russia and nascent nation-states like Serbia and Greece.

However, the empire's Balkan aspirations weren't solely about territorial aggrandizement. While they sought strategic footholds and the region's economic bounty, the leaders also had to grapple with internal resistance. Ethnic constituents within the empire, notably the Serbs and Croats, resisted its expansionist efforts. The empire's measures to suppress these nationalistic uprisings often escalated conflicts, making the Balkan region a veritable tinderbox.

Several events in the late 19th and early 20th centuries underlined the empire's challenges in the Balkans. The annexation of Bosnia and Herzegovina in 1908, previously an Ottoman territory, intensified regional tensions, especially with Serbia. While this annexation expanded the empire's territorial reach, it also planted seeds of broader discord, leading to the larger confrontations that would soon envelop Europe.

The tensions culminated with the assassination of Archduke Franz Ferdinand in Sarajevo in 1914, an event intrinsically linked to the empire's Balkan engagements. This assassination precipitated World War I, leading to the subsequent decline and dissolution of the Austro-Hungarian Empire.

Reflecting upon the Austro-Hungarian Empire's Balkan endeavors provides valuable insights into the complexities faced by 19th-century empires. It exemplifies the intricate balance between imperial ambitions, internal dynamics, and larger global tensions that would fundamentally shape the geopolitical landscape of the 20th century.

Italian Unification and Birth of a Nation State

As Germany coalesced into a formidable nation-state under Bismarck's stewardship and the Austro-Hungarian Empire grappled with its complex geopolitical entanglements, the Italian Peninsula experienced its own transformative journey. Rooted in the aspirations of the Risorgimento—the Italian resurgence—unification evolved as a monumental undertaking aimed at cohering a patchwork of independent states, duchies, and foreign-controlled territories into a singular, autonomous nation-state.

The peninsula, which had been divided since the fall of the Roman Empire, was a mosaic of competing sovereignties, including the Papal States, the Kingdom of the Two Sicilies, and smaller duchies like Modena and Parma. Further complicating matters were the Austrian territories in the north and French influence in various regions. The struggle for Italian unification was, therefore, not only a domestic endeavor but also an intricate interplay with the broader European power dynamics.

Leaders such as Giuseppe Garibaldi, Camillo Benso, Count of Cavour, and Victor Emmanuel II emerged as central figures in this process. Exploiting both diplomatic cunning and military prowess, they succeeded in bringing together these disparate elements through a series of expeditions, plebiscites, and treaties. The Franco-Austrian War of 1859 proved pivotal; its aftermath paved the way for annexations that would ultimately form the Kingdom of Italy in 1861.

However, the achievement of political unification did not instantaneously translate into a consolidated nation-state. The newly formed Italy faced internal divisions along cultural, linguistic, and economic lines. Additionally, the Roman Question—the issue of integrating the Papal States into Italy—lingered, only fully resolved with the capture of Rome in 1870. These challenges underscored the persistent tension between the ideals of national unity and the pragmatic difficulties inherent in amalgamating varied territories and populations.

In the wake of its unification, Italy was acutely aware of its geopolitical vulnerabilities and limited influence on the European stage. As a latecomer to the colonial competition, Italy sought to fortify its international standing through overseas expansion, primarily in Africa. Among its key ambitions was the annexation of Ethiopia, an independent African kingdom that had managed to resist European colonization. Governed by Emperor Menelik II, Ethiopia represented a unique opportunity for Italy to assert its imperial prowess, in line with its European peers. The First Italo-Ethiopian War, initiated in 1895, was marked by Italy's anticipation of an easy victory, heavily underestimating Ethiopian capabilities. Emperor Menelik II skillfully acquired modern weaponry and established a well-trained army, culminating in the Battle of Adwa in 1896, where Italian forces suffered a humiliating defeat. Italy's miscalculations were rooted in both a flawed assessment of Ethiopian military strength and an underestimation of the diplomatic acumen of Menelik II, who had deftly secured military aid and diplomatic recognition. This loss not only stymied Italy's colonial ambitions in East Africa but also damaged its reputation among European powers, reinforcing its status as a secondary power in the imperial hierarchy.

This experience would serve as a formative episode for future Italian leaders. Most notably, Benito Mussolini, who assumed power in the 1920s, sought to rekindle Italy's colonial aspirations, embarking on new imperial ventures in Africa, such as the invasion of Ethiopia in 1935. These later efforts were fueled, in part, by a desire to revise the narrative of Italian imperialism and to compensate for the past humiliations that had marked Italy as a lesser power. However, Mussolini's imperial aspirations in Ethiopia would ultimately lead to international isolation and contribute to Italy's downfall in World War II, demonstrating once again the precarious balance of imperial ambition and geopolitical reality.

Through its trials and triumphs, the formation of the Italian nation-state exemplifies the multifaceted challenges of building a unified country in the broader context of 19th-century European geopolitics. Italy's unification added another layer of complexity to the continental balance of power, affecting alliances and rivalries that would have far-reaching implications in the century to come.

19th Century:
The Nexus of Sociocultural Transformations

The 19th century, marked by rapid sociopolitical alterations, also witnessed deep-seated shifts in the cultural milieu and societal structures. These transitions, often intertwined, played instrumental roles in delineating the course of emerging and declining powers, mirroring the profound global changes of the era.

Nationalism's Dual-Edged Sword: Building States and Breeding Strife

As previously seen, at the forefront of 19th-century shifts was the ascent of nationalism, the conviction that a collective cultural or ethnic identity should predicate political self-determination. This ideology germinated widely across Europe, giving rise to centralized nation-states. While nationalism bolstered the creation of such entities, galvanizing them towards international prominence, it was not without its pitfalls. In multi-ethnic landscapes, fervent nationalist sentiments occasionally bred internal discord and externally, led to territorial expansions, exacerbating global confrontations.

Interestingly, the cyclical nature of history is evident in the recent resurgence of nationalism, often intertwined with populism, in contemporary Western societies. Motivated by factors ranging from economic disparities to cultural unease, this revival presents both an echo of the past and a challenge to modern international cohesion.

Parallel to political shifts, the 19th century's cultural sphere was animated by the Romantic movement. Valuing emotion, individualistic expressions, and connections with nature and heritage, Romanticism deeply permeated art, music, and literature. This movement's proponents—like Beethoven, Tchaikovsky, Scott, and Hugo—created works anchored in their national legacies, thereby strengthening national identities.

More than just domestic celebrations, these Romantic works had international ramifications. As these expressions found global audiences, they bolstered nations' soft power, subtly influencing international perceptions of their cultural gravitas.

The 19th century also heralded significant global migrations, propelled by multifaceted economic, political, and societal triggers. The Industrial Revolution's economic metamorphosis led to urbanization, drawing people to emerging urban hubs or colonies promising better prospects as covered in a previous chapter. Concurrently, political upheavals—ranging from wars to revolutions—instigated population movements.

These migrations had profound implications, both for the migrants' countries of origin and their destinations. Migrants carried with them a tapestry of cultural, linguistic, and traditional elements, fostering a global interconnectedness that would come to define the era.

To encapsulate, the 19th century's social and cultural evolutions were paramount in charting the course of global superpowers. As nationalism carved out potent nation-states, Romanticism enriched their cultural repositories and global appeal. Concurrently, migration patterns reshaped demographic landscapes, weaving a complex tapestry of global interdependence and influence.

Economic Paradigms: Global Networks, Capitalism, and Economic Turbulence

Emerging from the rich socio-cultural fabric of the 19th century — replete with waves of nationalism, Romanticism, and profound global migrations — were parallel and equally transformative economic currents. Just as the artistic and political realms experienced upheavals and evolutions, the economic landscape of this era underwent dramatic shifts, undergirded by new ideologies and punctuated by intermittent crises. These economic developments, while intrinsically linked to the century's sociopolitical changes, held their distinct narratives and consequences.

In the realm of global economics, the establishment of expansive trade networks was seminal. Facilitated by European imperial ambitions, these networks ushered in a new era of intercontinental commerce, facilitating the transfer of goods, innovations, and even cultural mores. Colonies, often relegated to peripheries, became essential cogs, feeding industrializing European powerhouses with raw materials.

Simultaneously, capitalism, with its ethos of private ownership and profit motivation, gained prominence. This economic model promoted innovation, fostering entrepreneurship and ushering in capital inflows. The resultant economic vitality was perhaps best epitomized by the Industrial Revolution, originating in 18th-century Britain and subsequently permeating Europe and other regions. The revolution, powered by technological novelties and advanced manufacturing techniques, transformed industries, augmenting productivity and generating unprecedented affluence.

Bank of England 1823

Yet, the era's economic narrative was not universally buoyant. Interspersed within this period of growth were significant economic downturns, reflective of the vulnerabilities inherent in the burgeoning globalized economic system.

The Panic of 1837 stands out as a particularly poignant illustration. Triggered in the United States by unrestrained speculation in land and infrastructure, its aftermath — bank collapses, insolvencies, and widespread economic distress — was felt globally, highlighting the interconnected fabric of the 19th-century economic milieu.

The Long Depression, spanning nearly two decades from the mid-1870s, further attests to the century's economic fragility. Enveloping multiple industrialized nations, this prolonged recession was marked by deflation, soaring unemployment, and resultant societal discord.

Such crises illuminated the interwoven nature of the 19th-century global economy. Economic tremors in one region often had ripple effects, impacting distant shores. These episodes not only underscored the need for improved economic foresight but also precipitated efforts in devising contemporary financial frameworks aimed at dampening future economic shocks.

As the 19th century ebbed, it left an indelible imprint on global economic structures. The interplay of burgeoning industrialization, capitalism, and recurring economic crises redefined societal structures, economic models, and geopolitical hierarchies. This intricate intermeshing of economic forces and events carved the path for the subsequent century, laying the groundwork for evolving quests for economic supremacy and international influence.

Political Movements and Revolutions

Intersecting the transformative economic currents of the 19th century—described in the preceding section—were the political ideologies that would come to define the era. The symbiotic relationship between economic paradigms and political ideologies can hardly be overstated; the structures of capitalism, industrialization, and global trade networks did not simply coexist with but were actively shaped by political beliefs and actions. As economic frameworks wrought societal shifts and influenced geopolitical power balances, they simultaneously acted as a fertile ground for the rise and proliferation of political ideologies. It is within this context of deeply intertwined economic and political landscapes that we turn our focus to the dominant political ideologies of the 19th century: Liberalism, Socialism, and Conservatism.

These belief systems, with their divergent visions of societal structure and governance, would influence global politics profoundly, setting the trajectory for future political evolutions.

Emerging from the Enlightenment's crucible, **Liberalism** espoused the tenets of individual rights, freedom, and minimalistic governmental interference. The intellectual foundation for liberalism was fortified by luminaries such as John Locke, Adam Smith, and John Stuart Mill, who championed representative governance, adherence to the rule of law, and the safeguarding of civil liberties.

The real-world manifestation of liberal principles can be discerned in epochal events such as the American Revolution of 1776, which culminated in the establishment of a nation underpinned by these tenets. The French Revolution, too, with its clarion call of "Liberté, égalité, fraternité," was emblematic of liberal aspirations, despite the tumultuous pathways it sometimes undertook.

In juxtaposition to liberalism's focus on individual freedoms, **socialism** germinated as a counter-response to the disparities and inequities birthed by the 19th century's industrial acceleration. The socialist paradigm emphasized collective ownership of productive resources and wealth redistribution to engender enhanced social and economic parity. This ideological edifice was constructed on the theoretical scaffolding provided by visionaries like Karl Marx and Friedrich Engels.

Socialism resonated profoundly within the precincts of labor movements and unions, which rallied for enhanced working conditions, equitable wages, and robust social safety mechanisms. Events such as the 1871 Paris Commune and the 1917 Russian Revolution epitomized the realization of socialist aspirations, albeit with varying degrees of success and longevity.

In contradistinction to the transformative zeal of liberalism and socialism, **conservatism** emerged as a bulwark against rapid and radical metamorphosis. It advocated for the sustenance of entrenched social stratifications and venerated institutions. Key figures, notably Edmund Burke, delineated conservative tenets, underscoring the imperative for incrementalism and deference to traditional paradigms.

The tangible impact of conservatism can be discerned in endeavors to reinstate established orders, such as the monarchical re-establishments post the Napoleonic epoch and the resistance to burgeoning liberal and socialist ideologies. The conservative doctrine profoundly influenced political institution-building and cultural heritage preservation.

Throughout the 19th century, this triad of political ideologies locked horns both theoretically and pragmatically. Debates concerning governance modalities, wealth stratification, and civil liberties delineated the century's political topography. In certain instances, these ideological clashes engendered seismic shifts, prompting revolutionary movements and engendering geopolitical reconfigurations.

The ideological legacy of the 19th century would cast a long shadow over the ensuing century. Liberal democracies, socialist regimes, and conservative movements would perpetually engage in ideological and sometimes physical confrontations. Their philosophical constructs would indelibly shape global political trajectories, testament to their enduring relevance and impact.

Conclusion:
End of the Century and Looking Forward

As the 19th century waned, a profound metamorphosis had suffused every facet of human society, sculpting the contours for the monumental events of the impending century. The global tapestry was marked by a rich tableau of geopolitical entities, each maneuvering for prominence. European powers, having cast expansive colonial nets, influenced vast swaths of territories. The British Empire's reach was especially noteworthy, stretching across numerous time zones, while empires like France, Germany, and Russia were not far behind in their colonial endeavors.

Asia presented a contrast: China's historical stature as the "Middle Kingdom" was ebbing, besieged by a mélange of internal tumult and external intrusions. Conversely, Japan was charting an ascendant trajectory, rejuvenating its institutional mechanisms and fortifying its military capabilities.

Parallel to these geopolitical shifts, the 19th century was emblematic of economic dynamism, with Western Europe and the United States at its vanguard. Technological marvels like the steam engine and the telegraph revolutionized manufacturing, transport, and communication, heralding an era characterized by capitalist-driven mass production. Yet, this economic renaissance was not without its fissures. While substantial sections experienced enhanced living standards, the era also exacerbated socioeconomic disparities. Economic downturns, notably the economic stagnation of the 1870s and the 1893 financial upheaval, highlighted the vulnerabilities of these burgeoning economic systems.

As the century's end neared, a confluence of geopolitical, socio-economic, and ideological currents began to manifest. The intense scramble among European dominions for colonial territories, especially in Africa, hinted at potential future confrontations. Diplomatic interventions, such as the 1878 Congress of Berlin, sought to mediate territorial disputes and recalibrate power dynamics. Yet, these endeavors further underscored the intricacies of alliance structures and territorial ambitions.

The resurgence of nationalism, invigorated by distinct ethnic identities and aspirations, further muddled the European political landscape, introducing new arenas of potential conflict. Coupled with this was an escalating militaristic fervor, particularly palpable between Germany and the UK. This arms race, marked by burgeoning naval and military outlays and novel military technologies, underscored an impending climate ripe for conflict.

The intricate lattice of alliances further complicated this landscape. European powers found themselves ensnared in a web of commitments, suggesting that localized disputes could potentially metamorphose into larger conflagrations.

As the 19th century segued into the 20th, the world stood at a transformative crossroads. Ideological paradigms of liberalism, socialism, and conservatism, which had been instrumental in shaping the century's political ethos, now faced imminent real-world challenges. The shifting geopolitical landscape, underscored by the emergence of new power hubs and the realignment of traditional ones, was poised to profoundly influence the accounts of the 20th century. While the era of the 19th century was undoubtedly one of progress and enlightenment, its concluding chapters were tinged with the shadows of impending conflicts. The world was on the brink of witnessing not just global wars of unparalleled scale but also a significant reconfiguration of global power dynamics. The legacies of the 19th century, in all their multifaceted glory and complexity, undeniably set the stage for the tumultuous century that was to follow.

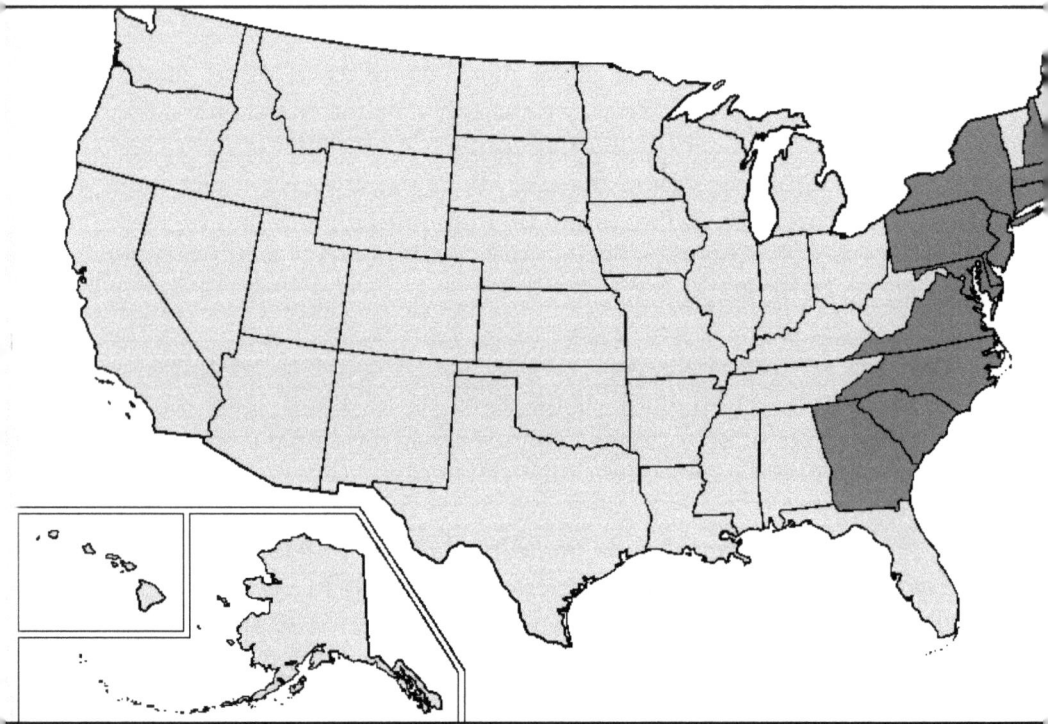

United States Now and Oriiginal Thirteen Colonies[29]

Chapter 21.
The United States: From Colony to Superpower (17th-21st Centuries)

Speak softly and carry a big stick

~Theodore Roosevelt

Introduction

The metamorphosis of the United States from a cluster of 13 disparate colonies to a global behemoth offers an enlightening case study in the rise of powers on the world stage. Positioned on the eastern seaboard of North America, these colonies were initially established primarily for mercantile and, to a lesser degree, religious purposes by European powers in the late 16th and early 17th centuries. The analysis of the factors that fostered unity among these colonies, notwithstanding their distinct regional cultures and economic systems, reveals a blend of geo-political, ideological, and economic drivers. As the 18th century drew to a close, a confluence of events – primarily the imposition of unsympathetic policies by the British crown – catalyzed a revolutionary spirit among these colonies, propelling them toward independence.

The subsequent history of the United States is replete with expansive territorial ambitions, deft diplomatic maneuvers, rapid industrial growth, and pivotal military engagements. The nation's westward drive, later termed as 'Manifest Destiny,' underscored an intrinsic belief in territorial and ideological expansion. The bitter Civil War in the mid-19th century, which threatened the very fabric of the young nation, eventually yielded a consolidated federal structure, with ramifications for the nation's subsequent global outlook.

Industrialization further catalyzed the United States' ascent on the global stage. By harnessing vast natural resources, adopting technological innovations, and fostering a robust entrepreneurial spirit, the U.S. rapidly transformed into an industrial powerhouse. As the 20th century dawned, the nation found itself drawn into global conflicts that would challenge and later cement its role as a dominant power. Its interventions in the World Wars, its leadership in establishing a new world order post-1945, and its ideological confrontations during the Cold War era underscore its meteoric rise to superpower status.

This chapter aims to elucidate the intricate processes and decisions that culminated in the United States' ascent from 13 fledgling colonies to a preeminent global power. By examining this trajectory within the broader context of global geopolitics and comparing it to other powers' journeys, we can gain invaluable insights into the mechanics of statecraft and power dynamics on the world stage.

Foundations:
The American Revolution and Independence

To understand the complexities that led to the United States' transformation from 13 disparate colonies to a unified, global power, one must delve into the seminal events that initially propelled these colonies toward independence. In particular, the culmination of British fiscal policies, regional economic dependencies, and the broader geopolitical landscape of the mid-18th century created a fertile ground for revolutionary sentiments.

The colonies, each with their unique economic and cultural attributes, coalesced into a single entity capable of challenging British hegemony, thereby setting in motion a series of events that would define their collective identity and global ambitions for centuries to come. New England, for instance, was characterized by its reliance on trade and shipbuilding, the Middle colonies by their multifaceted agricultural output, and the Southern colonies by their plantation economies anchored in crops like tobacco and cotton. Yet, these varied economic paradigms were intricately woven into the tapestry of the broader Atlantic trade system, a network that Britain predominantly orchestrated.

Britain's geopolitical maneuvers, especially its victory in the Seven Years' War (1756-1763), eradicated the looming French menace to its American possessions. However, the spoils of war came at a cost—Britain was saddled with a monumental debt. In a bid to offset this fiscal strain, Parliament, in a sequence of moves that might be perceived as myopic in the hindsight of history, enacted policies like the Sugar Act (1764) and the Stamp Act (1765), levying fresh duties on the colonies. The colonies, long accustomed to a modicum of legislative self-determination, construed these fiscal interventions as transgressions of their inherent rights. The sentiment was succinctly captured in their rallying cry, "no taxation without representation."

As the colonies grappled with their colonial overlords, it is worth noting that revolutionary impulses were not confined to North America. Although the French Revolution would not commence until 1789, years after the start of the American Revolution, the intellectual and cultural currents that would lead to that upheaval were already gaining momentum in Europe. As covered in chapter 18, the writings of Enlightenment philosophers, such as Voltaire, Montesquieu, and Rousseau, who questioned traditional authority and championed individual liberties, had gained considerable traction. Even though the direct impact of these European ideas on the American Revolution is a subject of ongoing scholarly debate, there is a consensus that the revolutionary spirit was part of a broader ideological shift that transcended national boundaries. This milieu of transformative thought contributed to the larger 18th-century narrative of challenging established structures of power, in which both the American and later the French revolutions were seminal episodes.

The colonial pushback against these British edicts was multifaceted. Economic boycotts, civil petitions, and radical actions such as the

Boston Tea Party coalesced to form a continuum of resistance. The British reaction, particularly with the implementation of the Coercive Acts in 1774, rather than calming the colonies, heightened the tensions. Thus, when the delegates of the First Continental Congress gathered later that year, there was a discernible shift from isolated regional agitations to a unified front against British overreach. The skirmishes at Lexington and Concord in April 1775 were emblematic of this transition, propelling the colonies from political dissidence to armed confrontation. April 1775 marks the official start of the American Revolution.

Boston Tea Party[30]

The war, spanning eight years, was not confined to the American theater. It drew into its vortex other global powers—France and Spain—who viewed the conflict as an avenue to undercut Britain. The American victory, ratified by the Treaty of Paris in 1783, was a product not solely of their martial competence but was significantly abetted by Britain's overextension in multiple theaters and by the diplomatic acumen of the American leadership.

With the yoke of colonial rule discarded, the nascent United States confronted an equally daunting task: the melding of thirteen diverse entities into a unified polity. The initial framework to achieve this, the Articles of Confederation, was found wanting, particularly in mediating fiscal and territorial disputes. The subsequent Constitutional Convention of 1787, therefore, was a crucible of negotiation and visionary statecraft. The outcome, the U.S. Constitution, fashioned a federal edifice with delineated powers and safeguards, thereby laying the institutional bedrock for the nation's future endeavors, both domestic and global.

In reflecting upon the American Revolution and the ensuing quest for nationhood, it is evident that the saga was underpinned by a complex matrix of local exigencies, overarching global geopolitics, and the strategic sagacity of its leaders. This intricate dance set the stage for the United States to both challenge and interface with established global powers in a multitude of arenas, a theme that will be recurrent as the narrative of its journey unfolds.

Westward Expansion and Manifest Destiny

The late 18th and 19th centuries in U.S. history were defined by an inexorable westward expansion, predicated on a potent blend of economic aspirations, geopolitical considerations, and a deep-seated ideological conviction, often articulated as 'Manifest Destiny.' This term, coined in the 1840s, encapsulated the belief that the United States was divinely ordained to spread its unique brand of republicanism and civilization across the North American continent.

The starting point of this westward trajectory was the Louisiana Purchase in 1803. Facing economic pressures and military challenges in Europe, particularly from Britain, Napoleon Bonaparte of France opted to liquidate his North American possessions. President Thomas Jefferson, recognizing the geostrategic value of the Mississippi River and New Orleans as crucial conduits for the agricultural produce of the American heartland, commissioned envoys to negotiate. The outcome surpassed their mandate: for a sum of $15 million, the United States acquired an expanse that nearly doubled its territorial size. This vast tract, stretching from the Mississippi River to the Rocky Mountains, not only bolstered the country's agrarian economy but also established a precedent for territorial acquisitions through diplomatic channels.

The annexation of Texas followed a more convoluted trajectory. Initially, a part of Spanish Mexico, Texas witnessed an influx of Anglo-American settlers during the early 19th century, often with the tacit encouragement of the Mexican authorities who sought to bolster the region's economy. However, cultural and political discord between the settlers and the Mexican government, especially after the centralization reforms of President Santa Anna, culminated in the Texan War of Independence (1835-1836). The Republic of Texas, established in the aftermath, angled for annexation by the United States. The process was protracted, fraught with concerns about the balance between slave-holding and free states, and the potential for conflict with Mexico. The eventual annexation in 1845 proved to be a catalyst for the Mexican-American War (1846-1848).

The Mexican-American War, spurred by territorial disputes in Texas and American ambitions in California and the Southwest, was a seminal moment in U.S.-Mexico relations. The Treaty of Guadalupe Hidalgo, which concluded the conflict, ceded vast territories, including modern-day California, Arizona, New Mexico, and parts of Colorado, Nevada, and Utah, to the United States. This acquisition further augmented the nation's territorial expanse and laid the groundwork for its transcontinental ambitions.

Parallel to these diplomatic and military endeavors was the migration along the Oregon Trail. Stretching over 2,000 miles from Missouri to Oregon, this route was traversed by settlers, often enduring arduous conditions, lured by the promise of fertile land in the Pacific Northwest. Their presence, and the concurrent British interest in the region, led to the Oregon Treaty of 1846, which established the U.S.-Canada border at the 49th parallel, ceding modern-day Washington, Oregon, and Idaho to the United States.

However, this westward push was not without profound consequences. Native American tribes, long the inhabitants of these territories, confronted a dual challenge: settlers encroaching on their lands and federal policies oscillating between assimilation and removal. The displacement of tribes, epitomized by events like the Trail of Tears, where the Cherokee Nation was forcibly relocated from the Southeastern United States to present-day Oklahoma, is a somber chapter in this narrative. The expansion also precipitated conflicts over the institution of slavery, setting the stage for sectional tensions in the nation.

In conclusion, the period of westward movement, championed by the concept of Manifest Destiny, critically molded the framework of the budding American nation. While it paved the way for the United States to establish its continental footprint and realize its economic potential, it also sowed the seeds for internal discord and posed ethical questions about its treatment of indigenous populations and the environment.

Civil War and Reconstruction

The period spanning the U.S. Civil War (1861-1864) and Reconstruction stands as a pivotal juncture in the nation's history, profoundly influencing its subsequent trajectory across the political, social, and economic spectrum.

The roots of the Civil War were deeply entrenched in the complex socio-economic fabric of the antebellum era. The institution of slavery was not merely a component of Southern society but its very foundation, underpinning the plantation economy and influencing cultural and political dynamics. By the mid-19th century, it had evolved beyond just an economic system, finding validation and defense through diverse means, from economic argumentation to religious justifications.

Yet, the factors precipitating the war were more nuanced than a simple dichotomy over slavery. As the Northern states rapidly industrialized, having largely phased out slavery, their interests began diverging from the agrarian South. This divergence manifested in numerous disputes, from tariffs and banking policies to investments in infrastructure. Amplifying these tensions was the growing abolitionist sentiment in the North, spurred by moral arguments and emblematic incidents, such as the wide-reaching impact of Harriet Beecher Stowe's "Uncle Tom's Cabin."

In tandem with these palpable disputes, a broader philosophical debate emerged, encompassing states' rights and federal authority. The South, with its robust interpretation of states' rights, contended that the Union was essentially a compact among sovereign states. According to this viewpoint, any perceived federal overreach could be contested, and in extreme cases, even nullified by individual states. This perspective was evident in events like the Nullification Crisis during the 1830s. During this crisis, South Carolina, under the leadership of figures like John C. Calhoun, asserted that it had the right to declare certain federal tariffs null and void within its borders. This challenge to federal authority foreshadowed the looming broader conflict over states' rights, which would be a significant spark igniting the Civil War.

The subsequent decade only heightened these rifts. The Compromise of 1850, aimed at settling issues related to the newly acquired territories from the Mexican-American War, and the controversial Fugitive Slave Act, which mandated the return of escaped slaves to their owners, were but fleeting solutions. However, rather than alleviating tensions, they added fuel to the fire.

In 1854, the passage of the Kansas-Nebraska Act further strained national unity. This legislation championed the idea of popular sovereignty, allowing settlers in these territories to decide whether they would allow slavery or not. This approach led to a bitter and violent contest in the Kansas Territory, known as "Bleeding Kansas," where pro-slavery and anti-slavery settlers clashed over the future status of slavery in the region.

The breaking point came with the 1860 election of Abraham Lincoln. While Lincoln initially took a stance against the expansion of slavery into new territories rather than disrupting it where it already existed, many in the South perceived him as an abolitionist. These fears, along with long-standing tensions over states' rights, led to secession by Southern states and the eventual formation of the Confederate States of America. This culminated in the outbreak of the American Civil War.

In the midst of these escalating tensions, the nation found itself at the precipice of a monumental conflict. The outbreak of the American Civil War in 1861 would come to define an era of unprecedented division and bloodshed. As North and South clashed on the battlefield over issues of slavery, states' rights, and the future of the Union, the war would exact a heavy toll on the nation. It was a conflict where ideals and ideologies collided, ultimately reshaping the destiny of the United States. When the war finally concluded in 1865, with the Union emerging victorious, it marked the end of an era and the beginning of a challenging period of Reconstruction.

The war's aftermath brought its own set of challenges. Reconstruction, stretching until 1877, sought to reconcile a broken nation and define the status of millions of freed African Americans. Initially, President Andrew Johnson's lenient policies, such as the Black Codes aimed at restricting freedmen's rights, faced vehement opposition. The Radical Republicans in Congress countered with policies enforcing equality and protecting the rights of African Americans. The resulting 14th Amendment in 1868 offered citizenship to all native-born or naturalized individuals, ensuring equal protection, while the 15th Amendment in 1870 was a step towards securing voting rights for African American men.

However, as Reconstruction progressed, resistance grew. The emergence of groups like the Ku Klux Klan sought to restore white supremacy through violence and intimidation. The Compromise of 1877, resolving the contentious 1876 presidential election, marked the end of Reconstruction, allowing the South to implement the "Jim Crow" laws, entrenching racial segregation and disenfranchisement.

Upon reflection, the Reconstruction era, despite its ambitious aims to reshape the nation's civic principles and extend rights to African Americans, leaves behind a complex legacy. The era's conclusion came prematurely, and this premature ending had lasting repercussions. It entrenched racial hierarchies in the South, where economic and infrastructural challenges stemming from the Civil War continued to hinder the region's growth and modernization for decades to come. This meant that many of the Reconstruction era's objectives were left incomplete, leaving a mixed and unresolved impact on the nation's history.

Industrialization and the Gilded Age

The period following the Civil War until the turn of the 20th century witnessed the United States' rapid transition from an agrarian society to an industrialized nation. This era, often referred to as the Gilded Age, was characterized by significant technological innovations, the growth of big business, and stark economic disparities. The fervent pace of industrialization, coupled with the challenges it posed, laid the groundwork for progressive reforms in the subsequent years.

Post-Civil War America provided fertile ground for industrial growth. The abundance of natural resources, a burgeoning population fueling labor and demand, an expanding transportation network, and influxes of foreign capital set the stage for rapid industrialization. Several inventors and innovations marked this era, underpinning the United States' emergence as a global industrial powerhouse.

In 1876, Alexander Graham Bell's groundbreaking invention of the telephone revolutionized communication, allowing people to connect across vast distances as never before. Thomas Edison, a prolific inventor, left an indelible mark on daily life and industrial processes. His innovations, which included the phonograph, the incandescent light bulb, and the development of a comprehensive electrical distribution system, transformed the way people lived and worked. These inventions illuminated homes, brought music and audio recording into households, and powered industries. Concurrently, the Bessemer process, pioneered and refined by industrialists like Andrew Carnegie, played a pivotal role in lowering the cost of steel production. This dramatic reduction in steel manufacturing costs catalyzed infrastructural and urban developments that reshaped the landscape of the United States during the Gilded Age.

The railroad industry epitomized the industrial boom. The completion of the transcontinental railroad in 1869 not only facilitated coast-to-coast travel but also expedited the movement of goods, people, and ideas. This, in turn, enabled the growth of industries and the opening of vast western territories to commercial exploitation.

The celebration of the completion of the first transcontinental railroad, May 10, 1869[31]

However, the transformative nature of the industrial revolution was not without its societal repercussions. Urban centers swelled, often leading to overcrowded and unsanitary living conditions. Laborers, including significant numbers of women and children, often worked in hazardous environments for meager wages, leading to calls for labor reforms and the birth of the American labor movement.

The latter part of the 19th century saw the ascendancy of powerful industrialists, often termed "robber barons" due to their ruthless business tactics. Figures such as John D. Rockefeller, Andrew Carnegie, and J.P. Morgan exemplified the era's capitalist ethos. Their endeavors led to the formation of vast corporate empires in oil, steel, and banking, respectively.

These magnates often utilized trusts and holding companies to monopolize entire industries. By controlling all aspects of production and distribution, they could dictate prices and sideline competitors. Such monopolistic practices often resulted in reduced competition, stymied innovation, and were detrimental to consumers and small businesses.

Public outcry against these trusts, combined with investigative journalism exposing corporate malpractices, known as "muckraking," laid the foundation for the Progressive Era reforms. The federal government responded by enacting antitrust legislation, such as the Sherman Antitrust Act of 1890, aimed at curbing monopolistic business practices. Subsequent legislations, like the Clayton Antitrust Act of 1914, further sought to promote competition and protect consumers, workers, and small businesses.

Furthermore, Progressive reforms tackled a range of societal issues exacerbated by rapid industrialization. Initiatives aimed at improving urban living conditions, advancing workers' rights, and promoting ethical business practices. The establishment of regulatory bodies, such as the Interstate Commerce Commission (ICC) and the Food and Drug Administration (FDA), exemplified the growing recognition of the need for regulatory oversight in an increasingly complex industrial society.

In sum, the Gilded Age, with its dramatic economic growth and associated challenges, set the stage for a series of reforms that sought to balance the benefits of industrial capitalism with its social costs. The push and pull between laissez-faire principles and regulatory interventions would continue to shape the American economic landscape in the decades that followed.

Ideological Intersections: U.S. Universalism Vs. European Balance of Power

The ascendency of the United States in the 19th and early 20th centuries was not merely an isolated phenomenon; it intersected and often clashed with prevailing European notions of international relations and statecraft, particularly the concept of the balance of power. European geopolitics, which had its roots in the treaties of Westphalia in 1648, was largely predicated on maintaining equilibrium among nations to prevent hegemony. This philosophy was institutionalized through a series of congresses and treaties, the most notable being the Congress of Vienna in 1815, which sought to create a balance of power among European states to avert the recurrence of Napoleonic imperialism.

Contrastingly, the United States, influenced by its own historical trajectory, manifested a kind of universalism that diverged from the traditional European approach. As exemplified by Theodore Roosevelt and later presidents, American universalism espoused the spread of democracy, free markets, and individual liberties both domestically and abroad. This ideological underpinning was a natural extension of the nation's founding principles and the Manifest Destiny that guided its continental expansion.

For the United States, this universalism was not merely an ideal; it was often operationalized through foreign policy. The Monroe Doctrine of 1823, for example, rejected European interference in the Americas, effectively countering the European balance of power with a form of hemispheric hegemony. Similarly, the Roosevelt Corollary expanded the Monroe Doctrine to justify American intervention throughout the Western Hemisphere, thus reinforcing the notion that American principles should hold universal applicability.

This ideological divergence had significant implications for both American and European approaches to statecraft and geopolitics. While the European powers engaged in complex alliances and counter-alliances to maintain equilibrium, the United States progressively moved toward a policy of interventionism, both in its hemisphere and beyond, as evidenced by its role in World War I and later conflicts.

It is crucial to note that the two approaches were not always mutually exclusive but interacted in complex ways. The United States, for instance, became a critical component of the balance of power during and after World War II, underpinning a new international order through institutions like the United Nations. Meanwhile, European nations began to incorporate elements of American universalism, especially as decolonization and the Cold War reshaped the global landscape.

In summary, the ideological underpinnings of the United States and European powers provided both contrasts and intersections that influenced international relations and the art of statecraft for centuries to come. By examining these ideological frameworks side by side, one can better understand the unique trajectory that propelled the United States from a nascent republic to a global superpower. The adoption, adaptation, and sometimes rejection of these ideologies offer vital insights into the intricacies of geopolitics and the complex web of factors that contribute to the rise and sustenance of global powers.

Conclusion:
Reflecting on the U.S.'s Tumultuous Journey

As this chapter has demonstrated, the transformation of the United States from a collective of 13 colonies into a global superpower unfolded through a series of interconnected developments, encompassing revolutionary fervor, territorial expansion, industrial prowess, and geopolitical maneuvering. The ideological foundation, rooted in the principles of democracy and individual liberty, provided the impetus for a distinctive form of universalism that contrasted markedly with the prevailing European philosophy of balance of power. These divergent frameworks had implications not only for domestic governance but also for international relations and geopolitics, thereby highlighting the United States as a critical case study in the broader canvas of the rise, reign, and, potentially, the decline of global powers.

Starting with the late 18th-century revolutionary aspirations for independence from British rule, the young nation evolved through the challenging terrains of Civil War and Reconstruction to forge a more cohesive and centralized governmental structure. These internal consolidations were paralleled by territorial expansions justified through the doctrine of Manifest Destiny, which had both pragmatic and ideological dimensions. This expansion came at significant human costs, particularly for Native Americans and Mexicans, whose lands were usurped and annexed.

The industrial era ushered in an unprecedented period of economic growth and technological innovation, setting the stage for the United States to become a significant actor on the global stage. The ideological paradigms that guided this ascent—captured, for instance, in Theodore Roosevelt's robust form of American universalism—interacted with, challenged, and at times even aligned with European models of statecraft, adding complex layers to international relations in the 19th and 20th centuries.

President Theodore Roosevelt, 1904[32]

In this narrative, it becomes apparent that the rise of the United States was not a straightforward or inevitable progression but a series of strategic choices, adaptations, and at times, fortuitous circumstances. The nation's journey is emblematic of the dynamic interplay of internal and external forces that shape the trajectory of global powers.

Thus, by examining the evolution of the United States within the complex milieu of domestic imperatives and international pressures, and by juxtaposing its ideological frameworks against those of European powers, this chapter contributes to a more nuanced understanding of the mechanisms of power dynamics on a global scale. It underscores the necessity of adopting a multifaceted approach to statecraft, one that incorporates not just military and economic dimensions but also ideological and cultural factors, to fully comprehend the cyclical patterns of rise, reign, and potential decline that characterize the histories of world powers.

Chapter 22.
World War I: The Shifting of Global Power (1914-1918)

The world must be made safe for democracy.

~Woodrow Wilson

Introduction:
The First Global War and the Imperial Stage

At the dawn of the 20th century, the world was dominated by mighty empires, their spheres of influence stretching across continents. The unfolding of World War I would mark a turning point, shaking the foundations of these empires and forever altering the global power dynamics.

The prelude to war was characterized by a delicate power balance among European nations, teetering on the edge of conflict. Imperial ambitions fueled by intense rivalries and entangling alliances served as combustible elements awaiting a spark. The stage was set for an unprecedented clash.

By 1914, tensions reached their climax. The assassination of Archduke Franz Ferdinand of Austria-Hungary in Sarajevo triggered a chain reaction of events, leading to a declaration of war. The Great War had begun.

Soon, major battles erupted in various corners of the globe, vividly illustrating the grandeur and vulnerability of empires. The Central Powers, led by the Austro-Hungarian and Ottoman Empires, faced formidable challenges along their frontlines. These empires struggled to maintain their grasp over diverse territories and navigate the intricate web of alliances formed against them. On the opposing side, the Allied Empires, including Britain, France, and Russia, found themselves entangled in a war that would test the limits of their power and influence. These empires deployed their vast resources and colonial troops to defend their interests and expand their reach. The battle lines stretched across Europe, Asia, and Africa, showcasing the immense scale of imperial warfare.

As the war progressed, the titans of empires began to crumble. The Austro-Hungarian Empire faced internal strife and ethnic tensions that ultimately led to its collapse. The Ottoman Empire, once a formidable force, saw its territories in the Middle East gradually slip away, planting the seeds for future dynamics in the region. Meanwhile, the Russian Revolution ushered in a new era of Soviet power, challenging traditional notions of empire and sparking ideological shifts that reverberated worldwide.

In the midst of this global conflict, a new power emerged on the scene: the United States. Initially reluctant to enter the war, America's involvement proved decisive in tipping the scales towards victory for the Allies. This emerging power signaled a shift in the balance of global forces and set the stage for its ascendance as a superpower in the following decades.

The aftermath of World War I witnessed the redrawing of empires. The Treaty of Versailles laid out the terms for peace, but its impact resonated far beyond Europe. Germany faced harsh sanctions, both economic and territorial, that left lasting scars. Additionally, mandates were established, and new nations emerged from the ashes of fallen empires. The clamor for self-determination grew louder as people sought to determine their own destinies in an age marked by decolonization and shifting allegiances.

World War I not only catalyzed the decline of empires but also brought about fundamental changes in the concept of sovereignty. As nations grappled with the consequences of imperial warfare, a new sense of national identity took hold. Boundaries were redefined, allegiances shifted, and aspirations for independence grew stronger. The legacy of World War I would linger on, shaping the trajectory of nations and serving as a poignant reminder of the fragile nature of empires when confronted with global conflict.

In this chapter, we embark on a journey through the pivotal events of World War I, exploring its catastrophic impact on empires and the subsequent reshuffling of global power structures. By examining key battles, the fall of empires, and the emergence of new powers, we shed light on the profound changes that swept through the world during this tumultuous time. World War I stands as a defining moment in the ongoing saga of empires through time, leaving an indelible mark on history's grand narrative.

The European Power Balance

As the 20th century dawned, the concept of the balance of power governed the intricate interplay of European states. Rooted in historical precedents dating back to the Treaty of Westphalia in 1648, which marked the end of the Thirty Years' War and laid the foundations for the modern international system, the balance-of-power mechanism operated as a fulcrum around which European states maneuvered. This European approach was geared towards maintaining stability by ensuring that no single power could dominate the continent, thus averting the concentration of hegemony and mitigating the propensity for conflict.

By the early 20th century, the political landscape of Europe was characterized by a complex network of alliances and treaties, buttressed by a web of diplomatic accords and military pacts. The Dual Alliance between Germany and Austria-Hungary in 1879, followed by the Triple Alliance with the inclusion of Italy in 1882, stood in direct opposition to the Franco-Russian Alliance of 1894 and later the Triple Entente, which added the United Kingdom to the Franco-Russian axis in 1907. These opposing blocs served as the cornerstone of European geopolitics, epitomizing the entrenched rivalries among the continent's leading powers.

While these alliances were ostensibly designed to deter aggression, they also had the unintended consequence of rendering the political environment increasingly brittle. The balance of power was now a precarious construct, susceptible to disruption by small-scale events due to the highly interdependent nature of the alliances. Adding to this complexity, military doctrines of the time, like Germany's Schlieffen Plan, were built on the foundation of rapid mobilization and offensive operations, which left little opportunity for diplomatic negotiations once the gears of war were set in motion.

Economic factors also shaped the European power balance, as industrialization had led to an arms race among major powers. Advances in weaponry and the mobilization of resources accentuated the stakes of any potential conflict. Britain's naval prowess, Germany's growing industrial might, and France's colonial resources all contributed to a sense of impending tension, effectively stoking the fires beneath the smoldering cauldron of European politics.

The balance-of-power system, which had historically served as a stabilizing force, thus faced unprecedented challenges as the 20th century commenced. Diplomatic failures, rapid militarization, and the rigidity of alliance systems made the European power balance increasingly vulnerable. This fragility set the stage for a conflict of epic proportions, the spark for which would arrive with the assassination of Archduke Franz Ferdinand of Austria-Hungary in June 1914.

In summary, the balance of power in Europe at the dawn of World War I was a highly complex and fragile construct. Its historical evolution had led it to a point where the mechanisms that had once served to prevent conflict were now paradoxically contributing to the geopolitical tension that would soon erupt into war. By understanding the intricacies of this European power balance, one gains critical insight into the motivations, constraints, and options that shaped the actions of states in the lead-up to the First World War. This foundational understanding enables a nuanced interpretation of the war's broader geopolitical context, thereby enriching our grasp of the ensuing shifts in global power dynamics.

Imperial Ambitions and Entangling Alliances

The period leading up to World War I was not solely characterized by the balance-of-power mechanisms and alliance formations examined in the previous section. It was further complicated by the imperial aspirations of European powers and the unique dynamics these ambitions introduced into the already fragile geopolitical balance. The ambitions were especially evident in Germany and Austria-Hungary, nations with internal and external agendas that affected their interactions within the alliance systems.

Germany, unified in 1871 and burgeoning as an industrial power, sought to expand its colonial footprint, in a quest often referred to as its "place in the sun." Such ambitions put Germany on a collision course with established colonial powers, notably Britain and France. The inherent tension from colonial rivalries introduced another dimension to the existing balances, one that extended beyond continental Europe and involved overseas territories and resources.

Austria-Hungary, dealing with internal ethnic dissensions, viewed territorial expansion, especially in the Balkans, as a remedy for its internal woes. This vision brought it into conflict with Russia, a nation similarly interested in the Balkans, but primarily as a proponent of pan-Slavism. Austria-Hungary's ambitions thus did not merely act as an external manifestation of imperial policy but also as a mechanism to cement internal cohesion.

These imperial endeavors were tightly woven into the alliance systems, thereby exacerbating the tensions. Germany's colonial ambitions, for instance, were part of the larger dynamics that influenced its participation in the Triple Alliance, which had originally been formulated for continental concerns. Austria-Hungary's Balkan ambitions, on the other hand, were in part enabled and emboldened by its assurance of German support through the Dual Alliance. This layered complexity revealed how entangling alliances were increasingly influenced by a wider range of strategic considerations than merely continental power balances.

The alliances themselves evolved in response to these changing geopolitical aspirations. Italy, initially part of the Triple Alliance, defected to the Triple Entente due to the allure of territorial gains promised by the Entente powers. This fluidity introduced further unpredictability into a system already fraught with complexities. Additionally, the financial aspect, manifested in forms such as French loans to Russia, added another layer of obligations and expectations among the allied powers.

When Archduke Franz Ferdinand was assassinated in June 1914, these overlapping complexities—imperial aspirations entangled with brittle alliances—came to the fore. Austria-Hungary's punitive action against Serbia activated a series of obligations among the European powers, escalating what might have been a localized Balkan conflict into a world war.

In summary, imperial ambitions were not standalone elements; rather, they were intricately integrated into the pre-existing framework of alliances and power balances. This multidimensional matrix heightened tensions and added layers of complexity to European geopolitics, ultimately rendering the balance of power untenable. It was this interplay between ambition and obligation, within the overarching construct of the European balance of power, that set the stage for the unprecedented scale of conflict that was World War I.

Major Battles: Frontlines of Empires

The battlefields of World War I were not merely theaters of military conflict; they were also the crucibles in which the strengths and vulnerabilities of empires were laid bare. From the attritional battles on the Western Front to the fluid engagements on the Eastern Front and the failed invasions at places like Gallipoli, the nature and outcome of these major battles had implications far beyond the immediate tactical or strategic gains.

The Western Front, characterized by trench warfare and a deadlock that lasted years, saw critical battles such as the Somme and Verdun.

Soldiers rest during the opening hours of the battle[33]

At Verdun, the French and Germans engaged in a grueling contest that resulted in hundreds of thousands of casualties, but ultimately a French victory. The aim of Germany's Chief of General Staff Erich von Falkenhayn was to "bleed France white," but the struggle revealed the limits of attritional warfare and exposed the vulnerabilities of both empires' military strategies. The Battle of the Somme, intended to be a decisive Allied victory that would break the German lines, instead became emblematic of the war's futility, with an infamous first day that cost the British Army 57,000 casualties for negligible gains. The failure to achieve breakthroughs on the Western Front contributed to a protracted conflict that drained resources and undermined the political stability of participating empires.

On the Eastern Front, battles like Tannenberg and Masurian Lakes showcased Germany's tactical brilliance against a Russian army plagued by poor leadership and logistical issues. The defeat of Russian forces in these battles diminished Russia's standing among the Allies and contributed to the revolutionary fervor that would eventually lead to the Russian Revolution. Germany's victories in the East allowed for the reallocation of resources to other fronts but also presented logistical and manpower challenges due to the vast territorial gains that required occupation and administration.

In other theaters of conflict, including the Middle East and Gallipoli, the course of battle was significantly influenced by both geographical limitations and imperial objectives. The Gallipoli campaign serves as a particularly illustrative example. This operation, conceived by the Allies to secure the maritime passage from Europe to Russia, ended in resounding failure and illustrated the limitations of naval prowess in achieving continental aims.

Notably, Winston Churchill, then First Lord of the Admiralty, shouldered a disproportionate share of the blame for the Gallipoli debacle, despite the reality that the failed campaign was the result of a complex array of decisions and miscalculations, many of which were beyond his direct control. This episode cast a long shadow over Churchill's political career, effectively relegating him to two decades of what could be termed political wilderness. Had it not been for Adolf Hitler's ascendancy and the ensuing global conflict, Churchill might have remained a relatively obscure and failed politician, rather than rising to become one of the most consequential figures of modern history.

Meanwhile, in the Middle East, the Ottoman Empire faced off against British forces in multiple campaigns, such as the Siege of Kut. Despite significant resource expenditure, the Ottomans succeeded in repelling British advances, thereby elongating their involvement in the conflict. While these campaigns did not decisively tip the balance of the war, they did underscore the strategic complexities introduced by imperial aims and geographical constraints, elements that further diversified the motivations and outcomes across different fronts.

The failed invasion of Italy by Austro-Hungarian forces at battles like Caporetto exposed the empire's waning military capabilities and further weakened its internal cohesion. Italy's subsequent entry into the war on the side of the Allies reflected the fluidity and impermanence of pre-war alliances, and their inability to dictate the course of military engagements.

Each of these major battles had implications for the balance of power among empires. Tactical victories or defeats were interpreted through the lens of national morale, resource allocation, and the sustainability of war efforts. Moreover, these engagements had long-term geopolitical implications. For example, the failure to knock out Russia quickly led Germany to unrestricted submarine warfare, a move that would eventually draw the United States into the conflict. Similarly, the draining attrition of the Western Front led to internal crises in both France and Germany, affecting their post-war stability and influence.

In summary, the major battles of World War I served as both indicators and influencers of the balance of power among the involved empires. They exposed the limitations of pre-war military planning, shifted the alliances and coalitions, and influenced the decisions that would shape the post-war world. By analyzing these key engagements, one gains deeper insight into the operational constraints and strategic imperatives that guided the conduct of empires at war.

The Fall of Titans

The First World War did not merely serve as a theater for military conflict; it also functioned as an accelerator for structural weaknesses within the participating empires, leading to significant shifts in global power dynamics. Among the most striking manifestations of this phenomenon were the collapses of the Austro-Hungarian and Ottoman Empires, each of which had implications for the balance of power in their respective regions and globally.

The Austro-Hungarian Empire, an amalgamation of diverse ethnic and linguistic groups, faced existential challenges even before the onset of war. Its involvement in World War I exacerbated these vulnerabilities. Initially, the Dual Monarchy anticipated that a swift victory would silence internal dissent and cement its territorial integrity; however, the reality proved far more complex. Military failures, most notably the failed invasion of Serbia and defeat at the Italian front, exposed the empire's operational shortcomings. Concurrently, the increasing difficulty of administering a multi-ethnic empire during a prolonged conflict led to internal discord. Czechs, Slovaks, and other minority groups started to envisage a future without Habsburg rule, aided by the rhetoric of national self-determination propagated by American President Woodrow Wilson. The political structure in Vienna became increasingly tenuous, culminating in the empire's dissolution and the proclamation of separate republics and kingdoms. The collapse of Austria-Hungary thus not only marked the end of a historical epoch but also fundamentally altered the geopolitical makeup of Central Europe.

The Ottoman Empire, already referred to as the "sick man of Europe" in the decades leading up to the war, saw its geopolitical standing further weakened by its military engagements. Initially aligning with the Central Powers to safeguard its territorial integrity, the empire faced multiple fronts, including the Arabian Peninsula, where it was combating an Arab revolt aided by British intelligence. Despite early successes in repelling Allied invasions, such as the Gallipoli Campaign and the Siege of Kut, the empire's military performance was inconsistent. The British-backed Arab Revolt and the capture of key cities like Baghdad, Jerusalem, and Damascus eroded Ottoman control over the Arab territories, a loss formalized in the post-war settlements. The empire's crumbling facade was no longer sustainable, and its disintegration was formalized through the Treaty of Sèvres, which dismembered the empire and left it a rump state, later to be replaced by the Republic of Turkey following the Turkish War of Independence.

The downfall of these titans fundamentally restructured the global balance of power. The collapse of Austria-Hungary created a vacuum in Central Europe, soon to be filled by newly independent states and an increasingly assertive Germany, setting the stage for further conflicts. The decline of the Ottoman Empire had profound repercussions for the Middle East, as its former territories were either granted independence or fell under colonial mandates, setting in motion a range of geopolitical conflicts that persist to this day.

In conclusion, the fall of the Austro-Hungarian and Ottoman Empires serves as a compelling lens through which to view the transformative power of World War I. These collapses were not only the outcomes of military defeat but were the result of longstanding structural vulnerabilities exacerbated by the strains of war. Their dissolution altered the architecture of international politics, and the vacuums left in their wake would serve as arenas for new conflicts and the redrawing of geopolitical boundaries.

The United States Enters the Scene

The United States' entry into World War I in April 1917 constituted a seminal moment in the nation's emergence as a global power. It also marked a significant alteration in the balance of power on the world stage, especially within the context of the decaying European empires. Prior to 1917, America had largely adhered to a policy of neutrality, a stance facilitated by its geographical isolation and underpinned by a national ideology that was skeptical of entangling alliances, especially those of the Old World. However, several factors, such as unrestricted submarine warfare by Germany and the interception of the Zimmermann Telegram, which proposed a military alliance between Germany and Mexico against the United States, made this neutrality untenable.

The initial American contributions to the war were largely financial and material, as the U.S. provided loans and resources to the Allies. American industrial capacity rapidly expanded to meet the demands of a full-scale war effort. However, it was the infusion of American troops, arriving in Europe at a time when the Entente Powers were nearing the point of exhaustion, that proved most pivotal. The American Expeditionary Forces, led by General John J. Pershing, participated in key offensives such as the Meuse-Argonne Offensive, which contributed to breaking the German frontlines. The morale boost provided by the arrival of fresh American troops should not be underestimated either; it was a material and psychological game-changer for the war-weary Allies.

Strategically, America's entrance into the war allowed it to assert its influence during the subsequent peace negotiations. President Woodrow Wilson's Fourteen Points, including the notion of national self-determination and the creation of a League of Nations, reflected a new vision for international relations and underscored America's departure from its previous isolationist policies. The post-war settlement at the Treaty of Versailles, while not fully embracing all American proposals, nevertheless offered the United States a seat at the table of great powers, as it were. Although the U.S. Senate ultimately rejected membership in the League of Nations, the very fact that such a global institution was an American idea marked a significant shift in the nation's role in international politics.

America's involvement in World War I had far-reaching implications for its standing in the world. The economic benefits were immediate: European indebtedness to the United States, along with the devastation of European infrastructure, allowed America to emerge as the world's leading economic power. The war had also given the United States a taste of what global leadership entailed, including the complexities and responsibilities that accompanied such a role. The country's intervention in the war indicated a willingness to shape global outcomes in accordance with American principles, even if the full implications of this newfound role would not become entirely clear until the events of World War II and the subsequent Cold War era.

In summary, the United States' participation in World War I was not just a military endeavor but rather a multi-dimensional enterprise that accelerated its emergence as a global power. Through financial, military, and diplomatic means, the United States began to weave the fabric of a new international system, one in which it would play an increasingly dominant role. This development had a profound impact on the balance of power, particularly as the old empires of Europe receded into history.

Treaty of Versailles: The Redrawing of Empires

The Treaty of Versailles, signed on June 28, 1919, represented a pivotal moment in the restructuring of international relations and the redrawing of imperial boundaries. It was negotiated among the Allied powers with little input from the defeated Central Powers, marking a decisive rupture in the pre-war status quo and serving as a lens through which the balance of power in Europe and beyond can be critically evaluated.

At its core, the Treaty was designed to incapacitate Germany as a military threat and to realign territorial boundaries. It imposed severe reparations on Germany and divested it of key territories, such as Alsace and Lorraine, which were returned to France. The provinces of Eupen and Malmedy were ceded to Belgium, and significant portions of Silesia went to Poland. The Saar Basin was placed under the administration of the League of Nations, while the city of Danzig (modern-day Gdańsk, Poland) was declared a free city. These territorial adjustments were accompanied by severe military restrictions designed to prevent Germany from re-emerging as a military power.

In terms of imperial realignments, the Treaty was instrumental in dismantling the Ottoman and Austro-Hungarian empires. New nation-states emerged in Europe, including Czechoslovakia, Yugoslavia, and Hungary, reflective of the principle of national self-determination, albeit often in discord with ethnographic realities. In the Middle East, the Treaty led to the partition of Ottoman territories under the Sykes-Picot

Agreement, laying the foundation for modern-day geopolitical tensions in the region. Mandates were established in Palestine, Iraq, and Syria, effectively placing them under British and French control.

While the Treaty aimed to create a more stable international order under the aegis of the League of Nations, its terms were largely punitive, sowing seeds for future conflicts. It failed to integrate the defeated powers into the new international system, leaving Germany humiliated and economically burdened by reparations. Additionally, the League of Nations lacked the enforcement mechanisms and universal membership necessary to maintain long-term stability. The United States, despite President Woodrow Wilson's advocacy for the League, never joined, weakening the organization and diminishing its effectiveness as a guarantor of collective security.

The Treaty of Versailles recalibrated the balance of power but did so in a way that laid the groundwork for future tensions and conflicts. The severe reparations and territorial losses imposed on Germany contributed to the economic and political instability that eventually led to World War II. Furthermore, the artificial boundaries drawn in the Middle East continue to be a source of geopolitical strife. Thus, while the Treaty closed the chapter on one global conflict, its provisions served as prologue to subsequent upheavals in the international system.

In summary, the Treaty of Versailles was a momentous episode in the redrawing of empires and the reshuffling of global power structures. While its immediate goal was to create a new balance of power more favorable to the victorious Allied nations, the punitive nature of its provisions and the asymmetries it introduced into the international system had enduring implications. It reshaped global geopolitics but did so at the cost of long-term stability, the ramifications of which were felt well into the latter half of the 20th century.

Conclusion:
From Imperial Warfare to National Identities

The aftermath of World War I witnessed a transformative shift in the political landscape, marking a departure from a system characterized primarily by multi-ethnic empires to one increasingly defined by nation-states. This seismic shift presented a novel set of opportunities and challenges for governance and international relations, reshaping the concept of sovereignty and propelling the emergence of national identities.

The disintegration of the Austro-Hungarian and Ottoman Empires is a case in point. These sprawling, multi-ethnic entities could not withstand the pressures exerted by war and internal discontents, leading to their collapse and the creation of new, more ethnically homogenous states. The Treaty of Saint-Germain and the Treaty of Trianon formalized the partition of the Austro-Hungarian Empire, giving rise to Czechoslovakia and Yugoslavia and creating independent states of Austria and Hungary, among others. Similarly, the dissolution of the Ottoman Empire facilitated the creation of modern Turkey and also laid the groundwork for the mandates in the Middle East under British and French control.

The collapse of empires offered fertile ground for the application of Woodrow Wilson's principle of national self-determination, albeit inconsistently and often with disregard for complex local ethnic configurations. This principle was embodied in the formation of several nation-states, often designed along ethnolinguistic lines, but sometimes failing to accommodate minorities, thus sowing the seeds for future ethnic conflicts.

Germany offers another compelling case study in the emergence of national identities post-WWI. The Weimar Republic, despite its democratic orientation, had to navigate a complex web of social and economic issues exacerbated by the Treaty of Versailles. The collective national humiliation felt due to the war and the subsequent treaty contributed to a form of nationalism that would later be harnessed by extremist elements, setting the stage for World War II.

In a similar vein, the Russian Revolution and the subsequent civil war replaced the Tsarist empire with a communist state that sought to forge a new Soviet identity, transcending traditional nationalism but promoting a different kind of ideological identity. Though it retained an imperial structure in its domination over various ethnic groups within its vast territory, the Soviet Union presented itself as a vanguard of a new form of social organization, adding a new ideological dimension to national identity.

Moreover, the role of colonial troops in the war began to challenge imperial narratives. Soldiers from British India, French West Africa, and other colonies served on various fronts. Their experiences and the exposure to different cultures and political ideas led to increased demands for self-determination and fueled anti-colonial movements, further complicating the relationship between imperial powers and their colonies.

The aftermath of World War I, therefore, was a crucible for the reconfiguration of national and imperial identities. As empires crumbled, newly independent states sought to define themselves in terms of language, culture, or ideology, often in opposition to their former rulers or neighboring states. The result was a new international system, composed of a complex mosaic of nation-states with their own aspirations and identities, held together by a fragile framework of international laws and institutions.

Thus, the shift from imperial warfare to the emergence of national identities post-World War I was not merely a change in political borders but a profound transformation in the understanding of governance, sovereignty, and international relations. It catalyzed the decline of empires as the primary actors in global affairs, making room for a new order characterized by nation-states, each with their unique set of challenges and contributions to the balance of power.

City and People, 1918 Oil painting by Joseph Kölschbach[34]

Chapter 23.
Interwar Era: Totalitarian Aspirants (1918-1939)

When diplomacy ends, war begins.

~Adolf Hitler

The Landscape of the Interwar Years

In the intricate puzzle of global history, the interwar years (1919-1939) occupy a critical juncture, serving as both an epilogue to the cataclysms of the First World War and a prologue to the impending upheavals of the Second. This period, dense with political recalibrations and ideological realignments, merits scrutiny not merely as an interlude between two monumental conflicts but as a transformative epoch in its own right.

The cessation of hostilities in 1919, marked most notably by the Treaty of Versailles, did not usher in an era of unalloyed peace or stability. Instead, the post-war landscape was strewn with the debris of erstwhile empires. The Austro-Hungarian, Russian, Ottoman, and German Empires, once colossal pillars of power, had either dissolved or were undergoing profound metamorphoses. Their disintegration created vacuums, both territorial and ideological, setting the stage for fresh entities and ideologies to contend for ascendancy.

Europe, the epicenter of these transformations, grappled with dual challenges. On one hand, it faced the Herculean task of physical reconstruction and economic rehabilitation. On the other, the ideological fabric of the continent was being stretched and re-woven. While the war's end saw the birth of numerous republics and the affirmation of democratic principles in many quarters, it simultaneously sowed the seeds of disillusionment. Disparities in war gains, perceived injustices in peace treaties, and economic hardships fermented public discontent. These conditions were fertile grounds for radical ideologies, with populations seeking alternatives to the liberal democracies that seemed unable to address their grievances.

This mosaic of shattered empires, nascent republics, and emerging ideologies provided a backdrop against which powerful personalities would craft their narratives, each aiming to sculpt a new empire from the vestiges of the old. As the interwar years progressed, the contours of these new empires began to manifest, revealing ambitions and aspirations that would set the trajectory for the latter half of the 20th century.

In comprehending this era, one must adopt a panoramic view, capturing not only the political machinations but also the societal, cultural, and economic undercurrents that propelled them. For, in these intricacies lay the groundwork for the empires that would shape the epochs to come, and in their stories reside lessons of power, resilience, and the cyclical nature of history.

The Ruins of the Great War: Setting the Stage

As the First World War reached its conclusion in 1918, a shattered European landscape grappled with the reverberations of an unprecedented conflict. This "war to end all wars" had not only redrawn geopolitical boundaries but also destabilized the very pillars of continental order. The aftermath confronted Europe with challenges that were as multifaceted as they were monumental.

One of the most immediate challenges was economic. The continent, once a beacon of industrial strength and technological advancement, now faced immense infrastructure damage. Cities that had thrived as hubs of commerce and culture were reduced to rubble, their industries disrupted and populations dislocated. War debts mounted, and the financial networks that once buttressed European economies were strained to the brink. Hyperinflation plagued nations like Germany, where people, in stark testimony to the nation's dire economic situation, found banknotes more valuable as wallpaper than currency.

Yet, beyond these tangible devastations, lay deeper political tremors. The Treaty of Versailles, intended to formalize peace, inadvertently sowed seeds of future discord. While the Allied powers viewed the treaty as a mechanism to ensure lasting peace by curbing German aggression, in Germany, it was perceived as a 'Diktat'—an imposed agreement. Punitive reparations, territorial losses, and military restrictions not only engendered economic burdens but also wounded the national pride of a once-formidable empire. This mix of economic hardship and perceived humiliation created an undercurrent of resentment, a potent milieu for extremist ideologies to take root and flourish.

Simultaneously, the war heralded the end of monarchies that had stood for centuries. The Romanovs of Russia, Hohenzollerns of Germany, and Habsburgs of Austria-Hungary—each of these dynastic titans crumbled under the pressures of war and its aftermath. In their places emerged new republics, each attempting to navigate the challenges of governance without the anchoring weight of longstanding monarchy. The Weimar Republic in Germany, for instance, encapsulated these challenges. Born amidst national humiliation and economic adversity, the republic was buffeted by both leftist and rightist extremist movements, reflecting the volatile spirit of the age.

This transition from established monarchies to fledgling republics symbolized a broader continental shift. Traditions were being questioned, and the status quo was no longer sacrosanct. As Europe endeavored to rebuild, the old was juxtaposed against the new, setting the stage for ideological battles and power struggles. The ruins of the Great War, thus, were not mere physical devastations; they represented a transformative phase in European history, where the past and future were engaged in a tenuous dance.

The Rise of Fascism in Italy: Mussolini's Empire Ambitions

The aftermath of World War I left Italy, akin to much of Europe, in a state of profound unease. Italian sacrifices during the war, measured in both economic and human terms, were substantial, but the rewards at the war's conclusion seemed disproportionate. The Treaty of Versailles, rather than satiating Italian territorial appetites, fanned the flames of dissatisfaction. The "mutilated victory" sentiment proliferated, a feeling that Italy had been deprived of its rightful territorial gains, particularly in the Adriatic region. This national disillusionment combined with rampant inflation, economic stagnation, and political fragmentation to create fertile ground for radical ideologies.

It is within this tumultuous environment that Benito Mussolini, a former socialist and journalist, recognized an opportunity to mold Italy's future. Drawing from nationalist sentiments and an aversion to both communism and weak parliamentary governance, Mussolini crafted the ideology of Fascism. Characterized by authoritarian nationalism, Fascism positioned itself as the antithesis to Marxism and liberal democracy, promising stability, strength, and an end to political factionalism. The paramilitary Blackshirt squads, loyal to Mussolini, began asserting themselves, violently suppressing socialist and communist movements.

Mussolini's charisma and the promise of a decisive leadership appealed to a populace wearied by economic hardships and political instability. By 1922, Mussolini felt confident enough to challenge the extant political order directly. The March on Rome, a show of strength by thousands of Blackshirts, culminated not in violent confrontation but in King Victor Emmanuel III's invitation to Mussolini to form a government. It was a testament to the state of Italian democracy at the time: rather than defending the democratic order, the monarchy and established institutions seemed to acquiesce to the very force that sought to upend it.

Once in power, Benito Mussolini swiftly embarked on the consolidation of his regime, effectuating the transformation of Italy into a one-party state. Political dissidents were suppressed, the plurality of the press was curtailed, and a meticulous cult of personality around

'Il Duce' was crafted to galvanize public sentiment. These domestic measures, however, constituted merely one facet of Mussolini's broader agenda. His ambitions were not confined to the Italian peninsula; rather, he sought to resurrect the grandeur of Italy on a geopolitical stage, invoking the historical legacy of the Roman Empire as an ideological anchor.

Central to this vision was the pursuit of territorial expansion, primarily targeting Africa and the Balkans. Mussolini envisioned Italy as the pre-eminent power in the Mediterranean, encapsulated in the slogan "Mare Nostrum" or "Our Sea." In Africa, this entailed more than simply maintaining Italy's existing colonial possessions like Libya, acquired in 1912, and Eritrea, secured in 1890. The invasion of Ethiopia in 1935, also known as the Abyssinia Crisis, aimed to expand Italy's African empire and was a critical episode in this imperial blueprint. Italy's modern military machinery, including air power and chemical weapons, overwhelmed Ethiopian defenses, leading to the capture of Addis Ababa in 1936. The campaign significantly strained Italy's international relations, particularly with the League of Nations, and marked a pivotal moment in the weakening of international cooperative security mechanisms of the interwar period.

In the Balkans, Mussolini sought to extend Italian influence by capitalizing on the power vacuum left by the weakening of the Ottoman Empire and the fractious state of Yugoslav territories. While less successful than his African endeavors, these Balkan aspirations nonetheless signified a wider strategy of Italian territorial aggrandizement.

This imperial vision was inextricably tied to Mussolini's domestic policy. The nationalist ethos propagated within Italy served as a psychological scaffolding for imperial ventures abroad, justifying expansionism as a natural extension of Italian greatness. This intermingling of domestic and foreign policy aims reveals the multi-layered complexity of Mussolini's ambitions, reflecting not just a quest for territorial gains but also a deeper ideological conviction to imprint Italy's mark on the international system.

The rise of Mussolini and Fascism in Italy marked the dawn of a new political era. An era where democratic institutions were eschewed in favor of authoritarianism, and where the dreams of empire and national glory replaced aspirations for liberal governance. The Italian experience was but a precursor to similar political developments in other parts of interwar Europe.

Imperial Japan: Ambitions In the East

Japan, unlike much of the global community during the interwar era, had undergone a transformation well before the onset of the 20th century. This metamorphosis was largely catalyzed by the Meiji Restoration of 1868. Prior to the Restoration, Japan had been a secluded, feudal society under the Tokugawa shogunate, resistant to foreign influences and outside engagements. However, the encroachment by Western powers, manifest in events like the arrival of U.S. Commodore Matthew Perry's Black Ships, underscored Japan's vulnerability. This realization instigated a monumental shift.

The Meiji Restoration was more than a mere change in leadership from the Tokugawa Shogunate to Emperor Meiji; it represented a conscious decision by Japan to modernize, to reform its societal structures, governance, economy, and military by absorbing selected Western practices. Industrialization was aggressively pursued, and a centralized, bureaucratic state structure was instituted. Samurai domains were abolished in favor of prefectures governed by centrally-appointed officials. A new conscription-based national army was established, and Japan sought to build a navy that could rival the Western powers. This embrace of modernity and rapid industrialization bore fruit, enabling Japan to stand toe-to-toe with global powers within a matter of decades, evidenced by its victory against Russia in the Russo-Japanese War of 1904-1905.

Entering the interwar era, Japan's appetite for expansionism grew, driven by both its economic needs and the allure of imperial prestige. The 1931 invasion of Manchuria (in the Northeastern part of China) was emblematic of Japan's new aggressive stance. Using a staged event, often termed the Mukden Incident, as a pretext, the Imperial Japanese Army moved swiftly to occupy Manchuria, subsequently establishing the puppet state of Manchukuo. This initiative was not merely a territorial conquest; it was a strategic move to secure vast natural resources, especially iron and coal, that the resource-poor Japanese archipelago sorely needed to sustain its industrial expansion.

Manchuria, however, was just the starting point. Japan's gaze soon turned towards the broader Asian mainland and the resource-rich Southeast Asia. The nation's leadership believed in the concept of the "Greater East Asia Co-Prosperity Sphere", a self-sufficient bloc of Asian nations led by Japan and free from Western influence. This vision, though painted with the brush of pan-Asian solidarity, was in essence a blueprint for a Japan-centric imperial order in the region.

In recapitulation, the interwar period for Japan was marked by an assertive, sometimes aggressive, pursuit of its regional ambitions. Driven by both the needs of its burgeoning industries and the siren call of imperial grandeur, Japan set on a path that would inevitably lead it to larger confrontations on the world stage.

Germany's Resurgence: Nazism and the Third Reich

He emerged as a decorated war hero, a passionate artist, and a charismatic patriot, but his legacy would come to embody pure evil. Adolf Hitler's ascent to power marked one of the most chilling and tragic chapters in human history. In the annals of infamy, he would stand as a symbol of the darkest depths to which humanity could descend.

Hitler's rise to prominence had its roots in the harrowing aftermath of the First World War, exacerbated by the profound political turmoil inflicted upon Germany by the Treaty of Versailles. In this tumultuous and unforgiving backdrop, the Weimar Republic emerged in 1919, symbolizing Germany's first tentative steps into democratic governance after the abdication of Kaiser Wilhelm II.

From its inception, the Weimar Republic was beleaguered with challenges. Hyperinflation between 1921 and 1923 decimated the German mark, leading to significant economic hardships for the populace. Moreover, the republic faced political instability, with frequent changes in government and a fragmented Reichstag, which was often polarized between the extreme left (Communists) and the extreme right (Nationalists and nascent Nazi factions). Adding to these internal challenges were the Republic's perceived associations with the Treaty of Versailles, the "November Criminals," and the perceived betrayal of the German people. Such perceptions rendered the republic vulnerable to extremist narratives that yearned for a return to nationalistic pride and power.

The hall where the Reichstag met[35]

Into this fraught political climate emerged Adolf Hitler and his National Socialist German Workers' Party (NSDAP), commonly known as the Nazi Party. Originally just one of many fringe political groups, the Nazis adeptly manipulated the widespread discontent, offering a potent mix of German nationalism, anti-Communism, and anti-Semitism. Hitler's charisma, oratory prowess, and the party's propaganda machine, led by Joseph Goebbels, amplified the party's appeal.

By the early 1930s, the Nazi Party had gained significant representation in the Reichstag. Through a combination of backroom deals, political maneuvering, and growing popularity, Hitler was appointed as the Chancellor of Germany in January 1933 through a legitimate democratic process. This seemingly routine political appointment would soon prove catastrophic for Germany and the world at large, serving as a haunting reminder that leaders who come to power through fair and democratic elections can, under the right circumstances, turn a legitimate democratic process into unspeakable pain.

With Hitler at the helm, the process of Gleichschaltung, or "coordination," was initiated, aimed at centralizing Nazi control over all aspects of German life. Key moments, such as the Reichstag Fire in February 1933 and the consequent Reichstag Fire Decree, allowed the Nazis to suppress opposition, curtail civil liberties, and arrest political adversaries, especially Communists. The Enabling Act of March 1933 further solidified Nazi control, granting Hitler the authority to enact laws without Reichstag involvement, effectively sidelining Germany's democratic structures.

By the mid-1930s, Germany under Hitler was transformed. The Nazis had successfully consolidated their power, rebuilt the economy, and re-armed the military, in defiance of the Treaty of Versailles. Through initiatives like the Nuremberg Laws and the Night of the Long Knives, Hitler had also purged perceived internal threats and further marginalized the Jewish community. As the decade drew to a close, Germany's new ambitions under the Third Reich were becoming manifest, signaling ominous implications for Europe and the global order.

Soviet Union: Stalin's Vision of a Communist Empire

In the annals of the 20th century, few figures rival the stature and influence of Joseph Stalin in shaping the trajectory of a nation. Following the cataclysmic events of the Russian Revolution in 1917 and the subsequent Russian Civil War, the Soviet Union, under Vladimir Lenin's leadership, endeavored to embed the tenets of Marxism-Leninism within its societal, economic, and political paradigms. Lenin's death in 1924 ignited a fierce contest for succession, with various factions vying for supremacy within the Communist Party.

Stalin, who initially occupied the role of General Secretary, a position ostensibly administrative in nature, demonstrated astute political acumen, systematically consolidating his influence by neutralizing potential rivals and maneuvering loyalists into key positions. By the end of the 1920s, he had marginalized his opponents, notably Leon Trotsky, and solidified his grip on power.

One of Stalin's hallmark endeavors was a rapid and intense industrialization drive. The Soviet Union, predominantly agrarian at the onset of the 1930s, was rapidly transformed via a series of ambitious Five-Year Plans. These plans, while successful in elevating the Soviet Union to the echelons of major industrial powers, came at considerable human cost. Forced collectivization led to widespread famine, notably the Holodomor in Ukraine, resulting in millions of fatalities.

Concurrently, Stalin perceived threats, both real and imagined, to his regime. This led to the infamous Great Purge (or Great Terror) of the mid-1930s. Political rivals, intellectuals, military officers, and ordinary citizens were subjected to arrest, execution, or internment in gulag labor camps. This campaign of political repression served to quash dissent and further reinforce Stalin's autocratic rule.

While these internal dynamics were unfolding, the Soviet Union was also maneuvering its position on the global stage. The 1930s witnessed a growing apprehension of Fascist and Nazi ideologies in Europe. With Germany under Hitler intensifying its expansionist aspirations, Stalin perceived the necessity of fostering diplomatic engagements. The Molotov-Ribbentrop Pact in 1939, a non-aggression treaty between Nazi Germany and the Soviet Union, exemplified Stalin's pragmatism, albeit short-lived, in navigating these external challenges.

Stalin's era, while marked by significant advancements in industrial and military prowess, was also characterized by widespread repression, purges, and an indelible alteration of the communist principles initially envisioned by Lenin. The Soviet Union, under his aegis, had metamorphosed into a global superpower, albeit with a deeply complex and often tumultuous internal landscape.

Spain's Fracture:
Civil War and the Dawn of Francoism

In the interwar period, the global political climate was marked not just by the rise of totalitarian regimes but also by nuanced ideological confrontations, and Spain stood as a poignant testament to this phenomenon. Post-World War I, while much of Europe grappled with the challenges of reconstructing nations and consolidating power, Spain underwent a period of intense political turmoil that eventually culminated in a bitter and devastating civil war.

The roots of Spain's upheaval can be traced back to the early 20th century. Spain was a nation with disparate identities, where regional nationalisms, notably in Catalonia and the Basque Country, vied for greater autonomy. Furthermore, the traditional bastions of power, namely the monarchy and the Catholic Church, were being increasingly challenged by burgeoning socialist and anarchist movements.

By 1931, these tensions reached a climax, leading to the establishment of the Second Spanish Republic. The new republic aimed to modernize Spain, embarking on ambitious reforms including land redistribution, secularization, and enhanced regional autonomy. However, these reforms antagonized conservative and traditionalist factions, leading to increased polarization.

This polarization set the stage for the Spanish Civil War, commencing in 1936. On one side stood the Republicans, a coalition of communists, anarchists, socialists, and regional nationalists. On the opposite front were the Nationalists, comprising conservatives, monarchists, Carlists, and fascists, led prominently by General Francisco Franco. This war, often viewed as a precursor to World War II, drew international attention and intervention. Nazi Germany and Fascist Italy provided overt military support to Franco's Nationalists, while the Soviet Union aided the Republicans. The war also drew international brigades, composed of volunteers, sympathetic to the Republican cause.

By 1939, Franco's forces emerged victorious, and Spain found itself under a dictatorship. Franco's regime, characterized by autocratic governance and a return to conservative Catholic values, sought to unify Spain under a singular identity, marginalizing regional languages and cultures. Interestingly, despite the assistance Franco received from Fascist and Nazi regimes, Spain remained neutral during World War II, though it did lean towards the Axis powers in terms of diplomatic engagements.

Franco's rule, which lasted until his death in 1975, marked an era where Spain, although distanced from the broader confrontations consuming Europe, was nonetheless deeply scarred by its internal conflicts. The nation's fracture during the civil war and subsequent decades under Francoist Spain left indelible imprints, the reverberations of which are still discernible in Spain's political and cultural milieu today.

Global Response to Rising Totalitarianism

Between the World Wars, the rise of totalitarian regimes fundamentally altered the geopolitical map. Europe, previously the epicenter of grand empires and global diplomacy, was now a terrain where radical ideologies took center stage. The responses of the global community to this wave of totalitarianism varied, driven both by ideological positioning and pragmatic considerations.

The Western democracies, primarily France and Britain, initially adopted a policy of appeasement towards the totalitarian states, especially Germany. Memories of the Great War still haunted the European psyche, and there was a general reluctance to confront these aggressive regimes directly, fearing it might instigate another devastating conflict. Britain's Prime Minister Neville Chamberlain's infamous "peace for our time" proclamation in 1938, after signing the Munich Agreement which permitted German annexation of Sudetenland, exemplifies this appeasement policy. Watching from the sidelines, Winston Churchill, who would later reshape Britain's response to the rising threats, declared, "You had a choice between war and dishonor. You chose dishonor, and you will get war." His words were prophetic. As totalitarian ambitions grew unchecked, the policy of appeasement increasingly came under scrutiny. By the late 1930s, democracies like Britain began accelerating military preparations, acknowledging the looming prospect of another major conflict and the need for a decisive leadership shift.

Parallelly, the League of Nations, established post-WWI to foster international cooperation and prevent future wars, found itself ill-equipped to counter the totalitarian surge. Absent of significant enforcement mechanisms and lacking the participation of the United States, the League was often reduced to a talking shop. Its inability to prevent Italy's invasion of Ethiopia in 1935 or curb Japanese aggressions in Manchuria in the early 1930s underlined its limitations in the face of assertive and expansionist regimes.

Global realpolitik of this era was characterized by a complicated web of agreements, some public and others secret. The Molotov-Ribbentrop Pact between Nazi Germany and the Soviet Union in 1939, for instance, was a non-aggression treaty that belied the deep ideological differences between the two nations. It paved the way for the joint invasion and partitioning of Poland, setting in motion the events of World War II. Yet, it was a pact rooted in pragmatism, with both parties seeking territorial gains and time. Similarly, while the Anti-Comintern Pact of 1936, which included Germany, Italy, and Japan, was anti-communist in principle, it was also an instrument to counterbalance the perceived threats from the Soviet Union and, indirectly, the Western democracies.

In essence, the interwar period saw a global community caught in a tumultuous cycle of aggressive territorial ambitions, uneasy alliances, and diplomatic maneuvers. The rise of totalitarian regimes was not merely a regional phenomenon; it reshaped the very structure of international politics. As the 1930s drew to a close, the stage was set for a conflict of unprecedented scale, the echoes of which would define global dynamics for decades to come.

Social and Cultural Impact

Amid the prevailing political and military maneuvers during the interwar period, the cultural and societal dimensions under the aegis of totalitarian regimes often remain underemphasized. However, these dimensions were no less significant in reinforcing the ideologies and solidifying the regimes' control over their respective populations.

One of the primary tools employed by these regimes was propaganda. Whether it was Mussolini's Italy, Hitler's Germany, or Stalin's USSR, propaganda was systematically utilized to craft and propagate a narrative that galvanized the public towards the state's objectives. Radios broadcasted state-sanctioned messages, and newspapers were rigorously censored or directly controlled to ensure a consistent dissemination of the state's perspective. Monumental architecture and public rallies, exemplified by Nazi Germany's Nuremberg Rallies, were orchestrated displays of power, designed to both awe and intimidate, signaling the indomitable might of the state and the purported unity of the people.

In the realm of the arts, literature, and cinema, the state's influence was palpable. Artists were often co-opted or coerced into producing works that glorified the state, its leaders, or its ideology. In Germany, films

314 | Empires Through Time

such as Leni Riefenstahl's "Triumph of the Will" were masterpieces of cinematography, yet they were fundamentally propaganda tools, extolling the virtues of the Nazi regime. The USSR, under Stalin, propagated Socialist Realism, where art and literature were expected to be accessible to the common man and invariably showcase the purported triumphs of communism. Those artists and intellectuals who defied these norms faced ostracization, exile, or worse.

Arguably, one of the most insidious intersections of state control was witnessed in the realm of education and youth indoctrination. Totalitarian states placed immense emphasis on molding the next generation. Youth organizations, such as the Hitler Youth in Germany or the Komsomol in the Soviet Union, were platforms where ideological indoctrination was married to paramilitary training. These organizations fostered loyalty to the state, superseding familial bonds. School curricula were overhauled, history was revised, and an entire generation was systematically conditioned to perceive the world through the lens crafted by the regime.

Consequently, the sociocultural imprints of these regimes extended far beyond their political and territorial ambitions. They sought nothing less than a complete transformation of societal values, norms, and perceptions. This comprehensive influence not only solidified their immediate control but also left an enduring mark, the ramifications of which were felt long after the regimes themselves had crumbled. The interplay of ideology, culture, and control during this period is a testament to the profound impact that governance models can exert on the very fabric of society.

Conclusion: The Shadows of Unchecked Power

Reflecting on the interwar era's unique challenges, it becomes evident that the historical ebb and flow of empires, as seen in global history, consistently presents patterns. Empires, through time, have often ascended to pinnacle positions during power vacuums, exploited opportunities, and then, over time, faced eventual decline due to a confluence of internal and external factors. The rise of totalitarian regimes during the interwar period mirrored this trajectory. Empowered by socio-political upheavals, these regimes expanded, exerting influence over vast territories and peoples. Yet, as with ancient empires, they too faced challenges, resistance, and eventual reckonings.

The legacy of totalitarian regimes and the prelude to global conflict serve as a stark reminder of the age-old principles of statecraft, governance, and societal dynamics. Even within the span of two short decades, the world witnessed the birth, reign, and initial signs of decline of some of these powers, echoing the cyclical patterns seen in empires across millennia.

Within two decades, nations oscillated between profound despair and dizzying hope. The wounds of the First World War were yet to heal, but the shadow of the Second was already taking form. In this crucible, the rise of totalitarian regimes in several nations was neither spontaneous nor arbitrary. They emerged in response to unique national challenges, be it the Treaty of Versailles's punitive measures, the socio-economic upheavals of the Great Depression, or the power vacuums left by collapsing monarchies. Yet, while their rise might have been contingent upon specific circumstances, their methods exhibited striking similarities: a concentration of power, rigorous propaganda, and an often-brutal suppression of dissent.

These regimes' impact was not confined to their national boundaries. Their actions, and equally significantly, the global response to these actions, reshaped the international order. While nations like the USSR aimed at a communist global vision, others like Nazi Germany pursued territorial expansion under the guise of racial supremacy. The policy of appeasement, adopted by many Western democracies, inadvertently facilitated these aspirations. The failures of collective security, epitomized by the League of Nations' impotence, further underscored the complexities of international diplomacy during this tumultuous period.

But, perhaps, the most profound legacy of the interwar era lies in the sociocultural realm. The period showcased how swiftly societies could be transformed, for better or worse, by determined leadership. It illuminated the potency of propaganda, the allure of ideology, and the perils of unchecked power.

Drawing lessons from this era, it becomes evident that history's course isn't merely the result of vast impersonal forces; it is shaped by human decisions, actions, and, often, inactions. The interwar years caution against complacency in the face of rising autocracy and emphasize the continuous need for global vigilance. For empires, nations, and societies, the balance between power and principle, ambition and restraint, remains a perennial challenge, one that history persistently urges us to navigate with wisdom and foresight.

And, as the early morning of September 1, 1939 dawned, the ramifications of unchecked power became brutally clear. Hitler's armies marched into Poland, plunging the world into chaos once again. Merely two decades after the end of the 'war to end all wars', humanity found itself on the precipice of an even more cataclysmic conflict.

Hitler watching German soldiers march into Poland in September 1939[36]

Chapter 24.
World War II: A Global Struggle For Supremacy (1939-1945)

If You're Going Through Hell, Keep Going

~Winston Churchill

The Flashpoints of Global Conflict

The cataclysmic events leading up to September 1, 1939, as Hitler's armies advanced into Poland, marked not just the consummation of escalating tensions from the interwar period but also the commencement of another chapter in global conflict. The reverberations of unchecked power, the dangers of appeasement, and the inescapable shadows of the past didn't dissipate but rather manifested in fresh geopolitical flashpoints. The end of one historical phase often naturally paves the way for the next, and as global events unfolded showcasing the dangers of unrestrained authority, preparations were underway for ensuing challenges.

The Interwar Era, intricately woven between the World Wars, epitomized the transference of historical lessons, old disputes, and the evolution of fresh tensions. While the Treaty of Versailles, with its imposed punitive measures against Germany, set forth a series of eventual confrontations, concurrent factors were shaping up across global territories. Economic upheavals, notably exemplified by the aftermath of the 1929 Great Depression, shook the very foundations of nations, fueling social discontent and paving the way for radical ideologies. Japan's imperialistic endeavors in Asia sowed seeds of discord with its neighbors. Concurrently, Europe remained a hotbed of territorial contentions, simmering ethnic animosities, and ideological confrontations.

Central to the unfolding drama were the dynamic leaders poised to navigate these treacherous waters. In Germany, Adolf Hitler's rise was not merely due to nationalistic fervor, but a result of a myriad of internal and external pressures. The UK, with Winston Churchill's unwavering vision, stood as a bastion against the looming threat of Nazism, even as much of the continent succumbed. Churchill's outsized influence was crucial, transforming a declining power into a moral compass and a beacon of hope for the free world. Across the Atlantic, Franklin D. Roosevelt's leadership foresaw the shifting global paradigms and adeptly prepared the United States for its eventual and inevitable involvement.

As nations geared up, ideological battles overshadowed diplomatic courtesies. The world, balancing on a knife-edge, teetered towards what would be a monumental clash. At the forefront of this impending confrontation were leaders whose decisions, influenced by both personal convictions and national imperatives, would determine the fate of millions and the future of empires.

Emerging from the backdrop of global intricacies, as previously delineated, the stage was set for a series of confrontations that would ripple across continents. The rapid annexation of territories by Nazi Germany began with the absorption of Austria in 1938. Shortly after, the Sudetenland, a region in Czechoslovakia with a significant ethnic German population, was also annexed, signaling Hitler's intent to restore and expand the German Reich. The Molotov-Ribbentrop Pact, a surprising alliance between Nazi Germany and Stalin's Soviet Union, further highlighted the pragmatic choices leaders were willing to make in pursuit of their ambitions. This non-aggression pact not only divided Eastern Europe into spheres of influence but also provided Germany with the strategic advantage it sought.

From Skirmishes to Global Warfare: Leaders at the Helm

With the machinery of war grinding into motion, Germany's swift and devastating invasion of Poland in September 1939 was a stark manifestation of the blitzkrieg tactics that would become synonymous with Nazi military campaigns. Hitler's momentum didn't stop there. In rapid succession, by mid-1940, Nazi forces overran Belgium and Holland and, capitalizing on strategic weaknesses, launched a sweeping invasion of France. This series of blitzkrieg victories culminated in the stunning fall of France in June, a seismic event that left Britain as the last major European power standing against Nazi Germany.

In Britain, the looming specter of another large-scale conflict became increasingly undeniable. However, the political atmosphere of the 1930s had been one of appeasement, led by Prime Minister Neville Chamberlain, who believed that conciliation with Nazi Germany could prevent war. In contrast, Winston Churchill, largely marginalized during this period, consistently voiced concerns about the Nazi threat.

Churchill's sidelining had its roots in the aftermath of World War I. As the First Lord of the Admiralty during that conflict, he had championed the Gallipoli campaign, which ended in a disastrous defeat for the Allies and precipitated his resignation. This failure led to two decades of political wilderness, during which he was viewed with skepticism by many of his contemporaries.

Yet, even in these years of reduced influence, Churchill's prescient warnings about Nazi Germany stood out. By the time Germany invaded Poland in September 1939, his predictions began to ring true. And with the swift German advances in Europe by mid-1940, Britain desperately needed strong leadership.

On May 10, 1940, Churchill was appointed Prime Minister. Upon his appointment, he poignantly reflected, "I felt as if I were walking with destiny, and that all my past life had been but a preparation for this hour and for this trial." While he had been right about Hitler, his appointment was not solely about his foresight. Although Churchill may not have been Britain's initial preference for leadership, as the nation's circumstances grew increasingly dire, it became evident that he became its last hope for survival.

Winston Churchill at a conference in Quebec[37]

The Second World War, thus, set the stage for a monumental duel between two giants: Adolf Hitler and Winston Churchill. Both had battled on opposite sides during the First World War —Hitler as a corporal in the German Army and Churchill in various roles, including that ill-fated stint as the First Lord of the Admiralty. Now, they both led their respective nations in a struggle that would decisively shape the 20th century. Their clash, driven by ideologies, strategies, and personalities, undoubtedly the most consequential in the modern era, determined the course of human history.

While Britain braced for the challenges ahead, Churchill's oratory, often compared to the eloquence of historical greats like Pericles and Cicero, resonated deeply with the nation. His speeches communicated the immediacy of the threat to the British people. Moreover, they sent a clear message to Hitler and the Axis powers: Britain would not capitulate easily. Defeating the nation would be a far more formidable task than their previous conquests. Churchill's wartime addresses are universally considered some of the most effective and inspiring in history, joining the ranks of the world's greatest orators.

Britain's determination was soon put to the test during the Battle of Britain (July-October 1940), where the British Royal Air Force fiercely defended the skies against the relentless German Luftwaffe. This aerial combat not only showcased Britain's tenacity but also marked the first significant check on Hitler's expansionist ambitions.

In the United States, the scars of World War I combined with the economic downturn of the Great Depression led to a pronounced inclination towards isolationism. Many Americans believed that European conflicts were not their concern and that the U.S. should focus on domestic challenges. This was reflected in a series of Neutrality Acts passed in the 1930s, designed to prevent the nation from being drawn into external conflicts.

Yet, as the 1930s drew to a close, the rapid expansion of Nazi Germany in Europe and the aggressive actions of Imperial Japan in the Pacific began to challenge this insular stance. President Franklin D. Roosevelt, ever the astute political observer, recognized the potential global implications of these developments. While he personally believed in supporting the Allies against the Axis powers, he had to tread carefully given the prevailing isolationist mood of the country.

Roosevelt's approach was to prepare the nation for the possibility of conflict while extending indirect support to those fighting against Axis aggression. His speeches, notably the 'Arsenal of Democracy' address in December 1940, emphasized the importance of supporting nations resisting the Axis, even if the U.S. was not directly involved in combat.

The Lend-Lease Act of 1941 was a watershed in this strategy. It allowed the U.S. to provide military aid to foreign nations during the war and be repaid after its conclusion. While technically maintaining neutrality, this act was a clear indication of the U.S.'s leaning towards the Allied cause.

Furthermore, tensions in the Pacific, especially regarding Japan's aggressive expansion and military campaigns in China, which began with the invasion of Manchuria in 1931 and escalated with the Sino-Japanese War in 1937, necessitated a strong American stance. Additionally, Japan's ambitions in Southeast Asia further strained its relations with Western powers. The U.S., in response to these actions, imposed embargoes on crucial materials like oil and steel, aimed at Japan. These measures signaled the American disapproval of Japan's expansionist actions and hinted at an impending conflict.

In sum, while the United States began the 1930s rooted in isolationism, the global realities, coupled with Roosevelt's leadership, initiated a marked shift in foreign policy. This transition set the stage for America's eventual and decisive entry into World War II following the attack on Pearl Harbor in December 1941.

As countries and leaders navigated this increasingly volatile geopolitical maze, the strategic choices they made, both individually and collectively, set the trajectory for the most extensive and consequential conflict in human history. The looming shadows of World War II were cast by a blend of age-old ambitions, emerging ideologies, and the inextricable web of global interdependencies.

The Widening Conflict: Major Theaters and Leaders' Legacies

The initial reverberations of the war, initially localized to Europe, soon echoed in multiple regions around the world. As nations declared allegiances or were drawn into the maelstrom by invasion or strategic necessity, the conflict's scope expanded exponentially, birthing multiple theaters of war, each with its unique challenges and strategic importance.

In the vast expanses of the Eastern Front, the world bore witness to a clash of titans as Hitler's war machine, emboldened by its early successes, turned its gaze towards the Soviet Union. The German invasion, Operation Barbarossa in June 1941, began as a swift campaign but soon ran into the indomitable resistance of the Soviet forces. Stalin, for all his earlier purges and iron-fisted rule, marshaled his nation's resources and spirit, ensuring the USSR became an immovable bulwark against Nazi ambitions. The ensuing battles, particularly in Stalingrad (Aug 1942-Feb 1943) and Kursk (Jul-Aug 1943), showcased not only the military might of both sides but also the significance of leadership in shaping strategic decisions. Stalingrad, particularly, became a testament to the devastating consequences of leadership egomania. Hitler, obsessed with capturing the city named after Stalin, directed vast resources and troops to the battle, even as strategic considerations might have advised otherwise. Stalin, in turn, was equally determined that the city bearing his name would not fall, ordering his troops to "Not one step back!" This dogged determination, combined with poor strategic decisions, led to catastrophic losses for both sides. Stalingrad alone saw nearly 2 million casualties, making it one of the bloodiest confrontations in human history. The sheer scale of the devastation bore witness to the dangers of leadership driven more by personal ego and vendettas than by tactical and strategic acumen.

Parallel to the events in Europe was the unfolding drama in the Pacific Theater. The Japanese Empire, driven by its need for resources and inspired by a vision of Pan-Asian dominance, embarked on a series of conquests. Territories like Manchuria were rapidly subjugated, but Japan's ambitions didn't halt there. Its subsequent actions, especially the surprise attack on Pearl Harbor in December 1941, pulled the United States fully into the war. The interaction between Emperor Hirohito's imperial ambitions and the tactical objectives of the Japanese military leadership underscored the intricate relationships within the Axis alliance.

Meanwhile, in the arid landscapes of North Africa, another crucial theater was taking shape. Axis and Allied powers vied for dominance, with control of the Mediterranean and the Suez Canal at stake from 1940 to 1943. Churchill, ever the strategic visionary, understood the significance of this theater. His directives and involvement, ranging from the selection of commanders to the intricacies of military logistics, reinforced North Africa as a pivotal front.

Across these theaters, leadership was paramount. Decisions made at the top echeloned reverberated through the ranks, influencing battle outcomes and, by extension, the broader course of the war. The complexities of global warfare demanded not only tactical genius but also the ability to galvanize nations, negotiate alliances, and, when necessary, make sacrifices for the greater good. In this vast tableau of conflict, the influences of leaders like Hitler, Churchill, Roosevelt, Stalin, and Hirohito were not mere footnotes but defining scripts shaping the narrative of World War II.

Major Battles and Turning Points: Decisions from the Top

As the Second World War progressed, several pivotal battles, influenced by strategic decisions from leadership, dictated the direction and momentum of the conflict.

Having already delineated the catastrophic Battle of Stalingrad, its ramifications reverberated throughout the Eastern Front, marking a significant turning point in the war. Hitler's obsession with capturing the city, and Stalin's steadfast resolve to defend it, highlighted how personal ambitions and vendettas of leaders could have profound military and geopolitical implications. The aftermath of Stalingrad significantly weakened the German Wehrmacht, laying the foundation for subsequent Soviet offensives.

In the Pacific Theater, the Battle of Midway in June 1942 emerged as a decisive naval combat that shifted the momentum against Japanese expansion. American codebreakers, having intercepted Japanese communications, provided invaluable intelligence that allowed U.S. naval forces to prepare for the impending assault. The subsequent victory at Midway was not merely a testament to American naval prowess but also showcased the significance of intelligence, timely decision-making, and strategic foresight in modern warfare.

On the Western Front, the D-Day landings in Normandy stand as a monumental military operation, exemplifying the fruits of Allied cooperation. The decision to open a second front in Europe was a contentious one, but the combined vision of leaders like Winston Churchill and Franklin D. Roosevelt, backed by meticulous planning and immense logistical efforts, made it a reality. The successful landings on June 6, 1944, marked the beginning of the end for Nazi Germany, as Allied forces initiated their inexorable push towards Berlin.

Across these battles, it becomes again evident that while military prowess and ground-level tactics were essential, the overarching strategies and decisions taken at the top echelons significantly determined the outcomes. The confluence of leadership decisions, often made under immense pressure and with incomplete information, played a crucial role in shaping the course of World War II.

Allied Strategy and Cooperation:
Navigating Power Dynamics

The intricate landscape of World War II, with its multiple theaters and shifting alliances, necessitated an unprecedented level of cooperation among the Allied powers. Central to this collaborative framework were the high-level strategic decisions, alliances forged, and, crucially, the personalities that shaped them.

At the outset of the conflict, while the United States remained officially neutral, the strategic importance of supporting the Allies, especially Britain, was recognized by President Franklin D. Roosevelt. As articulated in a previous section the Lend-Lease Act, signed into law in 1941, stands as a testament to Roosevelt's vision and ability to navigate domestic political constraints. The material aid from the Act, ranging from warships to food supplies, played a pivotal role in bolstering the Allied war effort, particularly during periods when the outcome of the conflict seemed uncertain.

While material support laid the foundation for collaboration, the nuances of strategy and post-war planning required in-depth deliberations. A series of high-profile conferences marked the wartime period, with leaders of the major Allied powers convening to align their strategies. Among these, the Tehran, Yalta, and Potsdam conferences stand out for their impact on the war and the post-war world order.

Winston Churchill's presence in these gatherings was marked by his distinctive blend of diplomacy, foresight, and a deep understanding of European history and geopolitics. His interactions with both Roosevelt and Stalin showcased his ability to balance the immediate military needs with longer-term political considerations. For instance, at Yalta, while military strategies were a focus, discussions also ventured into the post-war reorganization of Europe, the United Nations' establishment, and the fate of territories liberated from Nazi occupation. Churchill's emphasis on preserving a balance of power in Europe, his concerns over Soviet intentions in Eastern Europe, and his push for a united post-war Germany underscored his long-term vision for a stable and free Europe.

However, these conferences also laid bare the underlying tensions among the Allies. As the war progressed, divergent post-war ambitions became evident. While the unified objective of vanquishing the Axis powers bound the Allies together, the foundations for future tensions, especially between the Western democracies and the Soviet Union, were taking root.

In sum, the strategic cooperation during World War II was not merely a function of shared military objectives but was deeply influenced by the visions, ambitions, and interpersonal dynamics of the key leaders. Their ability to navigate the complex power dynamics, often putting aside deep-seated mistrust in favor of larger goals, played a crucial role in shaping the war's outcome and the post-war world.

Holocaust: Hitler's Dark Vision Realized

The Holocaust, perhaps one of the most haunting and profound tragedies of the 20th century, stands as a chilling testament to the extreme depths to which human malevolence can sink when unchecked. This atrocity was not the byproduct of impersonal historical forces but was driven primarily by the vision and fanaticism of Adolf Hitler and the Nazi leadership, deeply rooted in a toxic blend of anti-Semitism, racial purity theories, and a distorted sense of German destiny.

As the Nazis solidified their grip on German society and expanded their territorial conquests across Europe, the architecture for systematic persecution and extermination of Jews and other targeted groups was meticulously designed and implemented. At the core of this machinery of death was the "Final Solution," a euphemistic term that concealed the intent to annihilate the entire Jewish population of Europe. Under the guise of resettlement or work programs, Jews from conquered territories were rounded up, often with the complicity or direct involvement of puppet regimes or collaborators in various European countries.

The concentration camps, initially created for political prisoners, dissenters, and perceived "racial enemies," evolved into a vast network of forced labor and extermination centers. Among these, camps like Auschwitz, Treblinka, and Sobibor gained notoriety for their industrial-scale slaughter. The chilling efficiency with which these camps operated – from the transportation of victims in cattle cars to their systematic extermination in gas chambers, followed by the disposal of bodies in crematoria – showcased a mechanized approach to mass murder. The brutality wasn't limited to these established centers. Mobile killing units, or Einsatzgruppen, conducted mass shootings, particularly in Eastern Europe, leaving behind grim trails of mass graves.

The Holocaust also extended beyond Jews. Romani people, Slavs, communists, homosexuals, Jehovah's Witnesses, and others deemed undesirable by Nazi ideology were subjected to persecution, forced labor, and death.

It was only as the war concluded and Allied forces liberated these camps that the full extent of the Holocaust's horrors came to light. The post-war world was confronted with unimaginable scenes of emaciated survivors, mass graves, and testimonies that recounted the depth of Nazi barbarity.

In the wake of these revelations, the international community grappled with the challenge of justice. The Nuremberg Trials, where major war criminals were prosecuted, set a precedent, emphasizing that individuals, including heads of state and military leaders, could be held accountable for crimes against humanity. These proceedings, while met with various criticisms, underscored a global commitment to ensuring that such atrocities were neither forgotten nor repeated.

Yet, beyond the realm of legal proceedings and historical records, the Holocaust's legacy serves as a somber reflection on the fragility of human morality, the dangers of unchecked power, and the profound consequences of turning indifference into state policy.

The Home Front: Societal Changes and Leaders' Influences

While the global theater of World War II witnessed military confrontations of unprecedented scale, the profound societal changes unfolding on the home front were no less significant. These transformations, often influenced or directly orchestrated by national leaders, were both a response to and a driving force of the war effort.

As nations became embroiled in the conflict, the importance of maintaining a robust wartime economy became paramount. National leaders, recognizing the urgency, took measures to redirect their countries' industrial and agricultural outputs towards supporting the war effort. Factories, previously dedicated to civilian goods, were swiftly converted to produce arms, ammunition, and military equipment. Labor forces were reoriented, with wartime needs dictating shifts in employment patterns. In the U.S., President Franklin D. Roosevelt's administration orchestrated massive mobilization efforts, ensuring resources, both human and material, flowed seamlessly to support the Allies. Similarly, in Britain, Churchill's government implemented rationing, production controls, and other measures to ensure the nation's survival during its most challenging times.

Yet, among the many societal shifts, one of the most profound was the evolving role of women. With a significant portion of the male population engaged on battlefronts, women stepped into roles previously deemed outside their purview. They worked in factories, managed farms, served as nurses, and even took up roles in auxiliary military services. This wasn't merely a feature of the Allied nations. In the Soviet Union, under Stalin's directives, women not only took up industrial roles but also served on the frontlines, with some gaining renown as snipers or pilots. This change, born out of wartime necessity, catalyzed a broader reevaluation of gender roles and paved the way for post-war discussions on gender equality.

Parallel to these economic and social transformations was the omnipresent influence of propaganda. State-controlled media in Axis and Allied nations alike presented carefully curated narratives designed to boost morale, demonize the enemy, and justify national policies. Hitler's Germany utilized propaganda to an extreme, molding every aspect of German society to align with Nazi ideals. Radio broadcasts, films, posters, and newspapers were all harnessed to this end. Churchill, too, recognized the power of communication, not just in his famed speeches but also in the broader British media strategy that fostered unity and resilience.

As days turned into months and months into years, the daily life of civilians, whether in bombed cities or rural villages, was profoundly shaped by the war. Yet, beneath the surface of shared sacrifices, ration cards, blackouts, and air raid sirens, it was the leadership and decisions of a few that often influenced the many, shaping national trajectories in ways that would resonate long after the war's final shots were fired.

Conclusion: Endgame and Lessons from WWII

As World War II neared its conclusion, it stood as a testament to the strategic decisions and actions of key leaders, each leaving an indelible mark on global history. The profound tumult of this conflict touched virtually every region, taking tens of millions of lives and reshaping the geopolitical landscape.

Berlin, emblematic of Nazi ambitions and Hitler's vision, bore the brunt of a relentless siege, primarily from the Red Army advancing from the East. Stalin, with a keen eye on post-war Europe, prioritized Berlin's capture. As the intensity of the siege amplified and defeat became inevitable, on April 30, 1945, Adolf Hitler, the architect of a vision that had plunged the world into chaos and brought untold suffering, committed suicide. This act marked the end of one of the most devastating and tyrannical reigns in the history of humanity.

Yet, the battle for Berlin was more than a military conquest. It was a clash of ideologies, a testament to the resilience of nations under their leaders. With Berlin's fall in May 1945, the curtain began to drop on Nazi Germany, and the stage was set for Europe's division into Eastern and Western blocs, influenced heavily by Stalin's aspirations.

Parallel to the European theater's climactic moments, the Pacific front witnessed critical decisions. The advancing Allies had effectively cornered the Japanese empire. However, Japan's tenacity remained undeterred. Recognizing the prospective challenges of a ground invasion of Japan, Truman, inheriting Roosevelt's mantle, opted to deploy atomic weapons, a decision altering humanity's trajectory. The consequent obliteration of Hiroshima and Nagasaki in August 1945 precipitated Japan's capitulation, marking World War II's end.

However, the war's termination was not just about concluding military engagements. It facilitated profound geopolitical realignments. Leaders like Churchill, Roosevelt, and Stalin, with their post-war visions, played instrumental roles in these shifts. Europe, a nexus of the conflict, soon found itself partitioned by the Iron Curtain. The establishment of the United Nations reflected the collective aspiration to circumvent future global conflicts, encapsulating the enduring hope for diplomacy over war.

Economic transformations ensued in the war's aftermath. With Europe's financial frameworks devastated, the U.S. rose as a dominant economic entity. This economic metamorphosis was amplified by strategies like the Marshall Plan and by foundational systems such as Bretton Woods. On a societal front, accelerated shifts in gender dynamics were palpable, especially in regions where women were central to wartime economies.

World War II's broader legacies permeated beyond geopolitical and economic realms. The indomitable spirit of nations, often mirroring their leadership, manifested in societal reconstruction post-conflict. The lessons from this era, shaped by both heroic and malevolent leaders, remain enduringly relevant. As contemporary generations navigate global complexities, the pressing need for visionary leadership, moral integrity, strategic wisdom, and international collaboration is accentuated, drawing from the invaluable lessons of this epoch.

Churchill, Roosevelt and Stalin in Yalta on Feb. 4, 1945[38]

Chapter 25.
Decolonization:
The Wind of Change
(mid-20th century)

I cherish the ideal of a democratic and free society in which
all persons live together in harmony
and with equal opportunities.

~Nelson Mandela

Decolonization: The Fall of Empires

By the early 20th century, empires that had long dominated vast swaths of territories began to face significant internal and external challenges. In the industrial age, these empires had stretched their boundaries, harnessing resources and markets to fuel their burgeoning economies. Colonial subjects were invariably subjected to a life designed to serve the imperial center. Raw materials from the colonies were shipped to the metropoles to feed the ever-hungry factories, and the finished goods were then sold back to these very colonies. This dynamic, while enriching the colonial powers, often came at a grave cost to the colonized regions, both economically and socio-culturally.

However, by the mid-20th century, global dynamics began to shift. Numerous factors, ranging from the severe economic strains placed on colonial powers by the two World Wars, to the rise of nationalist sentiments in the colonies, were reshaping the global order. The British Empire, often described as "the empire on which the sun never sets" due to its vast expanse, began to feel the pressure of these winds of change.

While Britain was the most dominant colonial powers, it was not alone in facing the challenges of a changing world. Other European empires, such as the French, Portuguese, and Dutch, also began to witness a rise in anti-colonial sentiments within their territories. These sentiments were not mere spontaneous outbursts but were the culmination of years, sometimes centuries, of foreign rule and its associated exploitations.

As nations within these empires began to agitate for independence, they drew upon a rich tapestry of experiences, weaving together histories of resistance, adaptation, and survival under colonial rule. The stories of these nations, as they sought to break free from the yoke of colonialism, were marked by struggles and sacrifices. Each sought to define its identity, often drawing on ancient histories and cultures that predated colonial rule. And as these nations charted their paths towards independence, they were not merely reclaiming their territories but also reasserting their histories, cultures, and destinies.

Though Latin America's decolonization largely predates this era and the Middle East's modern borders had been delineated after the collapse of the Ottoman Empire post-WWI, their experiences provided precedents and contexts for the challenges and aspirations faced by nations in the second half of the 20th century. Key regions like India, Sub-Saharan Africa, Southeast Asia, and the Caribbean emerged as epicenters of this transformative process, each with its unique journey and challenges.

The aftermath of World War II provided a critical juncture in the decolonization narrative. The war had not only weakened the traditional European powers economically and militarily but also laid bare the inherent contradictions of empires that had fought for freedom and democracy abroad while suppressing those very ideals in their colonies. Colonized soldiers, fighting side by side with Europeans, returned to their homelands with an enhanced fervor for self-rule and equality.

Economic constraints in the post-war era further catalyzed the decolonization process. For many European powers, upholding and administrating distant colonies, especially amidst growing resistance, became increasingly unsustainable. At the same time, nationalist movements burgeoned within these colonies.

On the global stage, evolving ideologies played a significant role. The principle of self-determination, gaining prominence particularly after the inception of international bodies like the League of Nations and subsequently the United Nations, made the world less amenable to colonial subjugation. Additionally, the Cold War's geopolitical dynamics, with the U.S. and USSR vying for global influence, often manifested in support for decolonization, albeit driven by their respective strategic interests.

Beyond political and economic realms, the moral landscape was shifting as well. A burgeoning cadre of intellectuals, artists, and writers began critiquing colonialism's core tenets, highlighting its exploitative nature and intrinsic inequities. Their discourses, resonating globally, fortified the moral underpinnings of the decolonization movement.

These movements towards independence, however, were not devoid of challenges. The colonial powers had left indelible imprints on the political, economic, and social structures of these emerging nations. Institutions and frameworks, established during the colonial era, often presented both opportunities and hurdles. While they offered a semblance of administrative continuity, they also posed challenges in reconciling these structures with indigenous traditions and aspirations.

In essence, the decolonization era represented a profound shift in global dynamics. The age-old structures of colonial dominance were giving way to a world where nations, once subjugated and exploited, were now asserting their rightful places on the global stage. However, the path to true sovereignty required these nations to confront not just their colonial legacies but also the intricacies of a world rapidly transforming around them.

As the world stood on the cusp of a significant transformation, the once unchallengeable might of empires began to wane. The decolonization process that ensued would not only redefine global geopolitics but would also raise profound questions about identity, governance, and the very nature of power. The narratives of nations emerging from the shadows of empires would serve as a testament to the resilience of peoples and cultures in the face of prolonged subjugation.

Dynamics of Post-Colonial Transition

In the aftermath of decolonization, as the once-mighty empires receded, emerging nations grappled with the profound reverberations of colonial rule. This transition was not merely a shift in political power but a comprehensive metamorphosis that probed the very essence of newly formed nations.

The departure of colonial administrations often ushered in a governance vacuum. Many nascent states, in their quest for stability and order, faced the Herculean task of crafting a governance model suitable for their diverse populations. While some leaned towards parliamentary systems reminiscent of their former colonizers, others embarked on journeys to meld indigenous principles with contemporary governance structures. These decisions bore profound implications for the trajectory of these nations, often determining their stability and prosperity in subsequent decades.

Alongside these political recalibrations, economic transformations were paramount. For long, the colonial framework had relegated many regions to the margins, primarily casting them as resource suppliers. With newfound autonomy, there arose an imperative to recalibrate economies, pivoting away from singular commodity reliance. Countries undertook ambitious projects: initiating land reforms, nationalizing pivotal industries, and investing in indigenous manufacturing capabilities, all in a bid to extricate themselves from economic blueprints stamped by colonial predecessors.

On the global front, the Cold War's looming specter presented a fresh set of challenges. In a world increasingly defined by the bipolar contestation of the US and USSR, many post-colonial nations, aware of the perils of aligning too closely with either bloc, aspired for a more neutral stance. Figures like India's Nehru and Egypt's Nasser championed the Non-Aligned Movement, advocating for a path that balanced national sovereignty with the pragmatics of global geopolitics.

Yet, decolonization was not solely a political or economic phenomenon. Emancipation from colonial confines spurred a vibrant cultural resurgence. Nations, emerging from under the shadow of imperial cultural impositions, witnessed the rebirth of indigenous art, literature, and traditions. This period, marked by a fervent exploration of identity, saw nations marrying their historical legacies with contemporary aspirations, crafting narratives distinct to each.

However, the journey was fraught with challenges. The colonial legacy had left scars, some overt and others more insidious. Economic paradigms, linguistic legacies, and even educational structures established by colonizers persisted, often raising contentious debates about the true depth of newfound independence.

Furthermore, the specter of colonial cartography haunted many. Borders, often arbitrarily etched during colonial dominion, became flashpoints. Territorial disputes, rooted in these historical demarcations, instigated tensions, necessitating complex diplomatic interventions and, in some instances, leading to militaristic confrontations.

While the overarching narrative of decolonization was punctuated by these themes, it's essential to recognize the countless grassroots movements that operated beneath this grand tapestry. These localized, yet potent movements, often overlooked in the annals of global history, played pivotal roles in reshaping national trajectories.

In synthesizing these dynamics, it becomes evident that while the formal cessation of colonial rule was undeniably a monumental milestone, the subsequent journey was laden with complexities. As we delve deeper into the regional narratives, starting with India, the intricacies of these post-colonial trajectories will be further illuminated.

India: From British Raj to Independence

In the immediate aftermath of World War II, India found itself at a pivotal moment in its long struggle against British colonial rule. The war had significantly depleted Britain's resources, both materially and morally. The British had advocated for freedom and democracy abroad while actively suppressing these very ideals in their colonies, an irony not lost on Indian nationalists.

During this period, India was not simply a subject of colonial domination but also a focal point in the global dynamics of empire building and dissolution. Its value as the "Jewel in the Crown" meant that its independence would signal a decisive shift in the balance of global power. The Quit India Movement of 1942, led by the Indian National Congress, epitomized the heightened push for self-rule, revealing the weakening grip of the British Raj.

Leaders like Mahatma Gandhi, with his philosophy of non-violent resistance, Jawaharlal Nehru with his vision for a secular, modern India, and Muhammad Ali Jinnah, advocating for a separate state for Muslims, became instrumental figures. Their varying visions and the intrinsic religious and cultural diversities within India added layers of complexity to the decolonization process.

The culmination of divergent aspirations, particularly the vision of Muhammad Ali Jinnah for a separate homeland for Muslims, led to the heart-wrenching decision of partitioning the subcontinent. In 1947, the boundaries were drawn, birthing two nations: predominantly Hindu India and Muslim-majority Pakistan. This process, overseen hastily by the British and materialized by the Radcliffe Line, resulted in one of the largest mass migrations in human

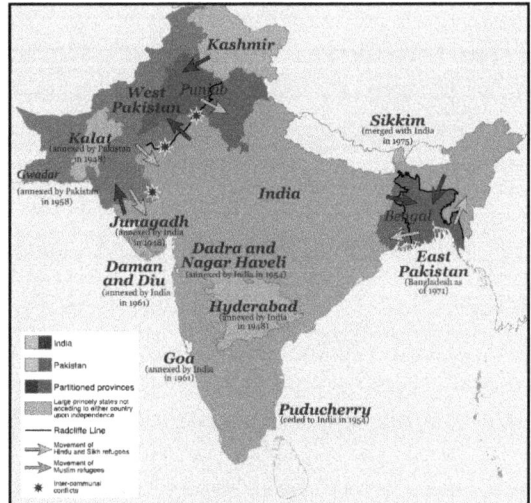

Partition of India 1947[39]

history, as millions sought to be on the side of the border that matched their religious identity. The hurried division, unfortunately, also ignited deep-seated animosities, leading to widespread communal violence, the scars of which linger in the subcontinent's psyche to this day. The partition not only reshaped the geopolitical landscape of South Asia but also underscored the inherent challenges and tragic costs tied to the dissolution of empires.

India's independence in 1947 did not just mark the end of British rule but also signified the decline of the British Empire itself. The narrative of India's independence, marred by the pains of partition, was a testament to the complexities involved in dismantling global empires. The colonial legacies, including the political and economic structures established by the British, continued to influence India's trajectory in subsequent years.

In sum, India's journey to independence exemplifies the intricate dance of the rise, reign, and decline of global empires. The subcontinent, once subjugated under the vast British Empire, emerged to assert its place in a rapidly changing global order, setting a precedent for other colonies and solidifying the inevitable decline of imperial dominance.

Sub-Saharan Africa

In the aftermath of India's path to independence, which set a precedent for colonial territories worldwide, Sub-Saharan Africa's aspirations for self-rule found renewed vigor. The decline of the British Empire in Asia resonated with the African anti-colonial movements, offering both inspiration and a tangible example of the waning European imperial might. Just as in India, the European powers, beleaguered by the demands of post-war reconstruction and shifting global dynamics, began to grapple with rising anti-colonial sentiments in their African colonies. These territories, rich in diversity and history, were no longer mere subjects of European domination but were increasingly becoming focal points in the broader narrative of the decline of global empires.

The struggle against colonial rule in Africa was multifaceted. Economically, the colonial extraction model had left many African countries impoverished, with economies tethered to the needs of their colonial masters. The shared experience of economic exploitation formed a collective consciousness among Africans about the need for self-rule and economic self-determination. Leaders such as Kwame Nkrumah in Ghana and Jomo Kenyatta in Kenya emerged as potent symbols of resistance against colonial subjugation.

By the late 1950s and throughout the 1960s, what began as a ripple in Ghana, with its successful quest for independence in 1957, transformed into a tidal wave. Nations across the continent, from Nigeria in the west to Tanzania in the east, embarked on their journeys towards self-rule. However, each transition carried its unique imprint.

In Algeria, the quest for independence from French rule was particularly violent and protracted. Starting in 1954, the National Liberation Front (FLN) led a guerrilla war against the French forces. This conflict, characterized by guerilla warfare, bombings, and large-scale battles, also witnessed atrocities and use of torture by both sides. The Algerian War for Independence, lasting nearly eight years, culminated in 1962 with the Evian Accords, leading to the official recognition of Algeria's sovereignty by France.

Similarly, in Angola, the struggle for independence from Portuguese rule was marked by a complex interplay of nationalist movements and Cold War geopolitics. Beginning in the early 1960s, multiple nationalist movements, including the Popular Movement for the Liberation of Angola (MPLA), the National Front for the Liberation of Angola (FNLA), and the National Union for the Total Independence of Angola (UNITA), initiated armed campaigns against Portuguese colonial forces. The intricacies of this conflict were further complicated by the involvement of major Cold War powers, with the U.S. and the USSR supporting different factions.

It's worth noting that Portugal's overseas wars in its colonies, such as in Angola, were one of the triggers for the Carnation Revolution back in Lisbon. This nearly bloodless coup in 1974 led to the downfall of Portugal's Estado Novo regime, ending decades of authoritarian rule. The revolution and the subsequent shift in the Portuguese political landscape expedited the decolonization process, as the new leadership was disinclined to sustain the empire's costly colonial endeavors. The Carnation Revolution, symbolized by civilians placing carnations in the muzzles of soldiers' rifles, not only transformed Portugal's domestic politics but also sent reverberations across its vast colonial territories, accelerating their paths to independence.

While some nations, like Botswana, navigated their way to independence relatively peacefully, others emerged from the shadows of prolonged and bloody conflicts, with the scars of these battles shaping their post-colonial trajectories.

Yet, the challenges for these newly independent nations were manifold. The artificial borders, drawn with little regard for ethnic or cultural considerations, became sources of internal strife. Furthermore, the Cold War era's geopolitical tug-of-war meant that many African nations found themselves pawns in the larger ideological battles between the US and the USSR.

In the overarching narrative of global empires, Sub-Saharan Africa's decolonization marked the decline of European imperial ambitions and underscored the region's resilience. The mosaic of African nations, each charting its path in a post-colonial world, symbolized the end of an era dominated by European colonial exploits and heralded the emergence of Africa's assertiveness in global geopolitics.

The Caribbean:
Chains of Colonialism to Chords of Independence

Following the wave of decolonization in Sub-Saharan Africa, the Caribbean began to resonate with calls for autonomy. The African experience, while geographically distant, held a symbolic significance for the islands. After all, many Caribbean societies were intricately tied to Africa through histories of the transatlantic slave trade and shared African roots. The triumphs of African nations against colonial rule provided both a blueprint and a beacon of hope for the Caribbean territories.

The Caribbean, with its mosaic of islands, each with a distinct colonial history, had been a stage for European power struggles for centuries. The Spanish, British, French, and Dutch had all etched their influence on these islands, leading to a complex web of linguistic, cultural, and political legacies. As World War II concluded and the colonial powers were reeling from its aftermath, the Caribbean islands sensed an opportunity to redefine their destinies.

Jamaica, under the leadership of figures like Norman Manley, began its march towards self-governance, culminating in its independence from British rule in 1962. Similarly, Trinidad and Tobago, under the guidance of Eric Williams, charted its own course away from colonial subjugation. These successes set off a domino effect across the region. By the mid-20th century, various islands, each in its own time and manner, began severing their colonial ties.

However, here too, the path to independence was not without its challenges. The economic dependency cultivated during the colonial era, especially in sectors like sugar and banana exports, posed significant hurdles. Moreover, the geopolitical significance of the Caribbean, especially during the Cold War, meant that the superpowers, particularly the United States, kept a close eye on the region. This was most evident in events like the Cuban Revolution and the subsequent tensions it ignited on a global scale.

In the broader saga of the rise, reign, and decline of empires, the Caribbean narrative underscores a crucial aspect: the lingering impact of colonialism on societies long after political independence is achieved. The Caribbean islands, while charting their paths in the post-colonial world, offered a stark reminder of the deep-seated imprints left behind by empires and the enduring quest of nations to navigate, and when necessary, challenge those legacies.

Southeast Asia: Embers of Empire and New Nationhood

Building on the momentum from the Caribbean and Sub-Saharan African decolonization movements, Southeast Asia emerged as another focal point in the narrative of the declining global empires post-World War II. The war had destabilized the once indomitable European colonial presence in the region, notably the French in Indochina and the British in Malaya and Burma. Moreover, the wartime occupation of many Southeast Asian territories by Japan had fostered nationalist movements and exposed the vulnerabilities of European powers.

In Vietnam, the aspirations for independence found voice in Ho Chi Minh and the Viet Minh movement. Despite facing a formidable French military, the Vietnamese, driven by nationalistic fervor and adept guerrilla tactics, achieved a decisive victory in the Battle of Dien Bien Phu in 1954. The conclusion of the Battle of Dien Bien Phu and the subsequent

Geneva Accords did more than just signal the end of French colonial rule. They divided Vietnam into North and South, setting the stage for a series of tensions that would eventually escalate into the Vietnam War. The North, under Ho Chi Minh, was determined to unify Vietnam under communist rule, while the South, with support from the United States and its allies, sought to establish a non-communist state. The Vietnam War, which ensued, was not merely a civil conflict but a manifestation of the larger Cold War tensions, with the United States and the Soviet Union supporting opposing sides. This war, a direct consequence of the decolonization process, became emblematic of the challenges many newly independent nations faced, as they became arenas for superpower rivalries, further complicating their paths to genuine sovereignty and internal cohesion.

Simultaneously, the Indonesian archipelago, having borne Dutch rule for centuries, witnessed a surge in nationalist sentiments. Leaders like Sukarno became instrumental in channeling these sentiments into a cohesive movement, eventually culminating in the Indonesian proclamation of independence in 1945. Although the Dutch initially resisted, international pressure and persistent Indonesian resistance forced their eventual withdrawal.

The British colonies in the region also underwent profound transformation. Malaya, buoyed by the Malayan National Liberation Army's resistance against British rule and the broader anti-colonial sentiment, moved towards self-governance, leading to the establishment of Malaysia in 1963. This formation initially included Singapore, but due to economic, political, and racial tensions, Singapore separated from Malaysia in 1965 to become an independent city-state. While Malaysia faced various challenges in its post-colonial journey, grappling with multi-ethnic governance and economic development, Singapore, under the leadership of Lee Kuan Yew, charted a remarkable course. With a focus on robust governance, economic liberalization, and education, Singapore transformed from a small port city to one of the world's most prosperous nations in a few decades. Meanwhile, Burma (now Myanmar) and the Philippines also navigated their unique colonial legacies towards sovereignty, each with its distinct challenges and trajectories.

However, like their counterparts in Africa and the Caribbean, these newly formed nations grappled with the challenges bequeathed by colonial rule. Ethnical and religious diversities, often manipulated during colonial times, emerged as sources of tension. Additionally, as seen before, the geopolitical significance of Southeast Asia, especially during the Cold War era, saw superpowers vying for influence, further complicating the post-colonial trajectory of these nations.

In the overarching context of empires, Southeast Asia's transition exemplified the intricate interplay between colonial legacies, nationalistic aspirations, and global geopolitics. These nations, once mere pawns in imperial designs, were now asserting their agency, reshaping the global tapestry in their quest for sovereignty and identity.

Conclusion: The Evolving Global Paradigm

As the sun set on empires, the latter half of the 20th century heralded a significant shift in the balance of global power. A world that had once been delineated by vast colonial territories and dominions began to reshape into a more multipolar landscape. This was not merely a shift in territorial control but a metamorphosis of the foundational paradigms governing international relations.

The decline of European colonial empires, whose dominance had shaped centuries of global politics, made room for two emerging superpowers: the United States and the Soviet Union. The ideological schism between these behemoths, one championing capitalism and the other communism, birthed the Cold War, covered in a subsequent chapter. The reverberations of this ideological tussle were felt across continents, influencing not just political allegiances but also economic, cultural, and social trajectories of many a newly independent nation.

However, focusing merely on the bipolar dynamics of the U.S. and USSR would be an oversimplification of the evolving global paradigm. The non-aligned movement, initiated by leaders like India's Jawaharlal Nehru, Egypt's Gamal Abdel Nasser, and Indonesia's Sukarno, epitomized the aspirations of many newly decolonized nations to carve out an autonomous space in global geopolitics, free from the overbearing shadow of superpower rivalry. The movement aimed to strike a middle path, focusing on developmental and post-colonial challenges rather than being ensnared in Cold War binaries.

Simultaneously, economic realities began to wield significant influence on global politics. The Marshall Plan, conceived by the United States to revitalize war-ravaged Europe, was not just an economic package; it was a strategic tool, fostering capitalist democracies that would align, both economically and politically, with the West. The formation of economic groupings and blocs, such as the European Economic Community, which would later evolve into the European Union, symbolized a shift towards regional integrations aimed at economic prosperity and political stability.

The decline of colonial empires also meant that global institutions started playing a more pivotal role. The United Nations, founded on the principles of collective security and international cooperation, sought to mediate conflicts and foster development. Yet, its effectiveness was often hamstrung by the veto powers of the permanent members of the Security Council, reflecting the continuance of power politics even in an age of internationalism.

The global stage was also witness to the emergence of significant players from Asia. Japan, rising from the ruins of World War II and renouncing militarism, charted a path that transformed it into an economic power-house by the close of the century. China, after the establishment of the People's Republic in 1949, embarked on a tumultuous journey, but by the turn of the 21st century, began asserting its place as a global actor, challenging the dynamics of a world that had, for long, been dominated by Western powers.

In conclusion, the latter half of the 20th century marked a significant departure from the established norms of global power. The rise, reign, and decline of empires were not just historical milestones but lessons underscoring the transient nature of power. As nations rose to prominence, others waned, but the constant was the ever-evolving nature of global geopolitics, characterized by a confluence of historical legacies, economic imperatives, ideological battles, and the indomitable aspirations of peoples and nations.

USSR_Republics_numbered_by_alphabet[40]
1. Armenia • 2. Azerbaijan • 3. Belarus • 4. Estonia • 5. Georgia • 6. Kazakhstan •
7. Kyrgyzstan • 8. Latvia • 9. Lithuania • 10. Moldova • 11. Russia • 12. Tajikistan •
13. Turkmenistan • 14. Ukraine • 15. Uzbekistan

Chapter 26.
Soviet Union: From Revolution to Dissolution (1917-1991)

Politicians are the same all over.
They promise to build bridges even when there are no rivers.

~Nikita Khrushchev

Setting the Stage For the Revolution

At the dawn of the 20ᵗʰ century, the vast expanse of the Russian Empire stood as a formidable presence in Eastern Europe and Asia. Yet, beneath the veneer of its territorial prowess, the empire was beset with profound socio-economic tensions that would soon bring it to a breaking point.

The Russian socio-economic landscape in the early 1900s was pre-dominantly agrarian. Over 80% of its populace resided in rural areas, engaged in agriculture. The peasantry, bound by semi-feudal relations and oppressive systems like the 'Mir' or the village commune, grappled with periodic famines, land shortages, and increasing indebtedness. The 1861 Emancipation Reform had liberated the serfs, but the benefits of this liberation were limited. Most peasants found themselves with insufficient land, and the better-quality plots often remained in the hands of the nobility.

Simultaneously, the turn of the century also marked Russia's tryst with industrialization, albeit belatedly. Cities like St. Petersburg and Moscow began to burgeon into industrial hubs. Factories, especially in the textiles and metallurgy sectors, mushroomed, attracting rural migrants in droves. However, the swift pace of urbanization was not matched with adequate infrastructure or labor rights. Working conditions in factories were deplorable, and urban workers, or the "proletariat", found themselves facing long hours, paltry wages, and hazardous environments.

While the lower strata of society grappled with these challenges, the Russian monarchy, led by Tsar Nicholas II (1894-1917), remained largely autocratic, resistant to substantive reforms. The political atmosphere was stifling, with limited avenues for dissent. The 1905 Revolution, a precursor to the more transformative revolution in 1917, was a manifestation of these socio-economic and political tensions. Though it led to certain concessions, including the establishment of the Duma or the legislative assembly, real power remained firmly with the Tsar.

In a broader global context, the early 20th century was a period of tumultuous change. The onset of World War I in 1914 further strained Russia's already fragile socio-economic fabric. The war effort exposed the empire's administrative inefficiencies and military vulnerabilities. As Russian soldiers faced defeats on the battlefield, discontentment grew at home, with food shortages and inflation exacerbating the populace's hardships.

In this evolving mosaic of internal strife and global upheavals, Russia stood on the precipice of monumental change. The long-simmering discontent would soon find an outlet, culminating in the 1917 revolutions – events that would not only reshape Russia but also leave an indelible mark on world history.

Rise of the Bolsheviks

Building up on the previous section the debacle of World War I, coupled with long-standing grievances against an autocratic regime, created a volatile environment. Into this milieu entered the Bolsheviks, a radical faction that would capitalize on the prevailing discontent to shape the destiny of the Russian Empire.

The undercurrents of dissatisfaction had been brewing for decades. The industrial workers, bearing the brunt of Russia's rapid but haphazard industrialization, agitated against oppressive working conditions and meager wages. The peasantry, reeling under the weight of exploitative land systems, aspired for agrarian reforms. And the intelligentsia sought political freedoms and an end to the Tsarist autocracy. The initial 1917 February Revolution, which led to the abdication of Tsar Nicholas II and the establishment of the Provisional Government, did not fully address these grievances, leading to a power vacuum and further discontent.

In this charged atmosphere, the Bolshevik Party, led by Vladimir Lenin, emerged as a potent force. Distinct from other socialist factions, the Bolsheviks adhered to a radical interpretation of Marxist thought, adapted to Russia's unique socio-economic context. Lenin's writings, especially his seminal work, "What is to be Done?" (1902), argued for a vanguard party that would lead the proletariat in overthrowing the bourgeoisie. He believed that only a dedicated elite could achieve the revolutionary consciousness needed to instigate change.

The return of Lenin from exile in April 1917 was pivotal. Under his leadership, the Bolsheviks propagated slogans like "Peace, Land, Bread," which resonated deeply with a war-weary and impoverished populace. Alongside Lenin, Leon Trotsky emerged as a key figure, especially in the negotiations and strategies surrounding the October Revolution. Trotsky's organizational acumen was instrumental in the success of the Bolshevik uprising.

In October 1917, leveraging the general disillusionment with the Provisional Government, especially its decision to continue with the war, the Bolsheviks staged a coup. Known as the October Revolution, this event saw the Bolshevik Red Guards take key positions in Petrograd, effectively placing the government under Bolshevik control.

However, the seizure of power was only the beginning. Russia soon plunged into a civil war that lasted from 1917 to 1922. The Bolsheviks, or the Red Army, led by Trotsky, found themselves pitted against a coalition of anti-Bolshevik forces, collectively known as the White Army. This coalition comprised monarchists, conservatives, liberals, and even some socialists, all united in their opposition to Bolshevik rule. The war was brutal, marked by atrocities on both sides.

The Civil War deeply tested the Bolsheviks' resolve and their aptitude to consolidate power. Employing a combination of military strategy, extensive propaganda, and sweeping socio-political reforms, the Red Army managed to outmaneuver its numerous adversaries.

But the conclusion of the Civil War did not simply mark a Bolshevik victory; it set the stage for the restructuring of Russia's political landscape. Lenin and the Bolshevik leadership recognized the need to integrate the various ethnic and national groups within the vast expanse of the former Russian Empire. As such, in 1922, they initiated the formation of a federative structure, integrating multiple national territories. The Russian Soviet Federative Socialist Republic, along with the Ukrainian, Belarusian, and Transcaucasian Soviet Socialist Republics, became founding members of this federation.

On December 30, 1922, these republics came together to sign the Treaty on the Creation of the USSR and the Declaration of the Creation of the USSR, effectively formalizing the establishment of the Union of Soviet Socialist Republics (USSR). This marked not only the end of the Russian Empire but also the inception of a new era: an ambitious socialist experiment that aimed to unify diverse nationalities under a single ideological and administrative umbrella. This union would eventually grow, incorporating various other Soviet republics, and it stood as a global superpower opposing the Western bloc, particularly the United States, throughout the Cold War era.

Establishing a New Order: Marxism-Leninism

Following the tumultuous events of the revolution and the civil war, the task before the Bolsheviks was monumental. They had to transform Russia from a predominantly agrarian society with a vast and diverse population into a unified, industrialized socialist state, guided by the principles of Marxism as interpreted by Lenin.

In the nascent years of the Soviet state, the Bolsheviks were keenly aware of the need to put Marxist theories into practice. Central to this was the establishment of a dictatorship of the proletariat. This entailed state control over the means of production, aiming to eradicate the bourgeoisie and ensure that power and resources resided with the working class. However, Russia's economic and social realities presented challenges. Its industrial base was still developing, and its large peasantry did not neatly fit into Marxist class structures.

To address these issues, Lenin introduced the New Economic Policy (NEP) in 1921. This policy allowed a degree of private enterprise while the state-maintained control over major industries. The NEP was seen as a pragmatic step to revive the economy after the ravages of war and revolution. Yet, it was always considered a temporary measure, a deviation from pure Marxist ideals to address immediate practical concerns.

However, the relative liberalization under the NEP was short-lived. The death of Lenin in 1924 precipitated a power struggle within the Communist Party. By the late 1920s, Joseph Stalin emerged as the undisputed leader, marking a significant shift in the direction of Soviet policies.

Stalin believed in the rapid industrialization of the Soviet Union and the collectivization of agriculture. To achieve these goals, he introduced the Five-Year Plans, focusing on the expansion of heavy industries. While these plans succeeded in rapidly increasing industrial output, they came at a considerable human cost, with forced labor, widespread famines, and the displacement of millions.

Parallel to economic reforms, Stalin embarked on a campaign to consolidate power and eliminate potential rivals. This period, often referred to as the "Great Purge" or the "Great Terror," saw the arrest, execution, or exile of millions, ranging from high-ranking party officials to ordinary citizens. Intellectuals, artists, and even military officials were not immune. The purges were characterized by show trials, forced confessions, and widespread paranoia.

Stalin's policies also extended to the realm of culture and society. He sought to forge a unified Soviet identity, emphasizing the virtues of socialism, patriotism, and sacrifice for the greater good. Efforts were made to promote a sense of common Soviet identity, transcending ethnic and regional differences. The Russian language was promoted, and a standardized educational curriculum was introduced.

Under Stalin, the Soviet state transformed dramatically. While it achieved significant economic progress and global prominence, this was achieved at a significant human cost. The ideals of Marxism-Leninism, as interpreted and implemented by Stalin, left an indelible mark on the Soviet Union, influencing its trajectory for decades to come.

Stalin's Iron Grip and Enduring Legacy

In the annals of the Soviet Union, few figures command the spotlight as formidably as Joseph Stalin. Though his policies facilitated the rise of the USSR as a formidable global entity, the strategies he championed, and the indelible mark he etched on the psyche of the nation determined its course for subsequent generations.

Stalin's zealous drive to solidify the state's influence was most starkly visible beyond his economic measures. While the achievements of the Five-Year Plans were evident in the impressive surge of industrial might, it was the societal cost of such rapid metamorphosis, as illustrated by the tragic famines in regions like Ukraine, that revealed the darker underbelly of Stalinist policies.

Moving from the economic arena to the intricacies of internal governance, Stalin's penchant for absolute control manifested in the haunting period of the Great Purge. Spanning the mid to late 1930s, this era saw the systematic extermination of any perceived threats to Stalin's dominion. The tentacles of this purge extended beyond political adversaries. Intellectuals, seasoned military personnel, and the general populace were frequently ensnared in its grip. Orchestrated by the NKVD, the state's security organ, the campaign's scope was vast, with its effects reverberating through millions of lives.

Yet, the machinery that bolstered Stalin's stature in the eyes of the masses was as sophisticated as it was relentless. An orchestrated cult of personality depicted him as the unerring guardian of Soviet ideals. From educational institutions to factories and domestic spaces, Stalin's visage and the accompanying narrative of his infallibility became omnipresent fixtures. These effusive displays of loyalty to Stalin weren't mere exercises in sycophancy; they were calibrated tools ensuring the state's omnipresence and, by extension, its omnipotence.

Assessing the Stalin era, one discerns a duality. While on one flank the Soviet Union ascended to unparalleled prominence on the global stage, internally, the populace contended with the specters of state-induced paranoia, vigilant surveillance, and an omnipresent climate of fear. And though Stalin's physical presence was extinguished with his death in 1953, his influence, akin to an elongated shadow, persisted. Successors grappled with the weight of his legacy, and even as they embarked on paths to de-Stalinize, remnants of his reign remained deeply interwoven in the fabric of the Soviet narrative.

Command Economy and the Industrial Push

The Soviet Union, under the direction of its leadership, recognized early on the importance of an independent and self-reliant economic framework. To this end, the initiation and implementation of the Five-Year Plans were not mere policy decisions, but a strategic maneuver to assert Soviet autonomy on the world stage.

While the previous section touched upon the broader objectives and consequences of these plans, delving deeper into the industrial push reveals a tapestry of meticulous planning, challenges, and the sheer will of a nation to transform itself. The focus here is not on the centralization itself but on the machinery that made this transformation possible.

The First Five-Year Plan, launched in 1928, was less about industrialization in isolation and more about constructing an interconnected web of industries. The plan aimed to make the Soviet Union self-reliant, reducing its need for western industrial imports. It emphasized heavy industries, including coal, iron, and steel. Simultaneously, efforts were made to construct infrastructural behemoths like the Moscow Metro and the Volga-Don Canal.

However, in this fervor to industrialize, agriculture was not left untouched. While the collectivization drive and its aftermath are detailed previously, it's crucial to note the economic rationale behind it. The Soviet leadership believed that modernizing agriculture was the key to financing its industrial ambitions. By consolidating farms and increasing grain exports, the state aimed to fund the required imports for industrialization.

Yet, this rapid march towards an industrial economy came with pitfalls. As factories mushroomed, urban areas swelled with a migrating population. The urban infrastructure, still in its nascent stages, struggled to accommodate this influx. Furthermore, the emphasis on quantity often overshadowed quality, leading to inefficiencies and wastages.

To navigate these challenges, the state relied heavily on its vast labor force. The Stakhanovite movement exemplifies this, promoting super-productivity and encouraging workers to exceed their targets. Named after coal miner Alexey Stakhanov, who mined 102 tons of coal in less than 6 hours, this movement was both an emblem of Soviet industriousness and a tool for propaganda.

In conclusion, the Soviet Union's economic journey, marked by its Five-Year Plans, was a testament to the nation's aspirations and resilience. While the strategies employed were monumental in reshaping the economic landscape, they also spotlighted the challenges of rapid industrial transformation in a vast and diverse nation. The intricate dance between agriculture and industry, urban and rural, and the state and its citizens would define the Soviet economic narrative for decades.

Transition and Transformation: Khrushchev and Brezhnev

Following the death of Joseph Stalin in 1953, the Soviet Union underwent a significant ideological and political transition. Two of the most consequential leaders during this period were Nikita Khrushchev and Leonid Brezhnev. Their tenures, while distinct, were characterized by attempts to both distance the nation from certain aspects of Stalin's rule and to consolidate the gains made during his time.

The ascendancy of Nikita Khrushchev to the leadership of the Soviet Union heralded a period known as the "Khrushchev Thaw." This era, spanning the late 1950s and early 1960s, was marked by efforts to de-stalinize the nation and to introduce liberal reforms. One of the seminal events of this period was Khrushchev's 1956 "Secret Speech" to the 20th Congress of the Communist Party, where he denounced the excesses of Stalin's rule, particularly the purges.

Khrushchev's agenda extended beyond mere political rhetoric. He released many political prisoners, closed down numerous forced labor camps, and sought to shift the focus of the state from heavy industry to consumer goods and agriculture. On the cultural front, there was a relative loosening of censorship, leading to a flourishing of arts, literature, and cinema. Works that had been previously banned or suppressed, such as those of Boris Pasternak, found their way to the public.

While the "Thaw" was significant, it was not without limitations. Khrushchev's tenure was punctuated by events like the Hungarian Revolution of 1956 and the Cuban Missile Crisis of 1962, which showcased the continued tensions of the Cold War era.

Leonid Brezhnev's leadership, which began in 1964 and spanned nearly two decades, is often contrasted with Khrushchev's. Where Khrushchev was seen as erratic and keen on reform, Brezhnev is remembered for what is termed as the "Era of Stagnation." However, it might be more apt to consider it as a period of stability, albeit one marked by economic and political rigidity.

Under Brezhnev, the Soviet Union reached the height of its global power. It witnessed the détente with the West, a brief thawing of Cold War hostilities. However, domestically, Brezhnev reversed many of Khrushchev's reforms. The state reasserted its control over arts and culture, and censorship was once again the order of the day.

Economically, the period saw the Soviet Union begin to lag. While it maintained its status as a superpower, the state's command economy began showing cracks. The focus on heavy industries continued, often at the expense of consumer sectors. By the late 1970s, this economic rigidity began to impact the average Soviet citizen, with shortages of essential goods becoming more common.

In essence, the transition from Khrushchev to Brezhnev marked a shift from an era of reform and thaw to one of consolidation. While Khrushchev's tenure was characterized by attempts to reshape the Soviet system in the aftermath of Stalin, Brezhnev's era was about solidifying the gains of the past while ensuring stability. Both periods, with their respective successes and challenges, were pivotal in shaping the trajectory of the Soviet Union during the Cold War era.

Winds of Change: Gorbachev's Reforms

The late 1980s signaled another transformative phase in the annals of the Soviet Union, driven principally by its then General Secretary, Mikhail Gorbachev. Recognizing the multifaceted challenges facing the USSR, both domestically and internationally, Gorbachev embarked on a series of unprecedented reforms. These measures, while intended to revitalize the Soviet system, inadvertently set the stage for its dissolution.

Glasnost, translating to "openness", was Gorbachev's clarion call to address the pervasive culture of secrecy and censorship that had characterized the Soviet state. This initiative sought to cultivate greater transparency in governance and foster a more open dialogue between the state and its citizens. The media, for years shackled by strict censorship, experienced relative liberalization. This newfound freedom saw the emergence of investigative journalism, which often shed light on issues previously considered taboo, from the inefficiencies of the Soviet bureaucracy to the darker aspects of Stalin's rule. This wave of openness, while ushering in a new era of public discourse, also exposed the myriad problems facing the Soviet system, stoking public discontent.

Perestroika, or "restructuring", was Gorbachev's ambitious plan to overhaul the Soviet Union's economic and political structures. Economically, Gorbachev recognized that the command economy, with its inherent inefficiencies, needed reform. He introduced measures to decentralize economic decision-making, giving enterprises greater autonomy from state directives. Additionally, he advocated for the establishment of private businesses and foreign investments, both radical departures from Soviet orthodoxy.

Politically, perestroika aimed to democratize the Communist Party and the state's governance mechanisms. Proposals were made to hold competitive elections, allow multiple candidates, and decentralize power, thereby granting greater autonomy to the Soviet republics.

Gorbachev's reforms cannot be divorced from the broader international context. The arms race, a defining feature of the Cold War, had drained the Soviet economy. The Chernobyl disaster in 1986 further accentuated the economic strains and emphasized the need for transparent governance. In this atmosphere, Gorbachev sought détente with the West. His foreign policy, characterized by a willingness to engage in dialogue, led to significant arms reduction treaties, notably the Intermediate-Range Nuclear Forces Treaty (INF) in 1987.

In summation, Gorbachev's tenure marked a significant departure from traditional Soviet policies. His twin pillars of reform, glasnost and perestroika, while designed to fortify the Soviet Union, inadvertently amplified its inherent contradictions. The push for openness exposed the system's flaws, and the drive for restructuring challenged its very foundations. By the end of the 1980s, these reforms had set the stage for a series of events that would culminate in the dissolution of the Soviet Union in 1991. Gorbachev's legacy, thus, is one of vision, reform, and unintended consequences.

The Path to Dissolution

The culmination of the Soviet era was not marked by a single event but rather by a concatenation of domestic and international dynamics that precipitated the USSR's dissolution. The 1980s witnessed a plethora of challenges, both socio-economic and political, which underscored the inefficiencies and contradictions inherent within the Soviet system.

The Soviet Union's economic model, while successful in its nascent stages, began exhibiting signs of strain by the 1980s. Centralized planning, once hailed as the backbone of the Soviet economic miracle, became synonymous with inefficiency, corruption, and stagnation. The economic challenges were palpable across the board, from declining growth rates to technological lag. These economic difficulties were compounded by social challenges, including rising alcoholism, decreasing life expectancy, and an overall sense of disillusionment among the populace. The inability of the state to address these issues effectively eroded public trust.

Another formidable challenge was the resurgence of nationalist movements within the various Soviet republics. For decades, the central Soviet apparatus had managed to suppress nationalist sentiments. However, as the central authority weakened, republics like Estonia, Latvia, Lithuania, Ukraine, and Georgia began voicing their aspirations for greater autonomy, if not outright independence. These movements, rooted in distinct cultural and historical identities, directly challenged the Soviet ideal of a unified socialist federation.

Externally, the Soviet Union was grappling with the pressures of the arms race and the economic drain it represented. The decision to intervene militarily in Afghanistan in 1979 further strained the USSR's resources and became its own quagmire, reminiscent of the United States' experience in Vietnam. Simultaneously, the drop in oil prices in the 1980s adversely impacted the Soviet economy, which was heavily reliant on oil exports.

While several events marked the decline of Soviet influence in Eastern Europe, few were as symbolic as the fall of the Berlin Wall in November 1989. The wall, which had stood as a stark representation of the Cold War divide, was brought down not by policymakers but by citizens yearning for freedom and reunification. Its fall signaled the beginning of the end for the USSR's dominance in Eastern Europe.

In tandem, these factors - socio-economic challenges, nationalist aspirations, external pressures, and the loss of Eastern European dominions - coalesced to create an environment ripe for change. By December 1991, this confluence of factors culminated in the dissolution of the Soviet Union, a monumental event that marked the end of an era in global geopolitics. The world's largest socialist state, which had stood as a superpower for much of the 20th century, dissolved, giving way to 15 independent republics, each charting its course in a post-Soviet landscape.

Conclusion: Legacy and Reflection

As the sun set on the Soviet Union, it bequeathed to history a complex legacy, punctuated by feats of industrialization, space exploration, and geopolitical prowess, but also marred by periods of repressive rule, economic challenges, and ideological rigidity.

In the pages of history, the Soviet Union emerges as both a beacon of human ambition and a testament to the complexities of statecraft. Its journey from the Bolshevik Revolution to its eventual dissolution offers invaluable lessons about the interplay of ideology, leadership, and socio-economic dynamics in shaping the trajectory of a superpower.

The USSR's establishment was not just a shift in political power but a profound statement in global geopolitics. As a superpower, it influenced diplomatic ties, ignited proxy wars, and set the stage for the Cold War. Its ideological zeal inspired numerous movements across continents, and its achievements in realms like space exploration were unparalleled. Yet, it was also a system punctuated by periods of stringent repression and economic challenges.

The transition from the Soviet behemoth to the Russian Federation was marked by significant upheavals. The "shock therapy" of the '90s, aimed at rapidly transitioning to a market economy, gave rise to vast socio-economic disparities. Politically, the task of embedding democratic practices while battling the legacies of centralized rule and corruption remained arduous.

For many, the Soviet period is imbued with nostalgia, symbolizing security and social welfare. For others, particularly those conscious of Stalin's excesses or the curtailed freedoms, it stands as a period of restraint. These contrasting perceptions extend beyond personal memories, influencing modern politics, popular culture, and international perspectives.

The Soviet Union, with its intricate blend of monumental achievements and profound challenges, indelibly shaped the 20th-century world order. While the empire dissolved, its echoes continue to reverberate, reminding us of the cyclical nature of empires and the persistent human quest for an equitable society.

As the Soviet Union etched its mark on the world stage, its intricate dance with another emerging superpower would define much of the latter half of the 20th century. This dance, characterized by tensions, proxy wars, and ideological confrontations, came to be known as the Cold War. While the Soviet Union's journey illuminates the internal dynamics of an empire's rise and fall, the Cold War era offers a macroscopic view of how superpowers navigate, negotiate, and occasionally clash in their quest for global dominance. In the upcoming chapter, we delve deeper into this high-stakes geopolitical contest, exploring the strategies, stakes, and the ultimate resolution of a conflict that held the world in suspense for decades.

PART IV: The New World Order

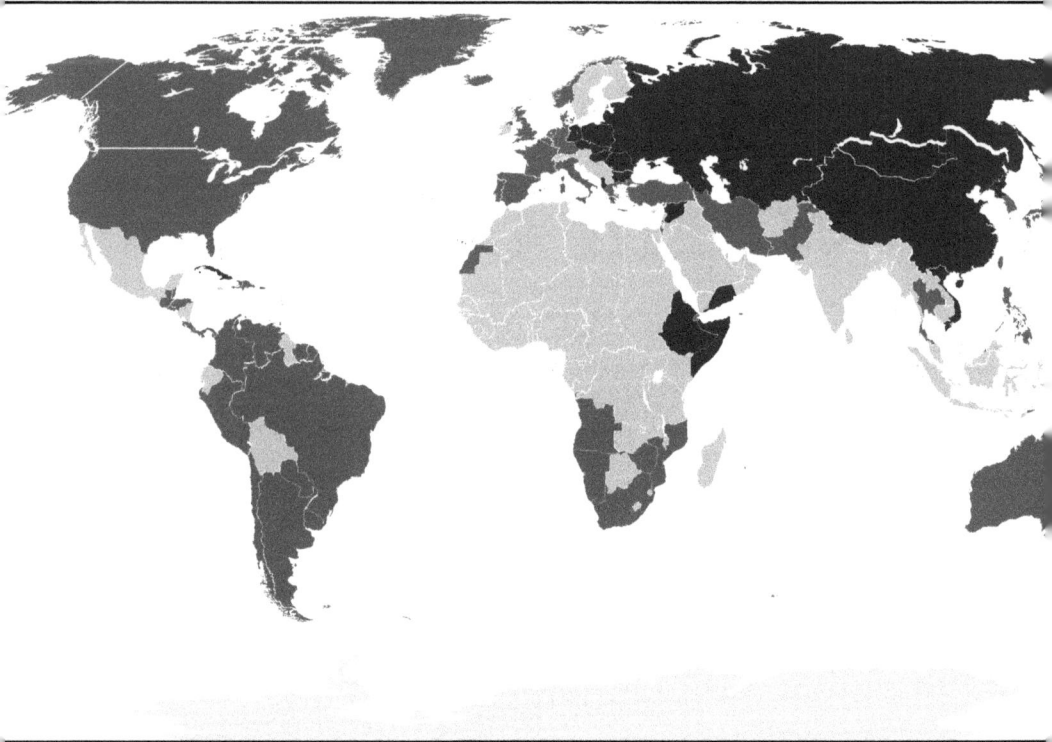

Cold War Alliances mid-1975[41]

Chapter 27.
The Cold War: Duel of the Titans (1947-1991)

From Stettin in the Baltic to Trieste in the Adriatic,
an iron curtain has descended across Europe...

~Winston Churchill

Setting the stage

In the aftermath of the devastation wrought by World War II covered before, the global geopolitical landscape underwent a significant reconfiguration. Historically, the dynamics of power have witnessed shifts and realignments, and the mid-20th century was no exception. As nations endeavored to rebuild from the ruins of conflict, two dominant powers emerged, heralding a new era in international relations.

The United States and the Union of Soviet Socialist Republics, by virtue of their military prowess, economic capacities, and political influence, ascended to positions of unparalleled prominence on the world stage. However, this wasn't merely a juxtaposition of two powerful nations; it was a profound ideological divide that would shape the contours of global politics for the better part of the century.

Capitalism, as championed by the United States, was predicated on principles of market economy, individual liberties, and democratic governance. The system advocated for minimal state intervention in economic matters, emphasizing private ownership and the free interplay of market forces to determine production, distribution, and consumption. Historically, the roots of capitalism can be traced back to the mercantile systems of Europe, which evolved over centuries, incorporating elements of industrialization and technological advancements. The United States, with its vast resources and innovative spirit, had become the epitome of capitalist success by the mid-20th century, offering a model that many war-ravaged nations found alluring.

Contrastingly, the Soviet Union was the standard-bearer for Communism, an ideology rooted in the writings of Marx and Engels. This system, emphasizing state ownership of means of production and a centrally planned economy, sought to eradicate class distinctions and promote communal welfare. Historically, while communism as a theory had its origins in the 19th-century critiques of industrial capitalist societies, its practical application on a large scale was a relatively novel experiment, led predominantly by the USSR. The promise of the Soviet model was not merely economic but also societal—a vision of a classless, egalitarian society where resources and opportunities were equitably distributed.

This ideological chasm between the two superpowers wasn't a mere academic debate but had profound implications for global governance, economic systems, and international diplomacy. As nations around the world sought to rebuild and redefine themselves post-World War II, they found themselves inadvertently drawn into this ideological vortex, often compelled to align with one superpower or the other.

Historically, the phenomenon of empires or dominant powers seeking to propagate their governance models, economic systems, and cultural values isn't unprecedented. However, the Cold War era presented a unique scenario: a bipolar world order where two superpowers, equipped with nuclear arsenals and entrenched in their ideological convictions, vied for global dominance. The stage was set for a complex ballet of diplomatic maneuverings, proxy confrontations, and strategic alliances that would dictate the course of world events for decades to come.

The Birth of the Cold War

The events culminating in World War II and its immediate aftermath played a pivotal role in the emergence of a bipolar world order. Although the major Allied powers—primarily the United States, the United Kingdom, and the Soviet Union—had collaborated extensively to counter the Axis threat, this cooperative facade belied underlying tensions and suspicions that had historical antecedents.

The conclusion of World War II saw a Europe ravaged by conflict, with political and physical landscapes profoundly altered. Major cities lay in ruins, economies were shattered, and societal structures disrupted. As the major Allies began the task of post-war reconstruction, ideological and strategic differences that had been momentarily overshadowed by the shared objective of defeating the Axis powers resurfaced. The United States and the United Kingdom, despite variations in their governance models, shared a broad commitment to capitalist economic structures and democratic governance as previously indicated. Conversely, the Soviet Union, with its Communist ideology, viewed the capitalist West with inherent suspicion, a sentiment reciprocated by the Western Allies.

Historically, the end of major conflicts has often been marked by conferences and treaties that outline the new order. In the aftermath of World War II, two significant conferences—Yalta (February 1945) and Potsdam (July-August 1945)—were convened to discuss post-war arrangements.

At Yalta, the key Allied leaders—Franklin D. Roosevelt of the U.S., UK's Winston Churchill and USSR's Joseph Stalin—centered their discussions on Nazi Germany's unconditional capitulation and post-war compensations. However, the conference also laid the groundwork for the division of Germany and Berlin into occupied zones. More broadly, it set in motion the arrangements for liberated European nations to hold free elections, though the interpretation of "free elections" became a contentious point, especially concerning Eastern European countries.

Potsdam, occurring after the fall of Nazi Germany, saw a change in participants with Harry Truman now representing the U.S. and Clement Attlee for the UK. The conference, while reiterating many decisions of Yalta, dealt extensively with the specifics of German disarmament, demilitarization, and denazification. Yet, beneath these agreements, there was a growing realization that the Allies' visions for post-war Europe were diverging rapidly.

Winston Churchill, in a speech delivered at Fulton, Missouri, in March 1946, uttered the phrase that would come to symbolize the Cold War divide: "From Stettin in the Baltic to Trieste in the Adriatic, an Iron Curtain has descended across the Continent." This metaphorical curtain represented the ideological, political, and physical barriers that were being erected between the Soviet-dominated East and the capitalist West.

Churchill's address, while prophetic, was not merely a product of foresight but a reflection of the already evident realities on the ground. The Soviet Union had quickly consolidated its influence over Eastern Europe, establishing Communist governments and suppressing opposition, effectively creating a buffer against the West.

Thus, the stage was set. Historical precedents, ideological disparities, and the practical realities of post-war Europe had converged to inaugurate an era characterized by deep mistrust, extensive militarization, and geopolitical maneuverings—the Cold War. This period, while devoid of direct military confrontation between the superpowers, would be marked by intensive economic, political, and ideological rivalries that would define global politics for the latter half of the 20th century.

Military Dominance and the Arms Race

The military dimension of the Cold War was multifaceted, characterized not only by an unprecedented arms race but also by regional confrontations, technological competition, and the looming specter of nuclear annihilation. This period represented a profound shift in military strategy and global geopolitics, influenced largely by advancements in technology and the overriding desire of the superpowers to achieve strategic dominance.

The bombings of Hiroshima and Nagasaki in August 1945 heralded the atomic age, marking the first use of nuclear weapons in warfare.

The overwhelming devastation caused by these bombs served as a stark testament to their destructive potential. The United States, having demonstrated its nuclear capability, held a temporary monopoly on this new form of warfare. However, this monopoly was short-lived. By 1949, the Soviet Union had conducted its first successful nuclear test, leveling the playing field and intensifying mutual suspicions.

The Cuban Missile Crisis of 1962 stands as a stark embodiment of the Cold War's nuclear tension. This crisis was precipitated when the U.S., under President John F. Kennedy, discovered Soviet ballistic missiles in Cuba, overseen by the Soviet Premier Nikita Khrushchev. For 13 harrowing days, the world was on tenterhooks as Kennedy, with advice from his Defense Secretary Robert McNamara, and Khrushchev, alongside his Foreign Minister Andrei Gromyko, engaged in a high-stakes diplomatic and military standoff. Through tense negotiations and back-channel communications, a resolution was reached: the Soviets agreed to remove their missiles from Cuba in exchange for the U.S.'s secret commitment to withdraw its missiles from Turkey. The Cuban Missile Crisis highlighted the precariousness of peace in an era bristling with nuclear arms and expedited efforts towards arms control agreements in the ensuing years.

The Cold War saw an exponential growth in nuclear arsenals as both superpowers embarked on a relentless pursuit to achieve nuclear superiority. The rationale was rooted in the concept of Mutually Assured Destruction (MAD): the idea that neither side would initiate a nuclear conflict for fear of reciprocation leading to total annihilation. Consequently, vast resources were allocated to develop sophisticated delivery systems, from intercontinental ballistic missiles (ICBMs) to submarine-launched ballistic missiles (SLBMs), ensuring a second-strike capability.

While the superpowers avoided direct military confrontation, regional conflicts often became arenas for their geopolitical rivalries. The Korean War (1950-1953) saw the U.S. and its allies supporting South Korea against North Korea, backed by China and the Soviet Union. Similarly, the Vietnam War (1955-1975) had the U.S. aiding South Vietnam against the communist North, supported by the Soviet Union and China.

These proxy wars, often rooted in local dynamics, became intertwined with the larger ideological and strategic objectives of the Cold War, resulting in prolonged conflicts and significant human and material costs.

As the 1960s dawned, the U.S. confronted the challenge posed by the Soviet Union's successful launch of the Sputnik satellite in 1957. This event marked the onset of the space race, with its profound ideological undertones. Recognizing the broader implications, President John F. Kennedy made a resolute commitment in 1961 to land an American on the moon before the decade's end. This ambitious objective spurred American scientific and technological efforts, leading to the monumental Apollo 11 moon landing in 1969. Beyond mere exploration and scientific feats, these space milestones served as demonstrations of missile deployment capabilities and emblematic assertions of each superpower's socioeconomic system, offering platforms for soft power projection.

In summation, the Cold War's military dimension was characterized by a complex interplay of direct confrontations, technological competition, and strategic posturing. The era was defined by its militarization, with both superpowers seeking to achieve dominance while navigating the intricacies of a nuclear-armed world.

Economic Maneuvering and Dominance

As with many historical epochs, the Cold War was not merely defined by overt military confrontations and ideological clashes but was deeply rooted in economic strategies and maneuvers. Both superpowers recognized the intrinsic link between economic vitality and geopolitical dominance, leading to a series of calculated economic initiatives aimed at consolidating influence, securing allies, and weakening adversaries.

In the post-World War II European landscape, ravaged by conflict and facing economic collapse, the United States envisioned a comprehensive recovery plan. The European Recovery Program, commonly known as the Marshall Plan (briefly outlined in a preceding chapter), named after U.S. Secretary of State George Marshall, was unveiled in 1947. This initiative proposed significant financial assistance to Western European nations, amounting to roughly $13 billion (over $140 billion when adjusted for inflation).

Historically, such largesse was not merely altruistic. The U.S. understood that economic stability in Western Europe was crucial for political stability and the prevention of communist inroads. Additionally, a revitalized European economy would serve American economic interests, facilitating trade and ensuring a receptive market for American goods and investments. The Marshall Plan, therefore, functioned not just as an economic aid package but as a strategic tool to cement U.S. influence in Western Europe and counteract the appeal of Soviet-style communism.

In response to the Marshall Plan and to consolidate its influence over Eastern Europe, the Soviet Union established the Council for Mutual Economic Assistance (Comecon) in 1949. Serving as a counterweight to Western European economic cooperation, Comecon aimed to facilitate economic collaboration among socialist states, promoting collective self-reliance and integration.

However, unlike the Marshall Plan's substantial financial injections, Comecon often involved barter agreements and trade at non-market prices. The Soviet Union utilized Comecon as a mechanism to exert control over the satellite states' economies, ensuring their dependence on Moscow. This economic strategy was reflective of the broader Soviet objective of creating a buffer against the West and consolidating the socialist economic model within its sphere of influence.

Beyond recovery initiatives and economic blocs, the Cold War saw the deployment of economic tools as instruments of statecraft. Economic sanctions emerged as powerful tools in the superpowers' arsenals. The U.S., for instance, instituted a comprehensive trade embargo on Cuba following Fidel Castro's alignment with the Soviet Union. Similarly, the Soviet Union utilized economic pressures, such as cutting off energy supplies, to exert influence or express displeasure with Eastern European states.

Such economic measures served dual purposes. They were aimed at weakening adversaries by disrupting their economies, but they were also symbolic, serving as clear signals of disapproval or retaliation without resorting to direct military confrontation.

In conclusion, the Cold War's economic dimension underscores the intricate relationship between economic strategies and geopolitical objectives. Historically, as evidenced in prior epochs, economic tools, whether in the form of aid, trade, or sanctions, have often been wielded to further strategic ends. The Cold War era, with its distinct bipolarity, only accentuated the use of economic instruments in the complex ballet of superpower rivalry.

The Opening to China: Realpolitik and Geopolitical Rebalancing

Within the complex dynamics of Cold War strategies, the U.S.'s overture to China in the early 1970s marked a significant shift in the global power equilibrium. Masterminded by President Richard Nixon and his National Security Advisor (later appointed Secretary of State), Henry Kissinger, this diplomatic maneuver was emblematic of the principles of Realpolitik. These principles, driven by considerations of power and national interest, rather than ideological affinities were reminiscent of 19th century European geopolitics.

The motivations behind this overture were multifaceted. First and foremost, by establishing closer ties with China, the U.S. aimed to exploit the evident Sino-Soviet split, thereby preventing a unified communist front. By doing so, Washington hoped to push Beijing and Moscow into a position where each would seek closer ties with the U.S. than they had with each other—a classic application of the Kissingerian principle of leveraging bilateral relationships to achieve a superior geopolitical stance.

Furthermore, China, with its vast population and undeniable strategic significance, was viewed as an indispensable player in global geopolitics. By engaging with Beijing, the U.S. aimed to draw China into a more integrated international system, thereby moderating its policies and actions. The immediate manifestation of this was in Vietnam, where it was hoped that China could be persuaded to exert its influence over North Vietnam.

The process culminated in Nixon's historic visit to China in 1972, a moment that symbolized the thawing of relations between two erstwhile adversaries. The subsequent Shanghai Communiqué, while acknowledging differences, laid the groundwork for cooperation and set the stage for China's eventual normalization of relations with the U.S. in 1979.

The implications of this strategic realignment were far-reaching. The Soviet Union was forced to contend with a resurgent China backed by U.S. diplomatic support, diluting Moscow's global influence. Moreover, by drawing China into the global economy, the foundations were laid for Beijing's eventual emergence as an economic juggernaut.

Henry Kissinger stands as one of the towering figures in the annals of 20th-century diplomacy. His intellectual foray into the realms of international relations was deeply influenced by a study of historical statecraft, drawing lessons from the strategies of past leaders. Among those, Otto von Bismarck, the Chancellor of the German Empire, was a particularly instructive figure. Bismarck's adeptness in navigating the European balance of power during the late 19th century, with a clear-eyed appreciation for the nuances of national interest and geopolitical realities, resonated with Kissinger's own philosophy. Such historical insights informed Kissinger's approach, enabling him to craft policies that transcended ideological boundaries in favor of strategic imperatives. In the U.S. opening to China, one observes a manifestation of this approach: a judicious blend of historical wisdom and present-day pragmatism, designed to reshape the global chessboard in a manner conducive to American interests.

Political Influence and Proxy Confrontations

Historical statecraft has always been marked by alliances, interventions, and the propagation of ideological constructs, and the Cold War exemplified these aspects in stark relief. While the era is punctuated by its avoidance of direct military confrontation between the superpowers, the geopolitical landscape was rife with strategic alignments, covert operations, and indirect confrontations, highlighting the depth and breadth of Cold War politics.

The inception of the North Atlantic Treaty Organization (NATO) in 1949 marked a significant development in post-World War II geopolitics. Founded on the principles of collective defense, NATO brought together North American and Western European nations in a formal alliance aimed at countering potential Soviet aggression. The charter underscored the principle that an act of aggression against any member would be viewed as an offense to all, pledging joint defensive actions.

In response, the Soviet Union, along with its Eastern European satellite states, established the Warsaw Pact in 1955. Mirroring NATO's collective defense principle, the Warsaw Pact cemented the military alliance of communist states in Eastern Europe, underscoring the bipolar division of the continent.

These two alliances, though defensive in their stated objectives, intensified the Cold War's politico-military divide, essentially drawing lines on the European map delineating spheres of influence and potential zones of conflict.

In the bipolar Cold War world, many newly independent states, particularly from Africa and Asia, sought to avoid alignment with either of the superpower blocs. This aspiration led to the formation of the Non-Aligned Movement (NAM) in 1961. NAM, with its foundational principles of mutual respect for sovereignty, territorial integrity, and non-aggression, aimed at promoting peace and cooperation without being ensnared in Cold War rivalries.

Historically, this movement represented the aspirations of post-colonial states to chart their own courses, free from external hegemonic pressures, and play a more significant role in international politics.

While direct military confrontations between the U.S. and USSR were rare, the era witnessed numerous interventions, often covert, aimed at furthering superpower interests or curtailing the influence of the adversary. The CIA-led coup in Iran in 1953, which overthrew Prime Minister Mohammad Mossadegh, and the U.S.-backed coup in Chile in 1973 that ousted President Salvador Allende, are emblematic of such interventions.

The Soviet Union similarly sought to consolidate its influence, notably in Eastern Europe, quelling uprisings and ensuring the dominance of Moscow-friendly regimes.

Beyond Europe and the traditional zones of Cold War confrontation, Africa, Asia, and Latin America became theaters for ideological propagation and geopolitical maneuverings. Both superpowers sought to back factions, movements, or regimes that aligned with their respective ideologies. This dynamic led to conflicts, sometimes prolonged, as seen in Angola, Nicaragua, and Afghanistan, where local disputes became intertwined with the broader Cold War rivalry.

In conclusion, while the Cold War is often viewed through the lens of the U.S.-USSR dichotomy, it was truly a global affair, affecting politics, alliances, and conflicts in virtually every corner of the world. The period exemplified the historical trend wherein major powers, driven by strategic and ideological objectives, seek to exert influence far beyond their borders, often with profound and lasting consequences.

Technological Advancement and Espionage

Throughout history, the acquisition and safeguarding of information has been fundamental to the strategies of nations. However, the Cold War period witnessed an unprecedented intensification of these endeavors, augmented by rapid technological advancements. The confluence of traditional espionage tactics with emerging technologies shaped much of the clandestine landscape during this era, with both superpowers deeply enmeshed in a shadowy dance of intrigue, surveillance, and counter-intelligence.

The intelligence agencies of the superpowers, notably the Soviet KGB (Komitet Gosudarstvennoy Bezopasnosti) and the American CIA (Central Intelligence Agency), became central actors in the Cold War narrative. These organizations, though historically rooted in earlier intelligence efforts, expanded their operations extensively during this period.

The KGB, with its vast network of operatives and informants, sought to penetrate the political, military, and technological bastions of the

West. Similarly, the CIA, established in 1947, embarked on a range of covert operations aimed at gathering intelligence, countering Soviet influence, and occasionally, effecting regime changes in regions deemed strategically significant.

These intelligence agencies, empowered by state mandates and often operating in secrecy, orchestrated a myriad of operations—ranging from human intelligence gathering to covert interventions.

As the 20th century progressed, technological innovations profoundly impacted the realm of espionage. Satellites, for instance, provided both superpowers with reconnaissance capabilities, allowing them to monitor military installations, troop movements, and missile sites from space. Such advancements rendered vast swathes of territory, which might historically have been considered safe from prying eyes, vulnerable to surveillance.

Additionally, the development of sophisticated electronic eavesdropping and signal interception tools enabled the monitoring of communications, often leading to the acquisition of invaluable intelligence. Cryptography and code-breaking, while not new, assumed renewed importance, with both sides investing heavily in deciphering each other's encrypted communications while safeguarding their own.

Beyond the cloak-and-dagger world of spies and covert operations, the Cold War was also a battle for hearts and minds. Propaganda—information, especially of a biased or misleading nature, used to promote a political cause or point of view—became a primary tool for both blocs. The aim was twofold: to bolster domestic support for government policies and to sway international opinion.

Radio broadcasts, such as the U.S.-backed Radio Free Europe or the Soviet-supported Radio Moscow, transmitted ideologically charged content across borders. Literature, film, and other cultural products were also co-opted into this informational warfare, each side showcasing its societal model's alleged superiority.

In tandem with these overt efforts, covert disinformation campaigns were also waged, with intelligence agencies planting false stories in the media to mislead, confuse, or discredit the other side.

In summation, the Cold War's clandestine aspect was as pivotal, if not more so, than its overt confrontations. Espionage, technological surveillance, and the constant battle for the narrative underscored the complexity of this era. These endeavors reflect a time-honored tradition in statecraft, albeit amplified by the unique circumstances of the Cold War: the continuous quest for knowledge, advantage, and influence in a constantly shifting geopolitical landscape.

Cultural Influence and Propaganda

As espionage and technological advancements were the covert instruments of the Cold War, culture emerged as the overt weapon in the ideological struggle. Drawing from historical antecedents, both superpowers tapped into various cultural avenues, from cinema and sports to music and literature, to project their narratives and vie for global influence.

The cinema, with its ability to reach and influence vast audiences, became a focal point in the Cold War's cultural arena. Hollywood, already a global cinematic powerhouse by the mid-20th century, produced films that often reflected the anxieties, values, and aspirations of the West. Movies like Red Dawn, Dr. Strangelove, and The Manchurian Candidate subtly and sometimes overtly engaged with Cold War themes, perpetuating notions of Western heroism, freedom, and the looming Communist threat.

Conversely, the Soviet film industry, while more state-controlled, produced works that championed socialist values, the resilience and solidarity of the Soviet people, and the purportedly aggressive intentions of the capitalist West. Films like The Cranes Are Flying and Ballad of a Soldier not only showcased the Soviet perspective on war and sacrifice but also sought to project an image of a modern, progressive USSR.

This cinematic rivalry was more than mere entertainment; it was an ideological contest, with each side leveraging the power of narrative to assert cultural supremacy and propagate its worldview.

The Olympic Games, historically a celebration of human athleticism and international camaraderie, assumed a distinct political hue during the Cold War. Both superpowers invested heavily in sports, viewing athletic achievements, especially Olympic gold medals, as validations of their respective societal models.

Events like the U.S. boycott of the 1980 Moscow Olympics and the subsequent Soviet boycott of the 1984 Los Angeles Olympics underscored the politicization of what was historically a non-political event. The medal count became an unofficial scorecard, a tangible metric of superiority in this ideological confrontation.

Literature, music, and the arts served as nuanced tools of soft power during the Cold War. American jazz, rock 'n' roll, and pop music became symbols of Western freedom and innovation, often penetrating the Iron Curtain and influencing Eastern European youth. Meanwhile, Soviet classical music, ballet, and literature were showcased as epitomes of high culture, discipline, and the intellectual depth of the Communist world.

Authors, composers, and artists, knowingly or unknowingly, became participants in this cultural dialogue. Western writers like George Orwell and Aleksandr Solzhenitsyn, with works such as 1984 and The Gulag Archipelago, critiqued totalitarian regimes. In contrast, Soviet literature, while often state-regulated, occasionally saw dissident voices highlighting the complexities and contradictions of life under socialism.

In essence, culture during the Cold War was not a peripheral domain; it was central to the broader struggle for influence and dominance. These cultural endeavors, reflecting the zeitgeist of the era, underscored the multifaceted nature of Cold War rivalries, reminding us that the battles of history are often fought not just on land, sea, or air, but in the minds and hearts of people.

Cracks in the Facade and Internal Challenges

Throughout the protracted duration of the Cold War, both superpowers, while externally presenting images of strength and unity, grappled with internal challenges. These fissures, often stemming from societal, economic, and political factors, provided insights into the vulnerabilities and complexities of each bloc. Historically, empires and superpowers, despite their external grandeur, have often faced internal dynamics that influenced their trajectories, and the Cold War superpowers were no exception.

The post-World War II era in the U.S. witnessed a profound societal shift as African Americans, buoyed by their contributions to the war effort and inspired by global anti-colonial movements, demanded an end to racial segregation and discrimination. The Civil Rights Movement of the 1950s and 1960s, with figures like Martin Luther King Jr. at the helm, exposed the contradictions of a nation promoting freedom abroad while denying it to many of its citizens at home. This internal struggle for racial equality highlighted the challenges the U.S. faced in presenting itself as a model of democracy and justice on the global stage.

The Watergate scandal of the early 1970s, culminating in President Richard Nixon's resignation, was indicative of deeper political vulnerabilities. This episode, involving a break-in at the Democratic National Committee headquarters and the subsequent cover-up by the Nixon administration, eroded trust in the U.S. political system and showcased the potential pitfalls of unchecked executive power.

The U.S. economy, while largely robust during the Cold War, faced periods of stagnation and recession. Economic downturns, often resulting from global dynamics, energy crises, or internal fiscal policies, challenged the U.S.'s image as an unassailable economic powerhouse.

As detailed in a previous chapter Leonid Brezhnev's tenure as the General Secretary of the Communist Party (1964-1982) is often characterized by the term "stagnation." Despite initial economic successes, the Soviet system faced declining growth rates, technological backwardness, and increased corruption. The state's heavily centralized planning model struggled to innovate and adapt, leading to widespread inefficiencies.

Dissident movements within the USSR, though often suppressed, provided a window into the underlying discontent. Intellectuals and activists, like Andrei Sakharov and Alexander Solzhenitsyn, criticized the regime's human rights abuses and the lack of political freedoms. By the 1980s, the calls for reform became more pronounced, eventually leading to Mikhail Gorbachev's policies of Perestroika (restructuring) and Glasnost (openness).

The oil crises of the 1970s, precipitated by geopolitical events in the Middle East, had profound implications for the global economy. Skyrocketing oil prices led to inflation, economic downturns, and altered the dynamics of global energy politics. Both superpowers, though to varying degrees, felt the impact. The U.S., with its oil-dependent economy, faced stagflation—a combination of stagnation and inflation. The Soviet Union, a major oil producer, initially benefited from the elevated prices, but its over-reliance on oil revenues exposed it to vulnerabilities when prices dropped in subsequent years.

In conclusion, while the Cold War externally appeared as a binary contest of monolithic blocs, a closer inspection reveals a mosaic of internal challenges, societal dynamics, and vulnerabilities. These challenges, rooted in historical, economic, and social contexts, played crucial roles in shaping the strategies, decisions, and eventual outcomes of this complex era.

The Thaw and the End of the Cold War

As this book has repeatedly illustrated, and in alignment with our central theme, empires and global powers traverse predictable cycles of ascent, consolidation, and eventual. decline. The Cold War, despite its prolonged and entrenched nature, was not immune to such cyclical patterns. By the late 20th century, a series of events and decisions led to a noticeable thaw in Cold War tensions, culminating in the dissolution of one of its primary protagonists—the Soviet Union.

The concept of Détente, rooted in the French word for "relaxation," emerged in the late 1960s and early 1970s. It was characterized by a mutual recognition by both superpowers of the need to reduce the risk of nuclear war and to stabilize their adversarial relationship. Several factors facilitated Détente:

The Cuban Missile Crisis had underscored the potentially catastrophic consequences of superpower confrontation.

Economic realities, including the cost of maintaining global military commitments and the need for trade, made continued hostility impractical.

Both powers faced internal and external challenges that required attention and resources.

Initiatives under Détente included strategic arms limitation talks (SALT) that led to treaties limiting the deployment of ballistic missiles. Diplomatic engagements, like the Helsinki Accords in 1975, aimed at improving relations and securing commitments on human rights and territorial integrity.

Mikhail Gorbachev's rise to the leadership of the Soviet Communist Party in 1985 marked a significant shift in Soviet policy. Recognizing the systemic challenges the USSR faced, Gorbachev introduced two fundamental reforms as detailed in the previous chapter: Perestroika (Restructuring) and Glasnost (Openness).

While these reforms were introduced to revitalize the Soviet system, they inadvertently accelerated its unraveling by exposing the depth of its problems and by emboldening critics and nationalist movements within the republics.

Fall of the Berlin Wall[42]

A symbolic and literal division between East and West, the Berlin Wall, began to face pressures by the late 1980s. Spurred by Gorbachev's reforms and growing demands for freedoms in Eastern Europe, peaceful protests escalated in East Germany. The government's decision in November 1989 to permit unrestricted travel for East Germans led to the Wall's breach by jubilant crowds. Its fall became emblematic of the larger collapse of Communist regimes across Eastern Europe, often referred to as the "domino effect."

The centrifugal forces unleashed by Gorbachev's reforms and the growing nationalist movements in Soviet republics, particularly in the Baltics, Ukraine, and the Caucasus, strained the Soviet federation. On December 25, 1991, Mikhail Gorbachev resigned as the Soviet president, and the Soviet Union was formally dissolved the following day.

In historical context, the end of the Cold War and the dissolution of the Soviet Union were not merely the results of short-term events or individual decisions. They were the culmination of long-term systemic issues, external pressures, and the inherent challenges of managing a vast, diverse empire. The end echoes the central theme of empires through time: even the mightiest entities, faced with internal and external challenges, are subject to the dynamics of rise, persistence, and eventual decline.

Conclusion: Legacy and Long-term Impacts

The tapestry of the Cold War, woven over nearly half a century, left indelible marks on the global stage. These marks, both overt and nuanced, shape the world we inhabit today. As this book has repeatedly illustrated, and in alignment with our central theme, empires and global powers traverse predictable cycles of ascent, stabilization, and eventual descent.

With the Soviet Union's dissolution, the United States, momentarily unchallenged, emerged as the world's preeminent superpower. Its military, economic, and cultural clout seemed unparalleled, casting a long shadow over global geopolitics. Yet, even as the U.S. enjoyed its newfound dominance, the landscapes of Europe were rapidly realigning. The eastward expansion of institutions like NATO and the European Union sought to knit former Warsaw Pact nations and Soviet republics into the Western fabric, a move that would sow seeds for future contentions with a resurgent Russia.

On the economic front, the demise of the Cold War heralded a pronounced shift towards neoliberal policies, emphasizing market freedoms, deregulation, and privatization. These policies, which gained ascendancy globally, would shape economic trajectories, influence political discourses, and, in many instances, redefine the very social contracts nations had with their citizenry.

Yet, beneath the triumphalism of liberal democracy and market capitalism, cracks were emerging. Russia, transitioning from its Soviet past, grappled with its new identity. While initial overtures between Russia and the West held promise, divergent geopolitical objectives, especially concerning Europe's eastern reaches, hinted at renewed tensions. The world watched as Russia oscillated between cooperation and confrontation, trying to carve a distinct space in the post-Cold War order.

The Cold War, while a defining epoch, stands in the broader tapestry of history as a reminder of the ever-shifting dynamics of global power. Its unique contours—shaped by the fervor of ideology, the race of technological innovation, and the nuances of individual and collective agency—echo patterns witnessed in past empires and geopolitical confrontations. The culmination of the Cold War was not so much an ending as it was a transition, paving the way for contemporary challenges that encompass not only geopolitical rivalries but also global concerns like pandemics and climate change.

Reflecting upon its legacy, the Cold War underscores the transient nature of dominance, the intricate balance of power, and the ceaseless interplay of forces that drive the destiny of nations. As we steer through the intricacies of the 21st century, this era not only serves as a chronicle of bygone tensions but also provides a prism, illuminating pathways forward. And, as the sun set on one superpower rivalry, the horizon began to glow with the emerging might of another: the meteoric rise of China.

China's Rise[43]

Chapter 28.
The Meteoric Rise of China (20ᵗʰ-21ˢᵗ Centuries)

It doesn't matter whether a cat is white or black, as long as it catches mice.

~Deng Xiaoping

Deng Xiaoping and the Opening Up

In China's modern history, especially post-1949, the late 1970s heralded an era of transformation under Deng Xiaoping, marking a significant departure from Mao Zedong's ideological governance. Deng's leadership, emerging after Mao's death in 1976, was characterized by a move towards pragmatism, a stark contrast to the preceding decades dominated by ambitious and often disruptive campaigns.

The Great Leap Forward (1958-1962), initiated by Mao, was a radical economic and social campaign aiming to transform China from an agrarian society into a socialist utopia through rapid industrialization and collectivization. Central to this was the establishment of "People's Communes," large cooperative entities that sought to increase agricultural and industrial output. However, the campaign's policies, combined with adverse weather conditions, led to one of the worst famines in history, with estimates of deaths ranging from tens of millions. Mismanagement, over-reporting of grain production, and an emphasis on steel production—often through rudimentary and ineffective means—further compounded the catastrophe.

Following this, the Cultural Revolution (1966-1976) was Mao's attempt to preserve Communist dogma and reassert his authority by removing capitalist, traditional, and cultural elements from Chinese society. It involved purging the "Four Olds": old customs, old culture, old habits, and old ideas. Mobilizing youth into Red Guard groups, Mao sought to target revisionists and capitalist roaders, leading to widespread purges, public humiliations, and even deaths. Intellectuals, teachers, and those associated with the West or traditional Chinese life were especially persecuted. The decade was marked by widespread upheaval, and the social, cultural, and economic fabric of China was profoundly affected.

Deng Xiaoping, having been purged during the Cultural Revolution only to be rehabilitated later, recognized the urgent need for reforms. He sought to extricate China from the consequences of these campaigns, especially the economic stagnation and socio-political turmoil left in their wake. With a vision for a modernized China, Deng steered the nation away from strict ideological adherence towards a path of economic rejuvenation, laying the groundwork for the nation's meteoric rise in subsequent decades.

When assessing Deng's motivations, it becomes evident that his primary impetus was the urgent need to course-correct China's trajectory. The nation's economy was largely agrarian, technologically lagging, and insulated from global markets. For Deng, the path to national rejuvenation lay in modernization and economic liberalization. Yet, this ambition wasn't merely a domestic aspiration. It was informed by a broader global context wherein free-market economies, particularly in the West, were witnessing robust growth and technological advancements.

However, Deng's pursuit of reforms was riddled with constraints. Firstly, there was the ideological inertia within the Communist Party—a faction that viewed economic liberalization as a betrayal of Maoist principles. Navigating this intricate party dynamic required Deng to tread cautiously, ensuring that his policies, while groundbreaking, were not portrayed as repudiations of Mao's legacy but rather as essential adaptations.

Deng's strategy involved a phased introduction of market mechanisms. Initiatives like the Household Responsibility System in agriculture allowed farmers to sell surplus produce in open markets after meeting state quotas. This not only boosted agricultural productivity but also augmented rural incomes. Similarly, the establishment of Special Economic Zones, particularly in coastal regions like Shenzhen, was a masterstroke. These zones, by offering tax incentives and a conducive regulatory environment, attracted a deluge of foreign direct investment, turning them into hubs of manufacturing and export.

Inextricably linked to these economic measures was Deng's broader vision of "Socialism with Chinese Characteristics." He astutely recognized that for China to thrive, it couldn't blindly emulate Western models of capitalism. Instead, it needed to craft an economic framework that, while embracing market mechanisms, remained under the overarching control of the Communist Party.

Positioning Deng's reforms within the global economic milieu of the late 20th century, one discerns a China eager to integrate with the world economy, yet on its own terms. The West, particularly the United States, with its technological prowess and vast consumer markets, beckoned as a lucrative partner. Yet, this integration wasn't merely transactional. As China opened its doors to foreign capital and technology, it also embarked on a subtle journey of learning and adaptation, gleaning insights from global best practices, and meticulously customizing them to fit its unique socio-political landscape.

In conclusion, Deng Xiaoping's era was not just about economic recalibration. It was a period of introspection and ambition, where China, acutely aware of its past setbacks and informed by global paradigms, sought to craft a future that harmonized its historical ethos with contemporary pragmatism.

Economic Reforms and Growth

Building upon Deng Xiaoping's foundational economic vision elucidated in the preceding section, China embarked on a journey of pragmatic implementation. This journey was characterized by a blend of
bold experimentation and strategic restraint, each initiative meticulously designed to fuel growth while preserving the Communist Party's
political dominance.

Central to this endeavor were the Special Economic Zones (SEZs).
While their genesis was covered in Deng's overarching strategy, their
meteoric rise and transformative impact on the Chinese economic
landscape deserve emphasis. Serving as controlled epicenters of mar-
ket-oriented reforms, these zones, especially Shenzhen, Xiamen, and
Zhuhai, drew significant foreign direct investment (FDI). The attrac-
tion was multifaceted: an amalgamation of fiscal incentives, simplified
bureaucracy, and access to a vast, cost-effective labor force. As a result,
SEZs became synonymous with China's manufacturing prowess and
were instrumental in pivoting the nation towards export-led growth.

Beyond the coastal SEZs, a strategic focus on coastal development
underpinned China's ambitions to integrate seamlessly into global
supply chains. Investments flowed into modern port infrastructure,
logistical networks, and allied industries, ensuring that the coastal
regions emerged as the forefront of China's economic renaissance. This
development had a ripple effect, stimulating economic activities further
inland.

However, while market dynamics began to play a pivotal role, the state
maintained discerning oversight. Instances where the economy showed
signs of excessive speculation or overextension were met with timely
interventions by the leadership. This prudence underscored the overarching philosophy: while economic growth was paramount, it should
never imperil the political equilibrium.

State-owned enterprises (SOEs), pillars of the old command economy,
underwent transformative changes. Rather than being sidelined in the
new economic order, they were modernized and repositioned. While
private enterprises made significant inroads, SOEs retained a dominant

presence in sectors deemed strategic, such as banking, energy, and telecommunications.

To conclude, this phase in China's economic journey was not solely about quantitative metrics like GDP growth or trade volumes. It was a nuanced endeavor, harmonizing Deng's vision of economic dynamism with the Communist Party's unwavering political ascendancy. This intricate balancing act facilitated China's rise as a global economic powerhouse by the dawn of the 21st century.

China Joins the World Trade Organization

The twilight of the 20th century bore witness to an event that would be instrumental in recalibrating global trade dynamics: China's accession to the World Trade Organization (WTO) in 2001. This integration was not an impulsive leap but the culmination of years of meticulous negotiations and strategic reforms, signaling China's unwavering commitment to embed itself within the global economic fabric.

Historically, the inception of the People's Republic of China in 1949 saw it adopt an insular economic stance. Guided by socialist principles, as articulated previously, the nation prioritized self-reliance, limiting its engagement with global markets. However, the economic reforms spearheaded by Deng Xiaoping in the late 20th century underscored a paradigm shift. China recognized that sustainable growth and development could be augmented by harnessing global trade's synergies. This realization set the stage for its aspirations to join the WTO, the epitome of the global trading order.

The journey to accession was by no means linear. China faced rigorous scrutiny, with existing WTO members demanding comprehensive market access commitments and adherence to the body's stringent trade norms. China's response was emblematic of its broader reformist ethos: it undertook wide-ranging modifications to its domestic trade policies, regulatory frameworks, and intellectual property rights regimes. These reforms were dual-faceted. While they aligned China's systems with WTO norms, they also synergized with the nation's internal agenda of modernization and efficiency enhancement.

China's inclusion within the WTO framework bore profound implications. Immediately, it cemented its position as a linchpin in global supply chains. The world, already enticed by China's labor market and burgeoning consumer base, now had reinforced confidence in its commitment to predictable and rules-based trade practices. The ensuing years witnessed a torrential inflow of foreign investments, further fueling China's export-led growth trajectory.

Moreover, this integration allowed China to influence, and occasionally challenge, the global trade discourse. While benefiting from the system, China also emerged as a vocal proponent of developing nations' interests within the WTO, often championing causes like technology transfers or differential treatment for economically disadvantaged states.

The dividends of WTO accession were palpable. China's share in global exports swelled, its industries scaled unprecedented heights, and its GDP experienced meteoric growth rates. However, beyond these tangible metrics lay a nuanced narrative: China's WTO membership was not merely about trade volumes or market access. It was a testament to its adeptness at synchronizing global integration with domestic imperatives. While opening its markets, China retained strategic levers to guide its industries, protect its nascent sectors, and ensure that the fruits of globalization were, to a significant extent, harmonized with its national priorities.

In retrospect, China's WTO membership can be viewed as a strategic masterstroke. It not only amplified its economic prowess but also positioned it as an indispensable actor within the global trade arena, capable of shaping, influencing, and occasionally contesting the tenets of international commerce.

Political Ascendancy

While China's economic metamorphosis captivated global attention, an equally significant transformation was unfolding within its political corridors. In the closing decades of the 20th century and the onset of the 21st, China meticulously reshaped its political terrain, weaving together centralization, stability, and contemporary governance.

As economic reforms gained momentum, the Chinese Communist Party (CCP) recognized the imperative of a stable political environment. China's historical tapestry, replete with periods of fragmentation and foreign subjugation, ingrained a deep-seated apprehension of chaos. This sentiment resonated within the CCP's ethos, driving its pursuit of a "harmonious society"—a societal state characterized by stability, prosperity, and the absence of disruptive elements.

This quest for harmony dovetailed with efforts to consolidate political power. Decentralized economic policies did not imply a relaxation of the CCP's political control. On the contrary, as market forces were unleashed, the Party intensified its grip on key political and administrative levers. The overarching narrative was clear: economic liberalization should, under no circumstances, precipitate political pluralism.

The turn of the millennium saw this consolidation coalesce around targeted anti-corruption drives. These campaigns were not merely disciplinary endeavors; they were strategic instruments, achieving dual objectives. First, they assuaged public discontent, projecting the Party as a guardian of public interest, relentlessly purging its ranks of malfeasance. Second, they subtly reconfigured power dynamics within the Party, ensuring that potential centers of alternative influence were systematically neutralized.

The rise of Xi Jinping heralded a new chapter in this political narrative. Ascending to the Party's helm in 2012, Xi's tenure is emblematic of a return to centralized leadership, reminiscent of the Mao era, albeit without its excesses. Under Xi, the CCP accentuated its role as the fulcrum of Chinese society. This centralization was enshrined both in policy and symbolism, with Xi's thought being incorporated into the Party constitution—a distinction reserved for a select few in China's political annals.

Xi's leadership also witnessed a recalibration of the Party's engagement with society. The emphasis shifted from sheer economic growth to a more holistic development model. Environmental sustainability, technological innovation, and cultural rejuvenation were integrated into the national discourse. Moreover, the Party, cognizant of the challenges posed by the digital age, adeptly interwove technology within its governance matrix, leveraging it for surveillance, information dissemination, and public engagement.

In examining China's political ascendancy, one confronts a paradox: a nation that, while embracing market dynamics and global integration, concurrently fortified its one-party political edifice. This duality, where economic liberalization coexists with political centralization, is integral to understanding modern China. The CCP's ability to deftly navigate this intricate balance has been pivotal, not only in ensuring its longevity but also in orchestrating China's resurgence on the global stage.

Military Modernization and Ambitions

China's resurgence as a global economic power was paralleled by its meticulous endeavors to rejuvenate its military capabilities. As the 20th century waned and the new millennium dawned, Beijing consciously embarked on a path of comprehensive military modernization, underpinned by two fundamental objectives: safeguarding its territorial integrity and expanding its strategic influence in the evolving global order.

Historical introspection elucidates China's military motivation. Historically, China's periods of vulnerability, from the Opium Wars to the 'Century of Humiliation', were inextricably linked to its military inadequacies vis-à-vis external powers. Consequently, in Beijing's strategic calculus, a robust military apparatus was not merely an instrument of power projection, but a bulwark against external subjugation.

Central to China's military modernization was the transformation of the People's Liberation Army (PLA). From an overwhelmingly ground-force-centric entity, the PLA underwent a metamorphosis, evolving into a multidimensional force with burgeoning naval, aerial, cyber, and space capabilities. Investment in advanced technologies, from stealth aircraft to missile defense systems, became the cornerstone of this transformation. Concurrently, doctrinal shifts emphasized joint operations, rapid deployment, and power projection beyond China's immediate periphery.

The South China Sea emerged as a focal point in China's military strategy. Historically a conduit for trade and cultural exchange, its contemporary significance transcended its economic value. Laced with contested territorial claims, the South China Sea became emblematic of China's broader geopolitical aspirations. Through a combination of island-building, naval patrols, and strategic posturing, Beijing sought to assert its dominance in these waters, positioning itself as the paramount regional power. These actions, while amplifying China's strategic depth, concurrently engendered apprehensions among regional stakeholders and the broader international community.

Of particular note in China's evolving military strategy is its increasingly assertive posture towards Taiwan. Since the end of the Chinese civil war in 1949, Taiwan has functioned as a separate political entity, albeit under the shadow of Beijing's claims of sovereignty. With China's military modernization, there has been a perceptible intensification in its approach to the Taiwan question. Beijing views the reunification of Taiwan as a core national interest, and its military enhancements, particularly in the domains of naval and missile capabilities, are often interpreted as tools to deter any formal declaration of independence by Taipei or intervention by external powers. Furthermore, there have been increased instances of PLA aircraft encroaching on Taiwan's Air Defense Identification Zone (ADIZ), signaling both a show of strength and a tacit warning against any drift from the long-held 'One China' policy. This assertive stance vis-à-vis Taiwan is emblematic of China's broader ambitions in the region and underscores the importance it places on territorial integrity and national reunification.

China's military endeavors were not confined to its immediate neighborhood. Its 'String of Pearls' strategy, characterized by establishing logistical hubs from the South China Sea to the African coastline, underscored its aspirations to safeguard its maritime trade routes and project power in the Indian Ocean Region—a critical artery for global commerce.

As China's military footprint expanded, so did its strategic dialogues. Military-to-military engagements, joint exercises, and defense collaborations became integral to Beijing's diplomatic outreach. Whether through the Shanghai Cooperation Organization or bilateral engagements, China emphasized a narrative of 'peaceful rise', assuaging concerns of a militaristic expansionist agenda.

In synthesizing China's military trajectory, one discerns a blend of historical lessons, geostrategic imperatives, and forward-looking ambitions. While its military modernization was unequivocally aimed at safeguarding its sovereign interests, it concurrently facilitated China's evolution from a regional player to a global strategic actor. In the intricate choreography of international relations, China's military maneuvers are both a response to and a shaper of the emerging multipolar world order.

Belt and Road Initiative: China's Grand Blueprint For Global Integration

The Belt and Road Initiative (BRI) stands as a testament to China's ambition for expansive intercontinental connectivity. Conceived in the early 2010s, the BRI aims to rejuvenate and expand upon ancient trade pathways. Specifically, the "Belt" focuses on overland corridors, reminiscent of the historical Silk Road, while the "Road" alludes to maritime shipping lanes connecting Asia, Europe, and Africa. This initiative envisions a comprehensive infrastructure network facilitating trade and cooperation across these vast regions.

The motivations underpinning the BRI are multifaceted. Economically, the initiative aims to catalyze regional development, particularly in China's landlocked western provinces, by facilitating access to international markets. Additionally, by investing in infrastructure projects abroad, China seeks to export its industrial overcapacity, ensuring sustained growth in sectors like steel, construction, and transportation. Strategically, the BRI serves as an avenue for China to diversify its trade routes, thereby reducing its dependence on specific transit routes. This is especially pertinent considering vulnerabilities associated with traditional maritime chokepoints, such as the Malacca Strait, a narrow but crucial waterway between the Malay Peninsula and the Indonesian island of Sumatra, through which a significant portion of China's imported oil passes.

Beyond these tangible benefits, the BRI encapsulates China's aspirations to sculpt a new global economic order. By fostering economic interdependence, China positions itself as a linchpin in global commerce. This enhanced economic leverage is complemented by the BRI's implications for soft power. Infrastructure development, coupled with cultural exchanges and academic collaborations under the BRI's purview, facilitates the dissemination of Chinese culture, values, and developmental models.

However, the projection of hard power through the BRI cannot be overlooked. Strategic investments, from ports to railways, not only enhance China's commercial access but also potentially offer logistical advantages, augmenting its military reach and strategic depth. Consequently, while the BRI is primarily posited as an economic venture, its geostrategic ramifications are palpable.

The international reactions to the BRI are a tapestry of intrigue, optimism, and apprehension. Many nations, envisaging the economic prospects offered by enhanced connectivity, have eagerly embraced BRI projects. Yet, concerns abound. The potential for 'debt diplomacy', where countries unable to repay Chinese loans cede control of critical assets, has emerged as a contentious issue. Such apprehensions have been exacerbated by instances like the Hambantota port in Sri Lanka, which, unable to meet its debt obligations, leased the port to China for 99 years. Moreover, the strategic implications of BRI projects, particularly those located in geopolitically sensitive areas, have elicited wary responses from global powers.

In summation, the Belt and Road Initiative is emblematic of China's evolving role in global geopolitics. It intertwines economic imperatives with strategic ambitions, encapsulating China's vision of a world where it stands not as a mere participant but as a principal architect. As nations navigate the opportunities and challenges posed by the BRI, it becomes evident that China's grand blueprint is not merely about roads and ports but about sculpting the contours of 21st-century global dynamics.

Technological Advancement and Global Leadership

In the latter half of the 20ᵗʰ century, China's technological realm was characterized primarily by its efforts to assimilate and adapt foreign technologies. Fast-forward to the dawn of the 21ˢᵗ century, and the narrative has transformed dramatically. China, once seen predominantly as a replicator of Western technological innovations, now stands at the forefront of numerous pivotal sectors, charting the course for global technological trajectories.

Foremost among these sectors is the realm of 5G telecommunications. With firms like Huawei and ZTE leading the charge, China has not merely developed 5G infrastructure domestically but has also exported its technology to various parts of the globe. This 5G leadership is not just about faster internet speeds. The ramifications extend to the broader digital ecosystem, impacting sectors from smart cities and the Internet of Things (IoT) — a network of interconnected physical devices that can collect and share data — to autonomous vehicles and telemedicine. As nations integrate 5G into their infrastructural fabric, dependence on Chinese technology grows, intertwining geopolitical considerations with technological choices.

Concurrently, China's strides in the domain of artificial intelligence (AI) have been remarkable. Recognizing AI's transformative potential, China's state-led approach, combined with vibrant private sector participation, has cultivated an environment conducive to rapid advancement. By harnessing vast data reserves and investing in research and development, China aspires to be the global AI leader by 2030. This AI prowess is manifest not just in consumer applications but extends to areas like surveillance, fostering a sophisticated state apparatus that melds technological sophistication with governance.

Space exploration provides another vista where China's ambitions are evident. From its 'Chang'e' lunar missions to its plans for a modular space station, China's extraterrestrial endeavors symbolize its aspirations to be a dominant spacefaring nation. These ventures, beyond their scientific merit, hold geopolitical significance, positioning China as a formidable player in the new space race.

The global implications of China's technological ascendance are multifarious. The most palpable of these is the technological competition with the United States. As both superpowers endeavor to secure technological hegemony, the world witnesses an unfolding tech-cold war, characterized by skirmishes in trade, intellectual property, and standard-setting. This rivalry, while fostering innovation, also risks fragmenting the global technological landscape, leading to potential bifurcations in standards, platforms, and ecosystems.

In analyzing China's technological journey, it becomes evident that its advancements are not isolated phenomena but are intricately linked to its broader strategic imperatives. As China continues to blaze its technological trail, it redefines the global tech order, shaping not just the future of innovation but also the geopolitics of the digital age.

China's Soft Power and Cultural Diplomacy

Amid the din of economic juggernauts and military might, another facet of China's global strategy has been steadily unfolding, albeit with a softer cadence: its endeavor to project cultural and ideological influence across the globe. While its economic and military pursuits are direct and often palpable, China's soft power ambitions operate on a more nuanced, subtle plane, seeking to shape perceptions, values, and narratives.

Central to this soft power strategy are the Confucius Institutes. Established across university campuses worldwide, these centers aim to promote Chinese language learning and foster an appreciation for Chinese culture. While they present themselves as benign cultural outposts, some critics perceive them as vehicles for Beijing's propaganda, especially given their close ties to the Chinese government. Nevertheless, their proliferation underscores China's intent to position its language and culture as integral components of global academia.

Beyond academic corridors, China's global media outreach has been expanding. State-backed media conglomerates like CGTN (China Global Television Network) and Xinhua have been amplifying China's narratives on global platforms. These outlets, equipped with significant resources, have correspondents stationed worldwide, ensuring that

China's perspective on global events gets disseminated. Such media endeavors are not just about news; they encompass documentaries, cultural programs, and other content genres that depict China's history, progress, and aspirations.

This cultural diplomacy extends to the cinematic world as well. With its burgeoning film industry, China has been creating movies that resonate not just domestically but also find audiences abroad. Collaborations with Hollywood, participation in international film festivals, and the construction of global cinematic infrastructures like theaters and distribution networks further this soft power projection.

Yet, it's not a one-dimensional projection. China has also been receptive, absorbing global cultural influences, be it in fashion, music, or cinema. This exchange ensures that while China projects its cultural identity outward, it also engages in a two-way dialogue with global cultures, fostering mutual understanding.

However, while these efforts have expanded China's cultural footprint, challenges persist. Skepticism regarding China's motives, concerns about freedom of expression, and the global promotion of values that may not always align with liberal democratic principles can sometimes limit the efficacy of its soft power initiatives.

Historically, nations have always sought to project their cultural and ideological prowess alongside their economic and military might. For China, this soft power strategy is a testament to its recognition of the intricate tapestry of global influence, where culture and ideology play roles as pivotal as commerce and defense.

Repercussions and Challenges

China's meteoric ascent on the global stage, while commendable, has not been devoid of intricacies and impediments. The nation grapples with a constellation of challenges that, in many ways, are the byproducts of its rapid transformation and international ambitions.

On the international front, human rights concerns remain a persistent point of contention. Reports of restrictive measures in Tibet, and more recently, allegations related to the treatment of the Uighur Muslim minority in Xinjiang, have generated considerable global scrutiny. China's approach to these issues has often been characterized by a juxtaposition of denial, stringent control on information dissemination, and diplomatic pushback against nations raising these concerns. These human rights issues, when viewed in the broader context of China's governance model, raise fundamental questions about the reconciliation of its domestic policies with its international image aspirations.

China's rapid industrialization, though an engine of its economic growth, has birthed significant environmental challenges. Cities shrouded in smog, waterways polluted by industrial effluents, and deforestation have become emblematic of the environmental cost of China's economic miracle. Recognizing these challenges, Beijing has been steering its policies towards green technologies, sustainable urban development, and international environmental cooperation. The nation's commitment to the Paris Agreement and its ambitious goals for carbon neutrality are reflective of this shift. However, the tangible implementation and scaling of these green initiatives remain to be observed.

Economic inequalities also present a formidable domestic challenge. While coastal cities like Shanghai and Shenzhen epitomize modernity and affluence, vast swathes of China's interior regions lag in development. The economic disparity between urban metropolises and rural hinterlands, and between coastal cities and inland provinces, poses not just socio-economic challenges but also has implications for social harmony and stability. Beijing's policies, like the "Go West" strategy, aim to address these regional disparities, but the task is Herculean, given the vastness and diversity of China's geography and demography.

It's imperative to understand that China's challenges, while significant, are not unique in the annals of history. Many emerging powers have faced similar, if not identical, impediments in their trajectories. What will define China's place in history is not the mere existence of these challenges but its strategies, adaptability, and resilience in navigating them. As the nation continues to carve its niche in the global order, its response to these challenges will be watched closely, shaping perceptions and influencing international relations.

Conclusion

China's remarkable journey from an insular nation to a global behemoth is emblematic of the fluidity inherent in the international hierarchy of power. Its trajectory not only underscores the cyclical nature of ascendancy and decline but also exemplifies how nations navigate and adapt within an ever-shifting geopolitical paradigm.

As earlier chapters delineated, superpowers such as the U.S. and the Soviet Union have shaped the post-WWII global order. China's rise, however, introduces a renewed dynamism into this equation. Its economic, military, and technological advancements can be seen, in part, as responses to the established global frameworks and power structures. For instance, the Belt and Road Initiative, while serving China's strategic interests, can also be perceived as an attempt to reconfigure global trade networks traditionally dominated by Western powers.

Furthermore, China's interaction with the U.S., particularly in technological sectors like 5G and artificial intelligence, highlights not just a competition for supremacy but also a deeper contention of values, governance models, and visions for the global future. This interaction resonates with historical patterns where emerging powers, as they ascend, often find themselves in a complex dance of cooperation and contention with existing dominant entities.

Yet, it's crucial to understand that China's rise is not merely about juxtaposition against other superpowers. Its ascent is rooted in its unique historical context, cultural ethos, and the strategic vision of its leadership. This blend of internal determinants and external interactions makes China's journey an illustrative chapter in the annals of global power dynamics.

As we reflect on China's evolution, it serves as a testament to the book's central theme: the transient nature of power. The world watched as China, harnessing its millennia-old civilizational legacy and fusing it with modern-day pragmatism, carved out a prominent niche in the global arena. Its story reaffirms that power dynamics, no matter how seemingly entrenched, are always in flux, subject to the push and pull of historical forces, strategic decisions, and global interactions.

Chapter 29.
Neo-Empires in a Post-Cold War Era (20ᵗʰ-21ˢᵗ Centuries)

Innovation distinguishes between a leader and a follower.

~Steve Jobs

Definition and concept of "Neo-Empires".

In an ever-evolving geopolitical landscape, the legacy of traditional empires, once manifested through territorial conquests and direct governance, has undergone profound metamorphosis. This transformation gave birth to the concept of "Neo-Empires" – a term capturing the essence of post-Cold War dominance.

In the ancient and medieval worlds, empires expanded their influence predominantly through the sword and colonization. Territories were annexed, populations subjugated, and resources directly extracted. This framework persisted, albeit with variations, until the mid-20ᵗʰ century. However, as decolonization movements gained momentum post World War II, and as the Cold War's ideological divide polarized the globe, direct territorial acquisition became less feasible and often less desirable.

This recalibration was not indicative of a decline in the pursuit of power or influence by dominant states or entities. Instead, it heralded the emergence of more subtle, yet equally potent, mechanisms of control. The post-Cold War era, characterized by economic globalization, technological advancements, and shifts in global politics, laid fertile ground for these Neo-Empires to flourish.

At the heart of the Neo-Empire concept lies the transition from direct territorial control to influence-based dominance. This influence manifests in various realms – economic, technological, cultural, and political. For instance, a nation no longer needed to colonize a territory to control its resources; economic instruments, from debt to trade agreements, could achieve similar outcomes. Similarly, cultural dominance was no longer anchored solely in language or administration but could be disseminated globally through media, brands, and academia.

Yet, it's pivotal to recognize that the evolution to Neo-Empires did not render traditional power dynamics obsolete. Military might, geopolitical strategy, and even old-fashioned diplomacy continued to play significant roles. However, they now operated within a broader toolkit, replete with instruments tailored for a globalized, interconnected world.

This nuanced approach to dominance is exemplified by the strategies of major powers in the post-Cold War era. The United States, for instance, leveraged its economic and technological prowess, alongside its military capabilities, to remain a preeminent global power. Similarly, China, while emerging as an economic behemoth, utilized mechanisms like the Belt and Road Initiative to expand its global footprint.

In conclusion, the concept of Neo-Empires underscores a continuum in the annals of global power dynamics. While the methods and tools of dominance have evolved, reflecting the complexities of contemporary geopolitics, the underlying impetus – the pursuit of influence and control – remains a constant.

Economic Dominance In a Globalized World

The late 20th and early 21st centuries witnessed the ascendancy of economics as a primary vector of global influence, profoundly reshaping power dynamics in a rapidly globalizing world. At the forefront of this evolution were entities previously deemed secondary actors in geopolitics: multinational corporations and international economic institutions.

As globalization accelerated, facilitated by technological advancements and liberalized trade regimes, corporations began operating on scales previously associated only with nation-states. Brands like Apple, Google, and Amazon saw their valuations not only surpass those of several countries but also exert influence in global policy-making, from data privacy standards to environmental protocols. The intertwining of corporate objectives with national interests became evident as countries vied for investments, technological hubs, and research centers, further underscoring the weight of economic power in contemporary geopolitics.

Parallel to the rise of these multinational corporations, international economic institutions such as the International Monetary Fund (IMF) and the World Bank began playing increasingly pivotal roles, extending their influence beyond their initial post-World War II reconstruction mandate. Originally established to foster global economic cooperation and facilitate post-war recovery, these institutions evolved into critical lenders and policy advisors for numerous nations, with their impact pronounced particularly in the Global South. While their objectives emphasize economic stabilization, development, and poverty reduction, the policy conditions accompanying their financial support have attracted criticism. Such conditions, which often include the imposition of fiscal austerity measures or market liberalization policies, have been contentious, inciting debates over national sovereignty and self-determination.

A notable case in point is the Greek financial crisis that began in 2009. The IMF, in conjunction with the European Union, orchestrated a series of bailouts for Greece, with the first package initiated in 2010. These bailouts were conditional upon Greece's implementation of extensive fiscal austerity measures and structural reforms. The intention was to restore fiscal balance and promote economic competitiveness. However, the austerity policies led to a deep recession, significant unemployment, and widespread public protests. The Greek situation exemplifies the complex dynamics at play when international institutions intervene in national economies. It raises important questions about the limits of such interventions and highlights the potential for socio-economic distress when externally mandated policies are at odds with the welfare of the citizenry. This example underscores the profound dilemmas facing states in the current international system, torn between the exigencies of financial stability and the imperatives of political autonomy and social stability.

China's Belt and Road Initiative (BRI), referenced in the previous chapter, presents a nuanced case study in this context. On the surface, the BRI appears as an infrastructure development and investment project spanning several countries and continents. However, when viewed through the lens of neo-imperialism, it mirrors historical patterns of influence through economic means. By providing critical infrastructure, investments, and loans, China positions itself as an indispensable economic partner for numerous countries. Yet, this partnership sometimes translates into geopolitical leverage, whether through the acquisition of strategic assets due to debt defaults or by aligning recipient countries' policies closer to Beijing's perspectives.

In synthesizing the facets of economic dominance in a globalized world, a complex tapestry emerges. While the tools of influence have expanded to include corporate strategies, investment flows, and developmental initiatives, the objective remains consistent with historical patterns: leveraging economic means to achieve broader geopolitical ends. The intricacies of this interplay, where economics melds seamlessly with strategy, underscores the dynamism and complexity of the Neo-Empire paradigm.

Digital Colonization and Technological Hegemony

The advent of the digital age heralded profound shifts in the conduits of global influence. With the proliferation of the internet and the emergence of digital platforms, the virtual realm began to parallel, and at times even eclipse, the physical world in terms of strategic importance.

This evolution ushered in new paradigms of dominance, notably "digital colonization" and technological hegemony.

The internet, initially perceived as a tool for global democratization and information dissemination, metamorphosed into a battleground for influence. Digital platforms, ranging from search engines to social media networks, not only became primary sources of information for billions but also potent instruments of narrative control. The ability to shape online discourses, influence digital algorithms, or control information flow endowed entities with unprecedented power. In essence, cyberspace became the new frontier where battles for hearts and minds were waged, where shaping perceptions could yield tangible geopolitical dividends.

In the sweeping digital era, tech behemoths, primarily originating from Silicon Valley in the West and tech hubs in China, have assumed a central role. Corporations like Google, Facebook, Tencent, and Alibaba, leveraging their massive user bases and integrated digital ecosystems, have wielded influence far beyond their national borders. Their platforms, dictating terms of information access, commerce, and communication, unintentionally evolved into instruments of soft power. This became evident in numerous ways: Facebook's alleged role in shaping political opinions during the U.S. 2016 elections; the dissemination of vaccine misinformation on various social media platforms influencing public sentiment regarding COVID-19 vaccinations; and conspiracy theories gaining ground via these vast networks. Such influences were especially pronounced in nations where indigenous digital alternatives were either in their infancy or simply absent, allowing these tech titans to mold digital consumer behaviors and, by consequence, socio-cultural norms.

Yet, the rise of these digital giants and the encompassing narrative of digital colonization has met with significant resistance. Global dialogues shifted to emphasize data sovereignty and the rights surrounding the digital realm. With data becoming an invaluable asset, often likened to "new oil", contentious debates emerged. Determining control over data, its processing protocols, storage locations, and its monetization became subjects of intense scrutiny. In response, countries, cognizant of data's strategic importance, initiated measures promoting data localization, instating rigorous regulatory frameworks, and intensifying oversight on foreign tech enterprises. Simultaneously, public discourses started echoing concerns about privacy, surveillance, and the freedoms in the digital domain, pressing both governments and corporations to tread a labyrinth of economic stakes, individual rights, and intricate geopolitical maneuvers.

The realm of digital colonization and technological hegemony underscores the complexities of the modern Neo-Empire era. While the mediums of influence have evolved to encompass bytes, algorithms, and digital platforms, the underlying imperatives remain anchored in historical constants: control, influence, and power. However, in this digital age, the dynamics are fluid, the stakeholders diverse, and the outcomes often unpredictable, reflecting the multifaceted nature of contemporary global power plays.

Cultural Proliferation In the Modern Age

Having traversed the history of global empires history in this volume, we recognize a recurring motif: the potency of cultural influence. From the oratory of ancient Athens to the trade-laden caravans of the Silk Road, culture has perennially served as a pivotal lever in the machinations of empires. As we transition into the modern era, it's evident that while the mediums and methods have evolved, the underlying principle remains intact: culture, as a vehicle of soft power, holds a profound sway over societies, transcending borders and influencing minds.

In an era marked by rapid globalization and interconnectedness, cultural vehicles have become central actors in the broader theater of neo-imperial dynamics. The age-old conduit of power now reflects a world where narratives are as influential as navies, where beliefs can be as binding as borders.

The global entertainment industry, with its reach and appeal, emerged as one such potent vehicle. Hollywood, with its cinematic behemoths, not only entertained global audiences but also subtly propagated values, ideals, and lifestyles reflective of the West. Films, series, and music subtly imprinted notions of democracy, freedom, and the 'American Dream' on global consciousness. Bollywood, originating from India, countered this with its vibrant tapestry of films that narrated tales infused with South Asian cultural, familial, and moral ethos. These entertainment giants, transcending their roles as mere content creators, became cultural ambassadors, forging connections, molding perceptions, and influencing global sociocultural landscapes.

Simultaneously, the globalization of food, fashion, and lifestyle underscored another dimension of cultural proliferation. Brands, whether they represented fast food, haute couture, or everyday commodities, transformed into symbols of aspiration, status, and identity. The ubiquity of brands like McDonald's, Starbucks, or Zara in cities across continents epitomized this cultural homogenization. Yet, this wasn't a one-way influence; the global popularity of sushi, yoga, or Latin dance attested to the reciprocal nature of cultural exchange in the modern era.

Education and academic institutions further bolstered this cultural exchange dynamic. Prestigious universities in the West attracted a global student body, becoming melting pots of diverse cultures, ideas, and aspirations. These institutions, while disseminating knowledge, also subtly inculcated values, perspectives, and biases, shaping the worldviews of future global leaders, policymakers, and influencers. Conversely, as Asian economies grew in prominence, their academic institutions began asserting their influence, drawing international students and forging global academic partnerships.

In evaluating the cultural dynamics of the contemporary age, one discerns a sophisticated tapestry of influence, marked by interplay, reciprocity, and at times, contention. Cultural elements, whether films, food, or academic curricula, serve as soft power tools in the arsenal of modern neo-empires, vying for global hearts and minds. Yet, unlike more overt forms of dominance, cultural proliferation often operates subtly, its influences seeping in gradually, molding perceptions and allegiances over extended temporal spans.

Geopolitical Strategies and Proxy Dominance

As detailed in the preceding section, the tools of empire-building have witnessed a shift from the overt might of military conquest to the more nuanced potency of cultural influence. Yet, while this realm of cultural influence has undeniably broadened, one must not discount the persistent role of traditional geopolitics, intelligence operations, and military strategy. The juxtaposition of these domains underscores the multifaceted nature of modern global dominance.

Yet we are still witnessing a departure from overt territorial ambitions to more covert strategies aimed at achieving regional dominance and global influence. This paradigm shift birthed a new lexicon of dominance, hallmarked by indirect interventions, proxy conflicts, and intelligence-driven operations.

Central to these strategies was the establishment and maintenance of military bases outside national territories. The United States, Russia, China, and several European powers established such military installations across strategic locations, notably in the Middle East, Africa, and the Indo-Pacific region. Ostensibly projected as facilitators of regional stability, these bases invariably served dual purposes. Firstly, they acted as logistical hubs, ensuring rapid deployment capabilities. Secondly, and more imperatively, they asserted influence, serving as palpable markers of presence and power, reminiscent of ancient fortresses overlooking conquered territories. Alongside, defense agreements, often cloaked in the garb of mutual cooperation, anchored these military forays, granting nations the legal frameworks to operate in foreign terrains.

However, the physical presence of military establishments was just one facet of this new-age geopolitical chess game. The theater of proxy wars emerged as another critical arena. Instead of direct confrontations, major powers often chose to back opposing factions in regional conflicts, transforming local disputes into global power plays. For instance, the Syrian conflict, ignited in 2011 as part of the broader wave of the Arab Spring protests, saw Russia and Iran ardently supporting the Assad regime, while the U.S., Turkey, and some Gulf states backed various rebel factions. In Yemen, the Houthi rebels, allegedly backed by Iran, have been in a protracted conflict with the government forces supported by a Saudi-led coalition, with both sides aiming for control and dominance. Meanwhile, in Libya, after the ousting of Muammar Gaddafi, a power vacuum ensued with different factions vying for control, drawing in external actors like Russia, Turkey, and the UAE, each supporting different sides. The Middle East, with its intricate web of alliances, rivalries, and resources, became a crucible for such engagements. Moreover, Africa, with its rich resources and strategic significance, wasn't immune either. The continent has witnessed external interventions masked as support for one faction or the other, further underscoring the expansive nature of modern proxy engagements.

Intelligence agencies, historically shadow players, took center stage in these complex dynamics. The role of agencies like the CIA, MI6, GRU, and Mossad transcended traditional espionage. In addition to gathering intelligence, they orchestrated covert operations, facilitated regime changes, and at times, even engaged in direct action. Their operations, often conducted under plausible deniability, added layers of complexity to global geopolitics, making it increasingly challenging to discern overt actions from covert agendas.

In summation, the contemporary era of geopolitical strategies is characterized by subtlety, complexity, and indirectness. Unlike the ancient empires, which exerted dominance through direct rule, modern neo-empires deploy a blend of military presence, proxy engagements, and intelligence operations to assert influence and achieve strategic objectives. In this intricate dance of power, the lines between offense and defense, between open engagements and covert operations, remain perennially blurred.

Environmental Control and Resource Wars

In the evolving narrative of neo-imperialism, environmental factors and natural resources have increasingly moved from the periphery to the center stage of global geopolitics. The twin pressures of climate change and the insatiable global demand for resources have redefined the contours of power dynamics and strategic priorities.

Climate change, transcending its environmental implications, has evolved into a platform for geopolitical maneuvering. While the global community grapples with the escalating ramifications of a warming planet, major powers vie for leadership in crafting and implementing solutions. The Paris Agreement, for instance, while being a multilateral effort to mitigate climate change, also witnessed subtle tugs-of-war over financial commitments, technology transfers, and responsibility attributions. As nations position themselves as champions of sustainability and environmental stewardship, the underlying currents are often driven by the desire to assert geopolitical influence and gain strategic advantages.

The Arctic region stands as a testament to the convergence of environmental change and resource-driven geopolitics. As global warming leads to the receding of Arctic ice, previously inaccessible natural resources, notably oil, gas, and minerals, have become increasingly attainable. This has ignited a scramble among Arctic nations and other interested powers to stake claims and establish footholds. The potential opening of new maritime routes, which could reshape global trade dynamics, adds another layer of strategic significance to the Arctic narrative.

Water, fundamental to life and civilization, has emerged as a potential flashpoint in the discourse on resources. With diminishing freshwater reserves and escalating global demand, transboundary rivers and aquifers have become subjects of contention and competition. The Nile, Mekong, and Indus basins, among others, witness intricate interplay between riparian states, balancing developmental aspirations with equitable resource sharing. These watercourses, historically lifelines of civilizations, are now potential battlegrounds, where disputes over access and control could escalate into larger regional conflicts.

In encapsulating the environmental and resource-driven imperatives of modern geopolitics, it becomes evident that the earth's physical and ecological attributes are intricately entwined with the strategies and ambitions of states. As nations grapple with the dual challenges of sustaining their populations and asserting global dominance, the environment and its resources become both arenas for cooperation and points of contention. In this delicate balance, the pursuit of sustainable solutions and the imperatives of geopolitical ambitions constantly intersect and interact.

International Organizations and Alliances

In the architecture of the post-World War II global order, international organizations and alliances have occupied pivotal roles. These institutions, while embodying the ideals of collective governance and multilateralism, have often been intertwined with the power dynamics of major states, raising intricate questions about their true nature and purpose.

The United Nations (UN), conceptualized as a bastion of global cooperation, embodies this duality. On one hand, the organization has facilitated collaborative efforts on a range of global issues, from humanitarian crises to sustainable development. On the other, its structure, notably the Security Council with its veto-wielding permanent

UN Headquarters in New York[44]

members, reflects the power dynamics of the post-war era, allowing major powers to exert significant influence on its decisions and actions. This dual role has, at times, prompted criticisms about the UN being used as an instrument of dominance by the major powers, while also being hailed as a beacon of global cooperation and norm-setting.

Similarly, the North Atlantic Treaty Organization (NATO), while originally conceived as a collective defense mechanism against potential Soviet aggression, has evolved in its role and reach. Post the Cold War, NATO's interventions in places like the Balkans, Afghanistan, and Libya have spurred debates about its purpose. Is it merely a tool for Western, particularly U.S., dominance? Or does it genuinely embody the principles of collective security in the face of evolving global threats?

Regional blocs, like the European Union (EU) and the Association of Southeast Asian Nations (ASEAN), offer a different lens through which to examine the interplay between cooperation and dominance. These organizations, rooted in regional identities and shared goals, strive to balance the imperatives of individual sovereignty with the benefits of collective action. The EU's economic and political integration, while fostering intra-regional cooperation, has also posed challenges, as member states grapple with the tensions between national autonomy and shared governance. ASEAN, with its emphasis on consensus and non-interference, underscores a different model, one that prioritizes regional harmony while allowing for significant diversity in its members' political and economic systems.

In recent times, the BRICS (Brazil, Russia, India, China, South Africa) grouping has emerged as a symbol of the shifting global order. Representing major economies from different continents, BRICS challenges the traditional Western-dominated economic and political frameworks, advocating for a more multipolar world. Its initiatives, such as the New Development Bank, are testament to its aspirations to create alternate global institutions that reflect the interests and perspectives of its members.

In summation, international organizations and alliances, while undeniably serving as platforms for cooperation and collective action, are not immune to the power dynamics inherent in global geopolitics. Their actions, policies, and very structures are reflective of the intricate balance between cooperative ideals and the strategic ambitions of their most influential members.

Challenging Sovereignty: Hybrid Wars and Information Warfare

The delineations of warfare and statecraft have evolved considerably in the contemporary era. Whereas traditional conflict largely revolved around overt military engagements, the present geopolitical landscape is characterized by a blend of conventional and unconventional tactics. These "hybrid" strategies often aim to challenge state sovereignties without necessitating outright warfare, marking a distinct shift in how dominance is pursued and resisted.

A salient feature of this hybrid warfare paradigm is the ascendancy of information warfare. The exponential proliferation of digital platforms and communication channels has engendered an environment where information, and its manipulation, has become a potent weapon. Disinformation campaigns, propelled by sophisticated algorithms and echo chambers, have the capacity to shape public perceptions, influence electoral outcomes, and sow discord. Nation-states, leveraging these tools, can wage covert wars on adversaries, destabilizing them without deploying conventional forces. The revelations about Russian interference in the 2016 U.S. elections stand as a testament to the potential ramifications of such campaigns.

Cyber-attacks further augment this spectrum of hybrid warfare. Infrastructure, financial systems, and critical state apparatuses, deeply integrated with digital networks, are vulnerable to sophisticated cyber assaults. These attacks, whether aimed at data theft, infrastructure disruption, or espionage, can inflict considerable damage on states, both materially and psychologically. Their often-anonymous nature, coupled with plausible deniability, makes them particularly appealing as instruments of statecraft.

The phenomenon of "Color Revolutions" in parts of Eastern Europe and Central Asia underscores another facet of this hybrid warfare paradigm. These popular uprisings, while rooted in genuine grievances, have often been viewed through the lens of geopolitics, with speculations about external influences and covert support. The interplay between grassroots movements and potential external instigations illustrates the complexities of modern political upheavals.

Media, both traditional and new, has assumed an increasingly central role in this evolving landscape. Beyond its function as a purveyor of news, media has become a tool in the strategic arsenals of states and non-state actors alike. Propaganda, narrative shaping, and perception management are conducted through media channels, with the aim of influencing both domestic and international audiences. The geopolitical tussles between major powers are often mirrored in their media narratives, each vying to shape global perceptions in line with their strategic objectives.

In synthesizing these dynamics, it becomes evident that the frontlines of modern geopolitical confrontations are as much in the digital realm and the domain of perceptions as they are on actual battlegrounds. In this intricate dance of influence, information, and intrigue, sovereignty is constantly negotiated, challenged, and defended.

Assessing Resistance and Autonomy

The 21st century, while punctuated by narratives of neo-imperial endeavors, has also borne witness to a spirited resurgence of resistance movements that challenge this dominant paradigm. These movements, propelled by an amalgam of historical, cultural, and economic factors, underscore the intrinsic human aspiration for autonomy and self-determination.

At the forefront of this wave of resistance are the burgeoning nationalistic movements observed across continents. While neo-imperial designs often operate on subduing or co-opting local identities for larger geopolitical or economic strategies, a counter-current of nationalistic fervor has risen to resist such overtures. This has manifested in calls for greater economic self-reliance, preservation of cultural heritage, and even in political realignments. For instance, the Brexit vote in the United Kingdom can be interpreted as a manifestation of such nationalistic sentiments, driven by perceived economic and cultural encroachments by supra-national entities.

Delving deeper, individual nation-states have exhibited concerted efforts to extricate themselves from stifling economic dependencies. Case in point, numerous African countries, traditionally reliant on Western aid and subject to its accompanying conditionalities, have started exploring south-south cooperation, gravitating towards nations like China, India, and Brazil for infrastructural investments and trade partnerships. Similarly, Latin American countries such as Bolivia and Ecuador have sought to renegotiate or even repudiate unfavorable economic agreements, aiming to regain control over their resources.

Parallel to these nationalistic and state-led efforts, the global arena has witnessed an intensifying push for indigenous rights and regional identities. Indigenous communities, historically marginalized and often bereft of a voice in the larger national dialogues, have begun to assert their rights. From the Maori in New Zealand to the Sami in Scandinavia, and the Native American communities in North America, the demand is clear: recognition, respect, and autonomy. These movements underscore a broader trend where localized identities seek to carve out spaces of self-governance and cultural preservation amidst the homogenizing tendencies of globalization.

Furthermore, regional groupings and blocs have emerged as bulwarks against neo-imperial tendencies. ASEAN (described in a previous section) in Southeast Asia, for example, while fostering economic integration, also serves as a platform to assert a collective regional identity and safeguard the interests of its member states against external hegemonic influences.

In sum, the modern landscape, while witnessing the nuances of neo-imperial endeavors, is equally characterized by multifaceted resistance movements. These movements, whether spearheaded by nation-states or grassroots communities, highlight the enduring spirit of autonomy and the intrinsic human yearning for self-determination amidst a rapidly changing global order.

History Has Not Ended: The 2022 Russian Aggression in Ukraine

In the aftermath of the Cold War, as the world transitioned into the 1990s, there emerged several theories about the direction global geopolitics would take. Central among these was Francis Fukuyama's 1992 work, "The End of History and the Last Man." Fukuyama hypothesized that with the Soviet Union's disintegration in 1991 and the widespread acceptance of Western liberal democracy, mankind might have arrived at a consensus regarding the most viable form of governance, suggesting a potential end to major ideological conflicts.

However, history's intricate patterns cannot be so easily unraveled or predicted. Margaret Thatcher, who led the United Kingdom from 1979 to 1990, was known for her assertive stances on the geopolitics of her time, and she cautioned against making deterministic assumptions about history's course, notably emphasizing that one should "never count history out." The unfolding events of the late 20th and early 21st centuries served as potent reminders of the complexities inherent in international relations.

The Russian actions in Ukraine in February 2022 became a quintessential example of history's persistent undercurrents. While the immediate precursor to this escalation can be traced back to the annexation of Crimea by Russia in 2014, the roots of Russian-Ukrainian dynamics delve much deeper, intertwining with centuries of shared histories, divergent nationalisms, and strategic geopolitics. Russia's military campaign, while undeniably embedded in the contemporary context of its strategic interests in Eastern Europe and its concerns about NATO expansion, also echoed the ambitions of historic empires and their quests for territorial dominance.

Russia's 2022 aggression was met with widespread international condemnation, leading to an array of economic sanctions spearheaded by the United States and the European Union. The crisis underscored the delicate balance of power in post-Cold War Europe and illustrated that while the nature of warfare and diplomacy might evolve, the fundamental drivers—territorial ambition, national interest, and strategic dominance—remain deeply entrenched in the annals of statecraft.

Conclusion: Reflection and Forward Look

The evolving dynamics of the post-Cold War era, marked by the emergence of neo-empires, beckons us to reflect on the persistent nature of power dynamics and the cyclical patterns of rise and decline. These neo-empires, while emblematic of modern tools and strategies, still harken back to historical imperatives of dominance and influence. Yet, as history has time and again demonstrated, such constructs, however powerful, are not immune to challenges, resistance, and eventual transformation.

Looking ahead, the global landscape presents an increasingly multipolar world. As power centers diversify, the prospects of a singular dominant neo-empire diminish. This multipolarity is not just a manifestation of state actors but is equally informed by non-state entities, transnational corporations, and grassroots movements, all exerting influence on the international stage. This complex interplay suggests that future neo-empires will have to navigate a far more intricate web of actors and interests.

Moreover, there's a palpable potential for a backlash against the very tenets of globalization and neo-imperial tendencies. As communities and nations grapple with the implications of external influence, whether economic, cultural, or technological, the calls for autonomy, self-reliance, and indigenous rights grow louder. This could herald a world that is increasingly skeptical of overarching dominance and more inclined towards regionalism, localized identities, and cooperative frameworks.

However, this doesn't necessarily portend a fragmentation of the global order. Instead, it offers an opportunity to reimagine a world order pivoted on genuine cooperation, mutual respect, and equitable growth. Such a paradigm would prioritize collective global challenges, from climate change to sustainable development, over narrow hegemonic pursuits.

In concluding this exploration of neo-empires in the post-Cold War era, it becomes evident that the undercurrents of power, influence, and dominance persist, albeit in evolved forms. Yet, so too does the indomitable human spirit for autonomy, justice, and equitable progress. As traditional empires have waned and neo-empires have risen, they too will face the inexorable dynamics of challenge, adaptation, and transformation. This continuity and change, reflecting the cyclical nature of power, resonate with the central theme of this book and underscore the intricate tapestry of global statecraft.

Storming of the US Capitol, January 6, 2021[45],

Chapter 30.
Contemporary America: Through the Historical Prism of Power

*Change will not come if we wait for some other person
or some other time.
We are the ones we've been waiting for.
We are the change that we seek.*

~Barack Obama

The Shifting Sands of Power

In the vast panorama of history, as powerful empires have risen, they have also inevitably faced decline. As we analyze contemporary America, it is instructive to employ the prism of history to identify and understand the forces that have precipitated the waning of mighty empires in the past. While Chapter 21 delved into America's meteoric ascent as a global hegemon, the motifs of decline discerned in Chapter 2 offer a profound context for comprehending the current trajectory of the United States.

Economic Strain. Historically, the apparent prosperity of empires has masked underlying economic vulnerabilities. The economic challenges faced by empires such as the Byzantines, burdened by external debts and reliant on complex trade networks, mirror America's present-day economic concerns. From growing national debts to challenges posed by international trade dynamics and economic rivals, the U.S. confronts an intricate web of economic pressures.

Internal Discord and Complacency. The tapestry of history is replete with empires that, at their zenith, grew complacent, believing their dominance unassailable. The Roman Empire, with its vast expanse, faced internal strife, political factionalism, and societal complacency, which weakened its foundational cohesion. Similarly, in the modern era, internal divisions, polarized political landscapes, and growing socioeconomic disparities have sown seeds of discord within American society, challenging the unity that once propelled its ascent.

Technological Standstill. Technological prowess has historically been a linchpin of an empire's dominance, from the engineering marvels of the Roman aqueducts to the naval innovations of the British Empire. However, resting on past laurels can lead to stagnation. As global centers of technological innovation shift and new powerhouses emerge, the once-uncontested dominance of American innovation hubs like Silicon Valley faces unprecedented challenges.

Overextension. The narratives of empires, from the Mongols to the Spanish, are tales of vast territories amassed but stretched thin. The logistical and administrative challenges of managing vast expanses, coupled with military overcommitments, have historically drained empires' resources. Contemporary America's global military commitments, spanning numerous bases and theaters of operation, echo these historical patterns of overextension.

External Threats. Empires, regardless of their might, have always faced external challenges. For the Romans, the relentless pressures came from the likes of barbarian groups and leaders like Vercingetorix. Similarly, America today finds itself navigating a world where new powers are emerging, challenging traditional spheres of influence and geopolitical norms.

Cultural Isolation. Cultural dynamism and adaptability have been strengths of many enduring empires. However, as history has shown, there's a risk of turning inward. The Han dynasty's eventual insularity offers a lesson in the dangers of cultural rigidity. In the contemporary context, America's once-universal cultural exports face challenges, hinting at a possible inward turn.

Environmental and Health Challenges. Beyond human-induced challenges, empires have historically grappled with environmental calamities and health crises. The destabilization of Mesopotamia's empires due to environmental degradation serves as a testament to nature's unpredictable power. In the recent past, the challenges posed to America by health crises, notably the COVID-19 pandemic, and environmental concerns exemplify this vulnerability.

Leadership Crisis. Strong leadership remains a linchpin of an empire's resilience. The decline of the Roman Empire, punctuated by leadership instabilities, and the fragmentation of empires post-Charlemagne and Alexander the Great, underscore the importance of visionary leadership. In the American context, leadership challenges, policy inconsistencies, and societal disillusionment with governance structures pose significant concerns.

In gauging America's current trajectory, it is paramount to understand that while history offers patterns, it doesn't dictate inevitabilities. America, with its deep-rooted democratic institutions, innovation legacy, and societal resilience, holds the potential to chart its course, informed by the past but not shackled by it.

Economic Strain:
The Ghost of the Great Financial Crisis

The architecture of contemporary American economic challenges possesses deep roots in the annals of recent history, notably the Great Financial Crisis of 2008. The cataclysmic event, ignited by the subprime mortgage bubble's collapse, cascaded through the global financial system, leaving few economies untouched. The ramifications of this crisis for the United States, while immediate in terms of bank failures, lost homes, and evaporated wealth, also manifested in long-term structural perturbations.

The 2008 financial crisis, often considered the most severe since the Great Depression of the 1930s, fundamentally rattled global economic structures. Its epicenter was the collapse of housing bubbles in the United States, where financial innovations, such as mortgage-backed securities (MBS) and collateralized debt obligations (CDO), were intertwined with risky subprime lending.

Lehman Brothers, a storied financial institution with a history dating back to the 1850s, became the most prominent casualty of the crisis. In September 2008, unable to secure additional financing or find a buyer, Lehman declared bankruptcy. This event sent shockwaves throughout the global financial system, exacerbating liquidity concerns and igniting fears of a systemic banking collapse.

In tandem, other financial stalwarts found themselves in precarious positions. Fannie Mae and Freddie Mac, government-sponsored entities responsible for a large portion of the U.S. mortgage market, faced insolvency. To prevent a total meltdown, the U.S. government placed them under conservatorship, effectively nationalizing them.

Beyond the housing and banking sectors, companies like General Motors (GM) and the insurance giant AIG teetered on the brink. AIG, heavily exposed to credit default swaps and facing massive collateral calls, required significant capital infusion. Similarly, GM's deep-rooted operational issues combined with the economic downturn threatened its very existence.

Recognizing the cascading threats to the economy, central banks worldwide, led by the U.S. Federal Reserve, adopted a series of unprecedented measures. The concept of Quantitative Easing (QE) was introduced, wherein central banks purchased government securities and other financial instruments to increase money supply and lower interest rates. The goal was twofold: to ensure liquidity in the banking system and to stimulate borrowing and investment.

The U.S. federal government's bailout measures, though controversial, were deemed necessary for systemic stability. The Emergency Economic Stabilization Act, enacted in October 2008, established the $700 billion Troubled Asset Relief Program (TARP) to purchase distressed assets and provide capital to banks. While essential, these interventions fomented public discontent, breeding perceptions of corporate cronyism. The notion that certain entities were "too big to fail" challenged longstanding beliefs about free-market capitalism, leading to profound debates on its very essence.

In sum, the 2008 financial crisis was not merely an economic downturn but a seismic event that reshaped perceptions, policies, and the global financial landscape. The reverberations of these events are still felt, underscoring the fragile interplay between financial systems, governance mechanisms, and public trust.

Simultaneously, the crisis accelerated certain global financial shifts that had been underway, albeit more subtly, in the preceding years. The U.S. dollar, long the dominant global reserve currency, faced challenges from emerging alternatives. The increased prominence of the Euro, coupled with discussions surrounding the Chinese Yuan's internationalization and the advent of decentralized digital currencies like Bitcoin, posed significant challenges to the dollar's hegemony. These developments had profound implications, as the dollar's dominance had long provided the U.S. with significant economic leverage and advantages in international trade dynamics.

Further exacerbating America's economic strains was the rise of parallel economies or the informal sector. Historically, the informal sector—comprising unregulated, untaxed, and often cash-based economic activities—was predominantly associated with developing nations. This sector includes activities ranging from street vending and casual labor to unregistered businesses and underground trading. In the U.S., as formal economic structures faced stressors and as certain industries contracted or underwent transformations, many individuals found themselves turning to these alternative means of livelihood. The motivations behind this shift included the search for supplementary income, the need for flexible work hours, and sometimes, the absence of viable opportunities in the formal sector.

Furthermore, technological advancements, particularly digital platforms, facilitated the growth of the gig economy, which, while not entirely informal, possesses characteristics that blur the lines between formal and informal employment. Platforms like Uber, Lyft, and Airbnb, for instance, allow individuals to monetize their assets (cars, homes) or skills without necessarily being part of a traditional employment setup.

Wealth disparities, already a contentious issue pre-crisis, widened further. The gains from the informal sector, typically sporadic and devoid of benefits like health insurance or retirement contributions, often did not offset the financial vulnerabilities it posed. Meanwhile, in the formal sector, while stock markets eventually rebounded, benefiting the asset-rich elite, wage growth remained stagnant. The labor market showed resilience with unemployment generally at record low levels in America, only witnessing a surge during the unprecedented challenges of the COVID-19 pandemic. Yet, as the pandemic abated, another economic concern surfaced—rising inflation, exacerbated by extensive fiscal spending during the crisis. This has further negatively affected purchasing power and trust in traditional institutions.

The resultant economic landscape has been one of contrasts: booming markets juxtaposed against struggling households with eroding purchasing power and record corporate profits in stark relief against beleaguered small businesses.

In assessing this era of economic strain, it's pivotal to comprehend that while the 2008 crisis was undeniably a seminal event, the ensuing economic challenges have been complex and multifaceted. These challenges were shaped not only by the immediate aftermath of the crisis but also by broader global shifts, technological advancements, and consequential internal policy decisions. This intricate interplay of factors determined the contours of America's economic trajectory in the years that followed, with effects that are palpable and significant in the contemporary period.

The Seeds of Internal Discord: From Trump to Turbulence

The economic tremors of the 2008 financial crisis, as delineated in the previous section, engendered not only financial and structural disruptions but also profound sociopolitical ramifications. One of the most palpable manifestations of this was the broad disillusionment with traditional institutions and the political establishment. This groundswell of discontent, catalyzed by perceptions of institutional failures, corporate cronyism, and the perceived detachment of the political elite from the common populace, set the stage for populist movements and leadership figures who promised to challenge the status quo.

The intricate tapestry of America's contemporary sociopolitical landscape bears witness to these sentiments, with the Trump presidency (2016-2020) serving as a prominent emblem. Historically, leaders and movements have emerged that, in attempting to address existing societal disparities, inadvertently amplify them. A parallel can be drawn to the Roman Republic and the era of the Gracchi brothers. Their populist interventions, while rooted in addressing genuine societal concerns, inadvertently exacerbated political divisions, leading to episodes of significant civic unrest.

Donald Trump's ascendancy to the American presidency echoed aspects of such historical populism. Riding on the wave of disillusionment from economic and institutional strains, his tenure, while addressing genuine grievances of a significant segment of the American populace, was marked by sweeping declarations that often lacked nuanced policy depth, fostering an environment of heightened political polarization.

Perhaps the apogee of the divisiveness of Trump's term was the events of January 6, 2021. This day marked an unprecedented episode in American political history when fervent supporters of the outgoing president violently sought to contest the electoral results. Such an overt act of insurrection underscored the dangers of deeply polarized political rhetoric. Drawing a parallel to Rome, the volatile political atmosphere during the Gracchi era witnessed street violence as a political instrument, exemplifying how leaders can inadvertently catalyze mass unrest.

Moreover, Trump's communication strategy frequently relied on repetition, which, while not a novel political tactic, drew uncomfortable parallels to Joseph Goebbels' maxim: "Repeat a lie often enough and it becomes the truth." Allegations of a 'stolen' election, absent substantive corroborative evidence, eroded trust in the democratic electoral process, destabilizing the foundational principles upon which the nation's democratic ethos stands.

Additionally, Trump's tenure was marked by a discernible shift in foreign policy rhetoric, which frequently alienated traditional allies. This alienation, coupled with America's perceived internal instability, precipitated an increasing sense of international isolation for the US. In this changing geopolitical milieu, traditional adversaries perceived an opportunity, emboldening them to adopt more assertive postures on the global stage.

Concurrent with these shifts, Trump's period in office witnessed the troubling ascendance of movements fueled by nativist, nationalist, and white supremacist ideologies. These groups, some of which openly advocated hate and isolationist sentiments, found resonance in an environment of heightened polarization and social unrest. They appeared to benefit from a climate that was at least tacitly permissive of extreme ideologies, contradicting the pluralistic and democratic values that have historically characterized the United States. While it would be an oversimplification to attribute this rise solely to Trump's presidency, the rhetoric and policies of this period did little to discourage such movements, and in some instances, seemed to embolden them. To contextualize, one might consider how the Weimar Republic's fractured political landscape facilitated the rise of extremist ideologies, including National Socialism, which exploited social divisions for political gain. The ensuing totalitarian regime in Germany led to catastrophic consequences, not only for the nation itself but for the entire world, including the horrors of World War II and the Holocaust.

In the immediate aftermath of Trump's tenure, America grappled with the ramifications of this heightened division. The political climate remained charged, with policy inconsistencies and an overarching disillusionment with federal governance becoming more apparent.

In synthesizing this period, one observes how singular leadership tenures, characterized by divisive rhetoric, can leave indelible marks upon the sociopolitical fabric of nations. This pattern, while unique in its details, aligns with broader historical cycles of rise, internal strain, and regretfully potential decline of a superpower.

Health and Denial:
The COVID-19 Mismanagement Legacy

The onset of the COVID-19 pandemic in 2020 presented an unprecedented global health challenge, the ramifications of which reverberated across social, economic, and political spheres. For the United States, historically seen as a beacon of scientific and medical advancement, the response to this crisis during the Trump administration became a subject of significant scrutiny and critique.

In the annals of public health, the proactive dissemination of accurate information and timely interventions are of paramount importance. However, during the initial stages of the pandemic, the Trump administration exhibited a marked skepticism towards prevailing scientific consensus. This manifested in public dismissals of the virus's severity, contradictory messaging, and, critically, delays in implementing robust testing and contact tracing infrastructures. Drawing a historical parallel, the Black Death in 14th century Europe, though vastly different in context, offers a chilling reminder of how misinformation and inadequate responses can exacerbate public health crises.

The ramifications of these policy choices and communication strategies were manifold. On a macro level, the US witnessed a prolonged duration of the pandemic with a significant number of infections and fatalities. The healthcare system, despite its advanced capabilities, found itself strained, particularly in hotspots where medical facilities were overwhelmed. Beyond the immediate health implications, the broader societal costs were significant. A beleaguered economy grappled with disruptions, resulting in job losses, business closures, and a general economic downturn. These economic strains were intertwined with health outcomes, as a weakened workforce faced prolonged recoveries, a surge in post-COVID complications, and an exacerbated mental health crisis.

While the United States is globally renowned for its cutting-edge medical technology, pharmaceutical innovation, and high-quality medical training, it stands as an anomaly among developed nations for its lack of universal healthcare. This absence is deeply ingrained in the American healthcare system, shaped by a historical preference for market-based solutions and a fragmented network of private and public healthcare providers. Unlike nations with socialized medicine or universal healthcare systems—such as Canada, Germany, or the United Kingdom—the U.S. system leaves a significant portion of the population without basic healthcare coverage. This systemic limitation significantly exacerbated the challenges posed by the COVID-19 pandemic. In the absence of comprehensive coverage, tens of millions of Americans faced formidable barriers to testing and treatment, which, in turn, impeded efforts to control the virus's spread. The uninsured and underinsured were more likely to delay seeking medical care, contributing to more severe health outcomes and thereby straining hospital resources further. The lack of universal healthcare also intensified the socioeconomic disparities laid bare by the pandemic.

However, the challenges were not solely physiological or economic. A discernible sociocultural shift emerged during this period, characterized by a growing skepticism towards science and expertise. This anti-science sentiment, which found resonance in certain sections of the populace, was bolstered by divisive political rhetoric and a proliferation of misinformation on digital platforms. The resultant mistrust in scientific institutions and experts presents a long-term challenge, as it impedes the nation's ability to effectively respond to future health crises and could potentially stifle advancements in medical research and public health.

In sum, the legacy of COVID-19 in the US, particularly under the Trump administration's purview, serves as a cautionary tale. It underscores the importance of evidence-based policymaking, timely interventions, and the crucial role of transparent, cohesive communication in navigating public health crises. It further emphasizes the intricate nexus between health, economic stability, and sociocultural dynamics, reiterating the interconnectedness of these domains in shaping a nation's trajectory.

Technological Standstill: Navigating the Shifting Tech Landscape

Throughout history, the United States has been a driving force behind technological innovation, shaping the course of the digital age. From the pioneering work at Bell Labs to the explosive growth of Silicon

Valley, the U.S. established itself as a crucible for technological advancement during the 20th and early 21st centuries. This culture of innovation, combined with a fertile entrepreneurial environment, gave rise to global tech giants like Apple, Microsoft, Google, and Facebook.

However, as the 21st century unfolded, a noticeable shift occurred in the landscape of technological dominance. The narrative of the post-Silicon Valley era, characterized by rapid advancements in areas such as quantum computing, biotechnology, and next-generation artificial intelligence, signaled that the United States was no longer the exclusive leader in global tech innovation.

Several factors contributed to this transition, each with its nuances. On one front, technological hubs outside the U.S. began to emerge organically. Regions in East Asia, such as China's Shenzhen and South Korea's Pangyo Techno Valley, rose to challenge Silicon Valley's supremacy. Europe, too, asserted its presence on the innovation map with burgeoning tech hubs in cities like Berlin and Stockholm. These regions weren't merely replicating American innovations; they were pioneering new frontiers, buoyed by supportive government policies, substantial investments in research and development, and robust collaborations between academia and industry.

The evolving landscape was further complicated by the challenges faced by American tech giants. While these companies had significantly shaped the digital age, they found themselves under increasing scrutiny, both domestically and internationally. Concerns related to antitrust issues, debates over data privacy, and ethical considerations surrounding technologies like facial recognition placed these corporations in the spotlight. On the global stage, gaining access to markets became challenging, particularly in countries that nurtured their domestic tech champions or implemented protective measures.

When juxtaposing America's earlier technological dominance with its position in the post-Silicon Valley era, one discerns an intricate mosaic of internal and external dynamics. Domestically, the innovation ecosystem remained vibrant, yet regulatory challenges and a sense of complacency hindered the pace of advancement. Externally, the global tech landscape became more multipolar, with various regions vying for leadership, each contributing its unique strengths and perspectives.

In conclusion, while the United States' leadership in technological spheres encountered challenges, it's crucial to recognize the cyclical nature of innovation. Historical precedents, from the scientific revolutions in Renaissance Europe to the technological innovations in Meiji-era Japan, suggest that leadership in innovation is dynamic. The future will reveal how the United States, with its deeply ingrained culture of innovation, navigates this evolving terrain in the years to come.

Overextension:
Military and Diplomatic Misadventures

Historically, empires and great powers have often succumbed to the perils of overextension. Whether it was the Roman Empire stretching its legions too thin or the Mongol Empire sprawling across vast territories, overreach has invariably strained resources and diluted focus. In a similar vein, America's post-Cold War trajectory showcased instances of overextension, particularly in its military and diplomatic domains.

In the aftermath of the Cold War, buoyed by its "unipolar moment", the United States embarked on a series of military endeavors, arguably under the banner of ensuring global stability or preempting threats. The invasions of Afghanistan (2001) and Iraq (2003) are emblematic of such interventions. While these incursions were initially justified on the grounds of counter-terrorism, nation-building, or countering weapons of mass destruction, their prolonged nature and ambiguous objectives strained American resources. Financially, trillions were expended, and the human toll, both in terms of American military casualties and civilian losses, added to the quagmire. More critically, these interventions lacked clear exit strategies, leading to protracted engagements that, over time, yielded diminishing strategic returns.

Diplomatically, the repercussions were multifaceted. America's unilateral actions, especially in the Middle East, often sidestepped established international frameworks or traditional allies, leading to strains in longstanding partnerships. NATO, for instance, witnessed fissures, not just because of military campaigns, but also due to divergent threat perceptions and burden-sharing debates. Moreover, the perception of the US engaging in interventionist policies, without clear mandates or goals, diminished its soft power globally. The narratives emanating from Abu Ghraib or Guantanamo Bay, for instance, provided fodder to critics, challenging America's moral high ground on global human rights and democratic values.

Furthermore, in regions like Asia-Pacific, while the US pivoted to counterbalance China's rise, its diplomatic endeavors occasionally lacked consistency. Allies, from Japan to Australia, often sought clarity on America's strategic commitment to the region, especially in the face of an assertive China.

In a recent interview, former U.S. Secretary of State Henry Kissinger, who recently celebrated his 100th birthday, made a sobering comparison between the current geopolitical tensions between the United States and China and the pre-World War I European landscape. His assessment carried a sense of urgency, as he suggested that the two global giants have a limited window of 7 to 10 years to avoid the catastrophic prospect of war. This assertion, rooted in the principles of Realpolitik that Kissinger masterfully practiced in the 1970s, prompts a critical examination of the evolving U.S.-China relationship and its implications for global stability.

Kissinger's Realpolitik was grounded in a fundamental principle: the United States should maintain closer relations with each of its adversaries than they have with each other. This strategic approach led to his landmark opening to China, a diplomatic feat that reconfigured the global power dynamics of the time. By establishing a relationship with China, the U.S. effectively isolated the Soviet Union during the Cold War, creating a dynamic where the U.S. was at the center of key diplomatic connections.

Fast forward to the present, and the geopolitical landscape appears to have reversed. The United States finds itself in a situation where it is less close to its adversaries, such as China and Russia, than they are to each other. This shifting balance of power has significant implications for global security and stability.

Recent events underscore the consequences of this shifting geopolitical landscape. Russia's aggressive actions, including the annexation of Crimea and the ongoing conflict in Ukraine, exemplify a growing assertiveness on the global stage. Simultaneously, China's increasingly assertive rhetoric and actions, particularly concerning Taiwan, indicate a desire to expand its influence in the Asia-Pacific region.

The danger lies in the emergence of rigid and fixed alliances, reminiscent of the pre-World War I European system. In an era marked by growing nationalism, these alliances could create a tinderbox where a small spark could ignite a catastrophic global conflict.

The internal divisions within the United States further complicate matters. Leaders, seeking to appeal to their political bases, often resort to tough rhetoric against adversaries. While this may play well domestically, it can inadvertently create mechanisms that escalate tensions and spiral out of control.

The key to averting such a catastrophic conflict lies in diplomacy. In an increasingly interconnected world, where the consequences of war are more devastating than ever before, diplomatic solutions must take center stage. This necessitates a united and coherent U.S. approach to foreign policy, one that transcends partisan divisions and emphasizes dialogue and cooperation over saber-rattling.

However, the United States currently faces challenges in projecting political and diplomatic clout on the global stage. Internal divisions and partisan gridlock hinder the development of a cohesive foreign policy strategy. To address this, the nation must prioritize unity and bipartisanship in matters of international importance.

In sum, as Henry Kissinger emphasized, the reverberations of history sharply illuminate the fragile nature of the present U.S.-China dynamics and its possible global implications. The United States must navigate this landscape with a renewed commitment to diplomacy and a unified approach to foreign policy. The lessons of history offer a path forward, one that prioritizes dialogue, cooperation, and the avoidance of catastrophic conflict. The stakes are high, and the time to act is now.

Navigating New Challenges:
Emerging Regional Powers and Cyber Threats

As the world evolves, so does the nature of external threats to the United States. Two significant challenges have emerged on the global stage: the ascent of united regional powers challenging American military, economic, and cultural dominance, and the increasing prevalence of cyber threats and espionage that undermine national security infrastructure, leading to widespread societal disruptions.

The post-Cold War era witnessed the rise of united regional powers that challenge traditional American dominance. These coalitions of nations, often with shared political, economic, and military objectives, have emerged as formidable players on the global stage. They seek to reshape the balance of power, challenging American influence in their respective regions and beyond.

This shift is evident in regions like East Asia, where China's assertive foreign policy and economic might have positioned it as a key competitor to American interests. China's Belt and Road Initiative, military modernization, and diplomatic initiatives have raised concerns about its intentions and capabilities.

In Europe, the European Union, although primarily an economic union, has also become a political and diplomatic force to be reckoned with. The EU's cohesive approach to foreign policy, trade negotiations, and security challenges presents a united front that can challenge American policies.

In the digital age, the threat landscape has expanded to include cyber threats and espionage that transcend traditional boundaries. These threats pose unique challenges to national security, as they target critical infrastructure, institutions, and data, causing widespread disruptions and compromising sensitive information.

Cyberattacks, whether state-sponsored or the work of criminal organizations, can have devastating effects. They can disrupt power grids, financial systems, and communication networks, leading to economic and societal chaos. Moreover, cyber espionage, often linked to nation-states, targets government secrets, intellectual property, and defense information, eroding national security.

Both of these challenges require the United States to adopt a multi-faceted approach, blending diplomacy, technological innovation, and robust security measures. Engaging with emerging regional powers through diplomatic channels, trade agreements, and cooperation on global issues can help manage competition and promote stability. Additionally, enhancing cybersecurity infrastructure, investing in advanced threat detection and prevention technologies, and fostering international collaboration to combat cyber threats are vital components of national defense.

In navigating these external threats, the United States must remain adaptable and forward-thinking, recognizing that the global landscape is continually evolving. By addressing these challenges proactively and strategically, the nation can safeguard its interests and maintain its position as a global leader.

Cultural Isolation: From Melting Pot to Simmering Cauldron

The United States has often prided itself on being a cultural melting pot, a nation that thrived on diversity and embraced global trends. However, as the 21st century unfolded, a subtle transformation began to alter the nation's cultural landscape. Gradually, the United States found itself straying from the vibrant tapestry of global cultural trends, embarking on a journey of gradual alienation.

This shift has been marked by the rise of inward-focused narratives that increasingly dominate the national discourse. Populist political rhetoric, with calls for "America First" policies, emphasize a prioritization of domestic issues over international ones, leading to skepticism towards international agreements, such as the Paris Climate Accord and the Trans-Pacific Partnership. Concurrently, the media landscape has undergone its own transformation. With the advent of digital platforms, echo chambers have begun to emerge, where individuals are frequently exposed to news and views that align with their pre-existing beliefs, limiting their exposure to a broader spectrum of perspectives.

Simultaneously, there has been a tangible shift in national sentiment towards immigration. Stricter immigration policies and heightened rhetoric around border security underscore a more guarded approach to external cultural influences. Discussions of building walls, both metaphorical and literal, have become emblematic of this change in sentiment. The irony has not been lost on many: where once Ronald Reagan stood in Berlin and boldly declared, "Mr. Gorbachev, tear down this wall," championing an open and interconnected world, now the narrative has shifted to insulating and guarding, suggesting a marked transition from an America that confidently engaged with and shaped the world to one seeking solace behind barriers.

Even the nation's educational institutions aren't immune. Moves to revise educational curricula have begun to surface, with emphasis on certain aspects of American history and culture, occasionally minimizing or excluding the contributions and narratives of immigrant and minority communities.

In totality, whether driven by political, economic, or social factors, these evolving narratives have contributed to a palpable sense of introspection. The nation, once renowned for its openness to external influences, has begun to turn inward, and in doing so, started to simmer in its own cultural cauldron.

One of the most conspicuous signs of this transformation has been the diminished export of American culture. The creative industries, which had long been synonymous with American soft power, began to experience a noticeable decline in global influence. Hollywood, once a beacon of cinematic innovation, found itself facing formidable competition from international film industries, particularly in Asia. The American music scene, while still influential, no longer holds the uncontested position it once did, as artists and genres from other regions gained international acclaim.

Furthermore, the global resonance of American literature, fashion, and visual arts have started to wane. American literature, which had produced literary giants like Hemingway and Fitzgerald, saw its prominence diluted in an increasingly global literary landscape. The fashion world, which had often dictated trends worldwide, started to share the limelight with designers from Europe and Asia. American visual arts, while still producing renowned artists, faced growing competition from emerging art scenes around the world.

In conclusion the consequences of this cultural transformation have been multifaceted. While it has not erased America's cultural significance, it certainly altered the dynamics. The nation, once an undisputed leader in shaping global cultural trends, has found itself sharing the stage with an increasingly diverse cast of cultural influencers. The patterns of cultural sway, much like history's consistent shifts, continue to transform in line with the unfolding nuances of the 21st century.

Concluding Thoughts: The Path Forward for America

As we explore the contemporary landscape of America through the lens of historical power dynamics, it becomes evident that the nation stands at a critical juncture. The preceding sections have detailed challenges encountered by past empires, each potentially influencing the course of the United States in the current century.

The shifting sands of power, both on the global stage and within the nation, highlight the need for astute navigation in a rapidly changing world. Economic difficulties, rooted in the enduring impact of the Great Financial Crisis, emphasize the complex interconnections of the global economy and the outcomes of neglect. The emergence of internal conflict, evident in the political upheavals since the Trump era, accentuates the value of cohesion and fortitude amidst domestic tribulations.

Health crises, exemplified by the COVID-19 pandemic, have exposed the critical significance of proactive governance, effective healthcare systems, societal resilience and willingness to support collective action. The technological standstill signals a need for innovation and adaptability, especially as the world hurtles toward new frontiers in quantum computing, biotechnology, and artificial intelligence. Overextension, both in military and diplomatic misadventures, cautions against overreach and the risks it poses to national interests.

Emerging regional powers and cyber threats pose external challenges that necessitate vigilance, adaptability, and strategic acumen. Cultural isolation, marked by an inward orientation, raises questions about America's role as a global influencer and the potential consequences of diminished cultural exports and global influence.

In this intricate mosaic of challenges and opportunities, history provides a guiding light. It reminds us that empires, despite their power, are not immune to decline. The path forward for America is one that requires introspection, adaptability, and a commitment to the principles that have defined the nation throughout its history.

History offers a glimmer of hope. It reminds us that empires have the capacity for rejuvenation and reinvention. The path forward for America is an open road, where its people, institutions, and leadership hold the compass. It is a path where history offers valuable lessons, not fixed destinies. The nation's journey continues to be written with each passing day, and the choices made today will shape the story of America for generations to come.

The data presented here serves as a compass, guiding through the complexities of a changing world and providing insights into the nation's journey. It invites to engage in critical discourse, to question assumptions, and to envision potential futures. The challenges ahead are formidable, and they echo the challenges that have tested empires in the past. Recognizing these challenges and addressing them with urgency is the key for America to maintain supremacy for generations to come.

As history unfolds, let us remember that the story of America is not one of stagnation but of evolution. It is a story of adaptation, innovation, and resilience.

Yet the rise, reign, and decline of empires are not mere historical abstractions; they are living lessons that remind us of the impermanence of power. The path forward for America is a choice—one that will determine whether it continues to rise, whether it remains in its reign, or whether it succumbs to the forces of decline.

Candido Portinari (1903 – 1962) created two murals entitled
War (east wall) and Peace (west wall) respectively.
The murals are placed outside the General Assembly Hall of the UN head-
quarters so that the delegates face War on their way into the building, and
Peace as they leave, functioning as a visual framework for negotiations.[46]

Epilogue:
Echoes in the Abyss

The farther backward you can look,
the farther forward you are likely to see.

~ Winston Churchill

The cyclical nature of power:
A reflection on history's lessons.

"History repeats itself, first as tragedy, second as farce." This observation by Karl Marx underscores a fundamental tenet: power dynamics, despite their unique contexts and actors, often exhibit recurring patterns. From the river valleys of Mesopotamia, where the foundations of civilization were laid, to the sprawling expanse of modern superpowers, the ebb and flow of dominance and decline remain a consistent motif.

Throughout this exploration of empires and superpowers, one discerns a remarkable continuity in the pursuit of power, prestige, and influence. Ancient empires, fueled by ambition and the desire for territorial expansion, laid down administrative, cultural, and economic blueprints that have been echoed, adapted, or sometimes rejected by their successors.

Yet, with every ascension to greatness, there were inherent vulnerabilities. As superpowers reached their zenith, internal and external pressures often culminated in periods of stagnation or decline. These cycles, with their individual peculiarities, serve as poignant reminders of the transient nature of power.

In the chronicles of history, while the actors, technologies, and ideologies evolved, the fundamental dynamics of ambition, strategy, and human agency remained at the core. As we have navigated this journey, from the earliest civilizations to the complex geopolitics of the 21st century, the lessons of history emerge not as deterministic paths but as guideposts, illuminating both the potential pitfalls and the avenues for resilience and rejuvenation.

By understanding the cyclical patterns of the past, contemporary societies can glean insights into their own position in the grand tapestry of time, fostering a nuanced appreciation for the legacies they've inherited and the futures they can shape.

Revisiting the Markers of Supremacy

As covered in Chapter 1, the attributes that define a superpower are multifaceted, often transcending singular dimensions like military might or economic prowess. From the earliest empires to the contemporary titans, certain core markers of supremacy have persistently emerged.

> Military strength has been constant. The Assyrian war chariots, Roman legions, and British naval fleets of yesteryears find echoes in today's intercontinental ballistic missiles, stealth aircraft, and cyber warfare capabilities. While the tools of warfare have evolved, the underlying principle remains steadfast: a superpower's military capability serves not merely for conquest but also as a symbol of deterrence and a tool for projecting influence.

> Parallel to this runs economic prowess. The ancient trade routes of the Silk Road and the mercantilism of European colonial powers laid the foundations for today's intricate global trade systems and complex financial markets. Throughout history, economic clout has

provided empires with the necessary resources to not only sustain their ambitions but also shape global agendas.

Politically, the ability to craft and navigate both internal and international landscapes is a hallmark of superpower status. Governance strategies, whether they were reflected in the Pax Romana or the 1815 Concert of Europe, find contemporary counterparts in diplomatic outreach, international treaty frameworks, and the intricate dance of global governance.

Technological innovation, a driving force behind many an empire's rise, has ranged from the infrastructural marvels like the aqueducts of Rome to today's groundbreaking advancements in the digital realm. Mastery over cutting-edge technologies not only grants economic and military advantages but also decisively shapes the trajectory of societal progress.

Lastly, the realm of cultural influence, though often subtle, carries profound weight. Whether it was the Hellenistic diffusion post-Alexander's conquests, the pervasive spread of Confucianism in East Asia, or the global dissemination of American pop culture in recent decades, cultural exports wield a form of soft power, crafting both admiration and aspiration across borders.

By synthesizing these markers across different epochs, it's evident that while their specifics might have transformed, their essence remained integral to the narrative of dominance. Recognizing these evolving markers not only offers insights into the trajectories of past empires but also provides a nuanced lens through which one might gauge the potential futures of contemporary superpowers.

The Ever-Present Shadows of Decline

While the markers of supremacy, as delineated in the previous section, illuminate the multifaceted attributes that have historically defined superpowers, they simultaneously cast a shadow of potential vulnerabilities. These attributes, while indicators of strength and influence, are not static; they are susceptible to erosion over time due to internal and external pressures. This juxtaposition of dominance and vulnerability is a recurring theme in the annals of history, illustrating the delicate balance that superpowers must navigate.

In the resplendent arc of any superpower's ascendancy lies an accompanying shadow, a subtle reminder of the vulnerabilities inherent to great power. Time and again, history has illustrated that the zenith of dominance is often followed by periods of stagnation or decline. These regressions, while influenced by distinct contemporary factors, echo familiar themes and challenges faced by their predecessors.

Internal strife has often been the silent eroder of empires. The sociopolitical unrest that plagued the later years of the Roman Empire, or the ideological fractures of the Soviet Union serve as testaments to the internal vulnerabilities even the most formidable powers grapple with. Dissent, economic disparity, and challenges to central authority can, over time, destabilize the very core of an empire, rendering it susceptible to external threats.

Externally, rising challengers, shifts in global trade routes, or technological revolutions have historically reshaped the balance of power. The Mongol invasions that challenged settled empires, the naval innovations that spurred European explorations and colonization, or the oil crises of the 20th century were all catalysts that altered the geopolitical landscape, often to the detriment of reigning superpowers.

Overlaying these tangible challenges are more intangible factors: complacency and hubris. The belief in the permanence of one's dominance can lead to strategic myopia, underestimating evolving threats or overextending one's reach.

Yet, amid these echoes of decline, there also lie lessons of resilience. Many empires, when confronted with existential threats, found ways to adapt, reform, and reinvent. These tales of rejuvenation, often overshadowed by narratives of downfall, hold invaluable insights for contemporary powers. In understanding the cyclical nature of ascendancy and decline, modern states can better navigate the complexities of the 21st century, drawing wisdom from the echoes of history's past downfalls and triumphs.

Facing the Global Abyss Together

As articulated throughout this book, world history is punctuated with tales of individual empires reaching unparalleled heights, only to confront the precipices of their own making. While these abysses often took the form of military overreach, economic crises, or internal disarray in bygone eras, the 21st century presents a new set of universal challenges that defy singular nation-centered solutions.

Climate change, arguably the most pressing issue of our time, stands as a testament to the interconnected fragility of our global ecosystem. The melting ice caps of the polar regions, the wildfires consuming vast stretches of continents, and the increasing frequency of extreme weather events are not constrained by national borders. Their repercussions are felt universally, from the smallest island nations to the most expansive continents.

Pandemics, too, as evidenced by the global spread of diseases in recent history, underscore the vulnerability of an interconnected world. Pathogens, indifferent to political boundaries, emphasize the necessity of collaborative health responses, shared research, and mutual trust.

The realm of cyber threats presents another frontier where traditional concepts of defense and sovereignty are being redefined. A single cyber-attack can cripple infrastructures, destabilize economies, and disrupt governance across multiple nations, necessitating a collective approach to cybersecurity and digital diplomacy.

In confronting these universal challenges, the traditional paradigms of power politics and hegemonic ambitions appear increasingly anachronistic. The global abysses of the modern era demand collective action, shared responsibilities, and a reimagining of what true leadership entails.

It is here that history offers both a warning and a beacon. The past chronicles of empires, in their quests for dominance, often neglected the collective good, leading to shared calamities. Yet, history also showcases moments of collaborative brilliance, where nations, cultures, and leaders came together to forge paths of shared progress.

As the world stands on the precipices of these global challenges, the lessons from the past resonate with renewed urgency. The future, it seems, hinges not on the dominance of a singular superpower but on the collective will of humanity to collaborate, innovate, and steer away from the abyss, towards a shared horizon of hope and resilience.

Remembering the Fallen: Lessons from the Ruins

In the complex dance of global dynamics, as underscored by the preceding section, while humanity confronts collective threats that defy national solutions, it must also grapple with individual nation-centered vulnerabilities reminiscent of past empires. This duality - of both shared and singular challenges - is at the heart of understanding the future trajectory of global powers.

As detailed throughout this book, history is as much a chronicle of empires that soared to dizzying heights as it is a record of those that faltered and faded into the annals of time. The ruins, both literal and metaphorical, left behind by these once-majestic entities offer somber reflections on the dual nature of power: its potential for greatness and its susceptibility to decline.

From the abandoned ziggurats of Mesopotamia to the overgrown temples of the Maya, the physical remnants of bygone empires stand as silent witnesses to their past grandeur and subsequent decline. These structures, while bearing testimony to the architectural and cultural zeniths of their eras, also evoke contemplations on the impermanence of even the most formidable powers.

Beyond these tangible relics, the intangible legacies of fallen empires often resonate with poignant lessons. The political intrigues that weakened the Abbasid Caliphate from within, the overextension of resources that plagued the Spanish Empire, or the resistance to technological advancement that hastened the Qing Dynasty's decline, all serve as cautionary tales. They underscore the multifaceted challenges empires faced, the internal and external pressures that could converge, and the often-thin line between continued dominance and precipitous fall.

Yet, amid these stories of decline and dissolution, there's also recognition of the invaluable contributions these empires made to human civilization. Whether in the realms of art, science, governance, or culture, the legacies of these fallen powers continue to shape contemporary thought and societal frameworks. Their innovations, philosophies, and cultural practices have been assimilated, adapted, and built upon by successive generations.

In reflecting upon the fallen, it's crucial to remember that their stories are not mere footnotes but integral chapters in the larger narrative of human progress. They serve as both reminders of the pitfalls of hubris and complacency and as repositories of wisdom and knowledge. For contemporary superpowers and emerging nations alike, these historical narratives emphasize the importance of self-awareness, adaptability, and the constant vigilance required to navigate the intricate dynamics of power, ensuring that past mistakes are not repeated, and history's lessons are duly heeded.

Conclusion: Predictions, Possibilities, and Paradigms

As we contemplate the intricate interplay between past, present, and future, a rich mosaic of potential trajectories for global order emerges. Although the act of prediction remains an inherently fraught enterprise, discernible patterns, trends, and emerging paradigms offer useful insights into the evolving dynamics of power and supremacy.

Technological advancements, notably in artificial intelligence, biotechnologies, and quantum computing, loom as more than mere tools. These technologies carry the potential to alter the very equations of power, albeit with ethical and societal challenges that necessitate collective deliberation.

Simultaneously, the democratization of the digital realm is facilitating a diversification of global narratives. This development heralds a more multipolar world, not solely in military or economic terms but extending into cultural and ideological spheres. Yet, such progress brings its own set of challenges, including the fragmentation of the digital space and potential resource scarcities, which demand a collective, perhaps even global, strategy.

One of the more provocative questions for the future centers on the evolving definition of what constitutes a superpower. Is it territorial or economic might, or could it be a leadership role in innovation, environmental stewardship, and global cooperation?

History demonstrates that the manifestations of power are fluid, perpetually subject to the shifts and ebbs of time. The stories of past empires provide cautionary tales replete with pitfalls of hubris, dangers of complacency, and perils of unbridled ambition. They also showcase the human capacity for innovation, adaptation, and resilience.

In this era marked by unprecedented challenges and opportunities, the lessons of history offer not merely guideposts but imperatives. These imperatives are not solely about the acquisition of power but concern its responsible and enlightened exercise.

In concluding this exploration, let us heed the words of the philosopher George Santayana: "Those who cannot remember the past are condemned to repeat it." As custodians of both our past and our future, the onus is upon us to remember, to learn, and to chart a course that respects history's lessons while forging a path of hope, unity, and shared prosperity.

May the echoes of history empower us to envision a future that, while respectful of its roots, aspires to heights of collective greatness, steering clear of past abysses and reaching, with shared purpose, towards a horizon radiant with promise.

View of the Earth taken on December 7, 1972, by the crew of the Apollo 17 spacecraft en route to the Moon at a distance of about 29,400 kilometres (18,300 mi)[47.]

References

Arrighi, G. (2007). *Adam Smith in Beijing: Lineages of the Twenty-First Century.* Verso.

Beard, M. (2015). SPQR: *A History of Ancient Rome.* Liveright.

Blair, T. (2010). *A Journey: My Political Life.* Knopf.

Braudel, F. (1979). *Civilization and Capitalism, 15th-18th Century, Vol. I: The Structure of Everyday Life.* Harper & Row.

Brzezinski, Z. (1997). *The Grand Chessboard: American Primacy and Its Geostrategic Imperatives.* Basic Books.

Churchill, W. (1948-1953). *The Second World War* (6 Vols.). Cassell & Co.

Clinton, B. (2004). My Life. Knopf.

Diamond, J. (1999). *Guns, Germs, and Steel: The Fates of Human Societies.* Norton & Company.

Fairbank, J. K. (1992). *China: A New History.* Belknap Press.

Ferguson, N. (2003). *Empire: How Britain Made the Modern World.* Penguin UK.

Foucault, M. (1975). *Discipline and Punish: The Birth of the Prison.* Pantheon.

Gaddis, J. L. (2005). *The Cold War: A New History.* Penguin.

Hobson, J. M. (2004). *The Eastern Origins of Western Civilization.* Cambridge University Press.

Hodgson, M. G. S. (1974). *The Venture of Islam,* Vol. 1-3. University of Chicago Press.

Kagan, D. (1991). *The Fall of the Athenian Empire.* Cornell University Press.

Keegan, J. (1993). *A History of Warfare.* Vintage.

Kissinger, H. (1969). *American Foreign Policy: Three Essays.* W.W. Norton & Company.

Kissinger, H. (1982). *Years of Upheaval.* Little, Brown & Co.

Kissinger, H. (1994). *Diplomacy.* Simon & Schuster.

Kissinger, H. (2014). *World Order.* Penguin.

Mann, M. (1986). *The Sources of Social Power: Volume 1, A History of Power from the Beginning to AD 1760.* Cambridge University Press.

McNeill, W. H. (1982). *The Pursuit of Power: Technology, Armed Force, and Society since A.D. 1000.* University of Chicago Press.

Mearsheimer, J. J. (2018). *The Great Delusion: Liberal Dreams and International Realities.* Yale University Press.

Modelski, G. & Thompson, W. R. (1988). *Seapower in Global Politics, 1494-1993.* University of Washington Press.

Morgenthau, H. J. (1948). *Politics Among Nations.* Knopf.

Obama, B. (2018). *The Audacity of Hope: Thoughts on Reclaiming the American Dream.* Crown.

Obama, B. (2020). *A Promised Land.* Crown.

Pomeranz, K. (2000). *The Great Divergence: China, Europe, and the Making of the Modern World Economy.* Princeton University Press.

Tilly, C. (1992). *Coercion, Capital, and European States, AD 990-1992.* Blackwell.

Waltz, K. N. (1979). *Theory of International Politics.* McGraw-Hill.

Weatherford, J. (2004). *Genghis Khan and the Making of the Modern World.* Crown.

Zakaria, F. (2008). *The Post-American World.* W.W. Norton & Company.

Image Attribution*

Images shown without reference are public domain

1. www.claudelorrain.org

2. thecollector.com

3. By KennyOMG - Own work, CC BY-SA 4.0, https://commons. wikimedia.org/w/index.php?curid=40998161

4. Getty images, Hardnfast/CC BY 3.0 <https://creativecommons.org/ licenses/by/3.0, via Wikimedia Commons>

5. Photo by Petar Milošević / CC BY-SA 4.0 <https://creativecommons. org/licenses/by-sa/4.0>, via Wikimedia Commons

6. By Charles J. Sharp - Own work, from Sharp Photography, sharpphotography, CC BY-SA 3.0, https://commons.wikimedia.org/w/ index.php?curid=32434567

7. Istockphoto.com, Thomas Guenther

8. By Cattette - This file has been extracted from another file, CC BY 4.0, https://commons.wikimedia.org/w/index.php?curid=113179532

9. Illustration By Bettmann, Getty

10. Juan Carlos Fonseca Mata, CC BY-SA 4.0 <https://creativecommons. org/licenses/by-sa/4.0>, via Wikimedia Commons

11. By Esiymbro - Own work / CC BY-SA 4.0, <https://commons. wikimedia.org/w/index.php?curid=83835819>

12. Map by worldmap.harvard.edu, vector graphics by vecteeezy.com, camels designed by Freepik, Marco Polo by Grevembrock

13. Simeon Netchev, CC BY-NC-SA 4.0, < https://www.worldhistory.org/ image/14624/the-greek-city-states-c-500-bce>

14. Steve Swayne, CC BY 2.0 <https://creativecommons.org/licenses/ by/2.0>, via Wikimedia Commons

15. By Map_Macedonia_336_BC-es.svg: Marsyas (French original); Kordas (Spanish translation)derivative work: MinisterForBadTimes (talk) - Translation of Map_Macedonia_336_BC-es.svg (data from R. Ginouvès and al., La Macédoine, Paris, 1992), CC BY-SA 3.0, https:// commons.wikimedia.org/w/index.php?curid=7398609

16. Istockphoto.com, TerryJLawrence

17. By Tataryn - Own work, CC BY-SA 3.0, https://commons.wikimedia. org/w/index.php?curid=19625326

18. Rabax63, CC BY-SA 4.0 <https://creativecommons.org/licenses/ by-sa/4.0>, via Wikimedia Commons

19. By Abraham-Louis-Rodolphe Ducros - This file was donated to Wikimedia Commons as part of a project by the Metropolitan Museum of Art. See the Image and Data Resources Open Access Policy, CC0, https://commons.wikimedia.org/w/index.php?curid=60841521

20. Istockphoto.com, Dimitrios Karamitros

21. Istockphoto.com, rakushka13sel

22. By Chamboz at English Wikipedia, CC BY-SA 4.0, https://commons. wikimedia.org/w/index.php?curid=89899000

23. By Rafy - info fromWorld map, by The Evil Spartan, Zaparojdik, Victor falk and Magog the OgreChinaPersiaSiam, CC BY 3.0, https:// commons.wikimedia.org/w/index.php?curid=15200374

24. By:Theodor de Bry - Scan from the original work, Public Domain, https://commons.wikimedia.org/w/index.php?curid=174364

25. Clipart courtesy FCIT, https://etc.usf.edu/clipart

26. By RedStorm1368 - Own work, CC BY-SA 4.0, https://commons.wikimedia.org/w/index.php?curid=135842890

27. Istockphoto.com, PeterHermesFurian

28. Universal History Archive/Universal Images Group Via Getty Images

29. By MaGioZal (this version), Brianski (Wikimedia Commons) (File:Map of USA-bw.png), Roke (Wikimedia Commons) and Brianski (File:Map of USA.png) - Derived from :Image:Map of USA-bw.png, which was in turn derived from File:Map of USA.png, CC BY-SA 3.0, https://commons.wikimedia.org/w/index.php?curid=37174306

30. Clipart courtesy FCIT, https://etc.usf.edu/clipart

31. By Andrew J. Russell (1830-1902), photographer - National Park Service. http://www.nps.gov/gosp/index.htm, Public Domain, https://commons.wikimedia.org/w/index.php?curid=708221

32. Granger, Cartoon by Clifford Berryman

33. Royal Engineers No 1 Printing Company/IWM/Getty Images

34. https://www.mutualart.com/Artwork/Stadt-und-Menschen/30651B119337749DBy Edward N. Jackson (US Army Signal Corps) - U.S. Signal Corps photo, Public Domain, https://commons.wikimedia.org/w/index.php?curid=6037445

35. By Bundesarchiv, Bild 102-10261 / CC-BY-SA 3.0, CC BY-SA 3.0 de, https://commons.wikimedia.org/w/index.php?curid=5664848

36. By Bundesarchiv, Bild 183-S55480 / CC-BY-SA 3.0, CC BY-SA 3.0 de, https://commons.wikimedia.org/w/index.php?curid=5369413

37. National Archives and Records Administration, Public domain, via Wikimedia Commons

38. STF/AFP/Getty Images

39. By Own work - This file was derived from:Hyderabad in India (1951). svgKalat Map.gifSaurashtraKart.jpg, CC BY-SA 4.0, https://commons. wikimedia.org/w/index.php?curid=56172721

40. By USSR Republics Numbered Alphabetically.png: Aris KatsarisUSSR map.svg: Saul ipderivative work: Master Uegly - Own work, recreation of Soviet Socialist Republics numbered by the Soviet constitution. png, Public Domain, https://commons.wikimedia.org/w/index. php?curid=68893861

41. By Vorziblix - Own work, CC0, https://commons.wikimedia.org/w/ index.php?curid=19317533

42. Gerard Malie/AFP / Getty

43. Illustration by Davide Bonazzi

44. Photo by Steven Bornholtz

45. By TapTheForwardAssist - Own work, CC BY-SA 4.0, https:// commons.wikimedia.org/w/index.php?curid=98667989

46. UN Photo/Lois Conner

47. By NASA/Apollo 17 crew; taken by either Harrison Schmitt or Ron Evans - http://tothemoon.ser.asu.edu/gallery/Apollo/17/ Hasselblad%20500EL%2070%20mm https://www.flickr.com/photos/ projectapolloarchive/21081863984/, Public Domain, https://commons. wikimedia.org/w/index.php?curid=114976945

* all coloured images were changed to greyscale

Index

C

D

www.ingramcontent.com/pod-product-compliance
Lightning Source LLC
Chambersburg PA
CBHW051255020426

42333CB00026B/3219